AT DEATH'S DOOR

NEW YORK, NEW YORK

AT DEATH'S DOOR

by

JILL THOMPSON

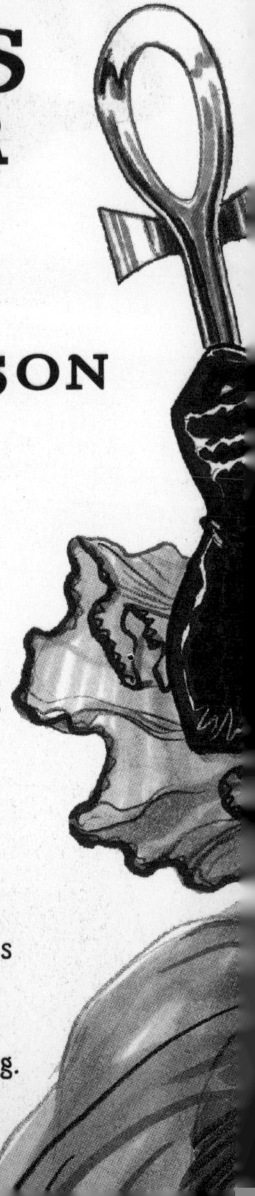

Separations by

LEE LOUGHRIDGE

NEIL GAIMAN

Consultant

Based on

The Sandman: Season of Mists

The Sandman is created by

Gaiman, Kieth, and Dringenberg.

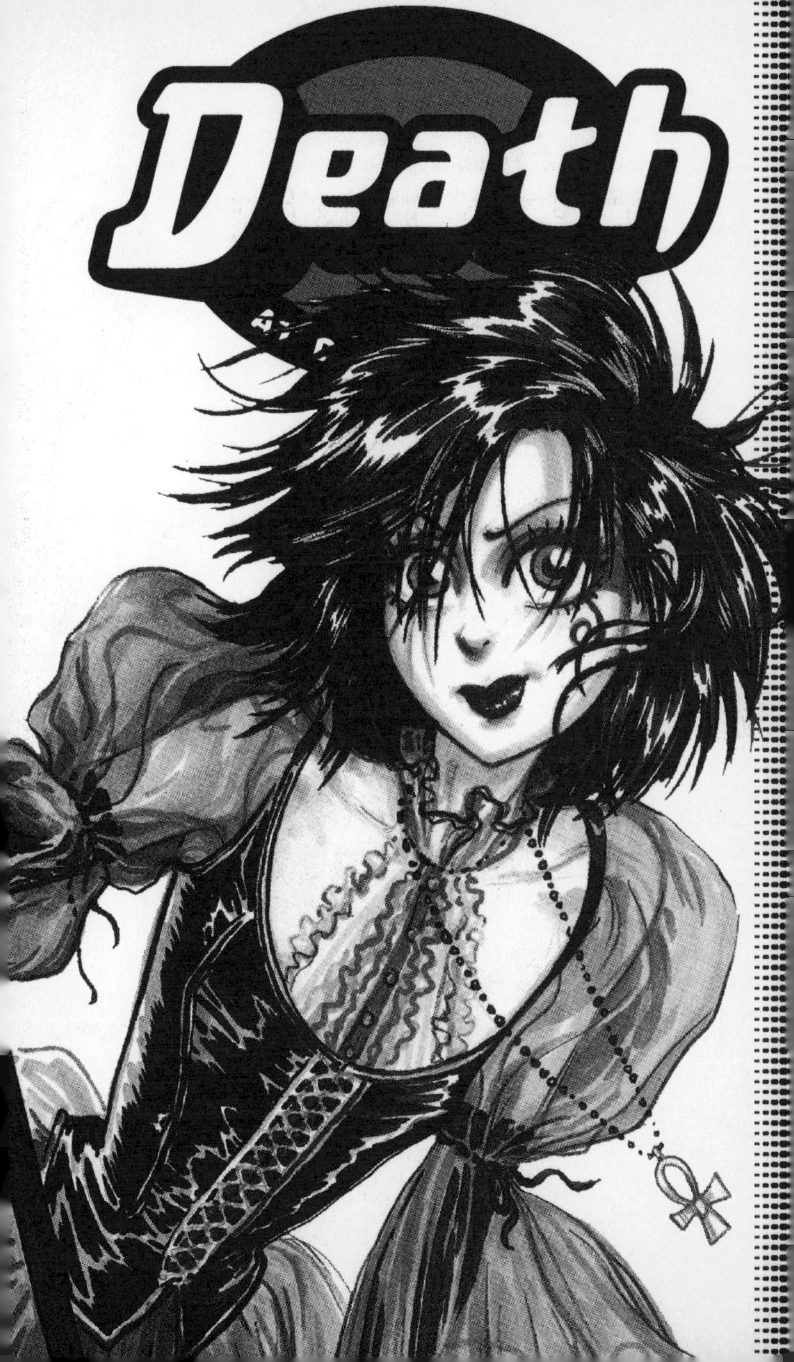
Death

DEATH #1: AT DEATH'S DOOR
Published by DC Comics,
1700 Broadway, New York, NY 10019.
Copyright © 2003 DC Comics. All Rights Reserved.
VERTIGO and all characters featured in this issue, the distinctive
likenesses thereof and all related indicia are trademarks of DC Comics.
The stories, characters and incidents mentioned
in this magazine are entirely fictional.
DC Comics does not read or accept unsolicited submissions
of ideas, stories or artwork.
ISBN 1-56389-938-8
Printed in Canada.
DC Comics, a Warner Bros. Entertainment Company

COVER PAINTING BY Jill Thompson
LOGO DESIGN BY Steve Cook

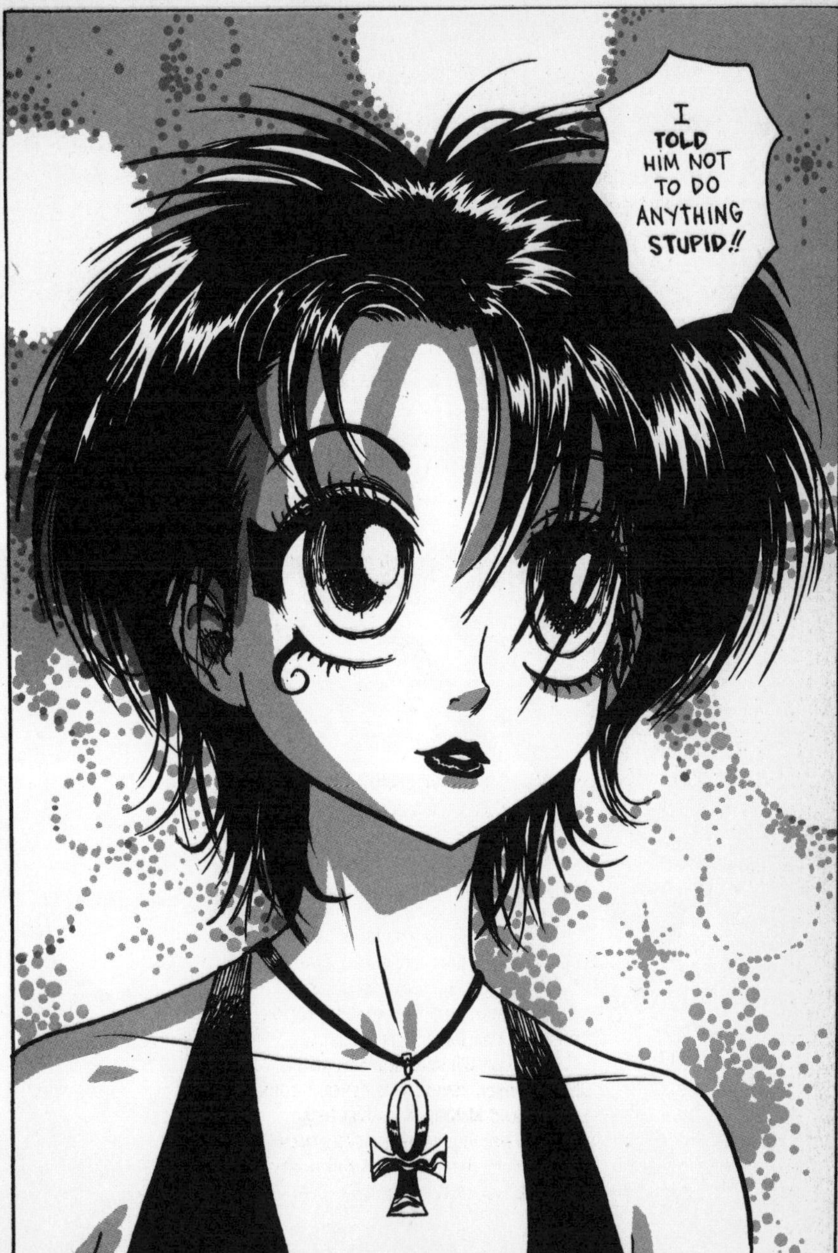
I TOLD HIM NOT TO DO ANYTHING STUPID!!

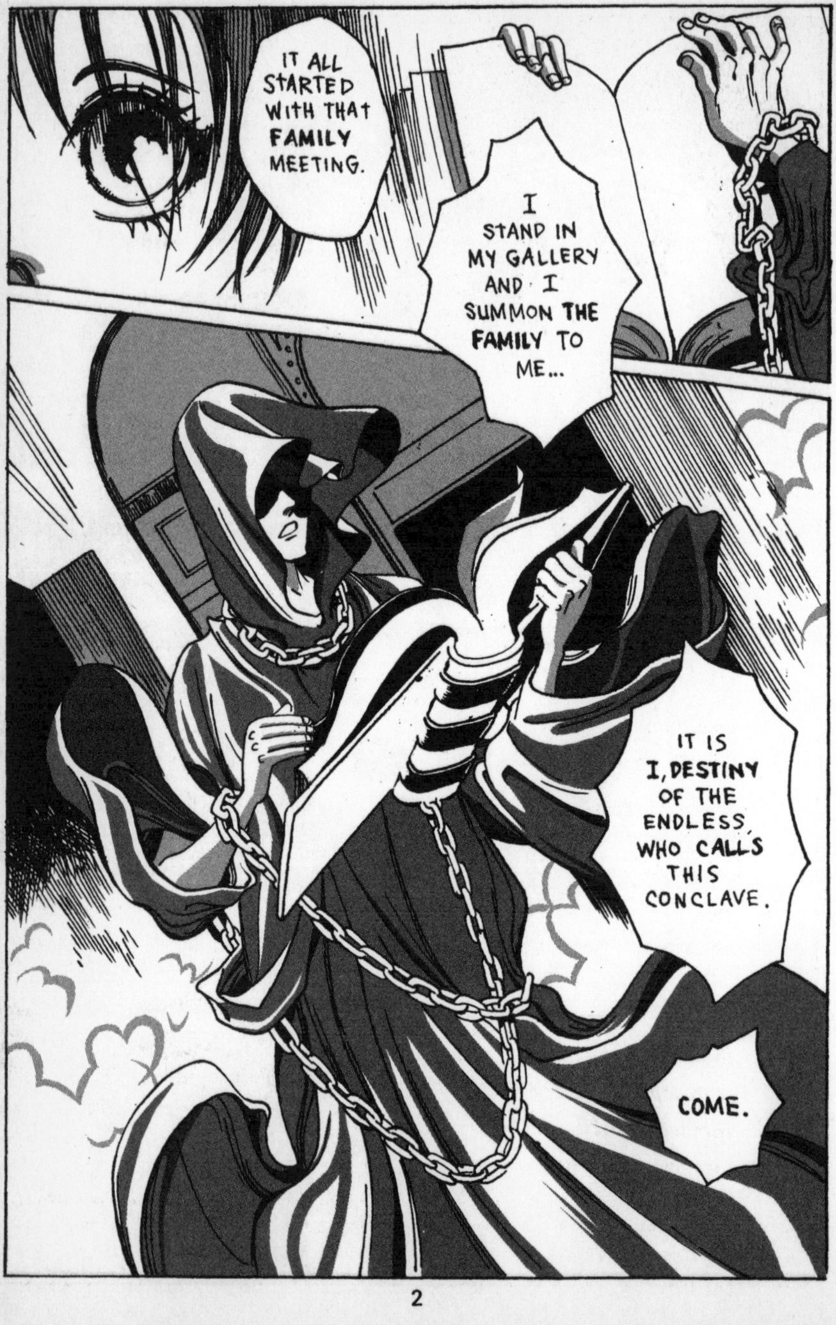
IT ALL STARTED WITH THAT FAMILY MEETING.
I STAND IN MY GALLERY AND I SUMMON THE FAMILY TO ME...
IT IS I, DESTINY OF THE ENDLESS, WHO CALLS THIS CONCLAVE.
COME.

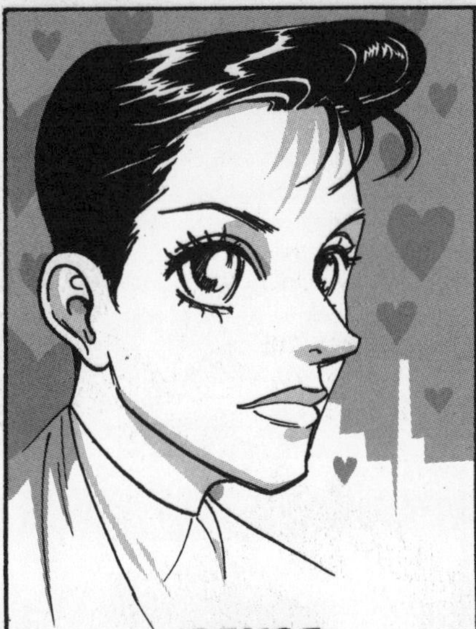

DESIRE

HEIGHT: medium
EYES : tawny, sharp as yellow wine
ODOR: summer peaches
FAVORITE COLOR: the color of sunset that makes you ache for lost love
HOBBY: being everything you've ever wanted
SPECIAL TALENT: casts two shadows, one black and sharp edged, the other translucent and wavering, like summer haze

DESPAIR

HEIGHT: shorter than desire, her twin
SKIN: cold and clammy
ODOR: none, but her shadow smells musky and pungent
EYES: the color of the sky on grey, wet days that leach the world of color and meaning
JOB: queen of her own bleak bourne, goddess of empty rooms
SPECIAL TALENT: patience

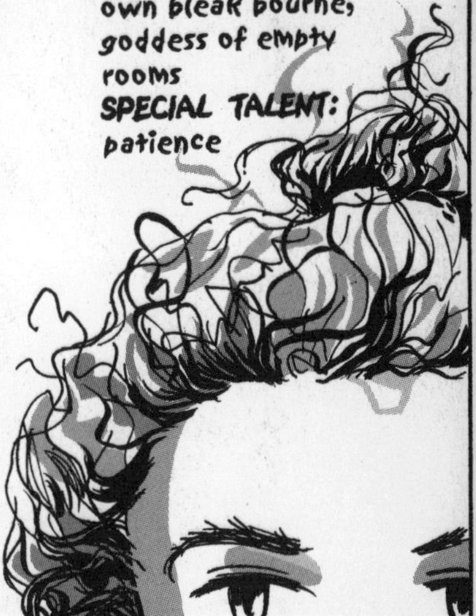

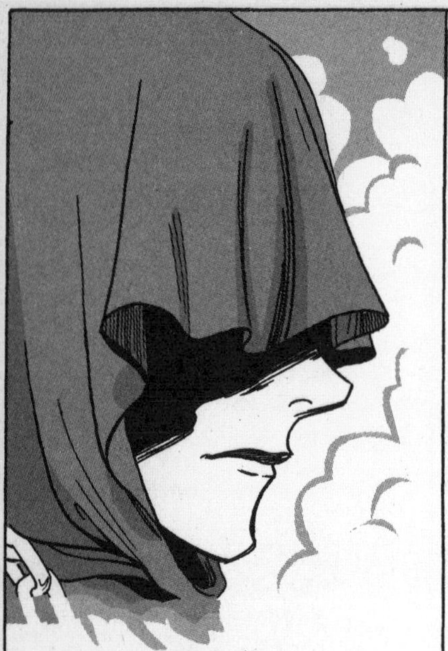

DESTINY

AGE: oldest of the endless
HEIGHT: tallest to mortal eyes
EYES: believed to be blind
SPECIAL TALENT: traveling far beyond blindness, watching the intricate patterns living things make on their journey through time, casting no shadow, leaving no footprints
ODOR: dust and the libraries of the night

DELIRIUM

AGE: older than suns, older than gods, but forever the youngest of the endless
EYES: one is vivid, emerald green with silver flecks, one is vein blue
FAVORITE COLOR: neon signs at 4 am
FAVORITE FOOD: little milk chocolate people with raspberry filling, fresh mango juice
LEAST FAVORITE FOOD: green mouse and telephone ice cream
ODOR: sweat, sour wines and old leather
SPECIAL TALENT: varied appearance, tangible shadow

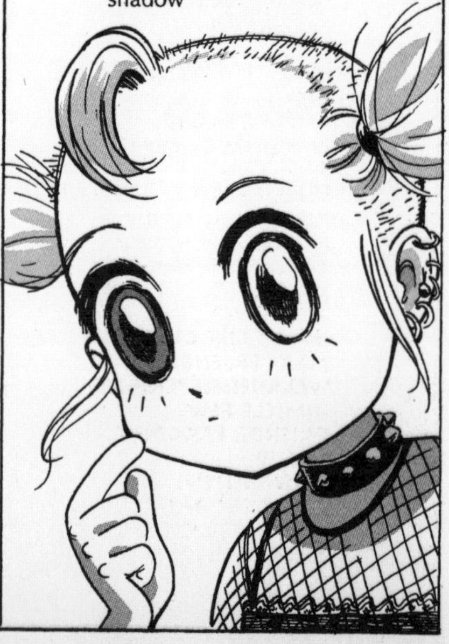

DREAM

WEIGHT: RAKE THIN
SKIN: THE COLOR OF FALLING SNOW
EYES: BLACK AS A MOONLESS, STARLESS NIGHT
FAVORITE FOOD: BANQUETS DREAMED BY SLEEPING CHEFS
LEAST FAVORITE FOOD: JUNK FOOD
JOB: LORD SHAPER, KING OF DREAMS
HOBBY: ACCUMULATING NAMES LIKE OTHERS MAKE FRIENDS
WEAKNESSES: PERMITS HIMSELF FEW FRIENDS, BROODING, PROUD
PERSONALITY: CONSCIOUS OF HIS RESPONSIBILITIES, METICULOUS

ALL OF MY SIBLINGS CAME...

DESTRUCTION

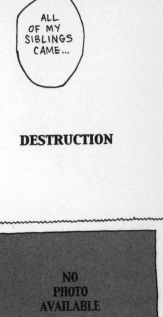

NO PHOTO AVAILABLE

EXCEPT FOR ONE.

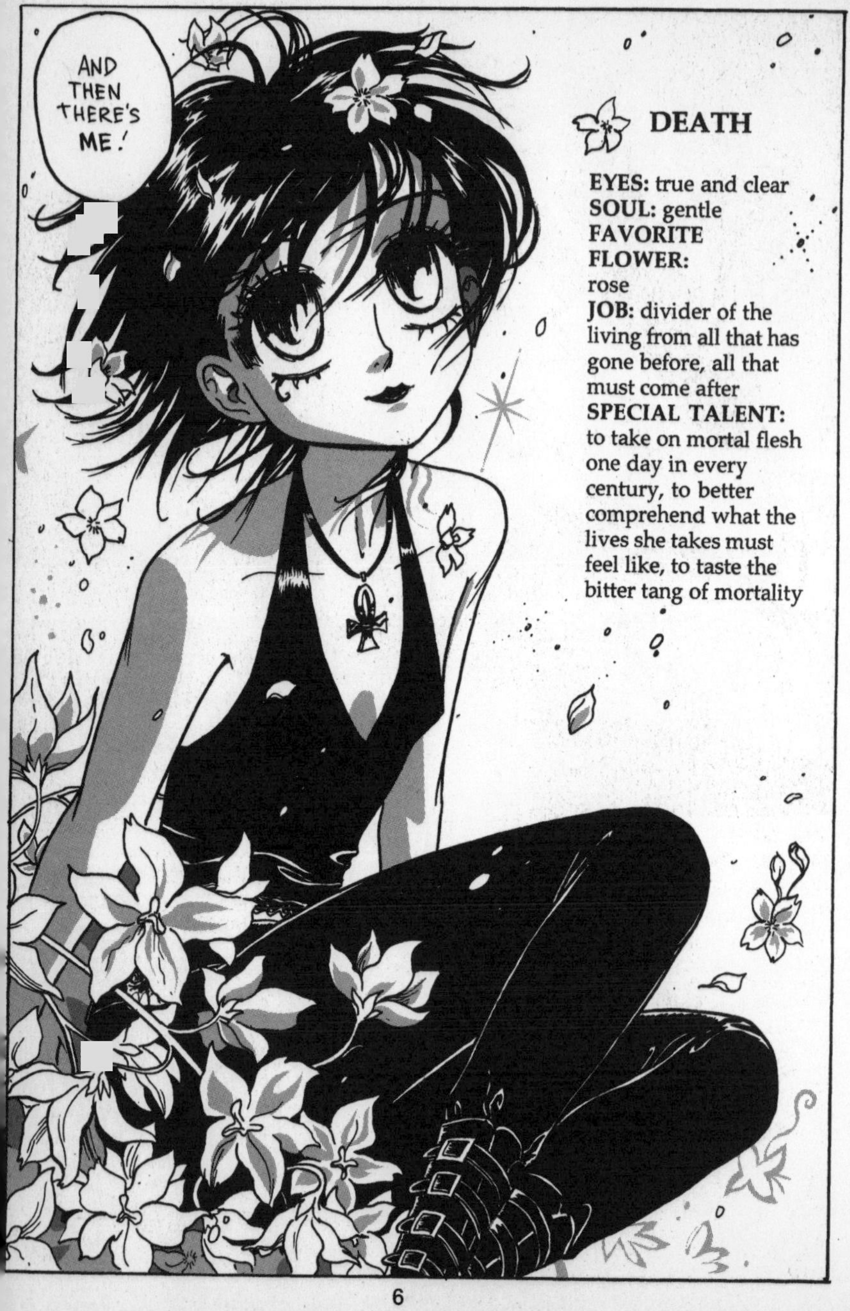
AND THEN THERE'S ME!
DEATH
EYES: true and clear
SOUL: gentle
FAVORITE FLOWER: rose
JOB: divider of the living from all that has gone before, all that must come after
SPECIAL TALENT: to take on mortal flesh one day in every century, to better comprehend what the lives she takes must feel like, to taste the bitter tang of mortality

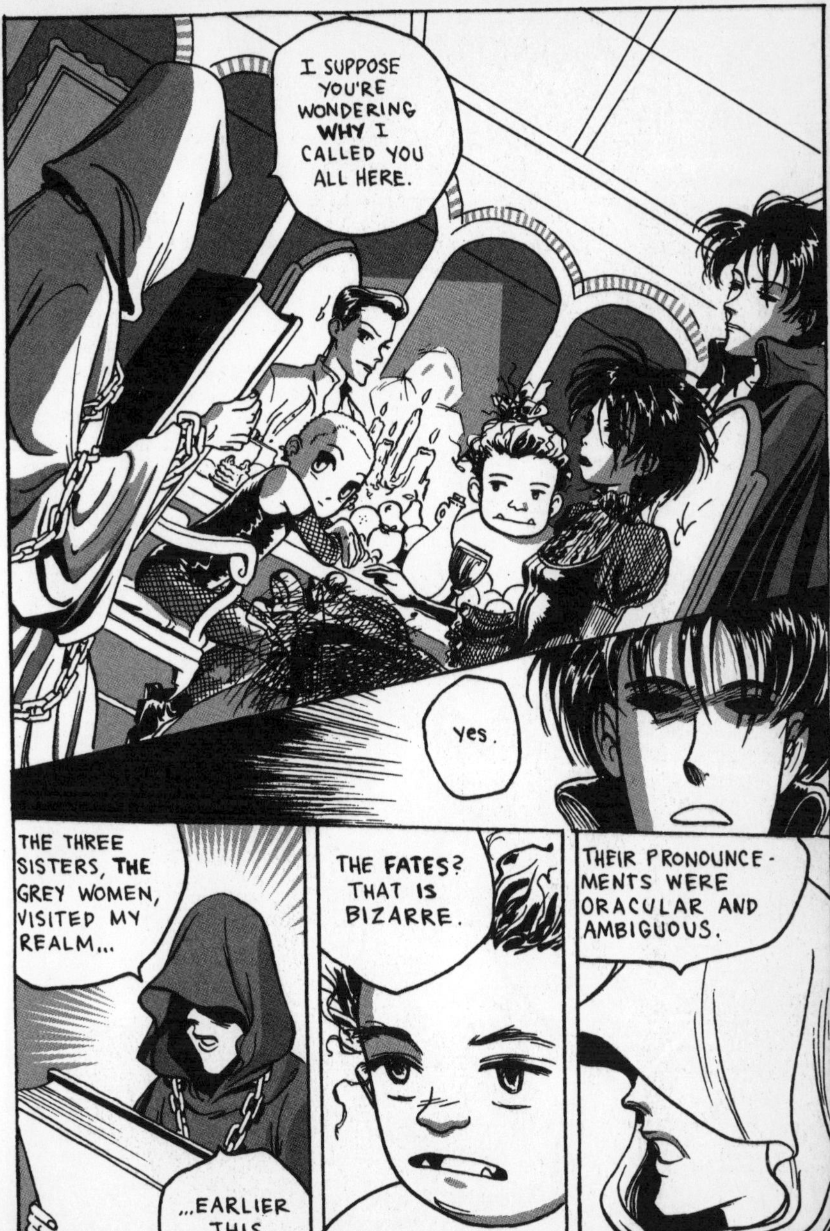
I SUPPOSE YOU'RE WONDERING **WHY** I CALLED YOU ALL HERE.
yes.
THE THREE SISTERS, **THE** GREY WOMEN, VISITED MY REALM...
...EARLIER THIS DAY.
THE **FATES**? THAT **IS** BIZARRE.
THEIR PRONOUNCE-MENTS WERE ORACULAR AND AMBIGUOUS.

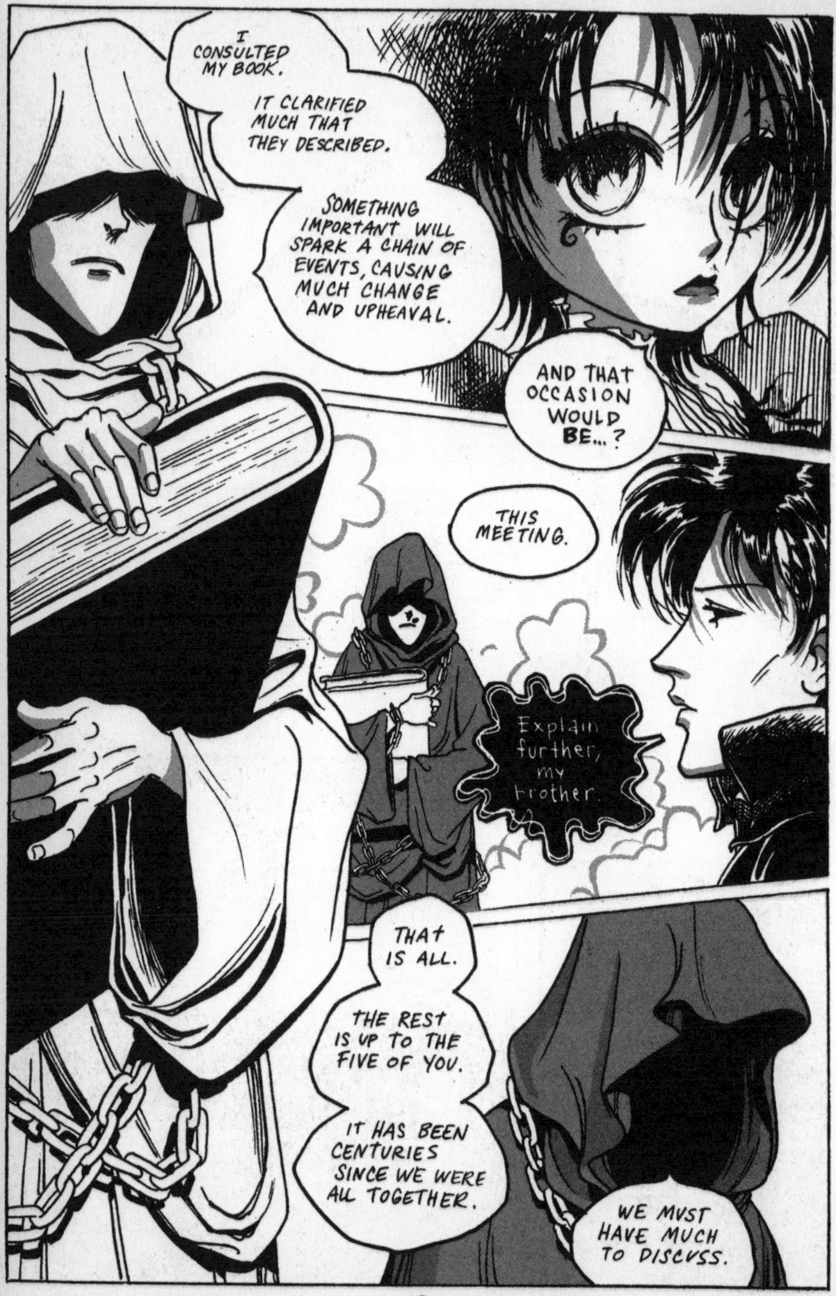
I CONSULTED MY BOOK.
IT CLARIFIED MUCH THAT THEY DESCRIBED.
SOMETHING IMPORTANT WILL SPARK A CHAIN OF EVENTS, CAUSING MUCH CHANGE AND UPHEAVAL.
AND THAT OCCASION WOULD BE...?
THIS MEETING.
Explain further, my brother.
THAT IS ALL.
THE REST IS UP TO THE FIVE OF YOU.
IT HAS BEEN CENTURIES SINCE WE WERE ALL TOGETHER.
WE MUST HAVE MUCH TO DISCUSS.

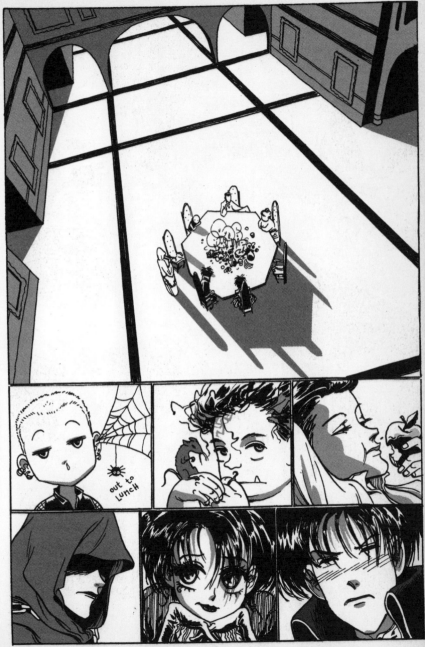

out to
LUNCH

9

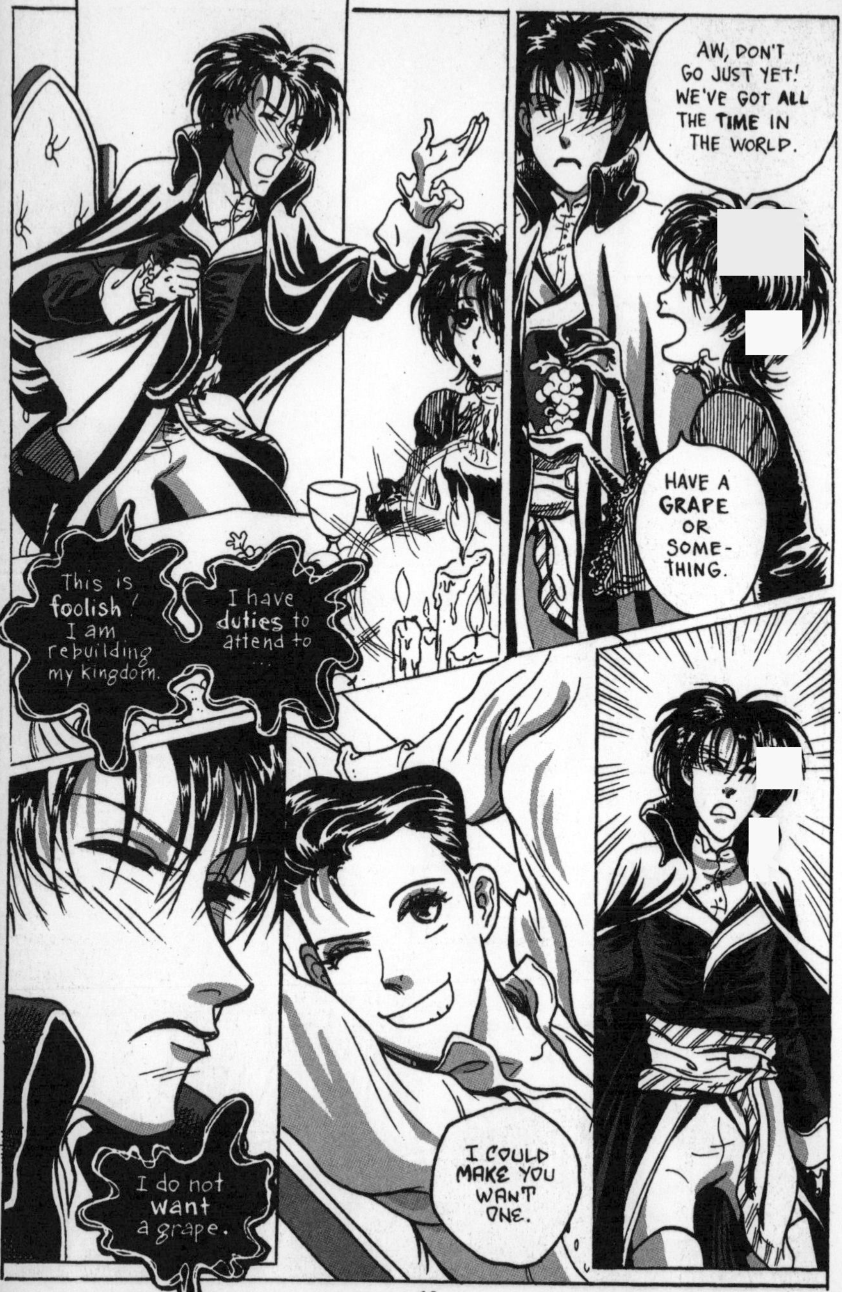
This is foolish! I am rebuilding my kingdom.
I have duties to attend to...
AW, DON'T GO JUST YET! WE'VE GOT ALL THE TIME IN THE WORLD.
HAVE A GRAPE OR SOMETHING.
I do not want a grape.
I COULD MAKE YOU WANT ONE.

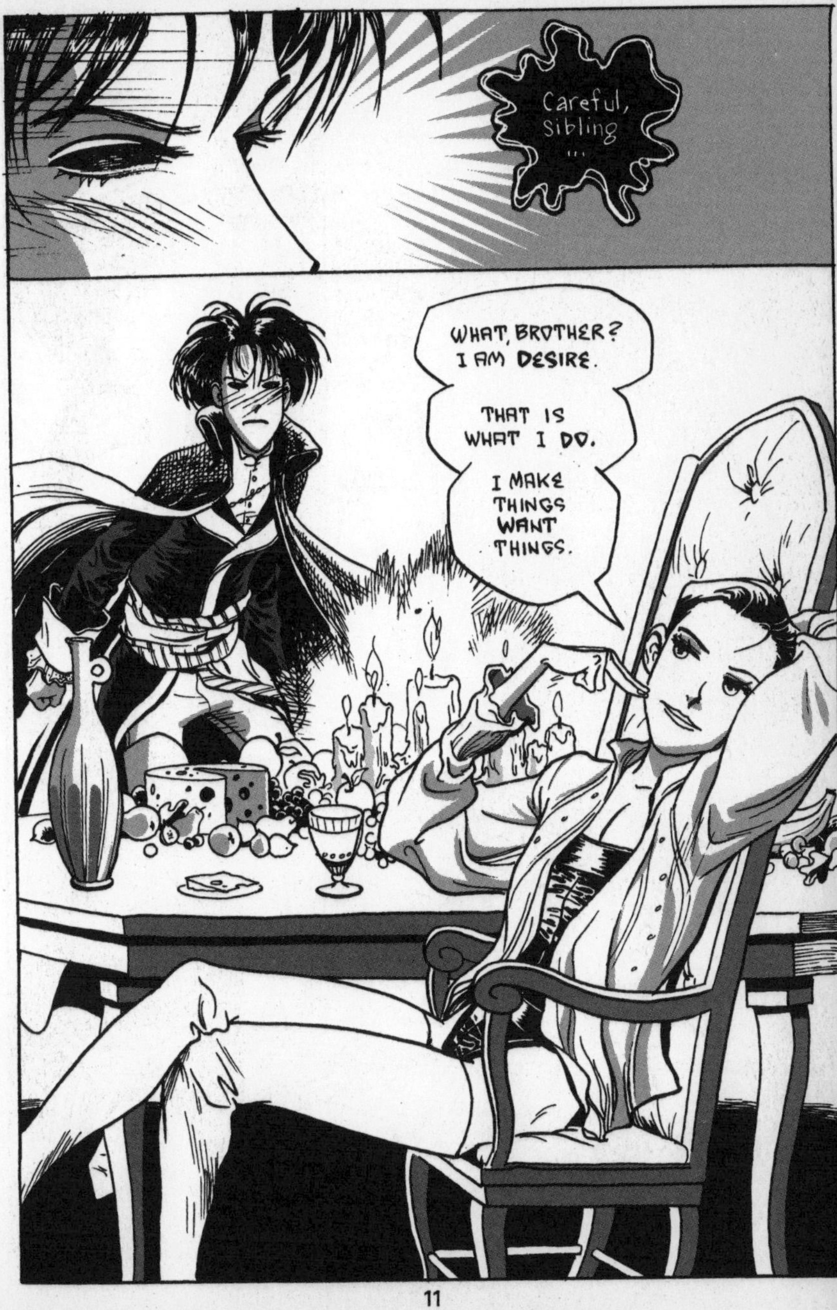
Careful, Sibling ...
WHAT, BROTHER? I AM DESIRE.
THAT IS WHAT I DO.
I MAKE THINGS WANT THINGS.

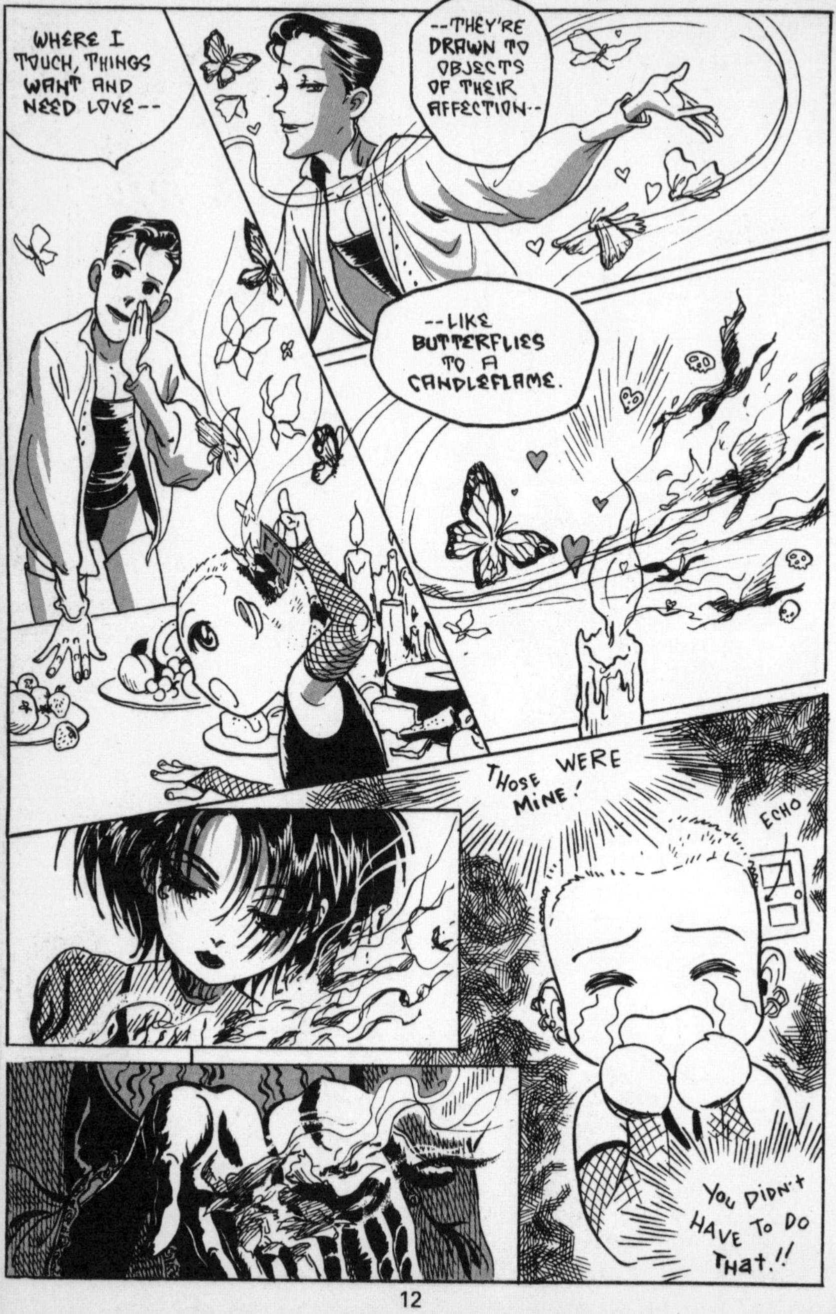
WHERE I TOUCH, THINGS WANT AND NEED LOVE--
--THEY'RE DRAWN TO OBJECTS OF THEIR AFFECTION--
--LIKE BUTTERFLIES TO A CANDLEFLAME.
THOSE WERE MINE!
ECHO
You DIDN'T HAVE TO DO THAT!!

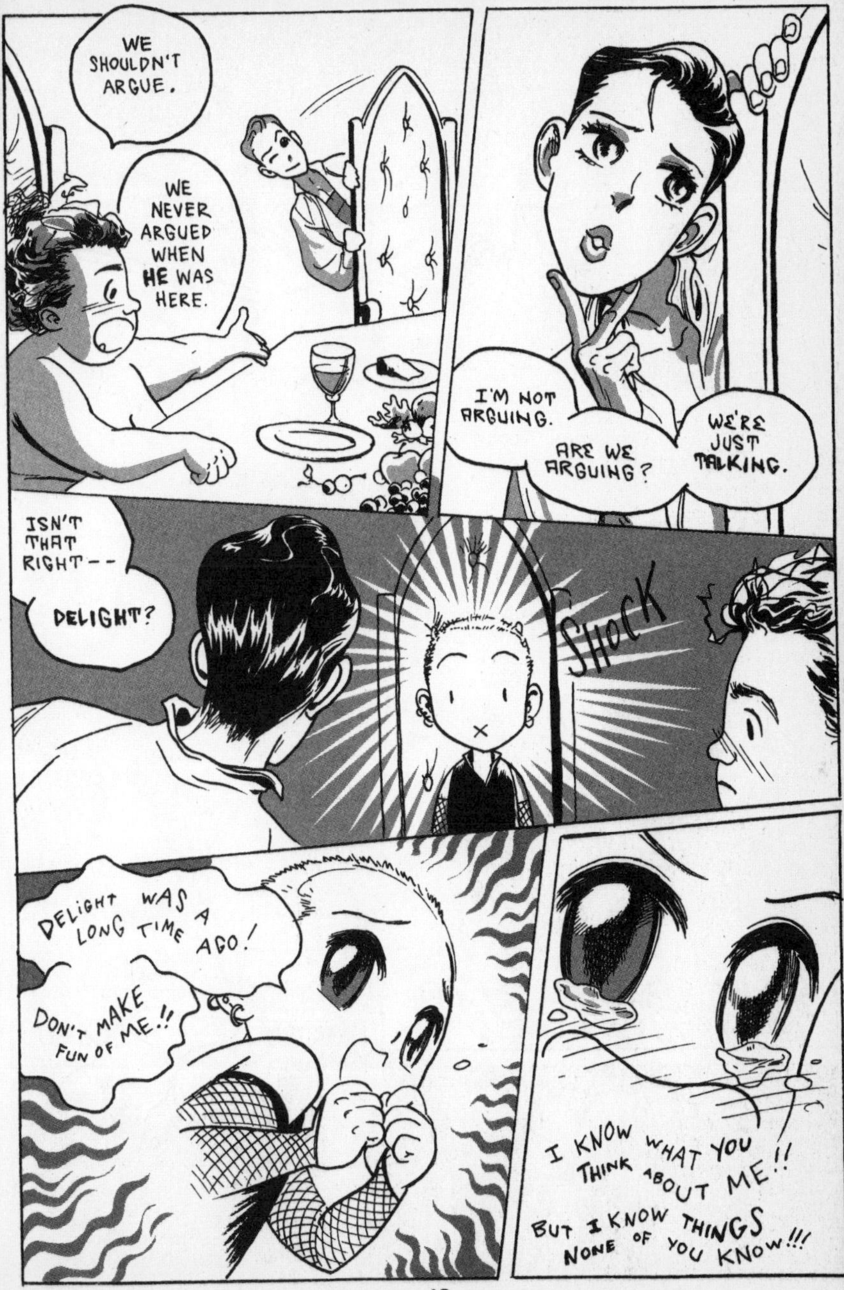
WE SHOULDN'T ARGUE.
WE NEVER ARGUED WHEN HE WAS HERE.
I'M NOT ARGUING.
ARE WE ARGUING?
WE'RE JUST TALKING.
ISN'T THAT RIGHT--
DELIGHT?
SHOCK
DELIGHT WAS A LONG TIME AGO!
DON'T MAKE FUN OF ME.!!
I KNOW WHAT YOU THINK ABOUT ME!!
BUT I KNOW THINGS NONE OF YOU KNOW!!!

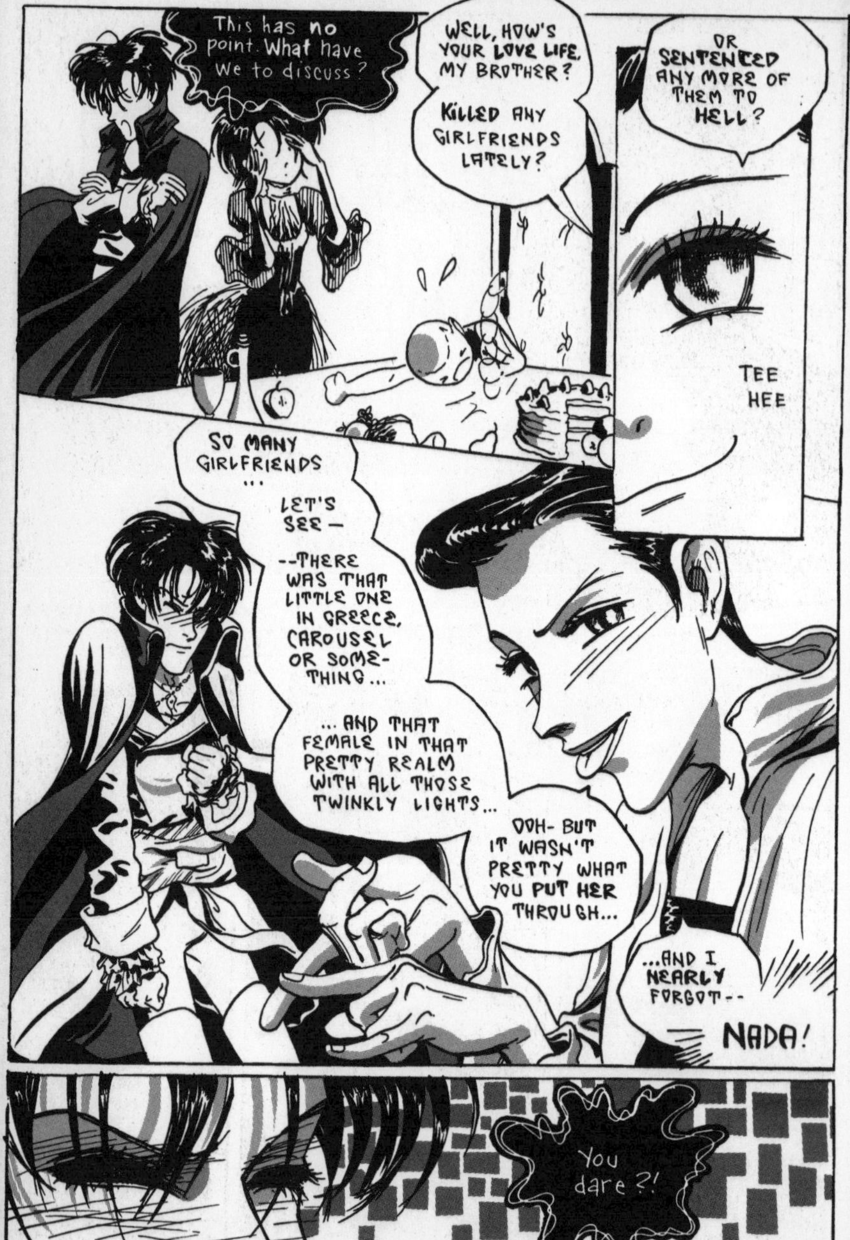
This has no point. What have we to discuss?
WELL, HOW'S YOUR LOVE LIFE, MY BROTHER?
KILLED ANY GIRLFRIENDS LATELY?
OR SENTENCED ANY MORE OF THEM TO HELL?
TEE HEE
SO MANY GIRLFRIENDS ...
LET'S SEE --
--THERE WAS THAT LITTLE ONE IN GREECE, CAROUSEL OR SOME-THING...
... AND THAT FEMALE IN THAT PRETTY REALM WITH ALL THOSE TWINKLY LIGHTS...
OOH- BUT IT WASN'T PRETTY WHAT YOU PUT HER THROUGH...
...AND I NEARLY FORGOT--
NADA!
You dare?!

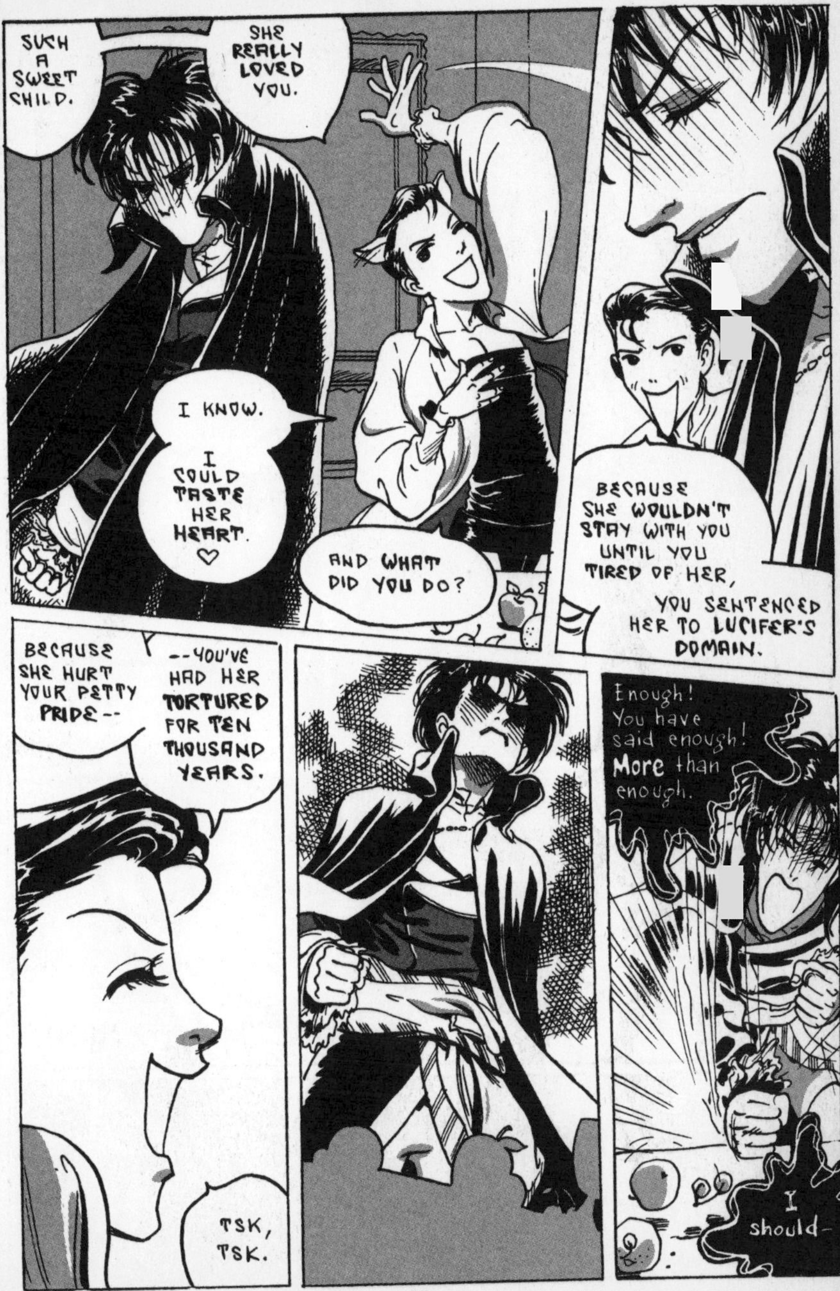
SUCH A SWEET CHILD.
SHE REALLY LOVED YOU.
I KNOW.
I COULD TASTE HER HEART. ♥
AND WHAT DID YOU DO?
BECAUSE SHE WOULDN'T STAY WITH YOU UNTIL YOU TIRED OF HER,
YOU SENTENCED HER TO LUCIFER'S DOMAIN.
BECAUSE SHE HURT YOUR PETTY PRIDE--
--YOU'VE HAD HER TORTURED FOR TEN THOUSAND YEARS.
TSK, TSK.
Enough! You have said enough! More than enough.
I should-

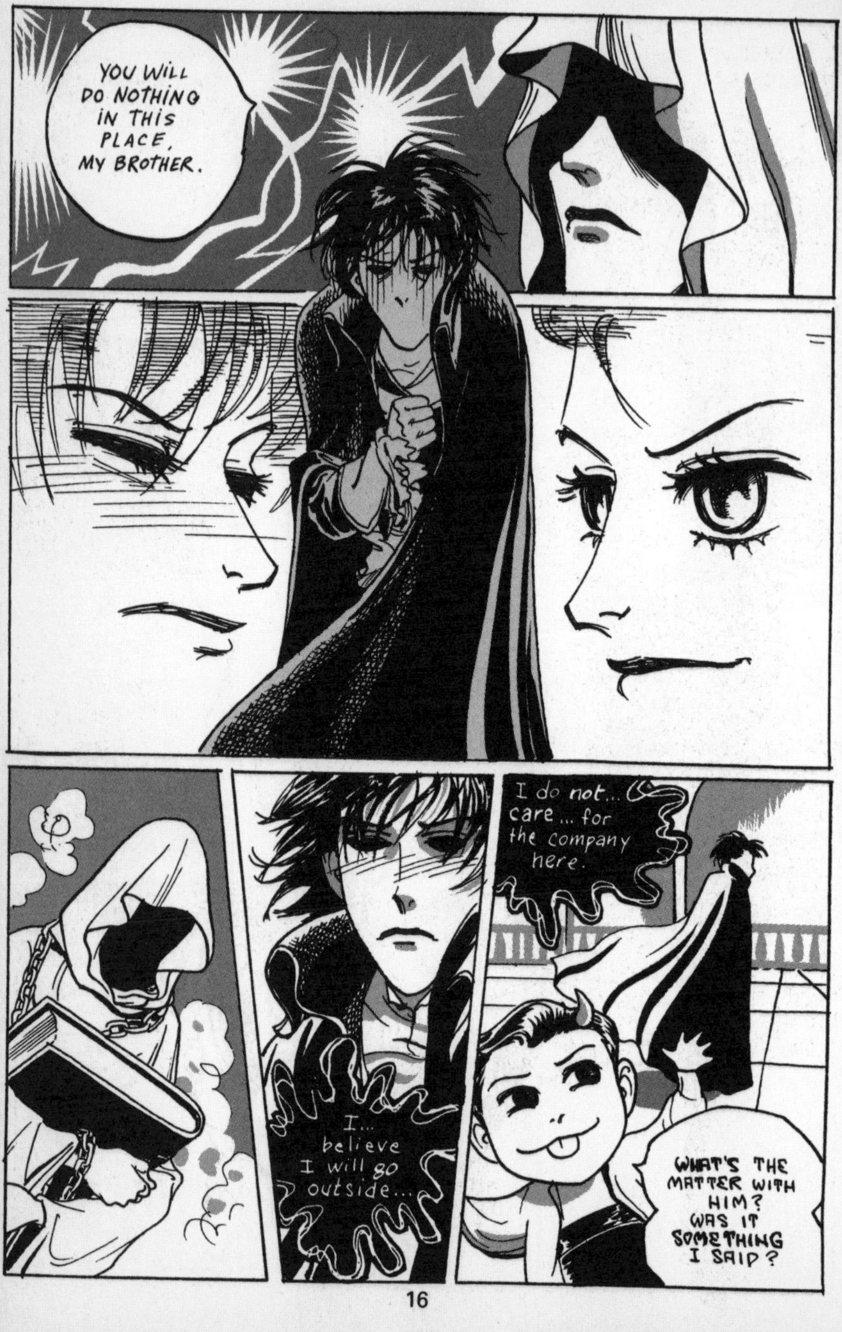
YOU WILL DO NOTHING IN THIS PLACE, MY BROTHER.
I do not... care... for the company here.
I... believe I will go outside...
WHAT'S THE MATTER WITH HIM? WAS IT SOMETHING I SAID?

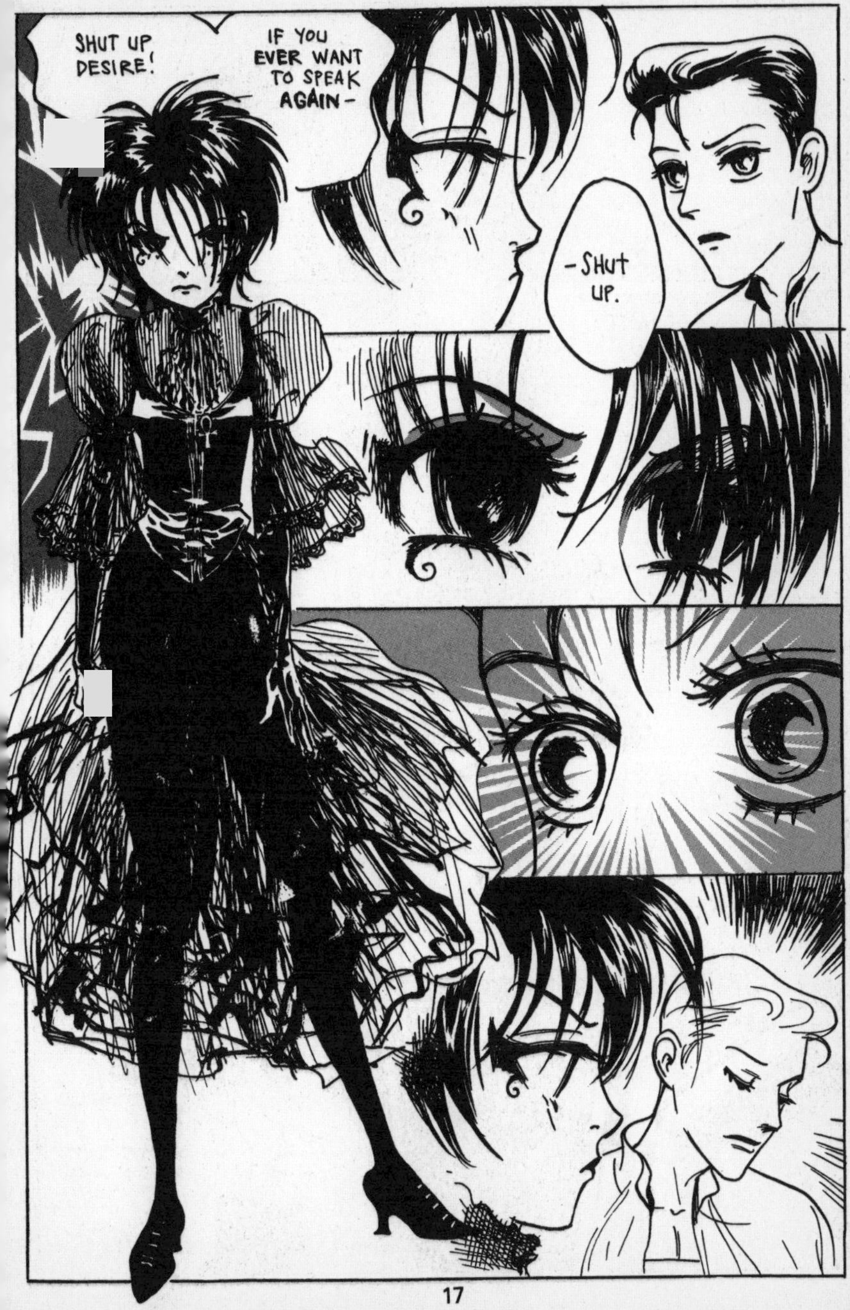
SHUT UP DESIRE!
IF YOU EVER WANT TO SPEAK AGAIN-
-SHUT UP.

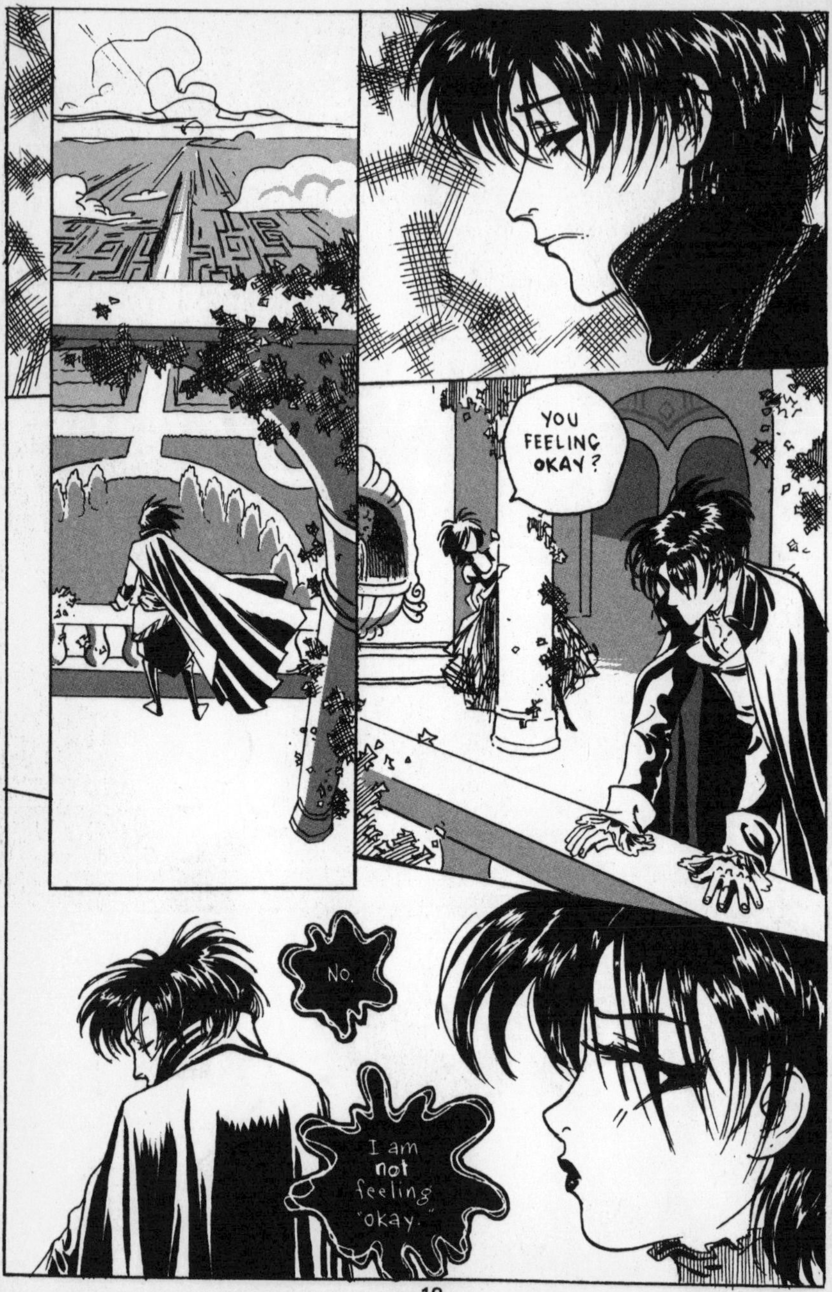
YOU FEELING OKAY?
No.
I am not feeling "okay."

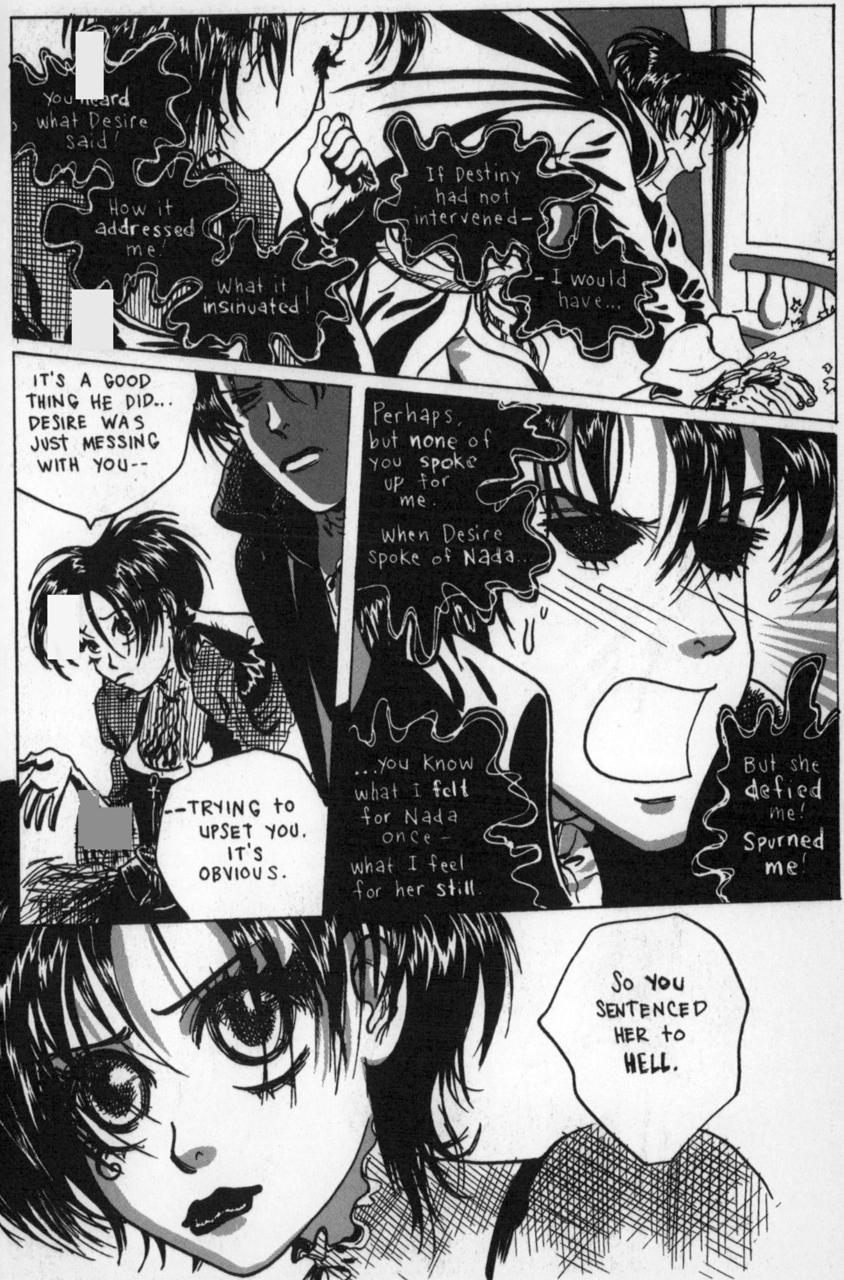

You heard what Desire said!
How it addressed me!
What it insinuated!
If Destiny had not intervened--
--I would have...
IT'S A GOOD THING HE DID... DESIRE WAS JUST MESSING WITH YOU--
--TRYING TO UPSET YOU. IT'S OBVIOUS.
Perhaps, but none of you spoke up for me.
When Desire spoke of Nada...
...you know what I felt for Nada once--
what I feel for her still.
But she defied me! Spurned me!
SO YOU SENTENCED HER TO HELL.

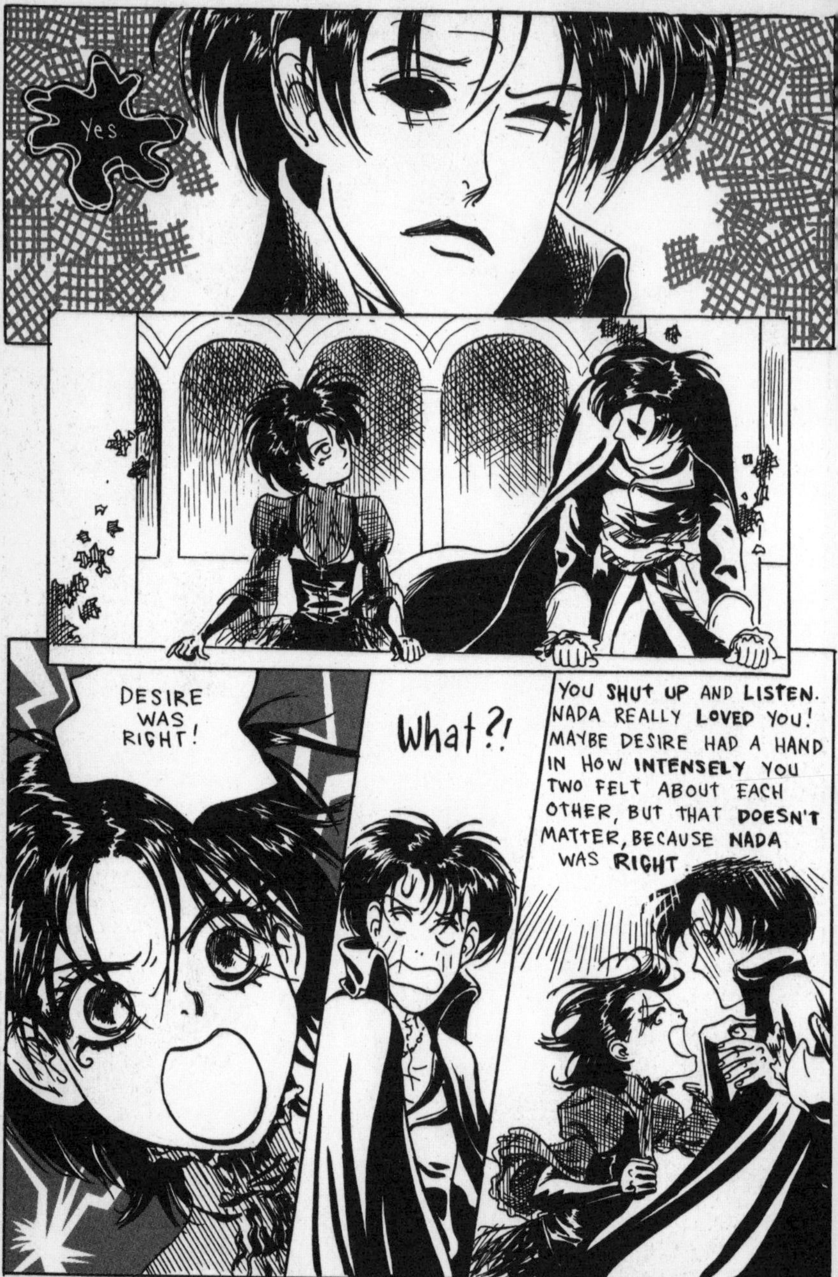
yes
DESIRE WAS RIGHT!
What?!
YOU SHUT UP AND LISTEN. NADA REALLY LOVED YOU! MAYBE DESIRE HAD A HAND IN HOW INTENSELY YOU TWO FELT ABOUT EACH OTHER, BUT THAT DOESN'T MATTER, BECAUSE NADA WAS RIGHT.

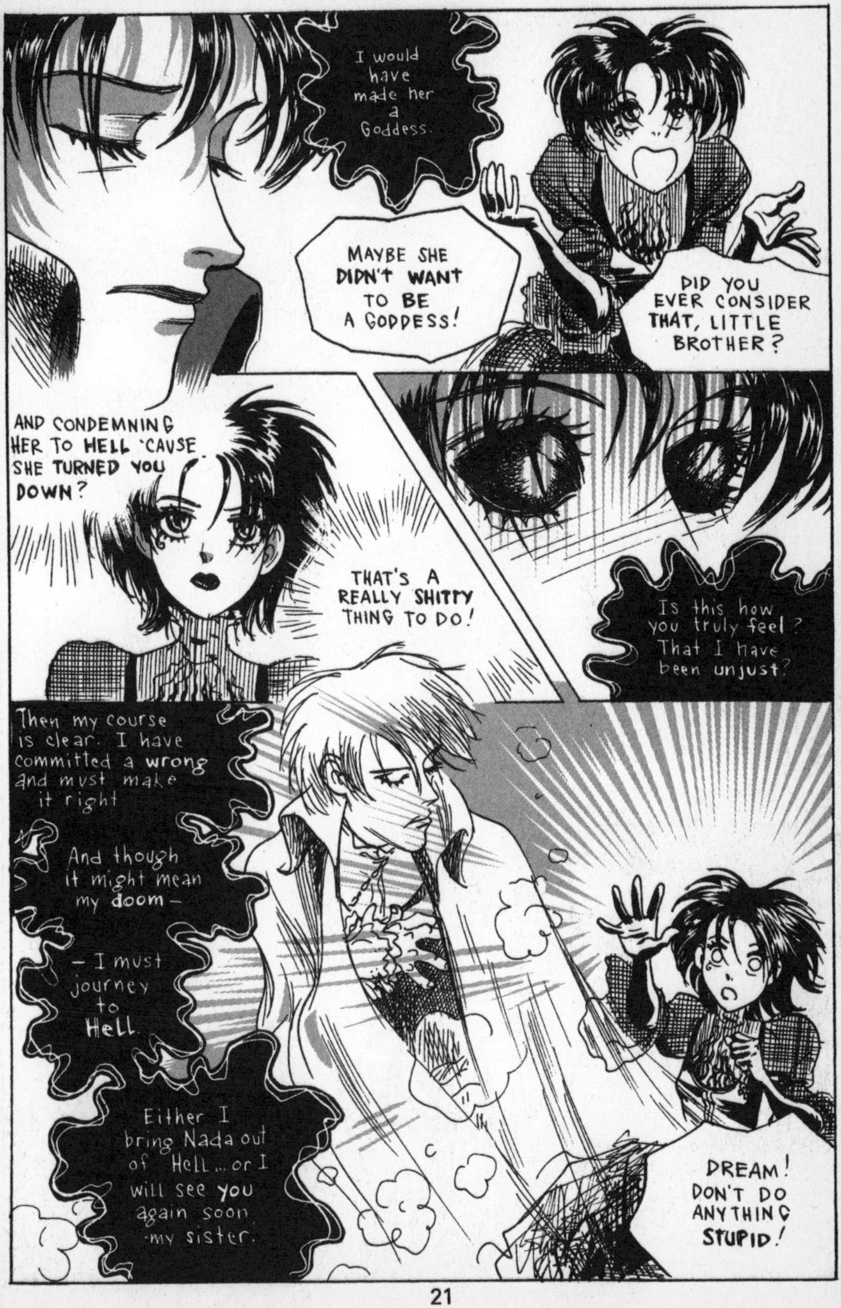
I would have made her a Goddess.
MAYBE SHE DIDN'T WANT TO BE A GODDESS!
DID YOU EVER CONSIDER THAT, LITTLE BROTHER?
AND CONDEMNING HER TO HELL 'CAUSE SHE TURNED YOU DOWN?
THAT'S A REALLY SHITTY THING TO DO!
Is this how you truly feel? That I have been unjust?
Then my course is clear. I have committed a wrong and must make it right.
And though it might mean my doom–
–I must journey to Hell.
Either I bring Nada out of Hell... or I will see you again soon, my sister.
DREAM! DON'T DO ANYTHING STUPID!

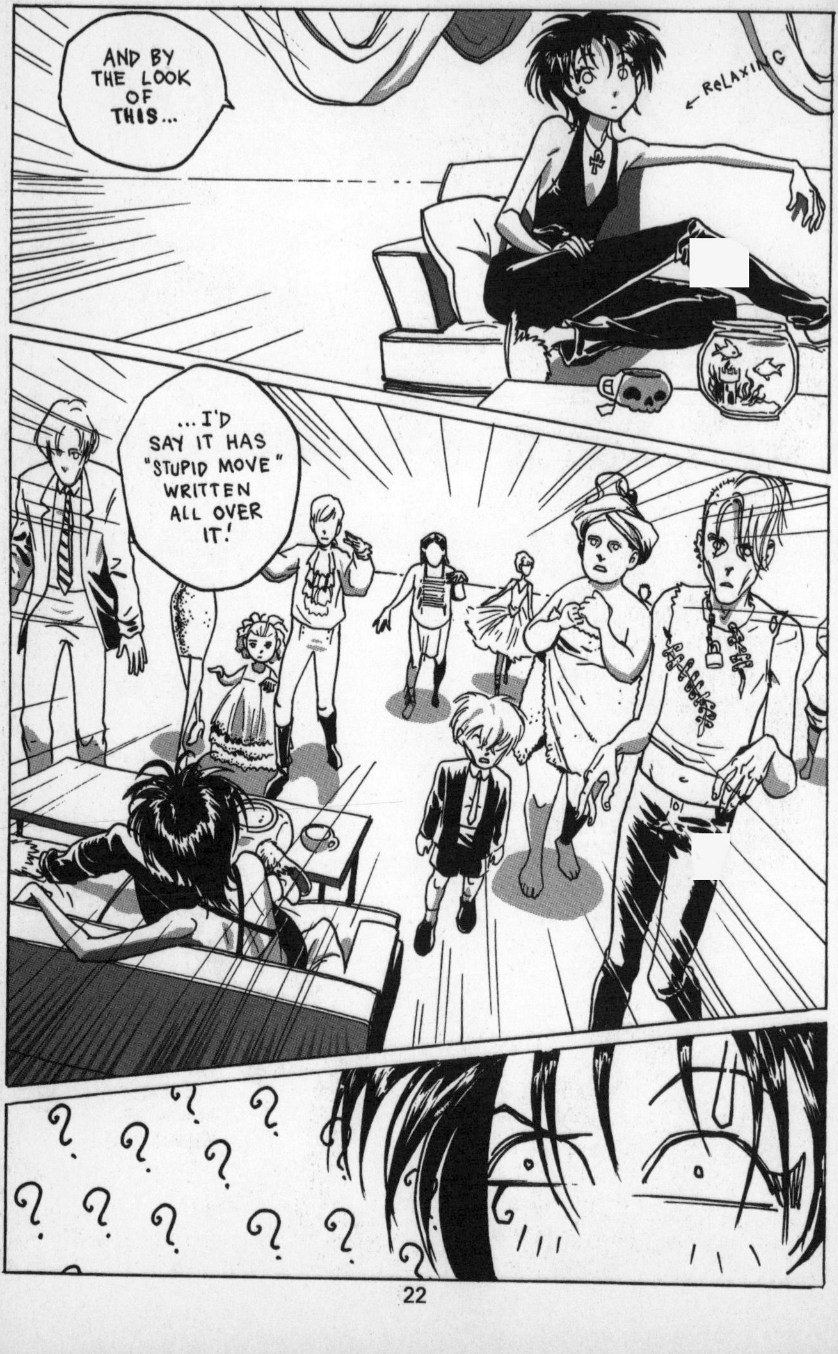
AND BY THE LOOK OF THIS...
RELAXING
...I'D SAY IT HAS "STUPID MOVE" WRITTEN ALL OVER IT!

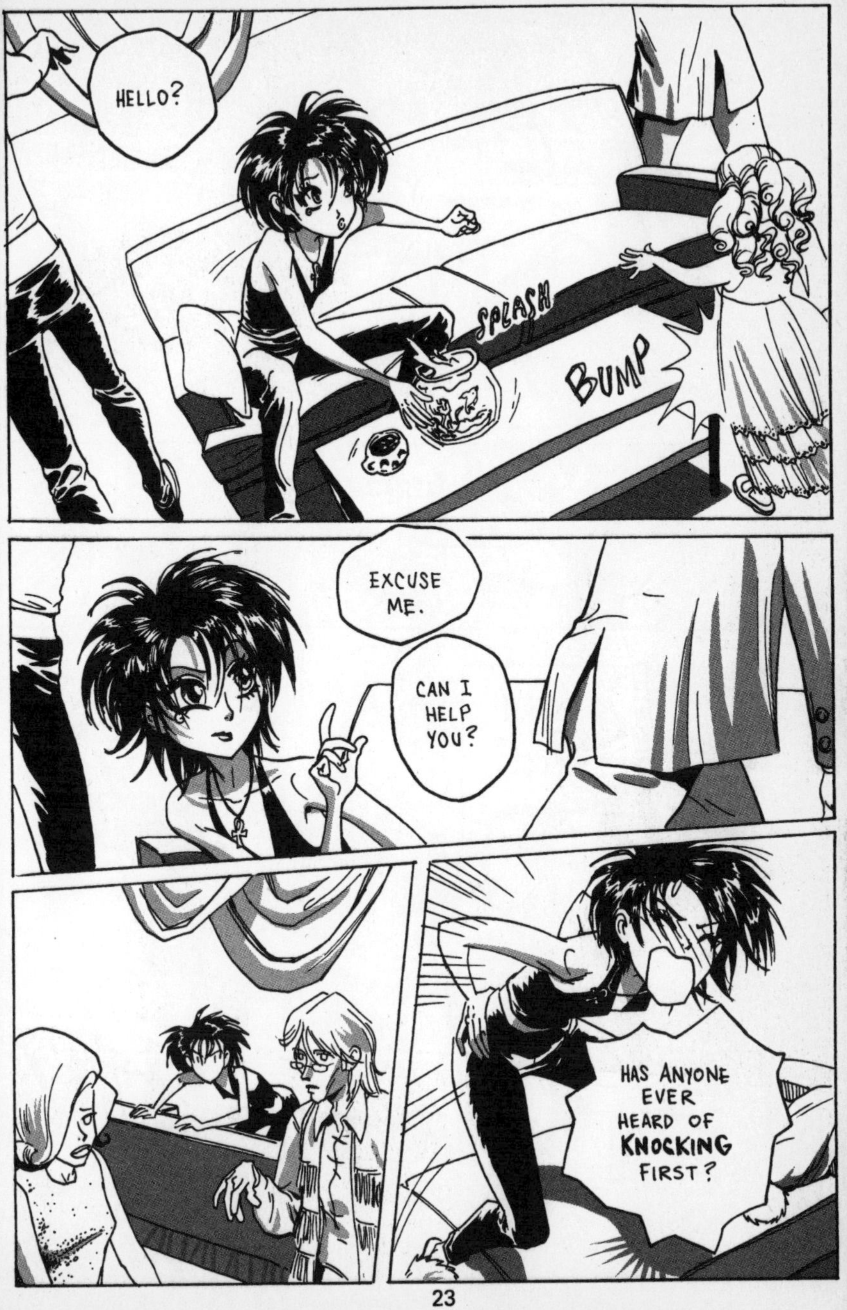
HELLO?
SPLASH
BUMP
EXCUSE ME.
CAN I HELP YOU?
HAS ANYONE EVER HEARD OF KNOCKING FIRST?

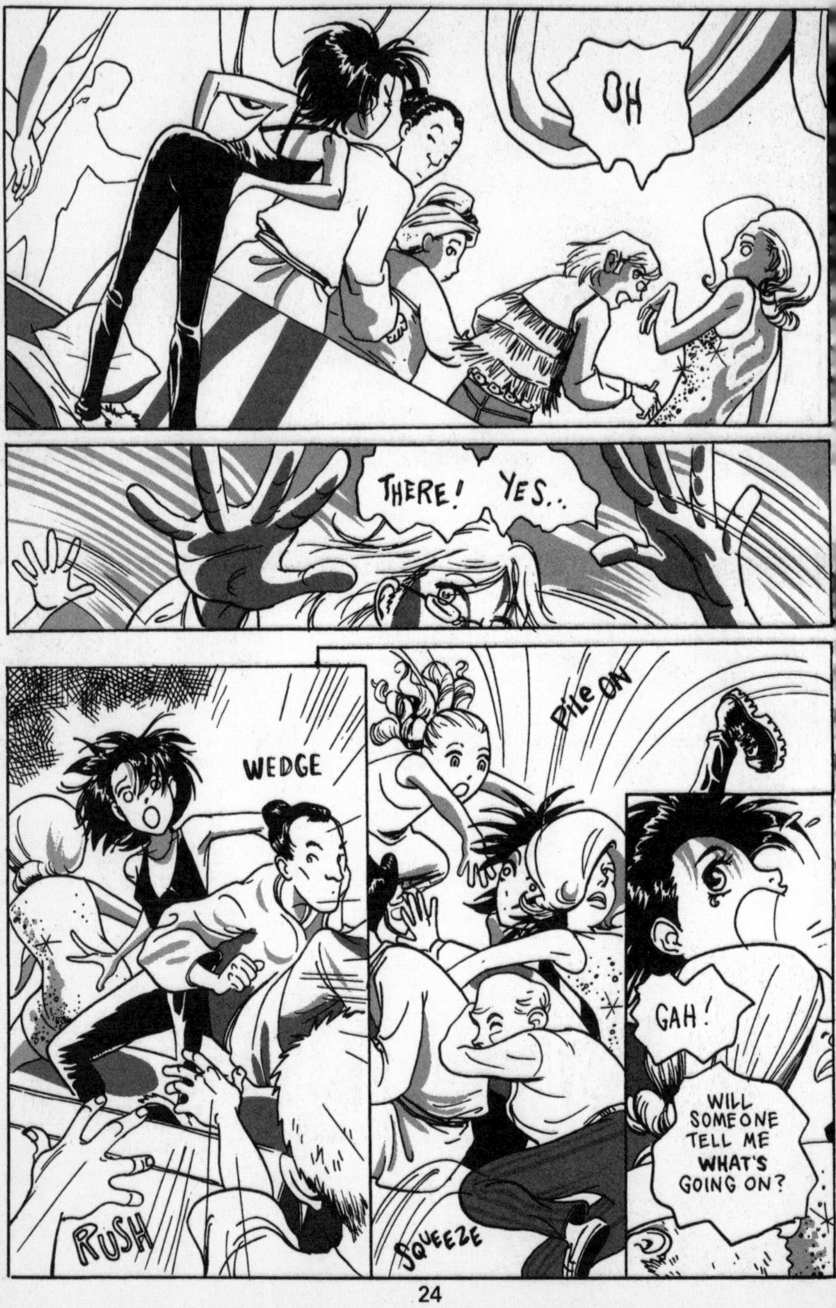
OH
THERE! YES..
WEDGE
RUSH
PILE ON
SQUEEZE
GAH!
WILL SOMEONE TELL ME WHAT'S GOING ON?

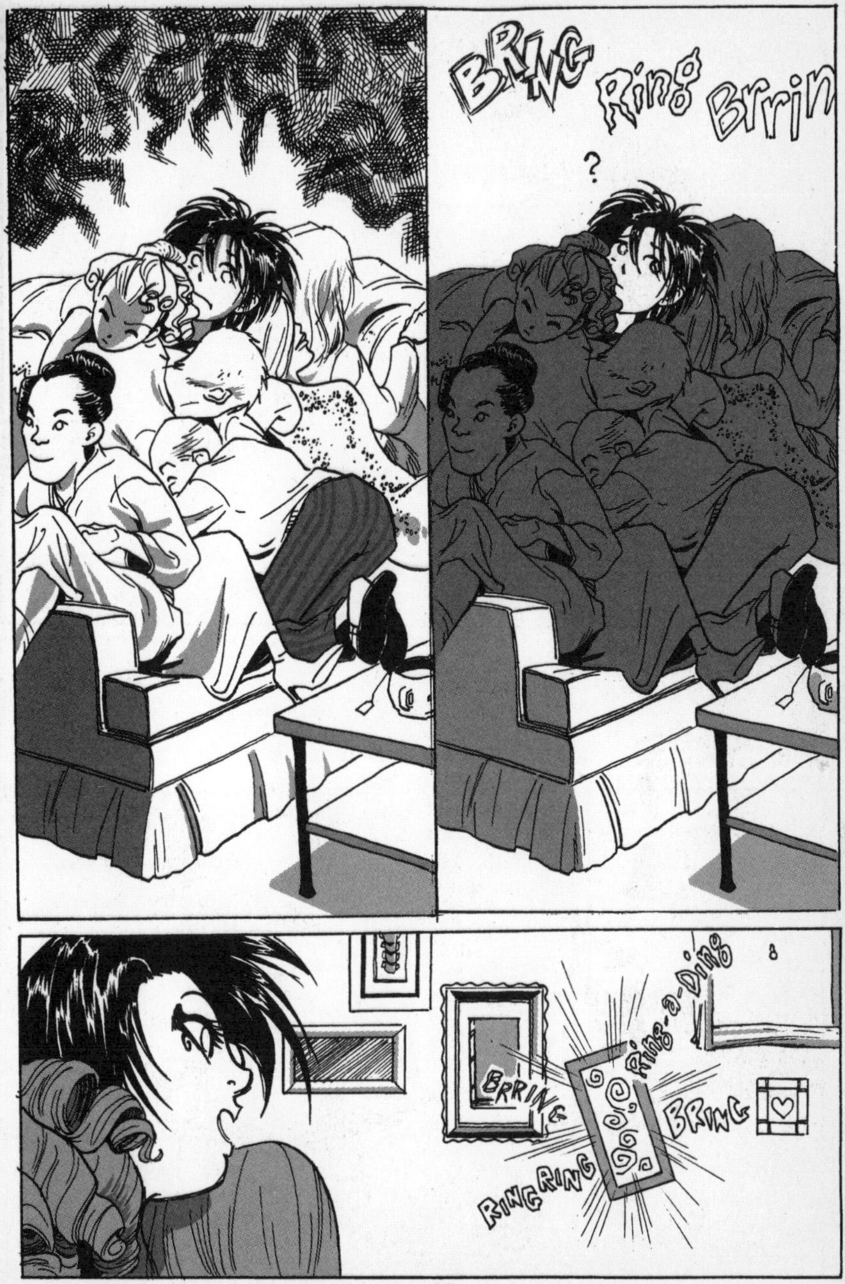
BRING
Ring
Brrin
?
BRRING
Ring-a-Ding
BRING
RING RING

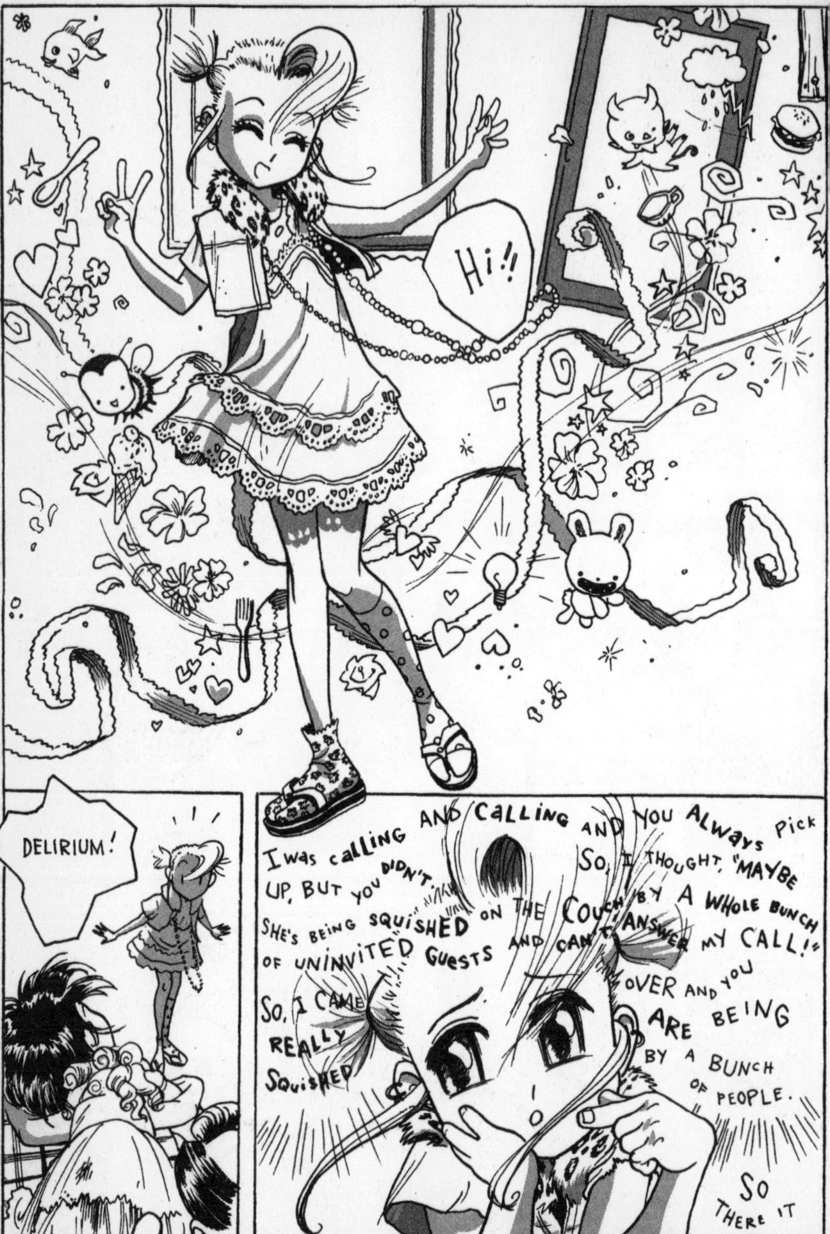
Hi!!
DELIRIUM!
I was calling and calling and you always pick up, but you didn't. So, I thought, "Maybe she's being squished on the couch by a whole bunch of uninvited guests and can't answer my call!"
So, I came over and you are being really squished by a bunch of people.
So there it is.

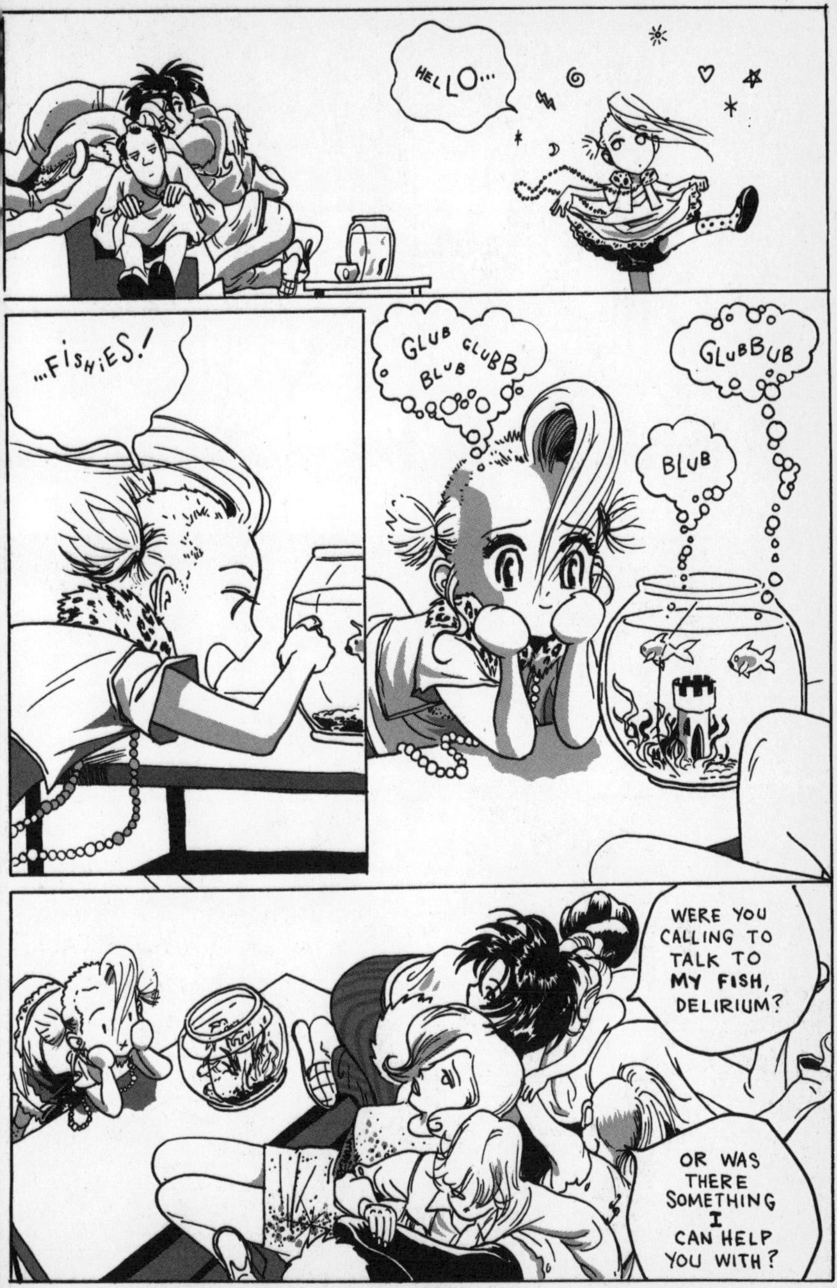
HELLO...
...FISHIES!
GLUB BLUB GLUBB
BLUB
GLUBBUB
WERE YOU CALLING TO TALK TO MY FISH, DELIRIUM?
OR WAS THERE SOMETHING I CAN HELP YOU WITH?

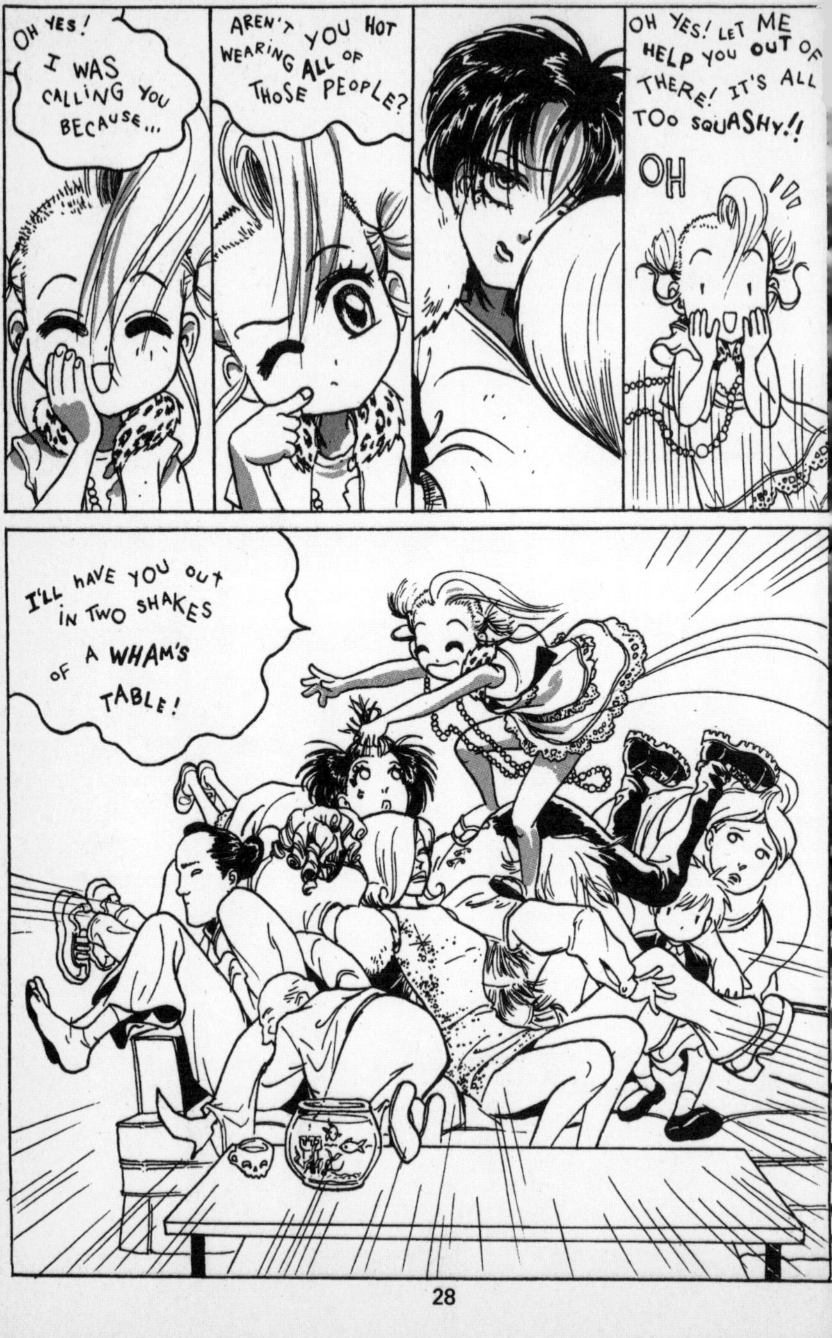
OH YES! I WAS CALLING YOU BECAUSE...
AREN'T YOU HOT WEARING ALL OF THOSE PEOPLE?
OH YES! LET ME HELP YOU OUT OF THERE! IT'S ALL TOO SQUASHY!!
OH
I'LL HAVE YOU OUT IN TWO SHAKES OF A WHAM'S TABLE!

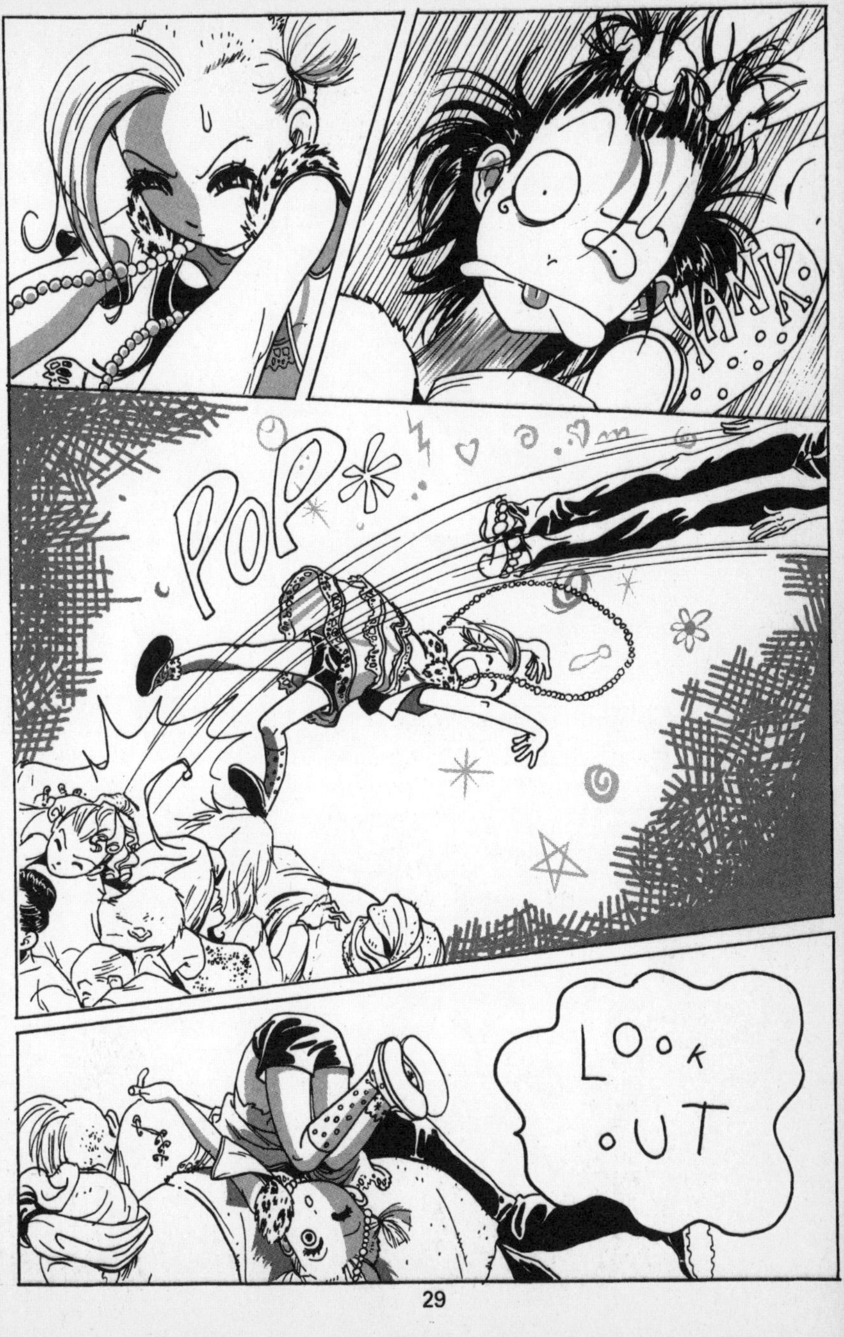
YANK
POP
LOOK OUT

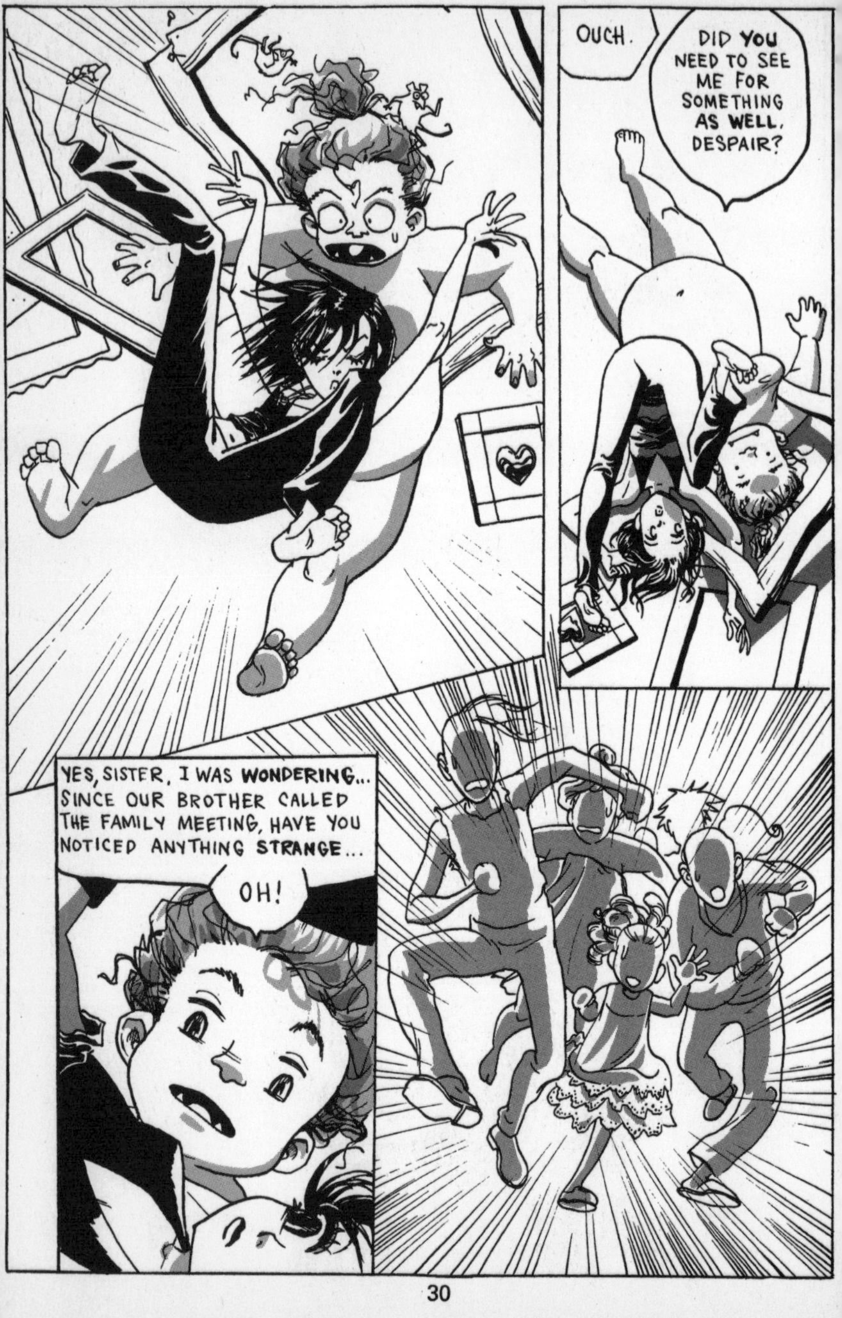
OUCH.
DID YOU NEED TO SEE ME FOR SOMETHING AS WELL, DESPAIR?
YES, SISTER, I WAS WONDERING... SINCE OUR BROTHER CALLED THE FAMILY MEETING, HAVE YOU NOTICED ANYTHING STRANGE...
OH!

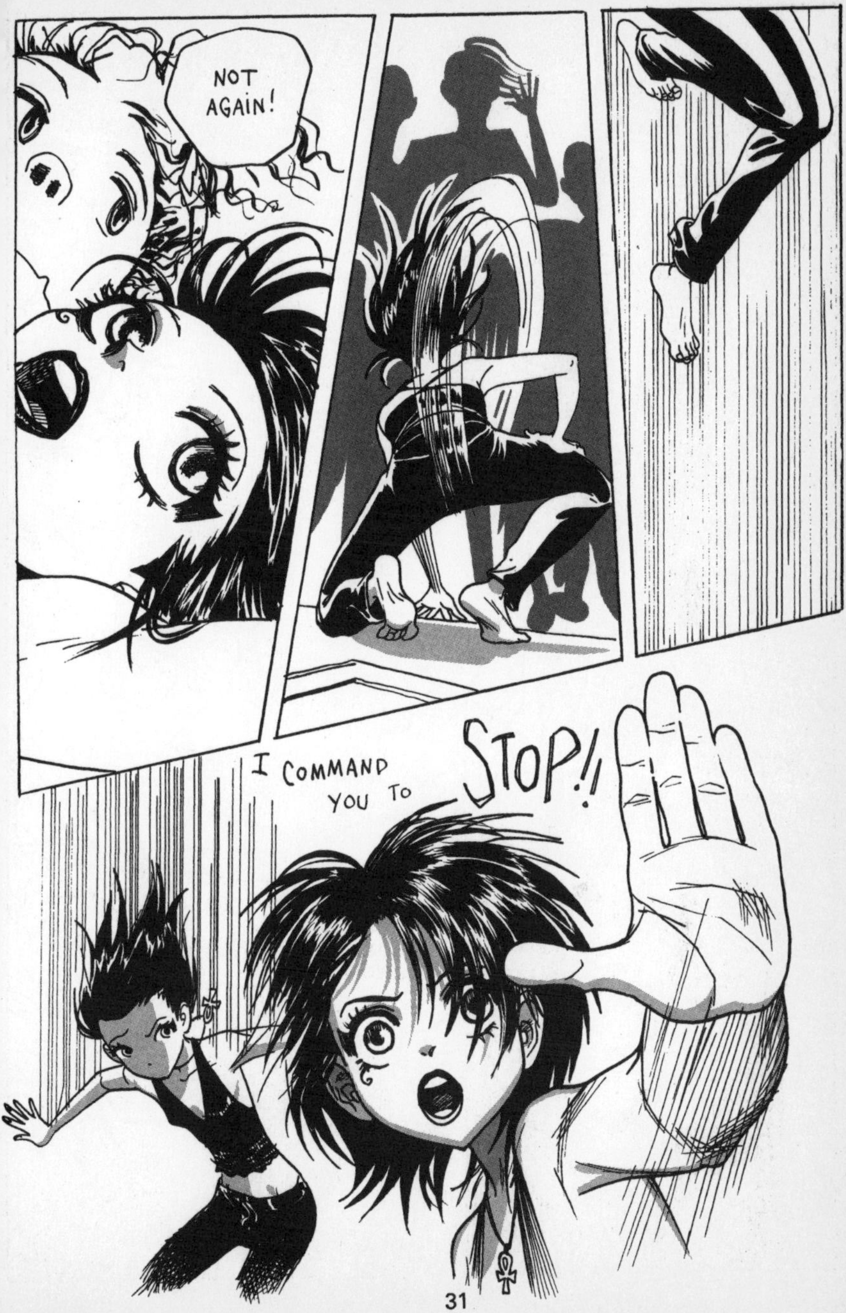
NOT AGAIN!
I COMMAND YOU TO STOP!!

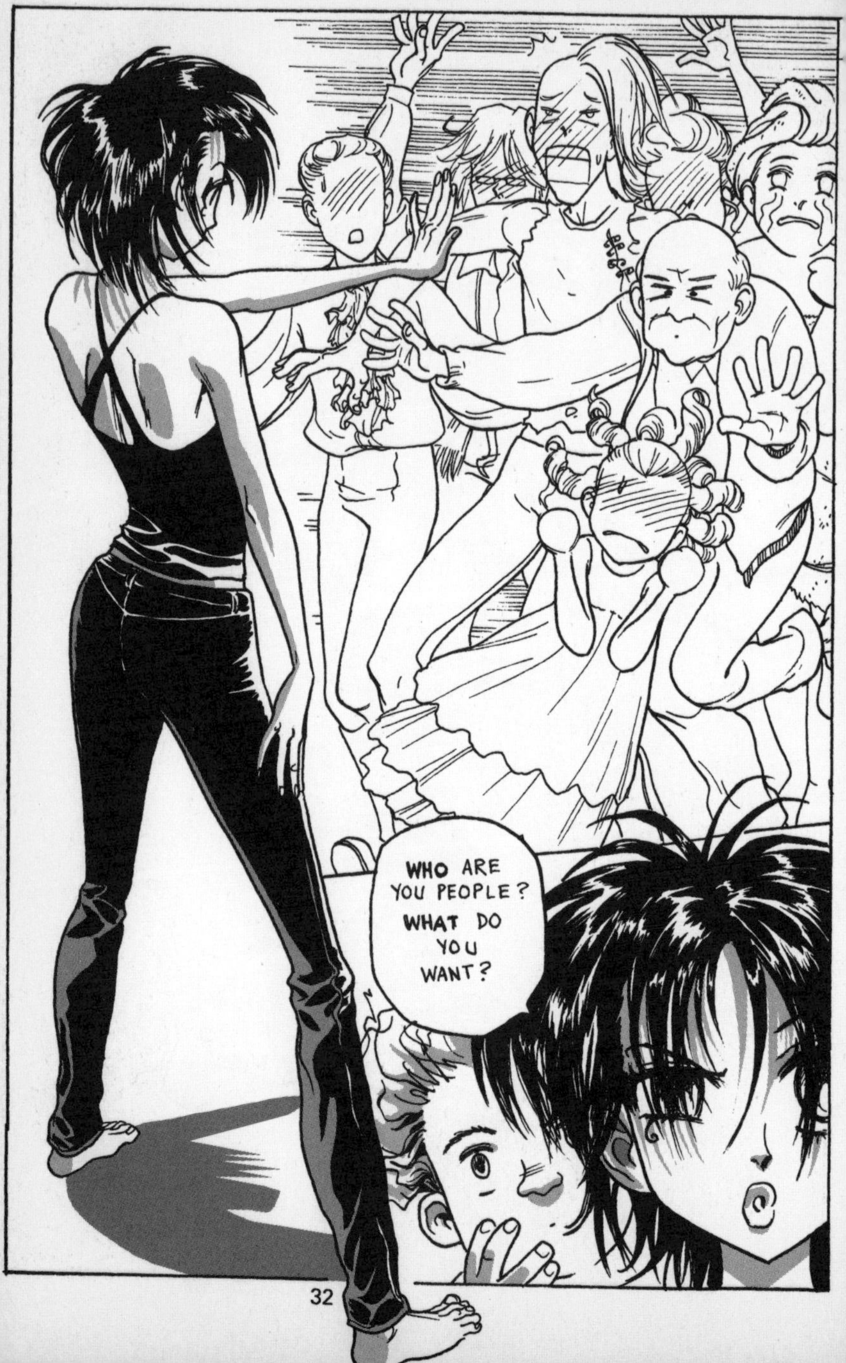
WHO ARE YOU PEOPLE? WHAT DO YOU WANT?

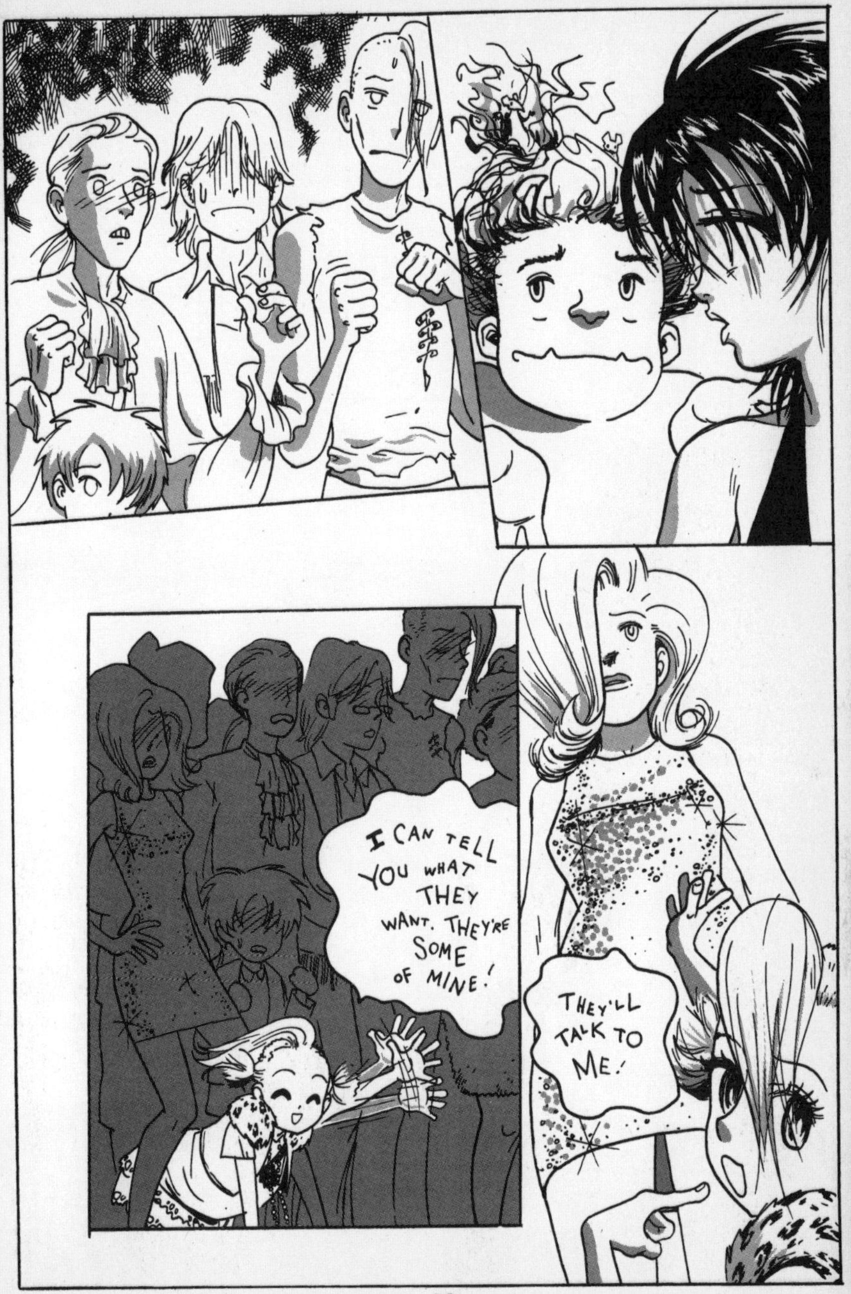
I CAN TELL YOU WHAT THEY WANT. THEY'RE SOME OF MINE!
THEY'LL TALK TO ME!

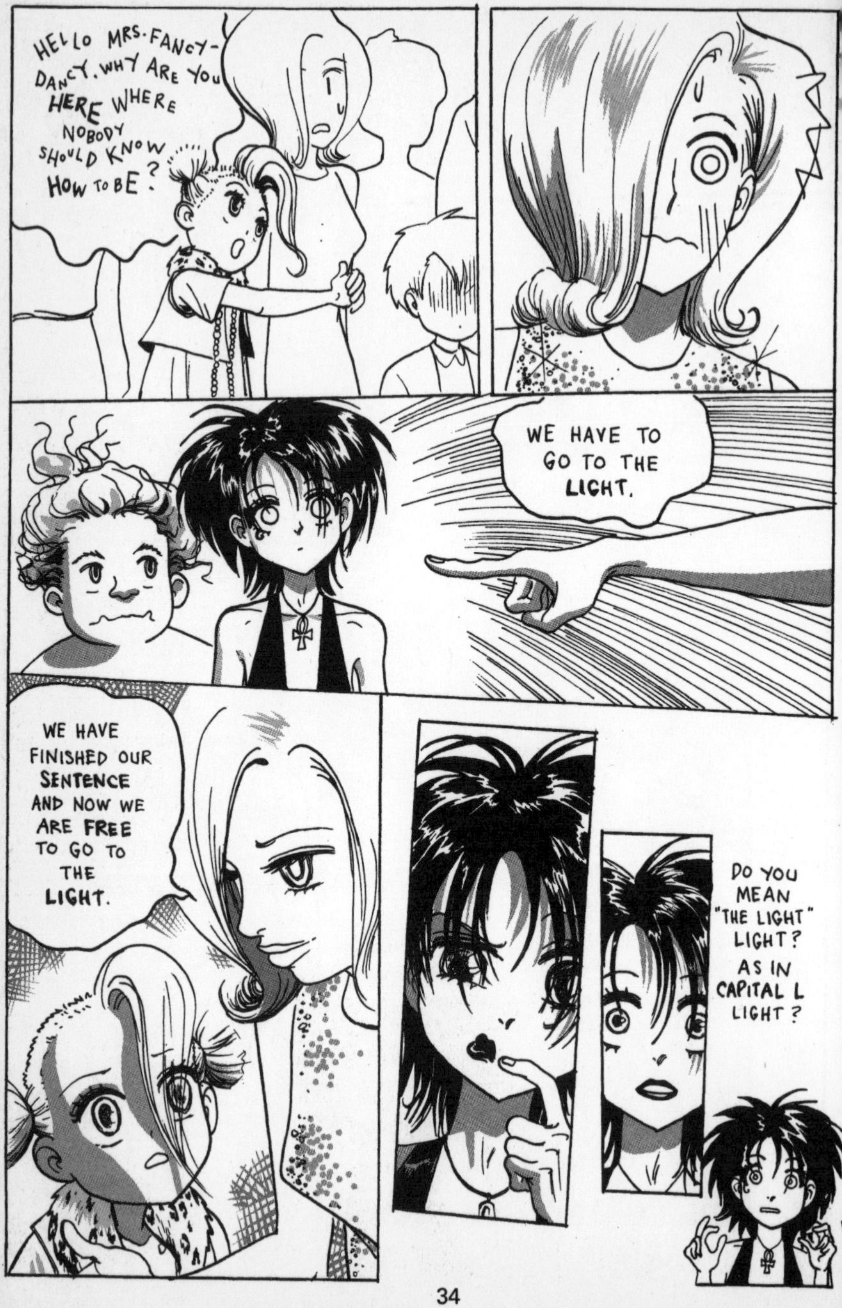

HELLO MRS. FANCY-DANCY. WHY ARE YOU HERE WHERE NOBODY SHOULD KNOW HOW TO BE?
WE HAVE TO GO TO THE LIGHT.
WE HAVE FINISHED OUR SENTENCE AND NOW WE ARE FREE TO GO TO THE LIGHT.
DO YOU MEAN "THE LIGHT" LIGHT? AS IN CAPITAL L LIGHT?

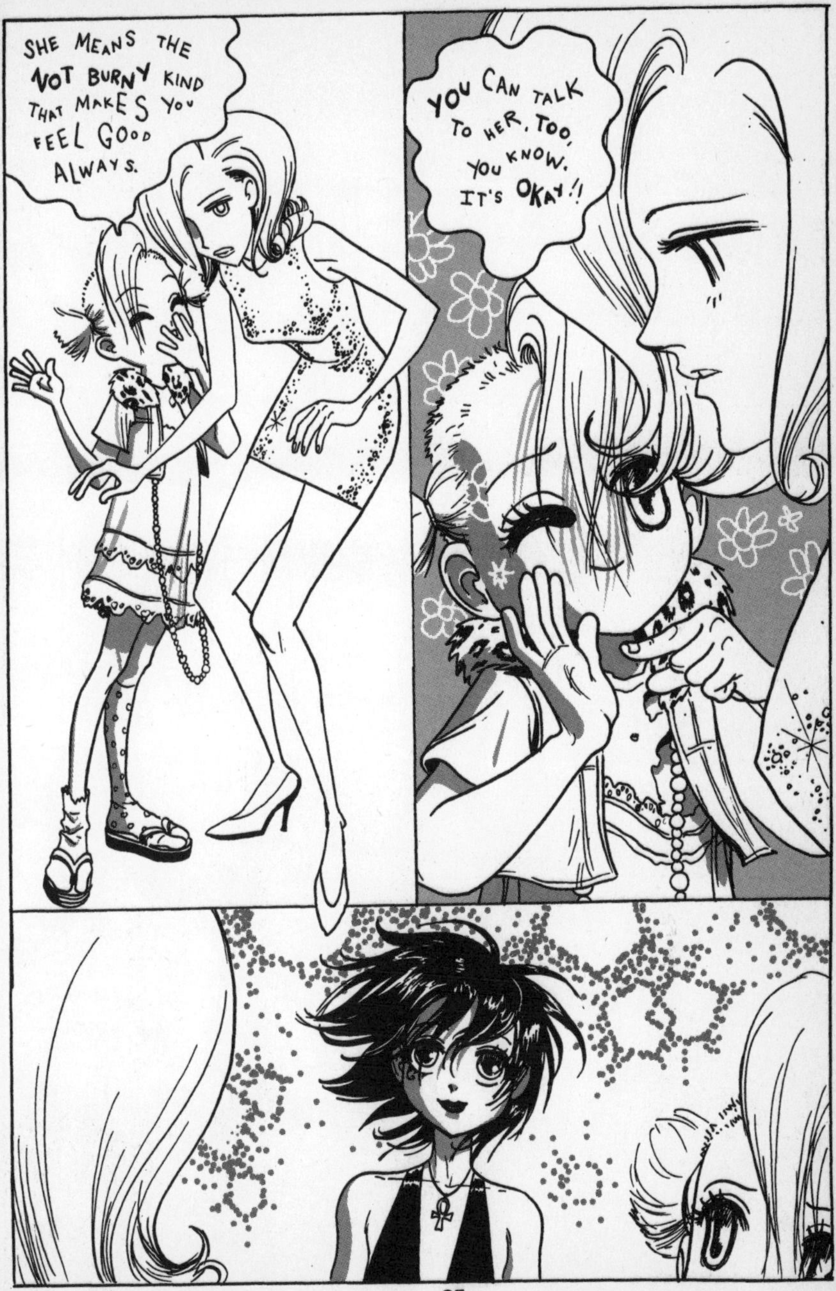
SHE MEANS THE NOT BURNY KIND THAT MAKES YOU FEEL GOOD ALWAYS.
YOU CAN TALK TO HER, TOO, YOU KNOW. IT'S OKAY!!

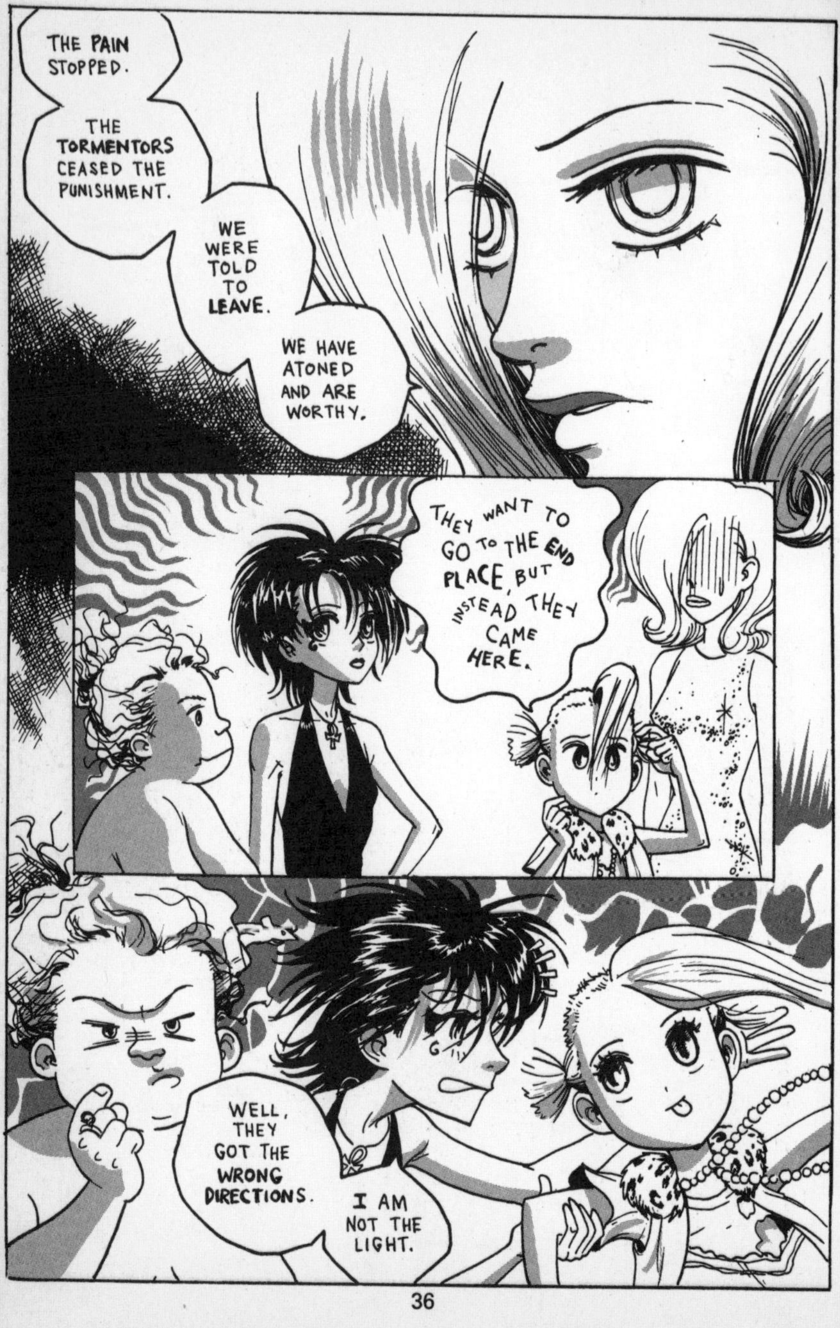
THE PAIN STOPPED.
THE TORMENTORS CEASED THE PUNISHMENT.
WE WERE TOLD TO LEAVE.
WE HAVE ATONED AND ARE WORTHY.
THEY WANT TO GO TO THE END PLACE, BUT INSTEAD THEY CAME HERE.
WELL, THEY GOT THE WRONG DIRECTIONS.
I AM NOT THE LIGHT.

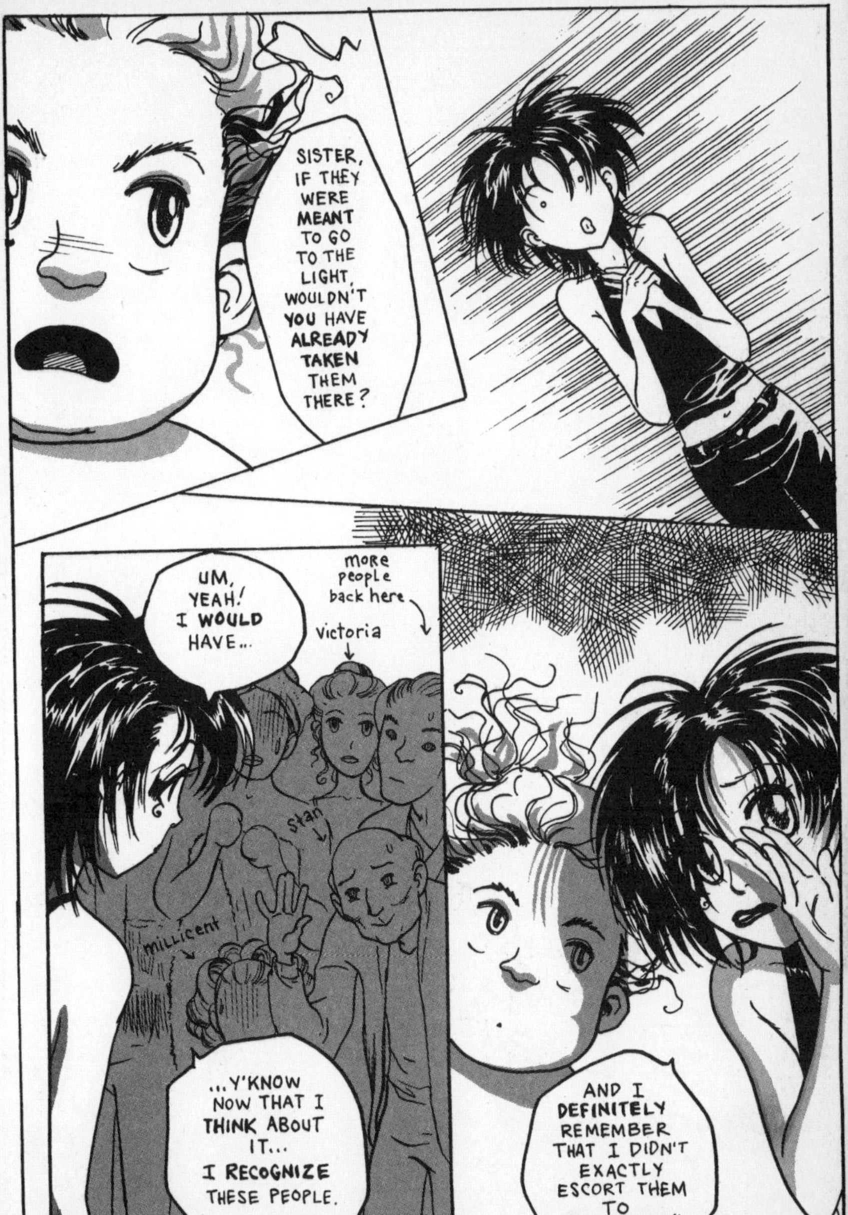
SISTER, IF THEY WERE MEANT TO GO TO THE LIGHT, WOULDN'T YOU HAVE ALREADY TAKEN THEM THERE?
UM, YEAH! I WOULD HAVE...
more people back here
victoria
stan
millicent
...Y'KNOW NOW THAT I THINK ABOUT IT... I RECOGNIZE THESE PEOPLE.
AND I DEFINITELY REMEMBER THAT I DIDN'T EXACTLY ESCORT THEM TO THE "LIGHT."

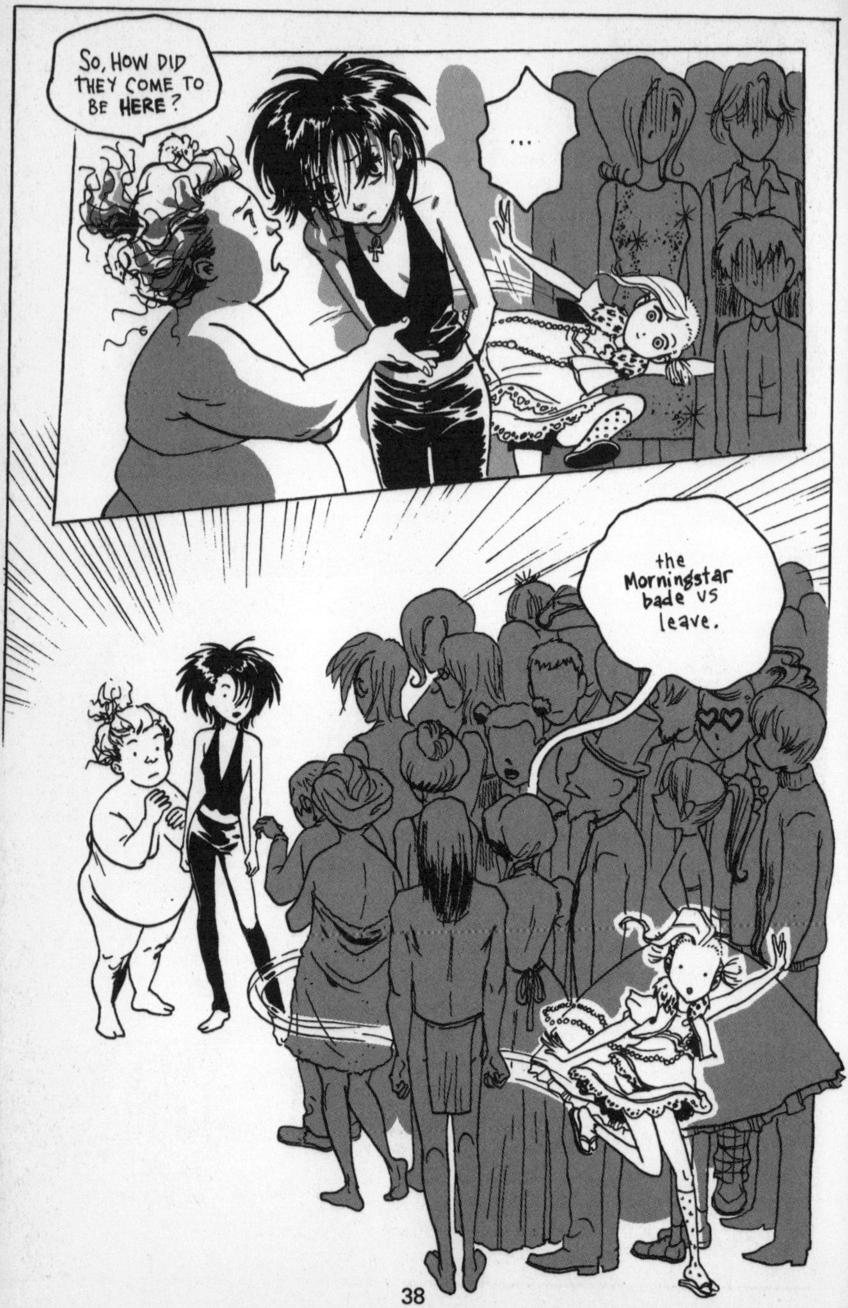
So, HOW DID THEY COME TO BE HERE?
...
the Morningstar bade us leave.

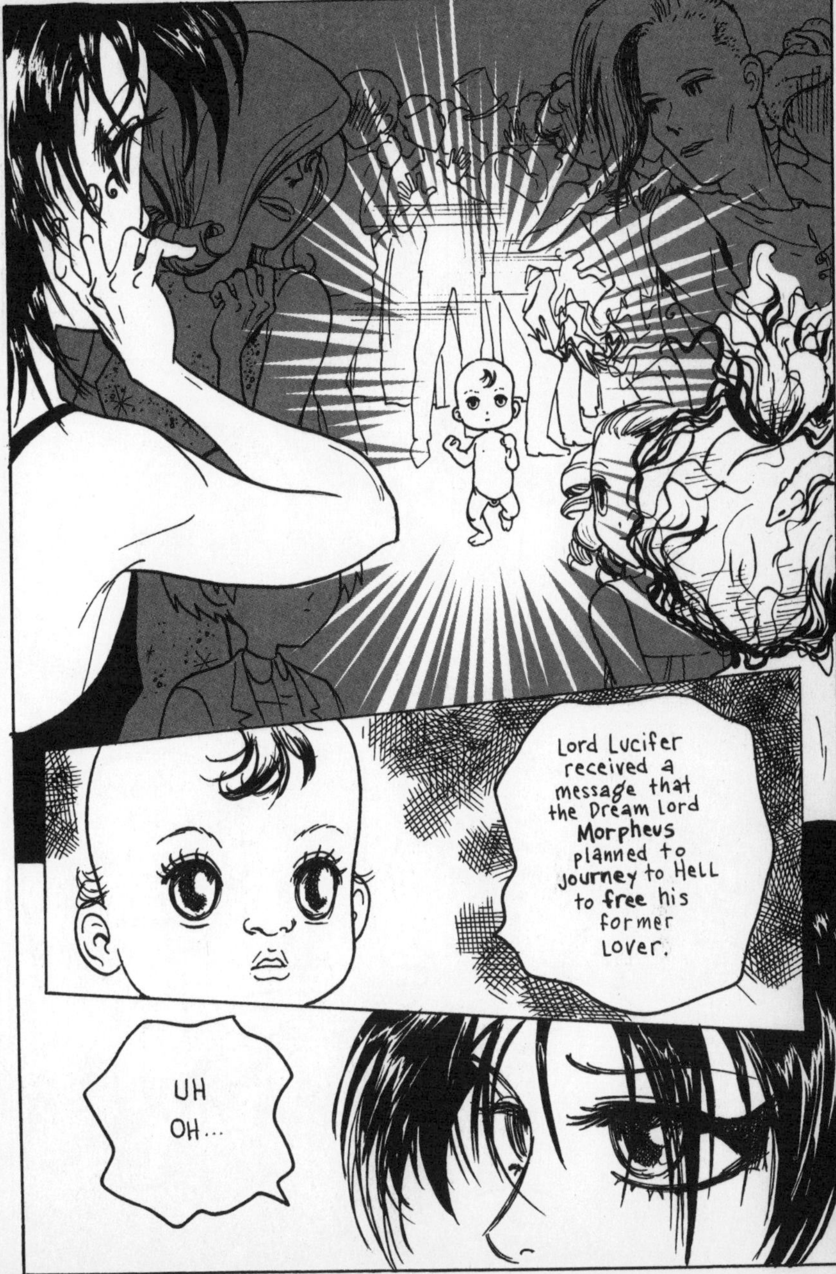
Lord Lucifer received a message that the Dream Lord Morpheus planned to journey to Hell to free his former lover.
UH OH...

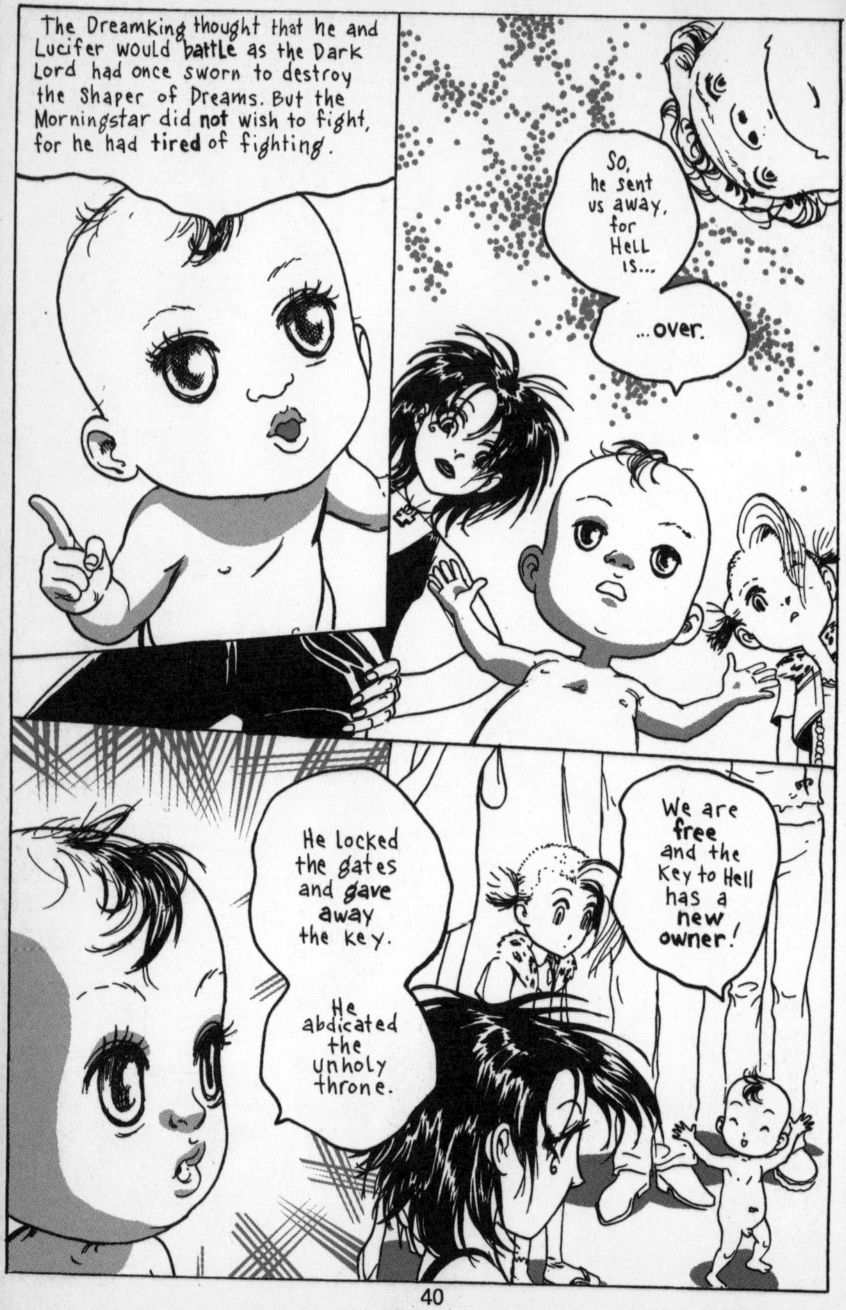
The Dreamking thought that he and Lucifer would battle as the Dark Lord had once sworn to destroy the Shaper of Dreams. But the Morningstar did not wish to fight, for he had tired of fighting.
So, he sent us away, for Hell is...
...over.
He locked the gates and gave away the key.
He abdicated the unholy throne.
We are free and the key to Hell has a new owner!

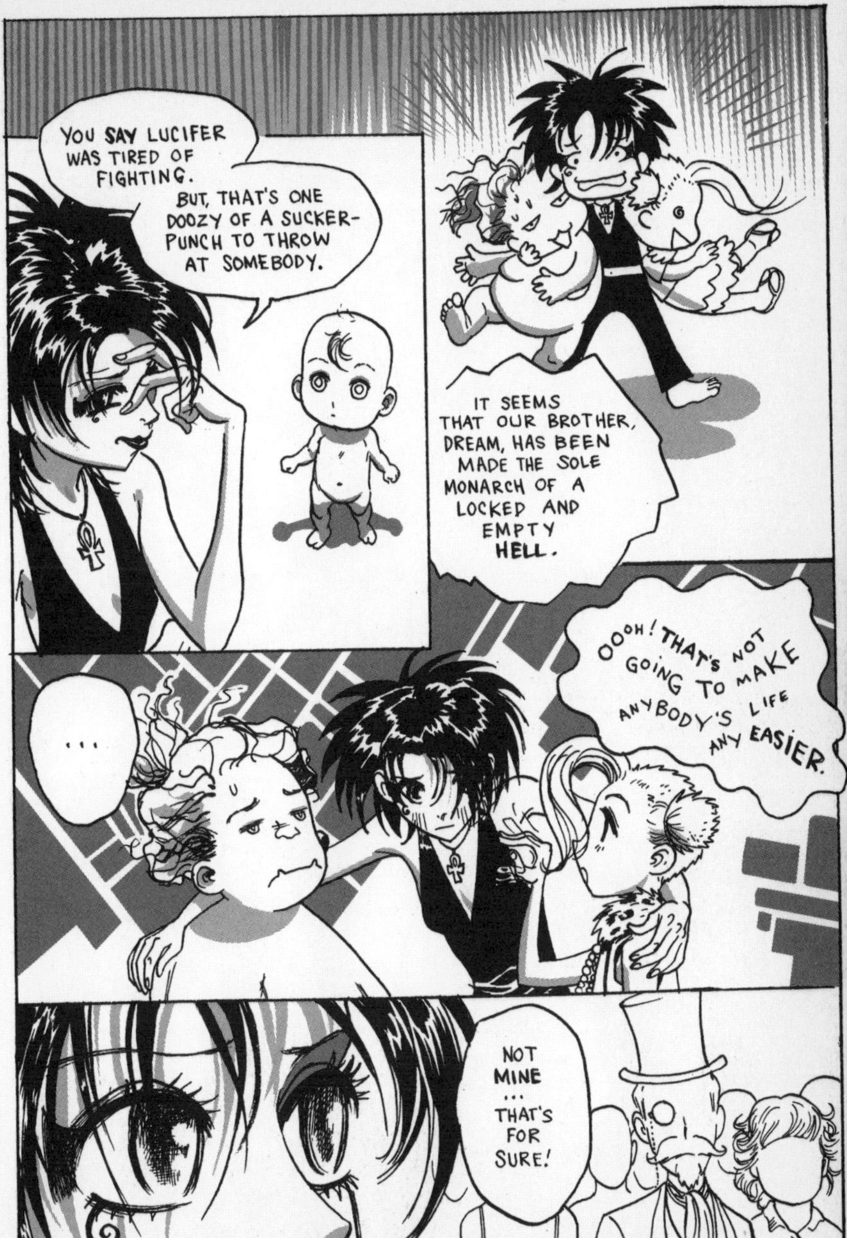
YOU SAY LUCIFER WAS TIRED OF FIGHTING.
BUT, THAT'S ONE DOOZY OF A SUCKER-PUNCH TO THROW AT SOMEBODY.
IT SEEMS THAT OUR BROTHER, DREAM, HAS BEEN MADE THE SOLE MONARCH OF A LOCKED AND EMPTY HELL.
OOOH! THAT'S NOT GOING TO MAKE ANYBODY'S LIFE ANY EASIER.
...
NOT MINE ... THAT'S FOR SURE!

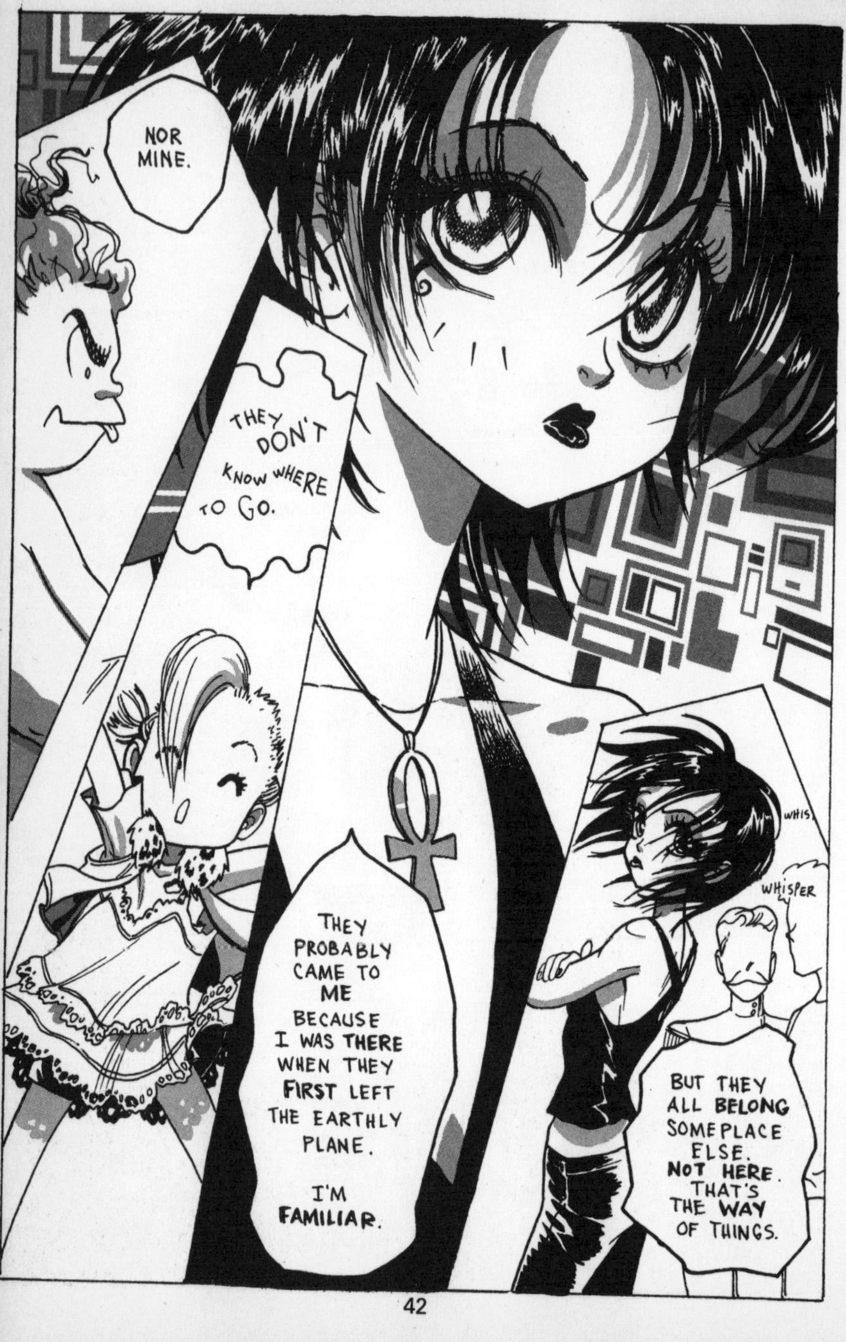
NOR MINE.
THEY DON'T KNOW WHERE TO GO.
THEY PROBABLY CAME TO ME BECAUSE I WAS THERE WHEN THEY FIRST LEFT THE EARTHLY PLANE.
I'M FAMILIAR.
WHIS
WHISPER
BUT THEY ALL BELONG SOMEPLACE ELSE. NOT HERE. THAT'S THE WAY OF THINGS.

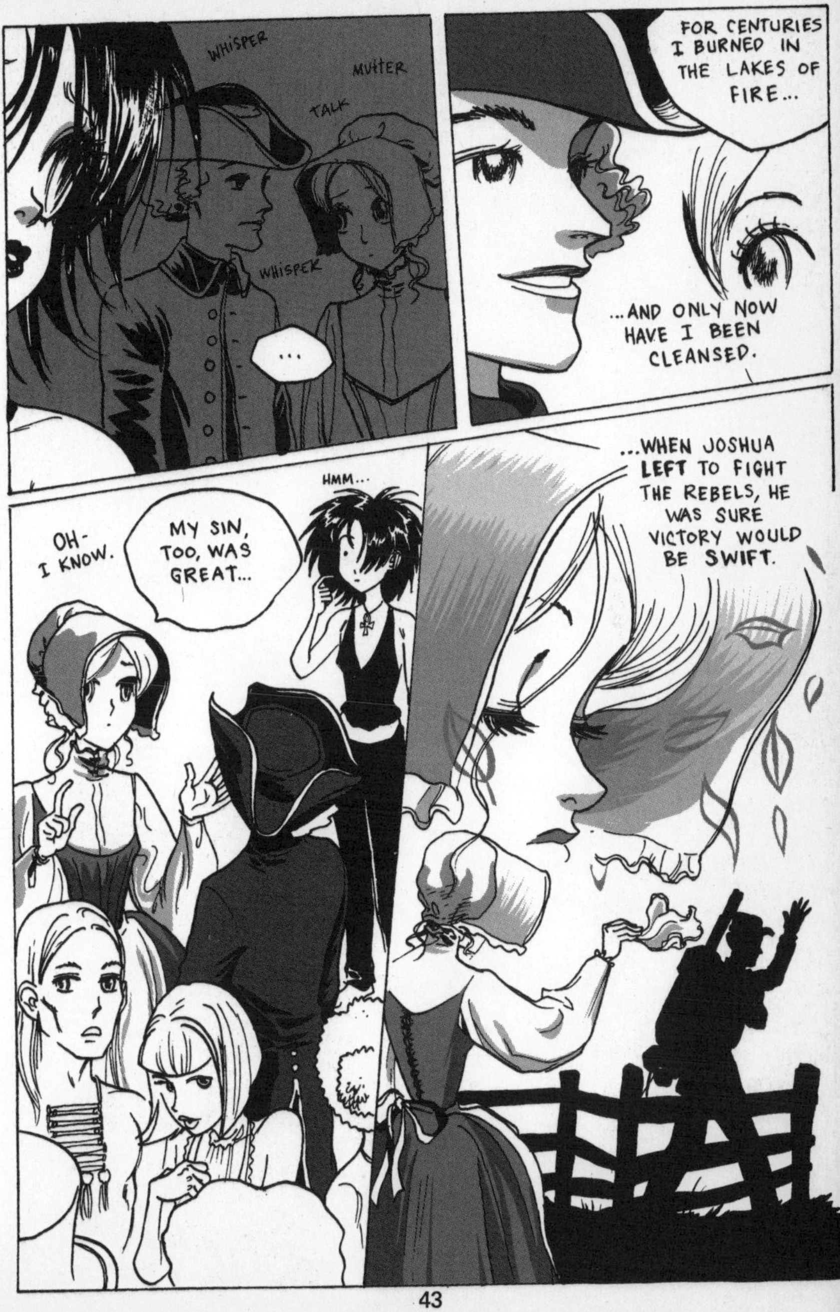
WHISPER
MUTTER
TALK
WHISPER
...
FOR CENTURIES I BURNED IN THE LAKES OF FIRE...
...AND ONLY NOW HAVE I BEEN CLEANSED.
OH- I KNOW.
MY SIN, TOO, WAS GREAT...
HMM...
...WHEN JOSHUA LEFT TO FIGHT THE REBELS, HE WAS SURE VICTORY WOULD BE SWIFT.

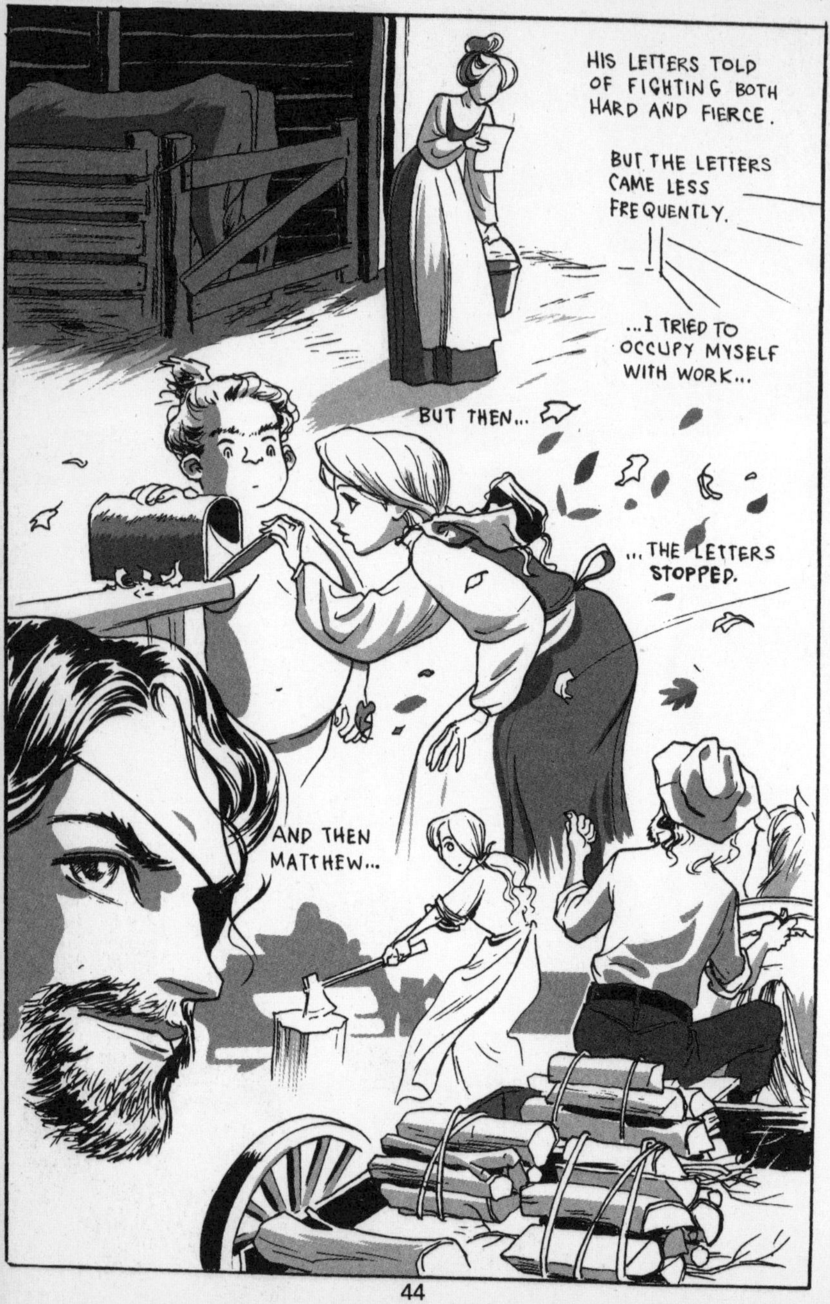
HIS LETTERS TOLD OF FIGHTING BOTH HARD AND FIERCE.
BUT THE LETTERS CAME LESS FREQUENTLY.
...I TRIED TO OCCUPY MYSELF WITH WORK...
BUT THEN...
...THE LETTERS STOPPED.
AND THEN MATTHEW...

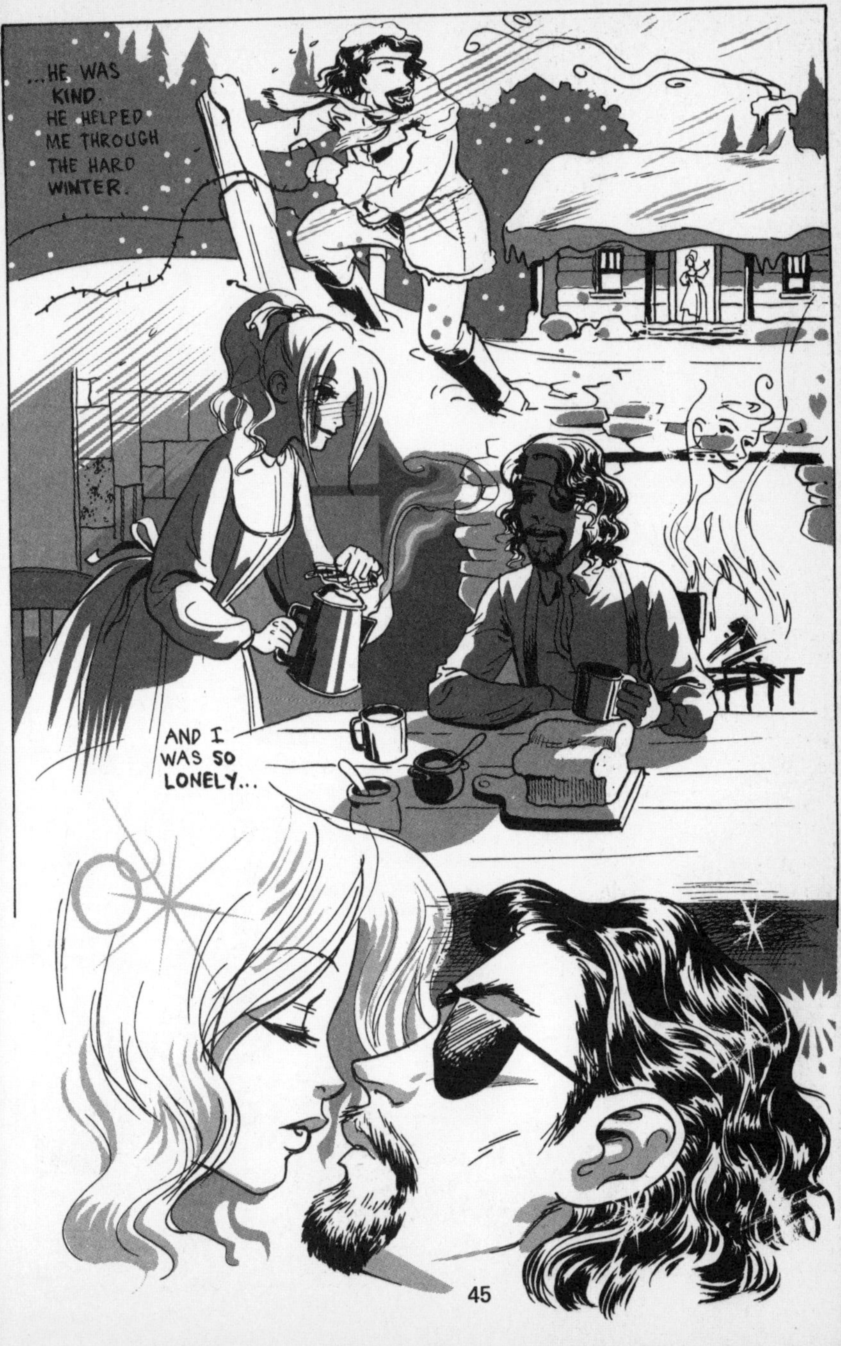
...HE WAS KIND. HE HELPED ME THROUGH THE HARD WINTER.
AND I WAS SO LONELY...

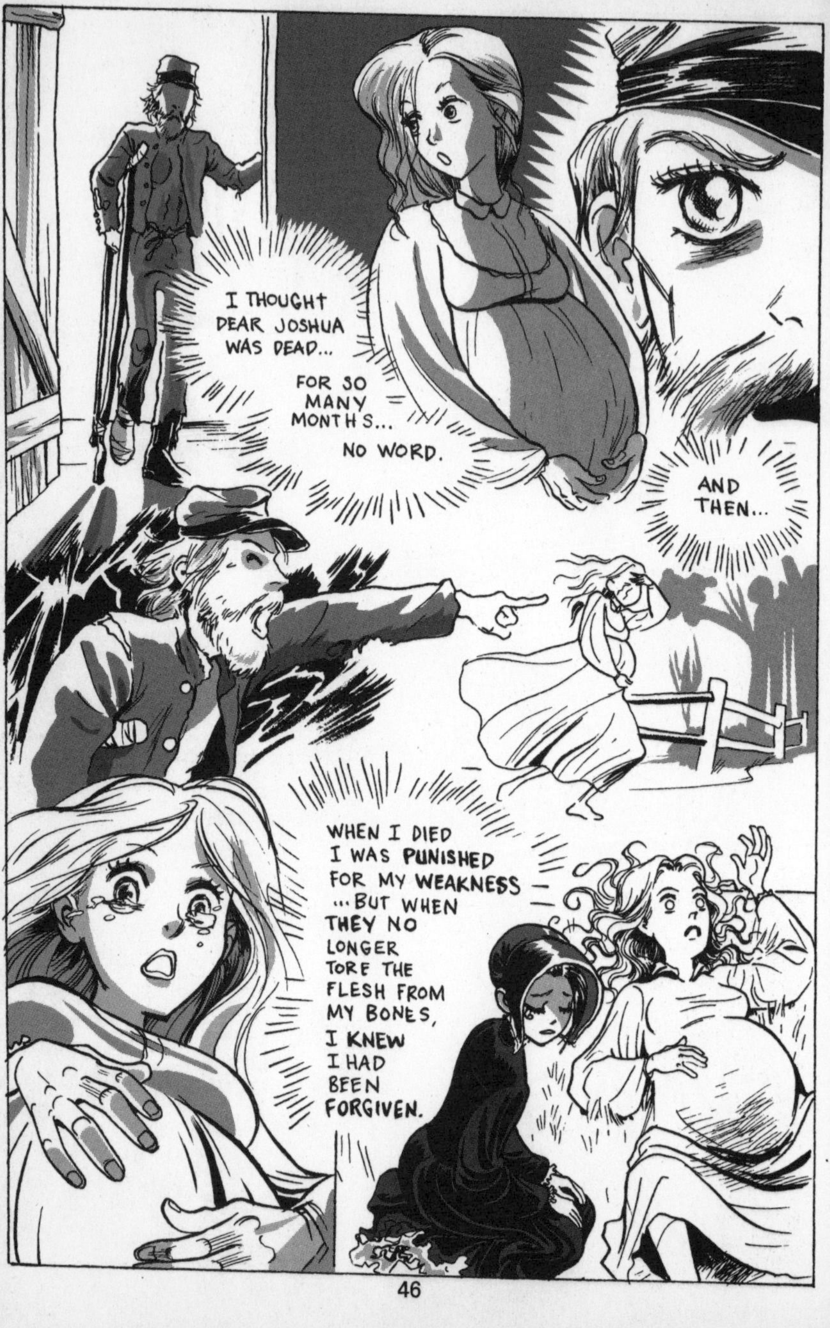
I THOUGHT DEAR JOSHUA WAS DEAD...
FOR SO MANY MONTHS...
NO WORD.
AND THEN...
WHEN I DIED I WAS PUNISHED FOR MY WEAKNESS ...BUT WHEN THEY NO LONGER TORE THE FLESH FROM MY BONES, I KNEW I HAD BEEN FORGIVEN.

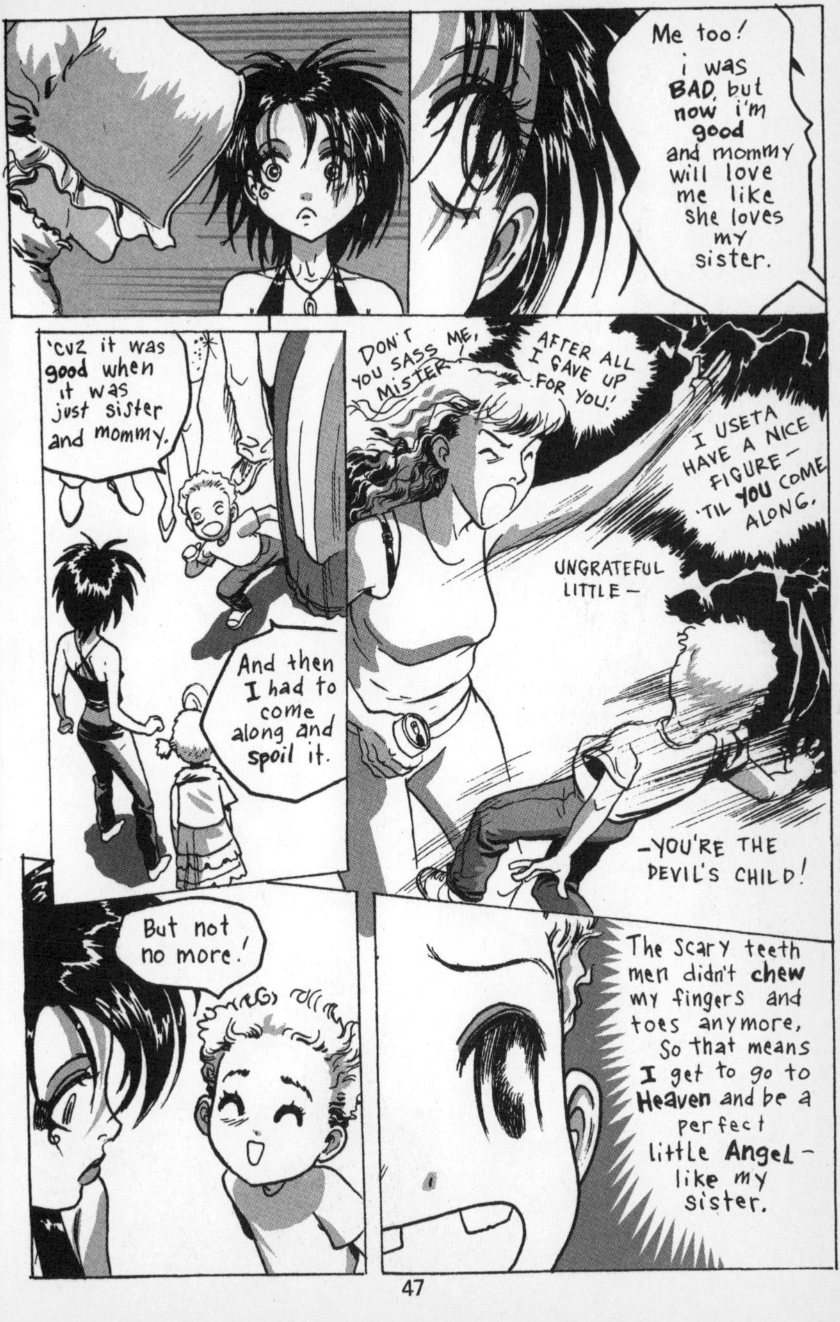
Me too! i was BAD, but now i'm good and mommy will love me like she loves my sister.
'cuz it was good when it was just sister and mommy.
And then I had to come along and spoil it.
DON'T YOU SASS ME, MISTER!
AFTER ALL I GAVE UP FOR YOU!
I USETA HAVE A NICE FIGURE— 'TIL YOU COME ALONG.
UNGRATEFUL LITTLE—
—YOU'RE THE DEVIL'S CHILD!
But not no more!
The scary teeth men didn't chew my fingers and toes anymore, So that means I get to go to Heaven and be a perfect little Angel— like my sister.

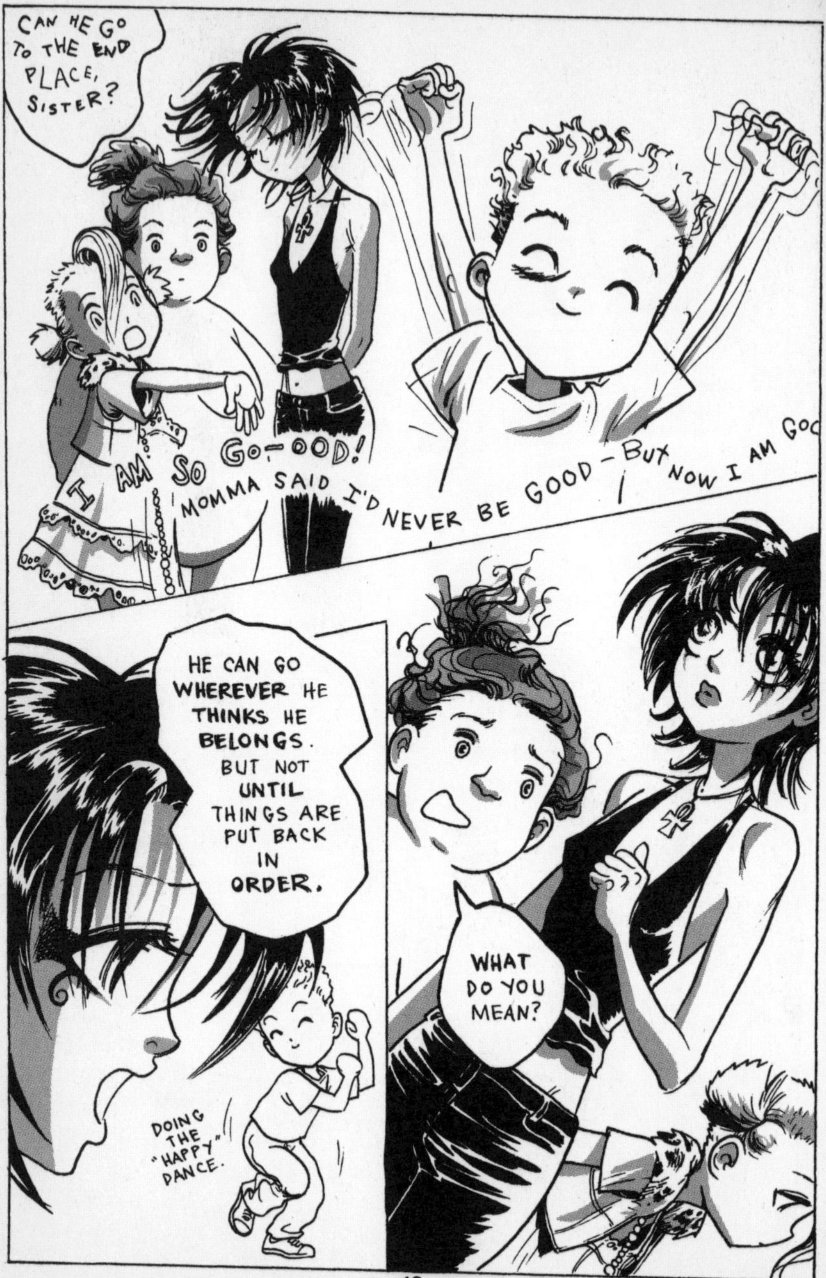

CAN HE GO TO THE END PLACE, SISTER?
I AM SO GO-OOD!
MOMMA SAID I'D NEVER BE GOOD - BUT NOW I AM GOO
HE CAN GO WHEREVER HE THINKS HE BELONGS. BUT NOT UNTIL THINGS ARE PUT BACK IN ORDER.
DOING THE "HAPPY" DANCE.
WHAT DO YOU MEAN?

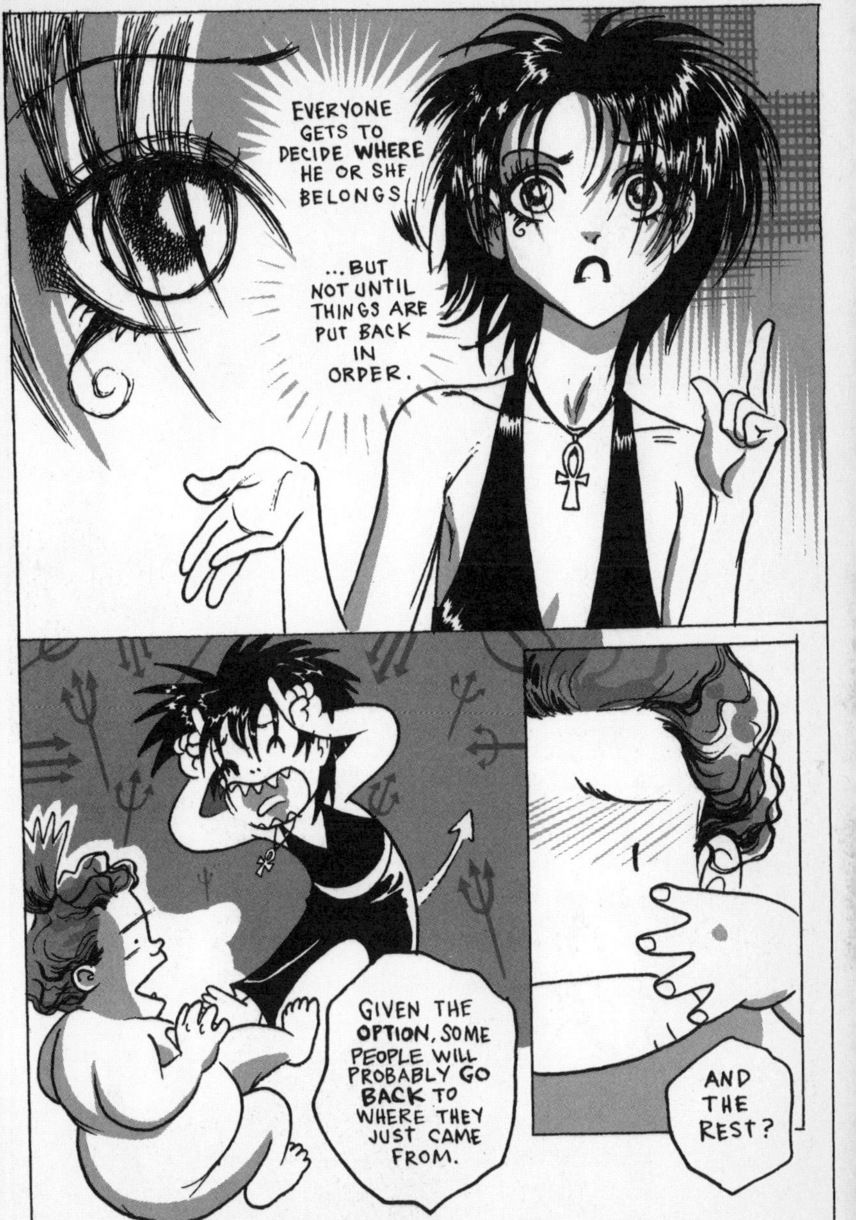
EVERYONE GETS TO DECIDE WHERE HE OR SHE BELONGS...
...BUT NOT UNTIL THINGS ARE PUT BACK IN ORDER.
GIVEN THE OPTION, SOME PEOPLE WILL PROBABLY GO BACK TO WHERE THEY JUST CAME FROM.
AND THE REST?

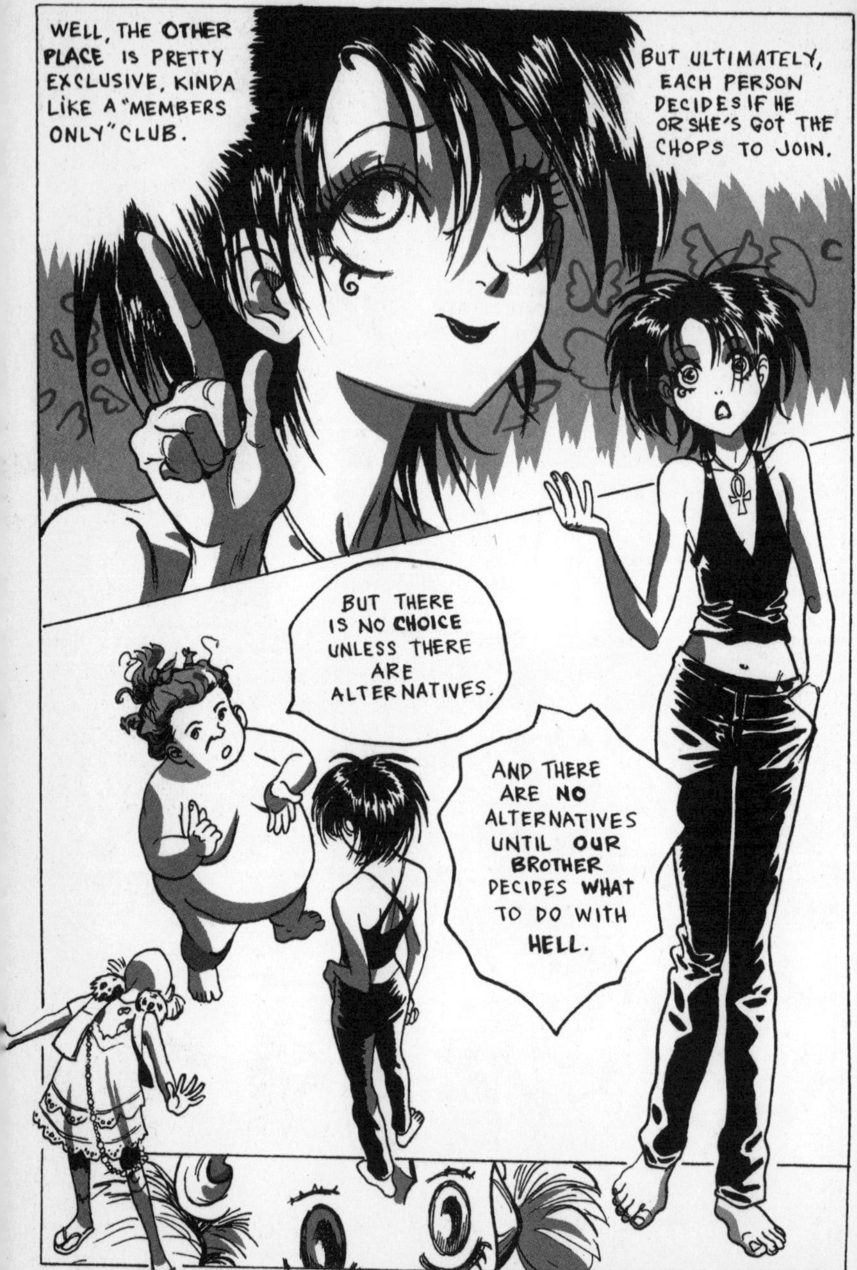
WELL, THE OTHER PLACE IS PRETTY EXCLUSIVE, KINDA LIKE A "MEMBERS ONLY" CLUB.
BUT ULTIMATELY, EACH PERSON DECIDES IF HE OR SHE'S GOT THE CHOPS TO JOIN.
BUT THERE IS NO CHOICE UNLESS THERE ARE ALTERNATIVES.
AND THERE ARE NO ALTERNATIVES UNTIL OUR BROTHER DECIDES WHAT TO DO WITH HELL.

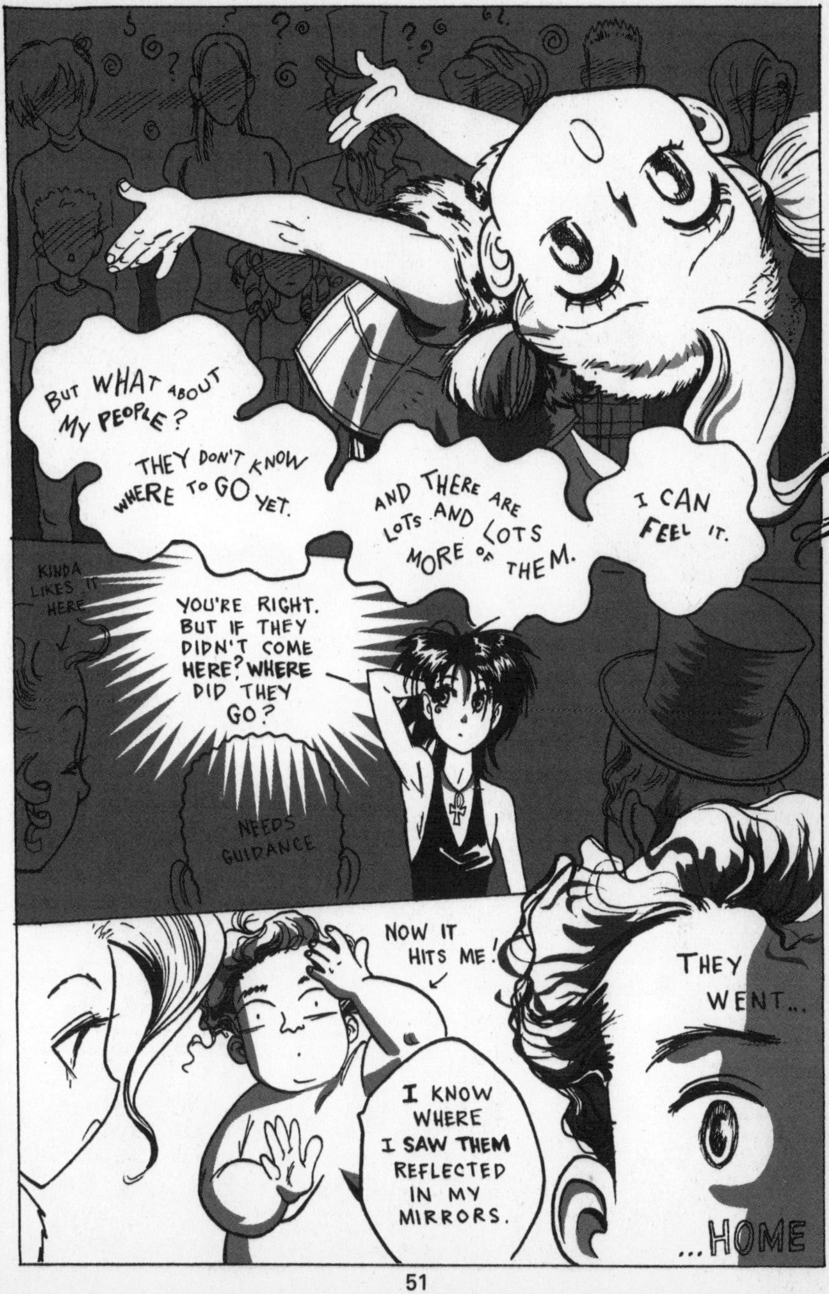
BUT WHAT ABOUT MY PEOPLE?
THEY DON'T KNOW WHERE TO GO YET.
AND THERE ARE LOTS AND LOTS MORE OF THEM.
I CAN FEEL IT.
KINDA LIKES IT HERE
YOU'RE RIGHT. BUT IF THEY DIDN'T COME HERE, WHERE DID THEY GO?
NEEDS GUIDANCE
NOW IT HITS ME!
I KNOW WHERE I SAW THEM REFLECTED IN MY MIRRORS.
THEY WENT...
...HOME

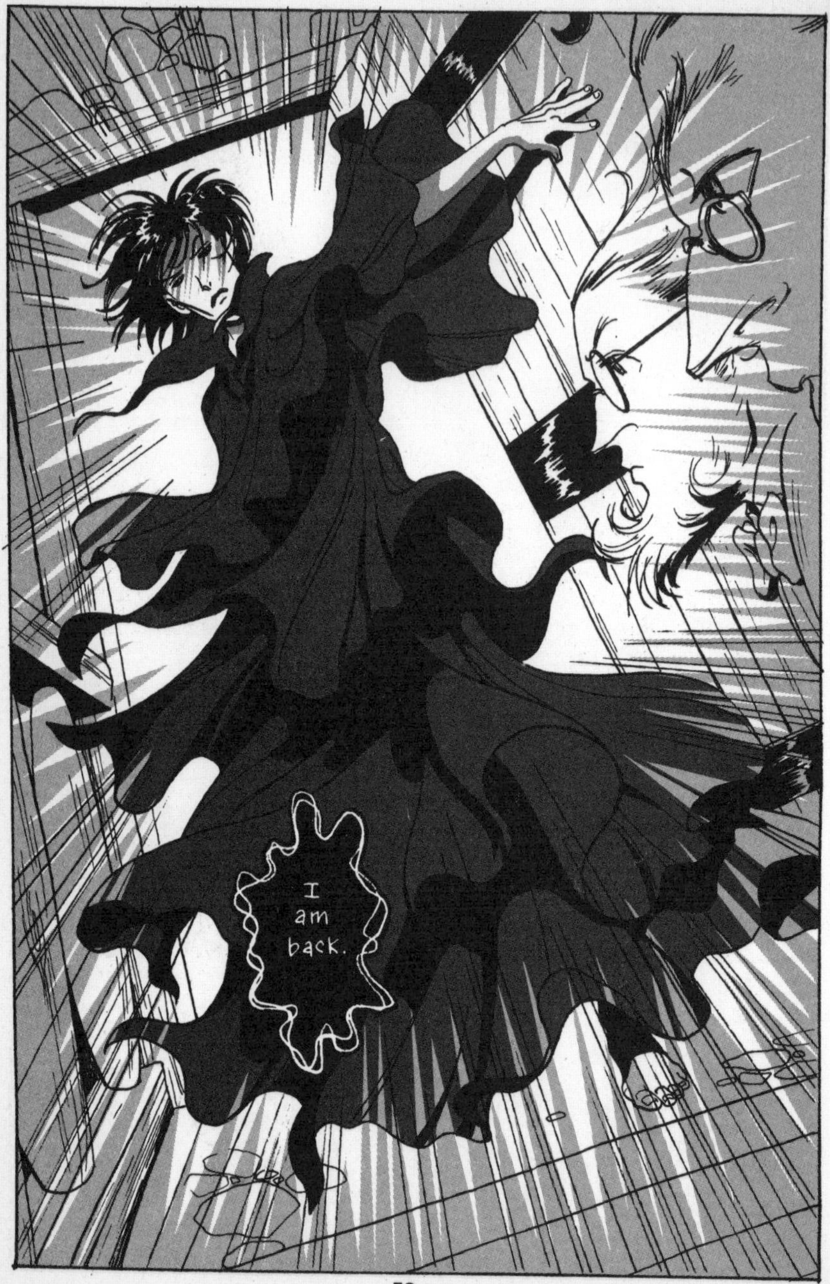
I am back.

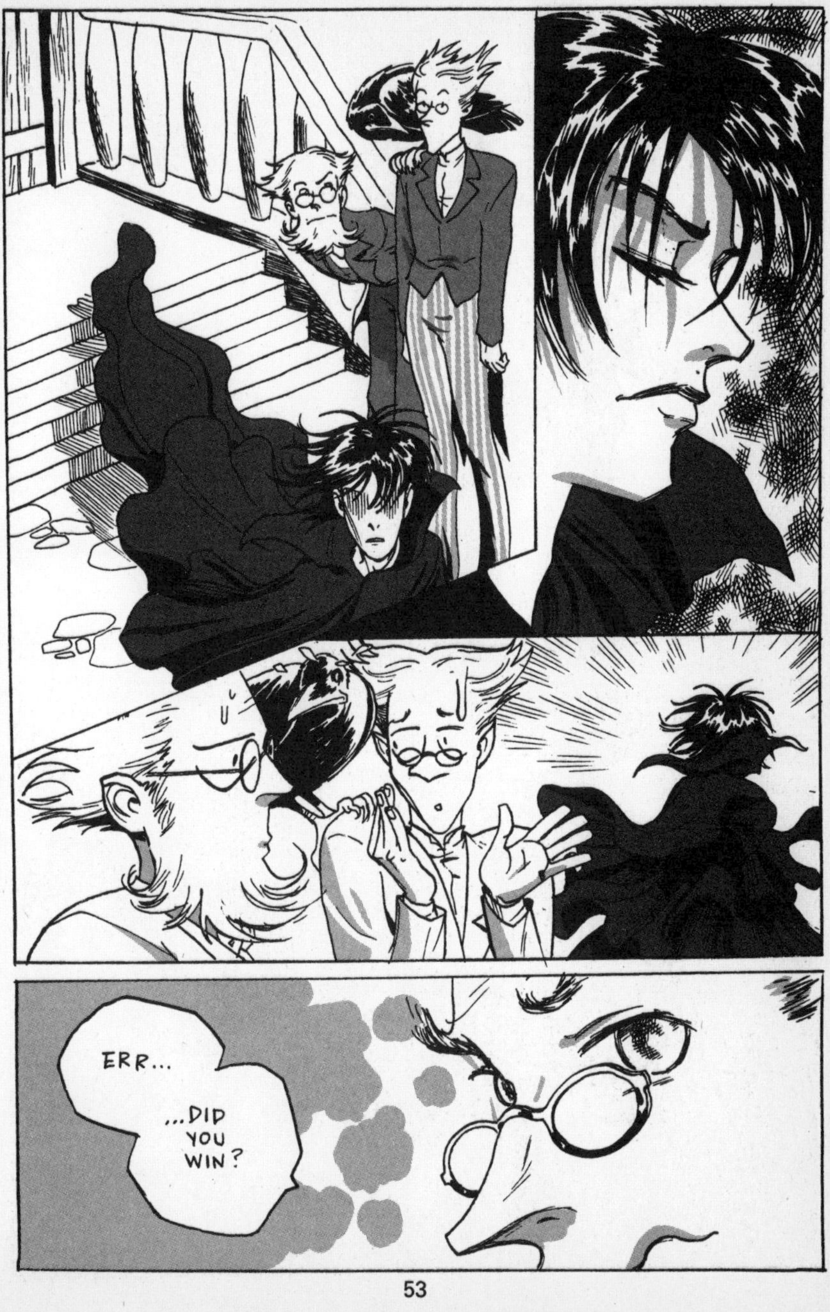
ERR...
...DID YOU WIN?

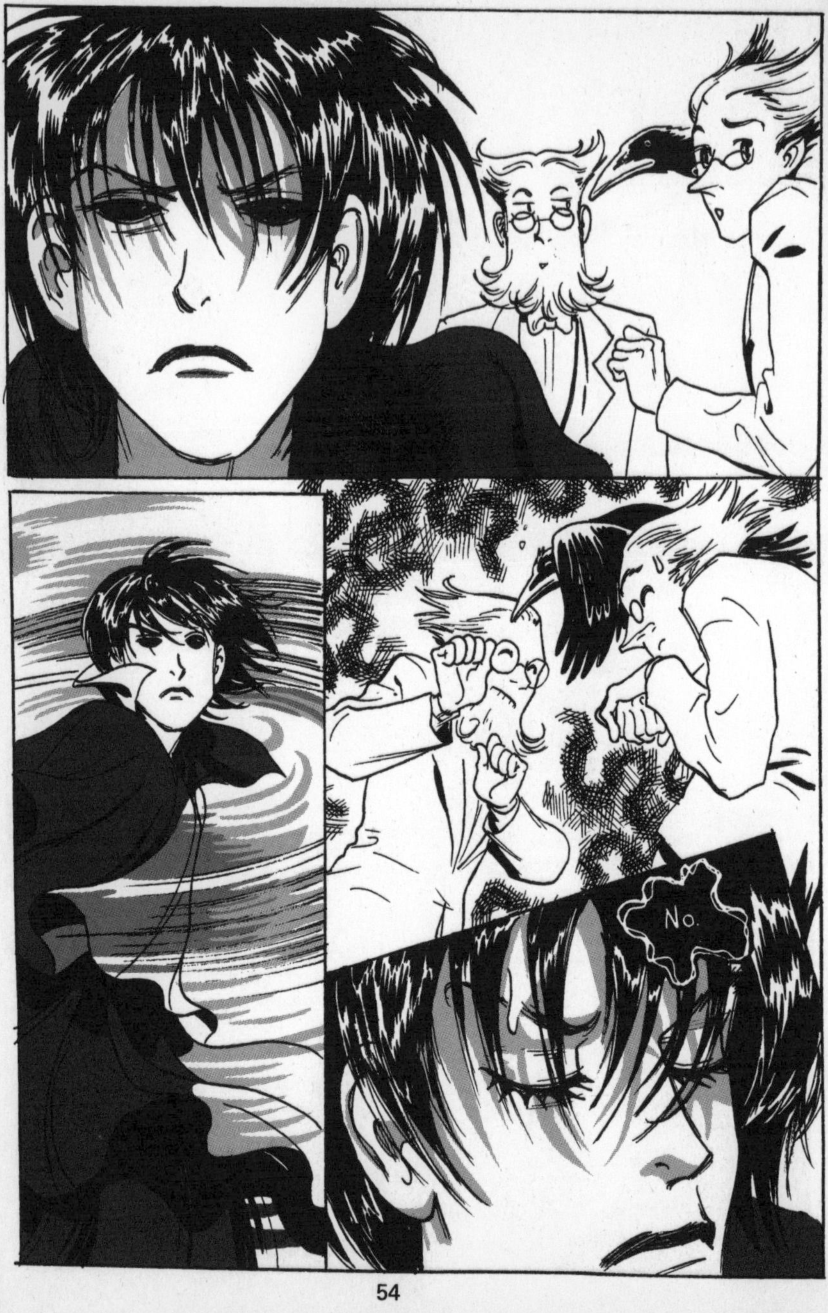
No.

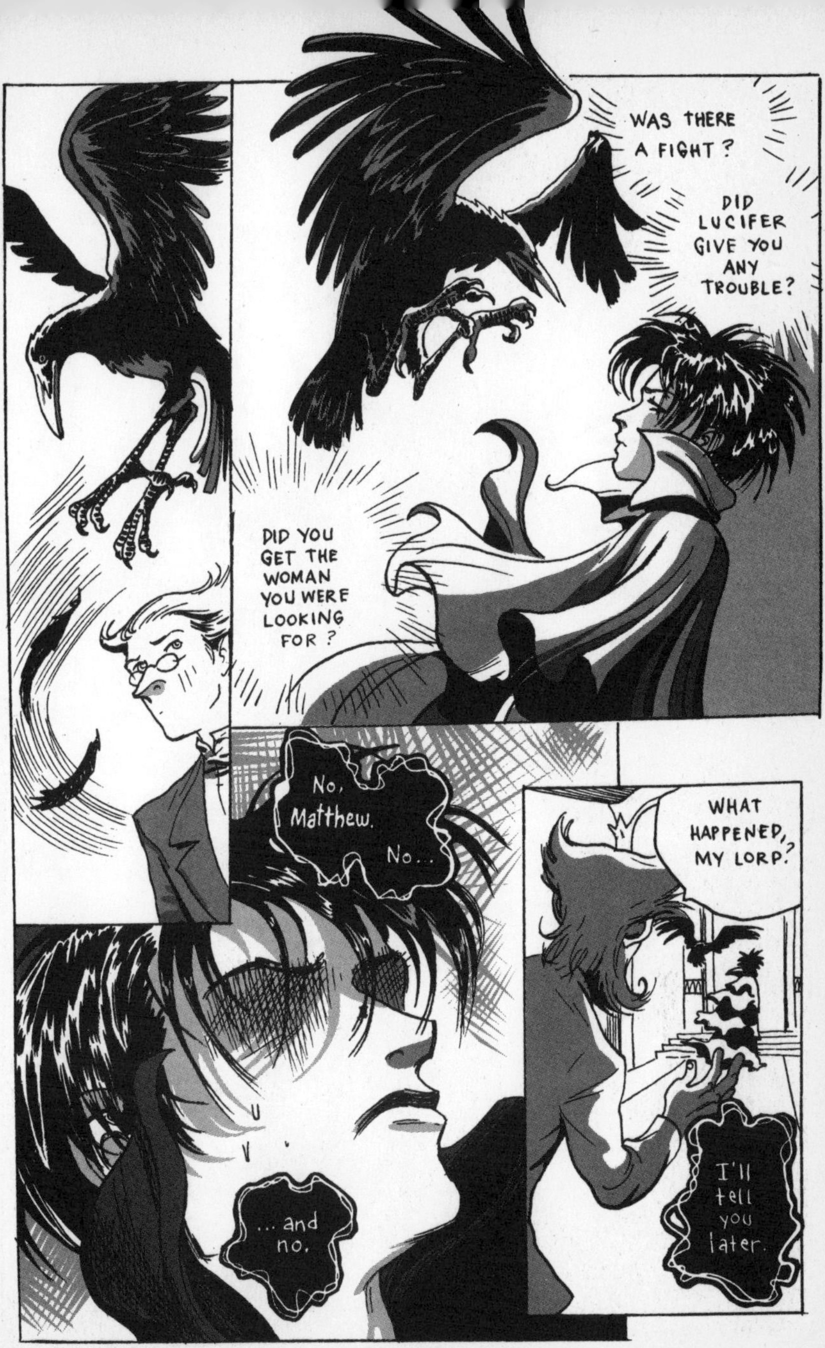
WAS THERE A FIGHT?
DID LUCIFER GIVE YOU ANY TROUBLE?
DID YOU GET THE WOMAN YOU WERE LOOKING FOR?
No, Matthew. No...
WHAT HAPPENED, MY LORD?
...and no.
I'll tell you later.

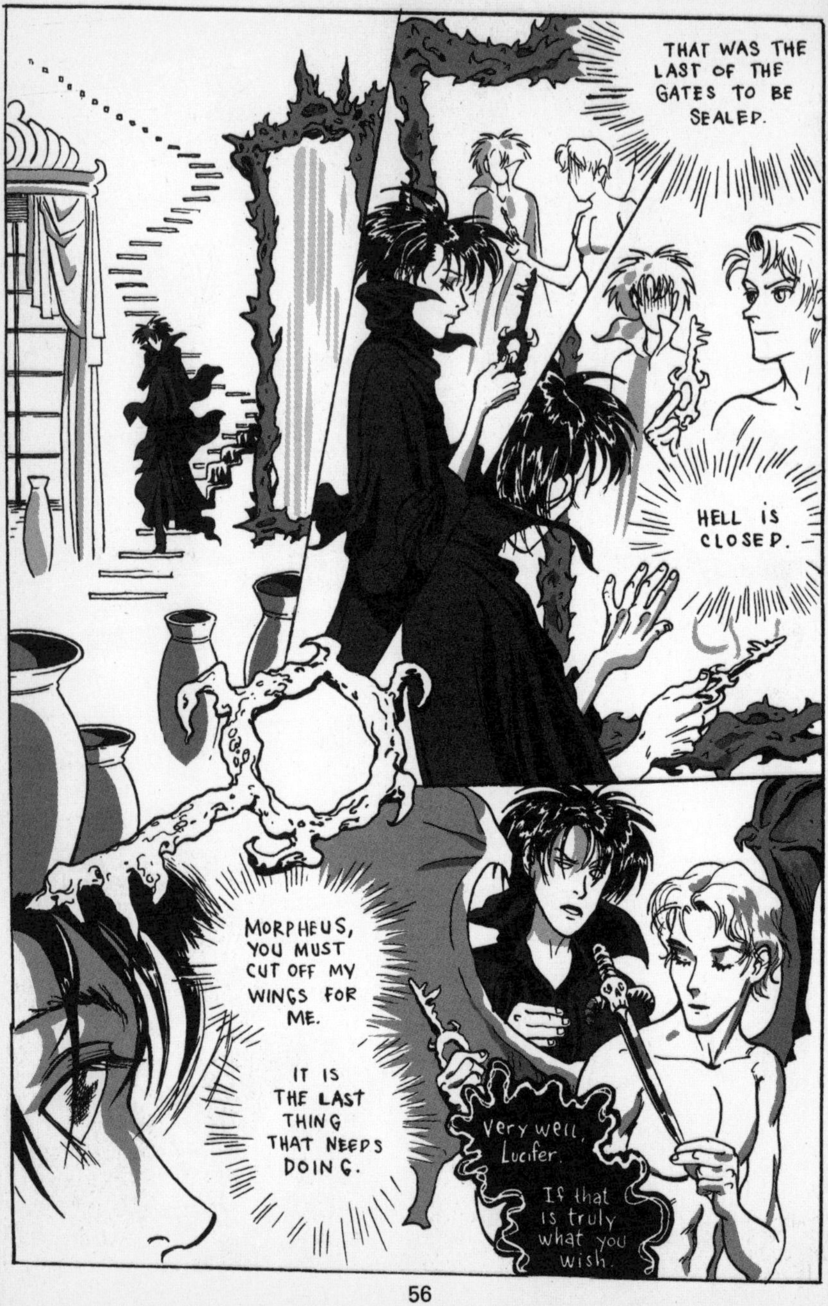
THAT WAS THE LAST OF THE GATES TO BE SEALED.
HELL IS CLOSED.
MORPHEUS, YOU MUST CUT OFF MY WINGS FOR ME.
IT IS THE LAST THING THAT NEEDS DOING.
Very well, Lucifer.
If that is truly what you wish.

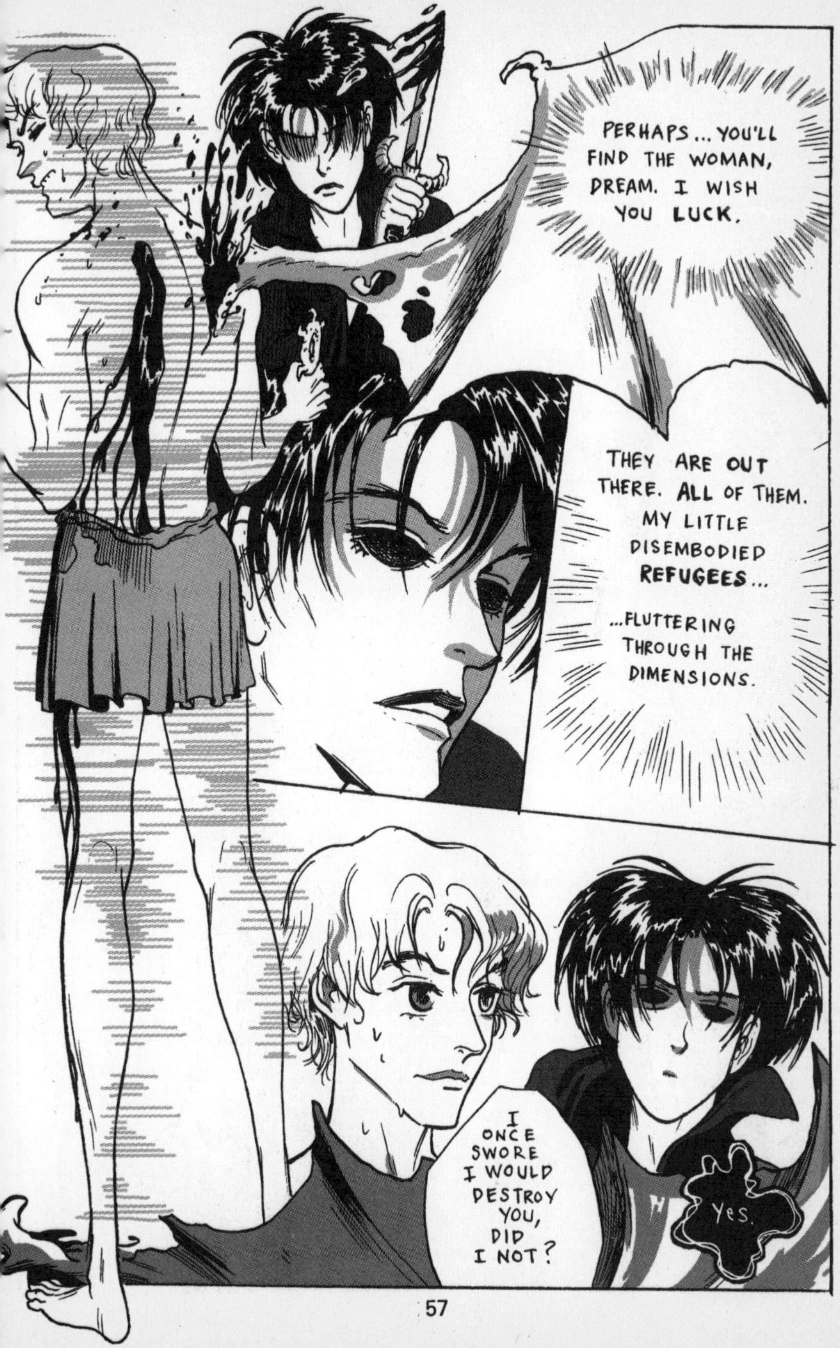
PERHAPS... YOU'LL FIND THE WOMAN, DREAM. I WISH YOU LUCK.
THEY ARE OUT THERE. ALL OF THEM. MY LITTLE DISEMBODIED REFUGEES...
...FLUTTERING THROUGH THE DIMENSIONS.
I ONCE SWORE I WOULD DESTROY YOU, DID I NOT?
Yes.

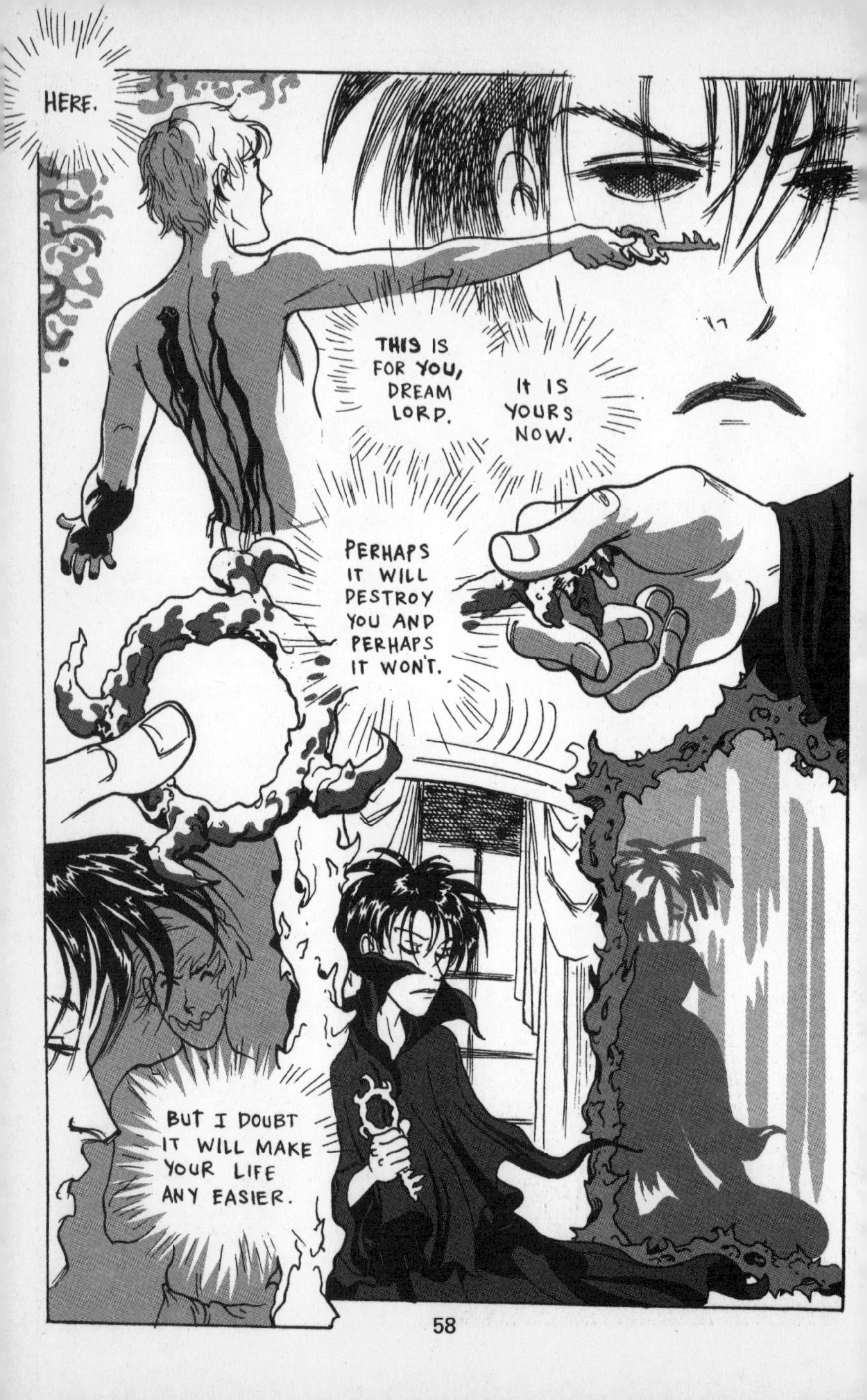
HERE.
THIS IS FOR YOU, DREAM LORD.
It IS YOURS NOW.
PERHAPS IT WILL DESTROY YOU AND PERHAPS IT WON'T.
BUT I DOUBT IT WILL MAKE YOUR LIFE ANY EASIER.

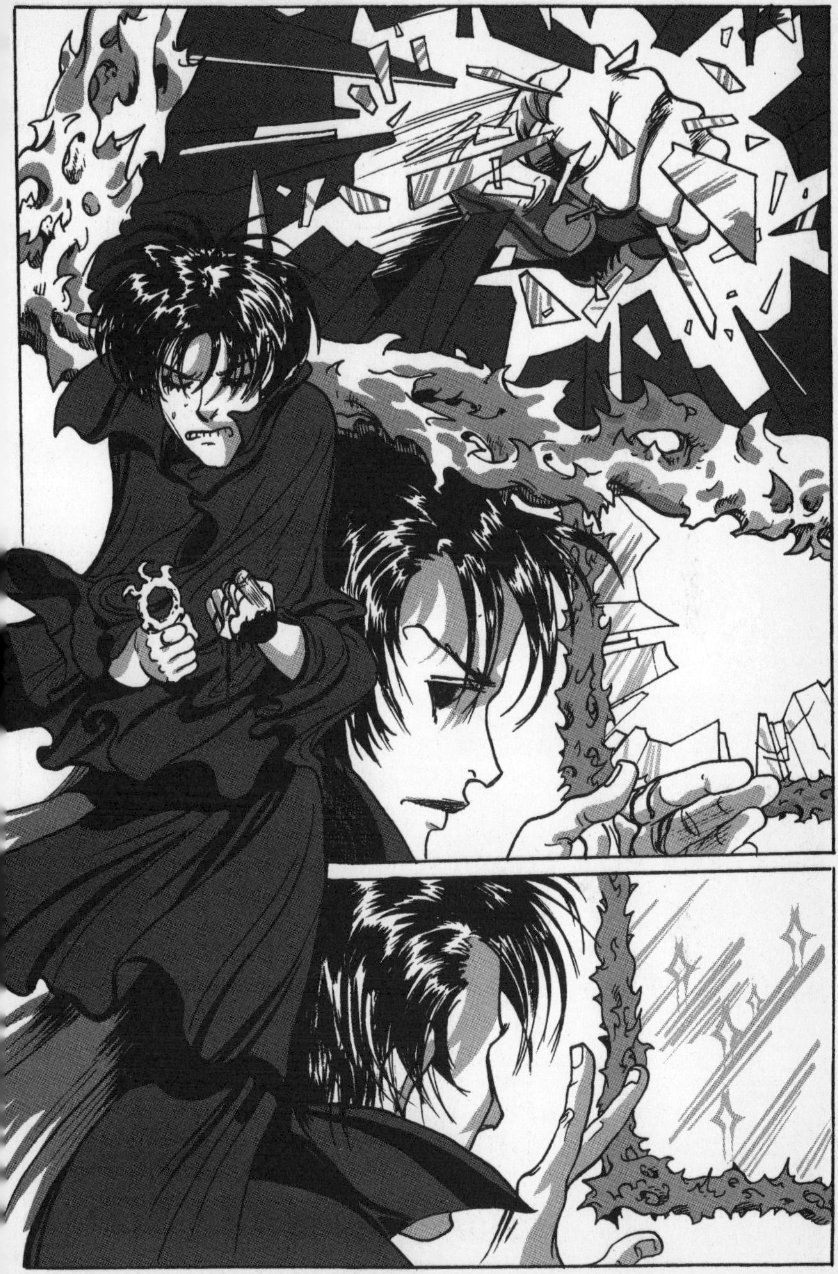

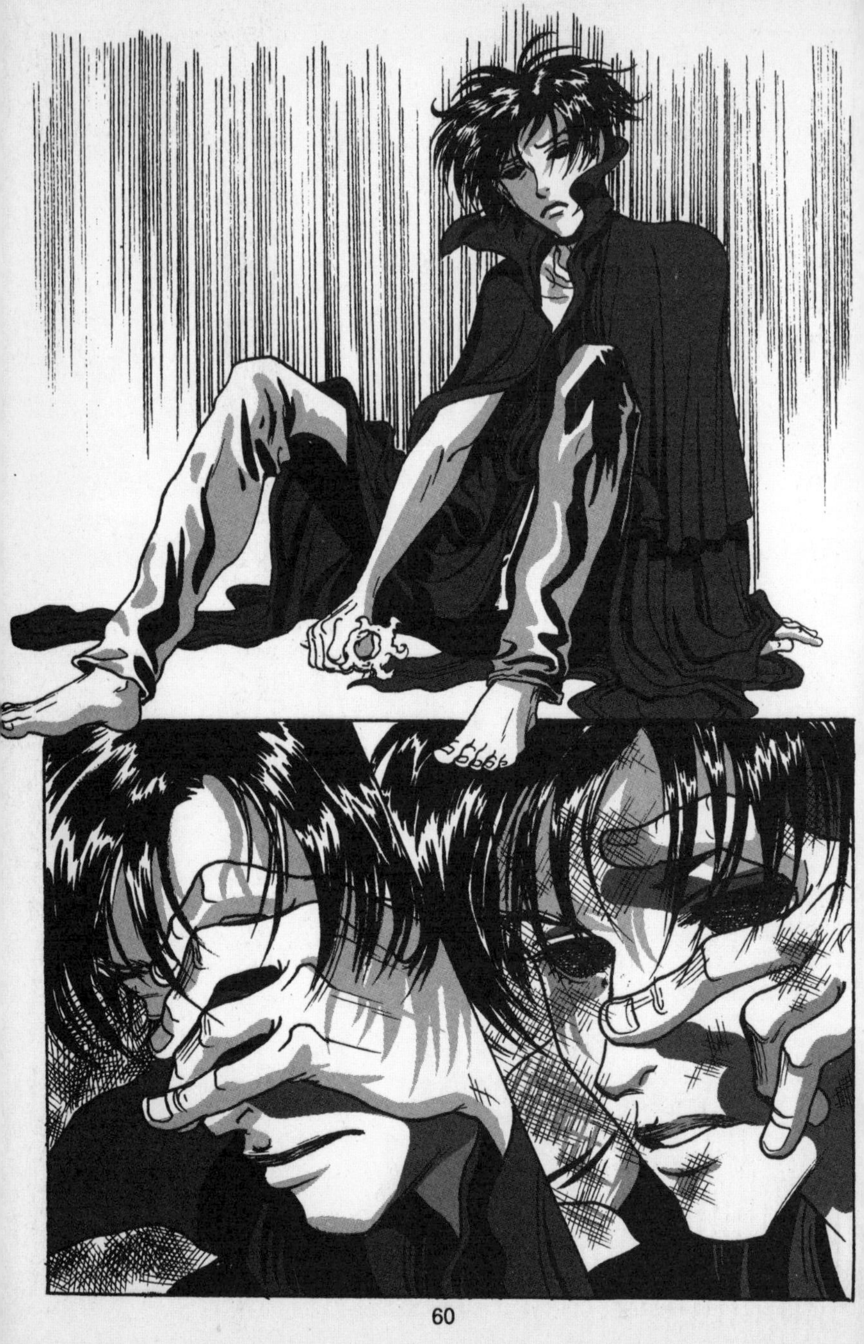

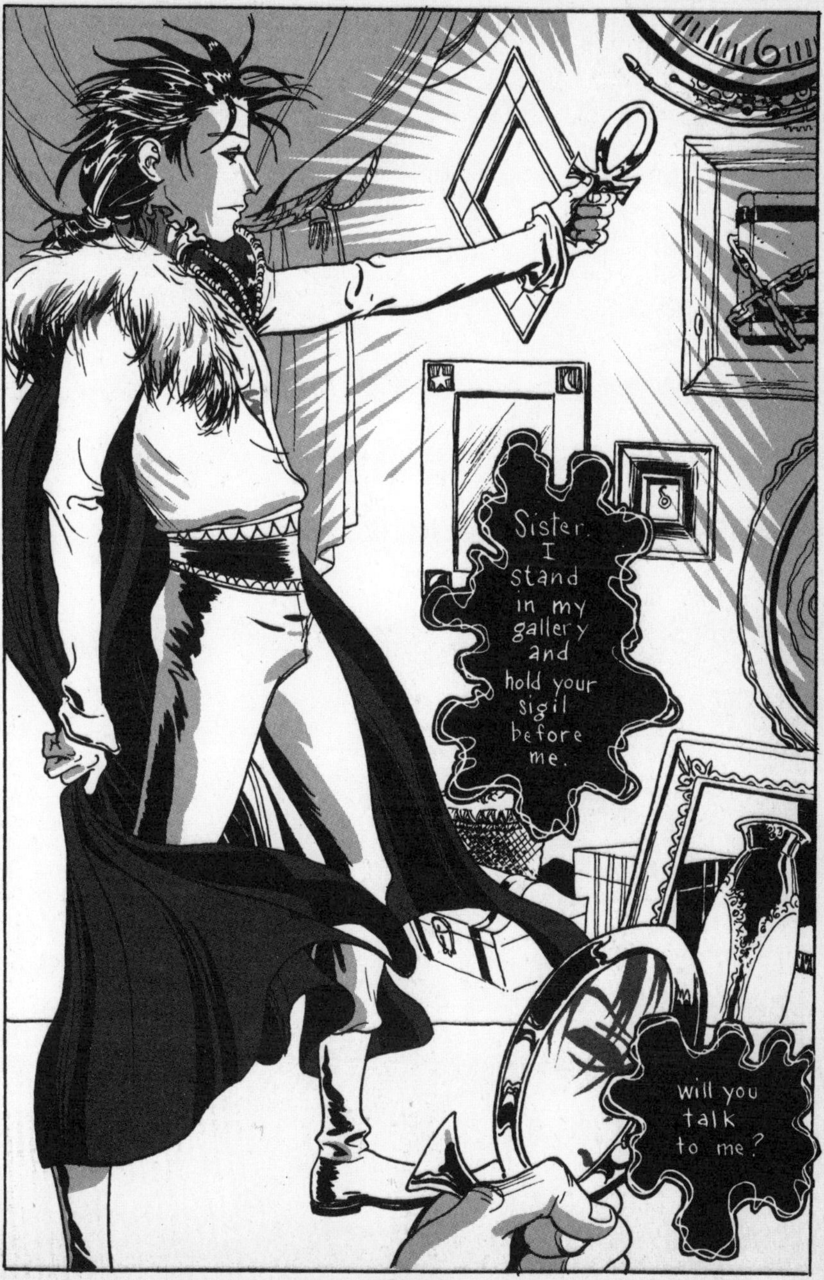
Sister. I stand in my gallery and hold your sigil before me.
will you talk to me?

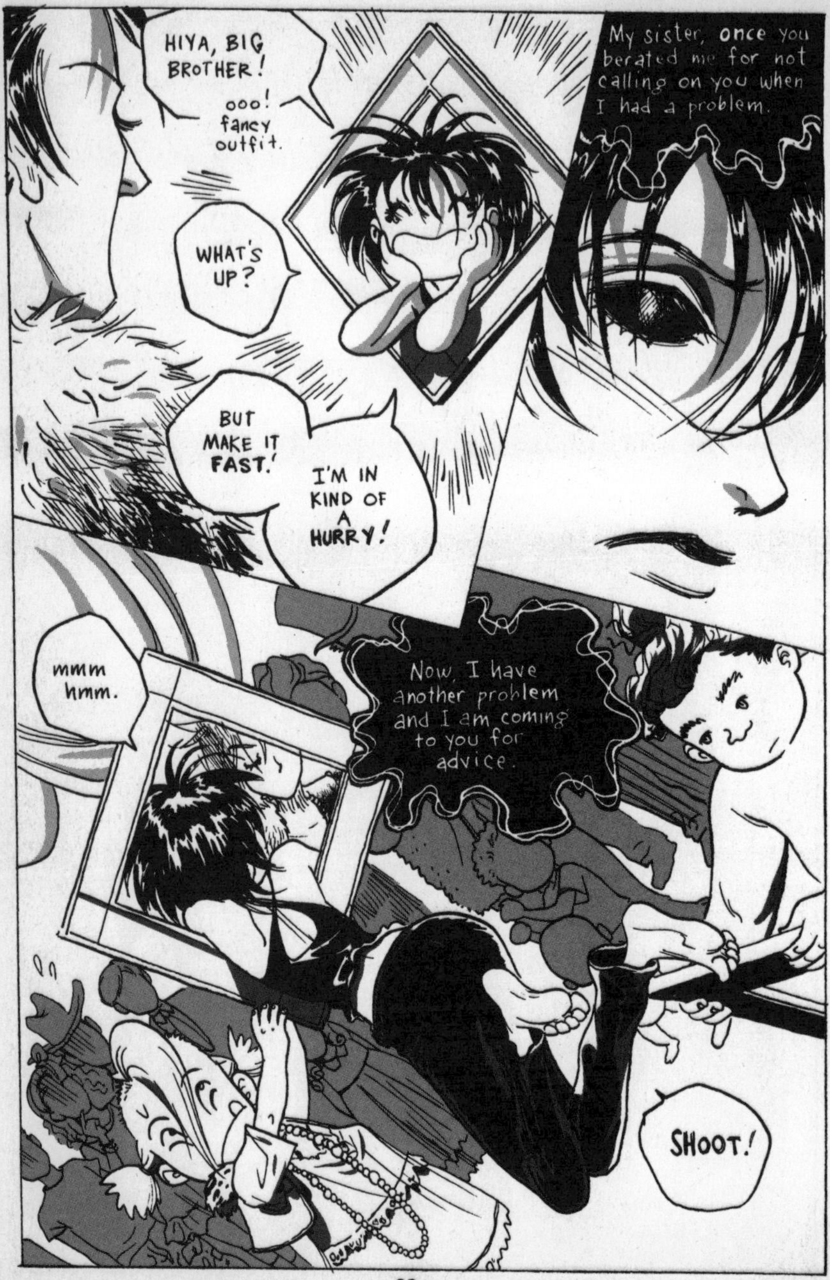
HIYA, BIG BROTHER!
ooo! fancy outfit.
WHAT'S UP?
My sister, once you berated me for not calling on you when I had a problem.
BUT MAKE IT FAST!
I'M IN KIND OF A HURRY!
mmm hmm.
Now, I have another problem and I am coming to you for advice.
SHOOT!

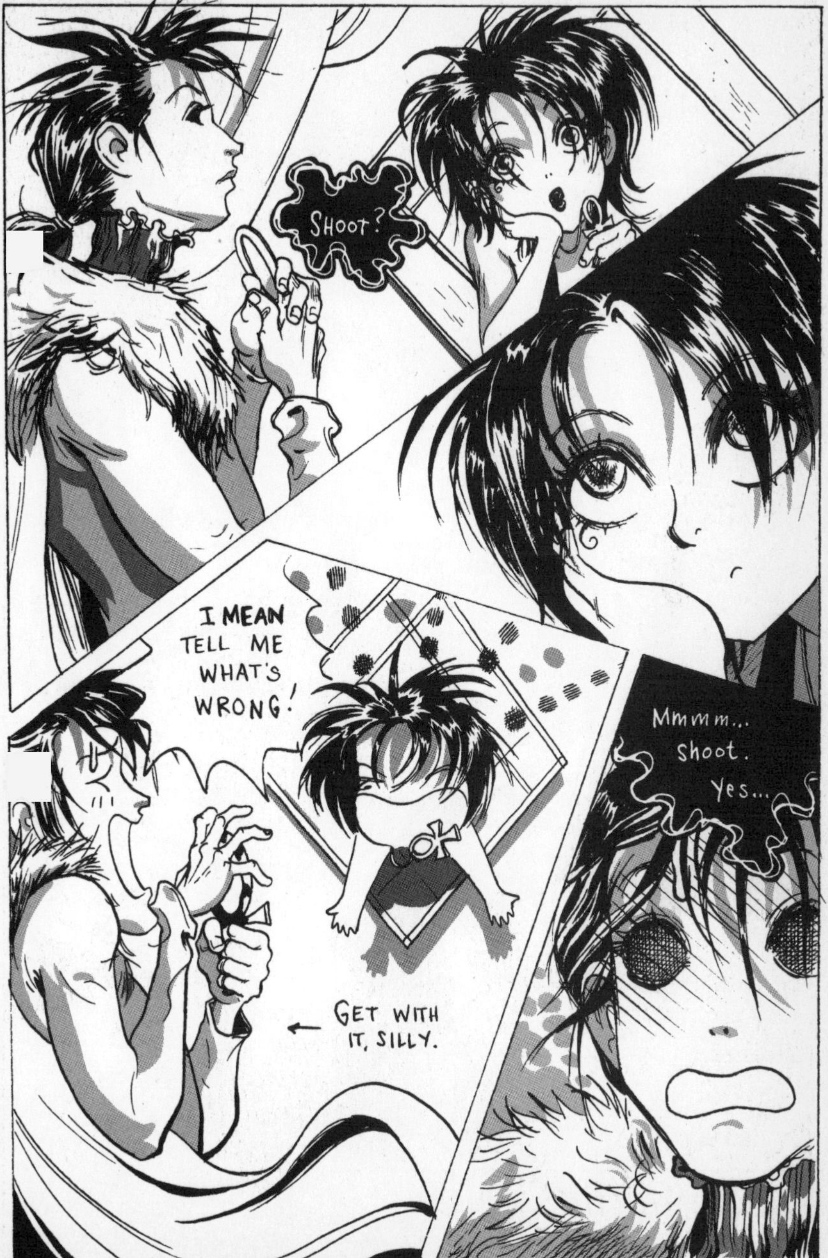
SHOOT?
Mmmm... shoot. yes...
I MEAN TELL ME WHAT'S WRONG!
GET WITH IT, SILLY.

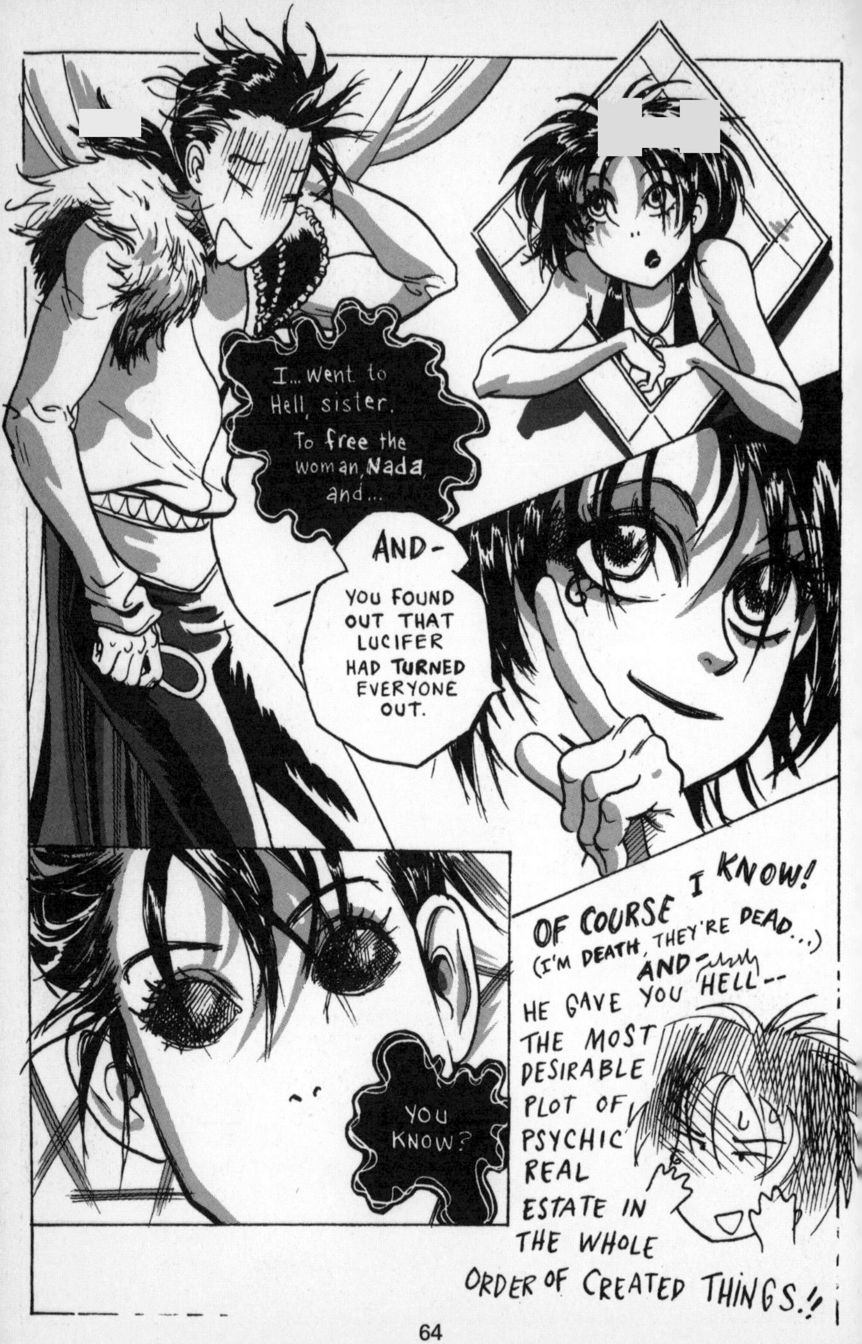
I... went to Hell, sister.
To free the woman, Nada, and...
AND-
YOU FOUND OUT THAT LUCIFER HAD TURNED EVERYONE OUT.
...
YOU KNOW?
OF COURSE I KNOW!
(I'M DEATH, THEY'RE DEAD...)
AND-
HE GAVE YOU HELL-- THE MOST DESIRABLE PLOT OF PSYCHIC REAL ESTATE IN THE WHOLE ORDER OF CREATED THINGS.!!

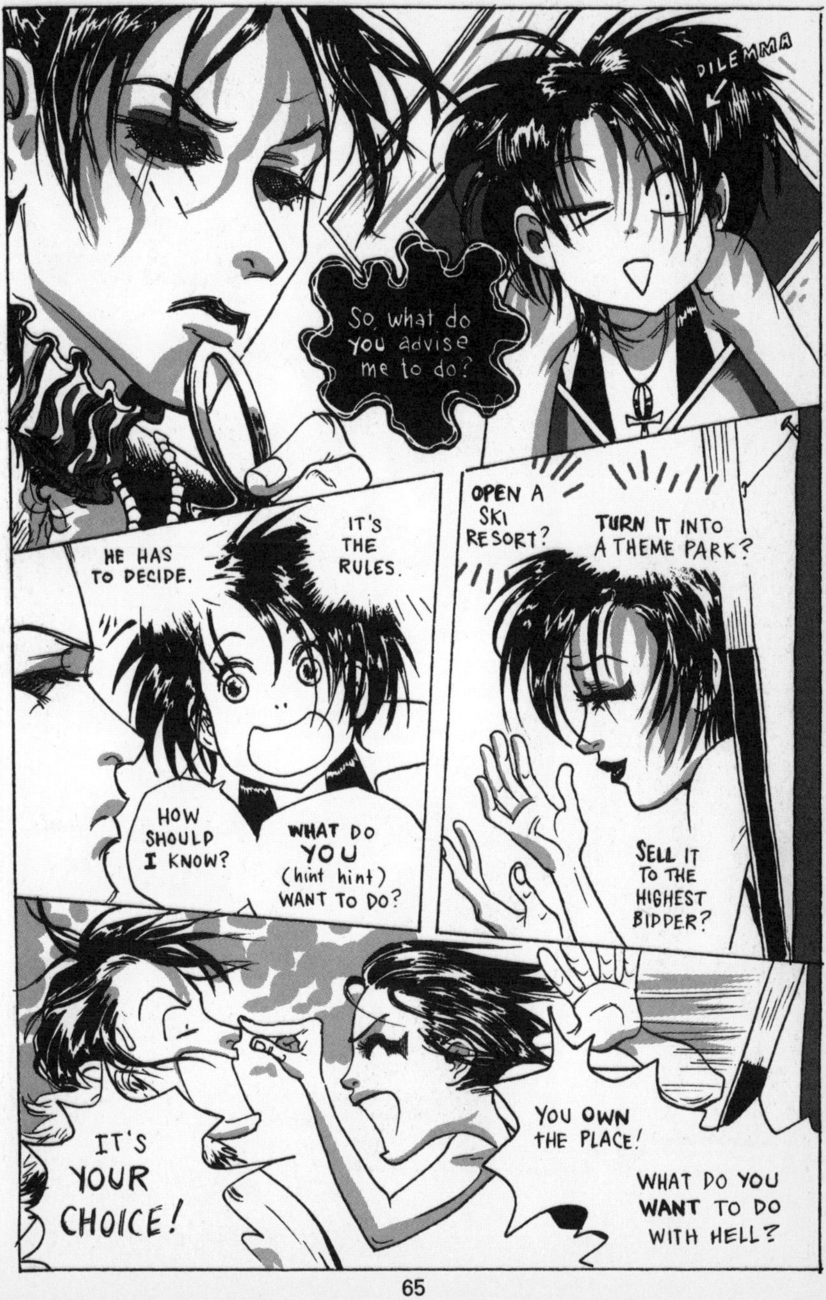
DILEMMA
So, what do you advise me to do?
HE HAS TO DECIDE.
IT'S THE RULES.
HOW SHOULD I KNOW?
WHAT DO YOU (hint hint) WANT TO DO?
OPEN A SKI RESORT?
TURN IT INTO A THEME PARK?
SELL IT TO THE HIGHEST BIDDER?
IT'S YOUR CHOICE!
YOU OWN THE PLACE!
WHAT DO YOU WANT TO DO WITH HELL?

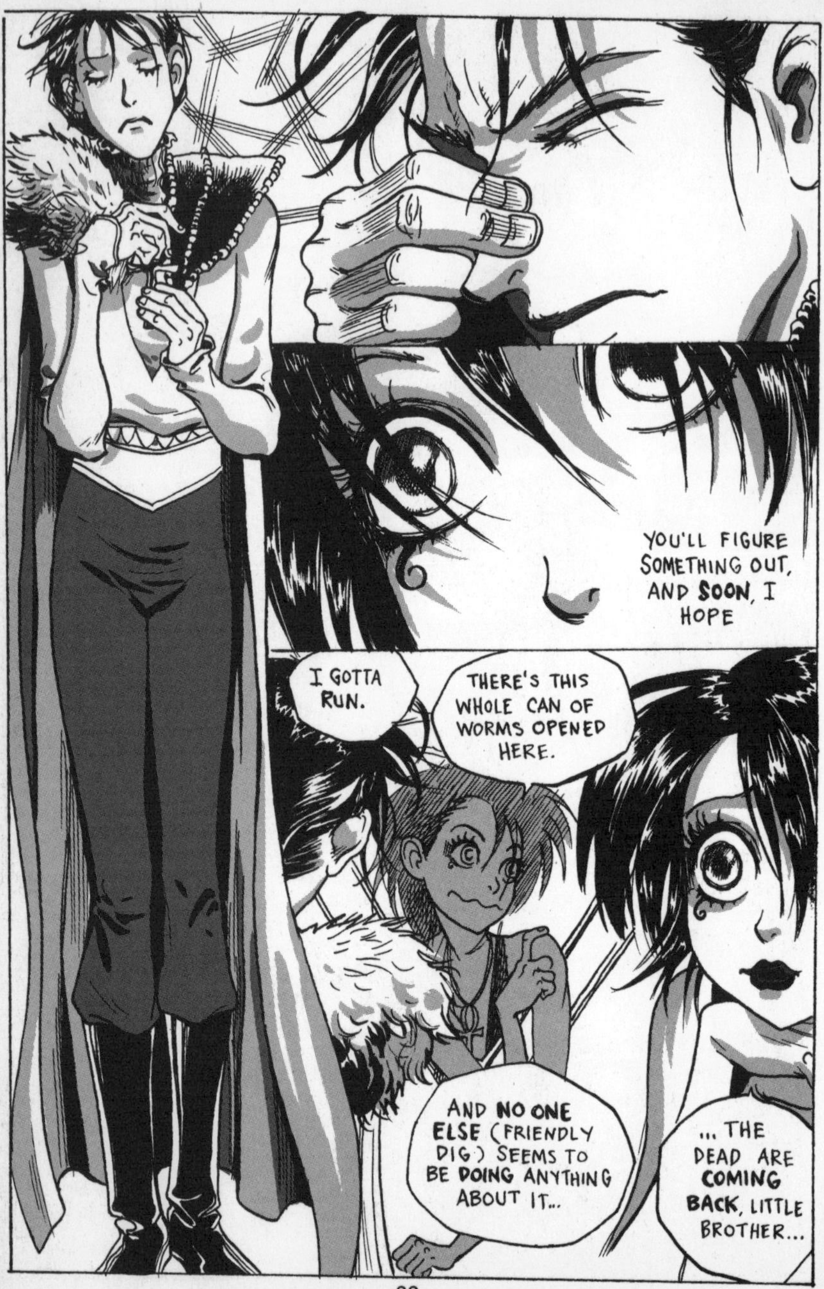
YOU'LL FIGURE SOMETHING OUT, AND SOON, I HOPE
I GOTTA RUN.
THERE'S THIS WHOLE CAN OF WORMS OPENED HERE.
AND NO ONE ELSE (FRIENDLY DIG) SEEMS TO BE DOING ANYTHING ABOUT IT...
... THE DEAD ARE COMING BACK, LITTLE BROTHER...

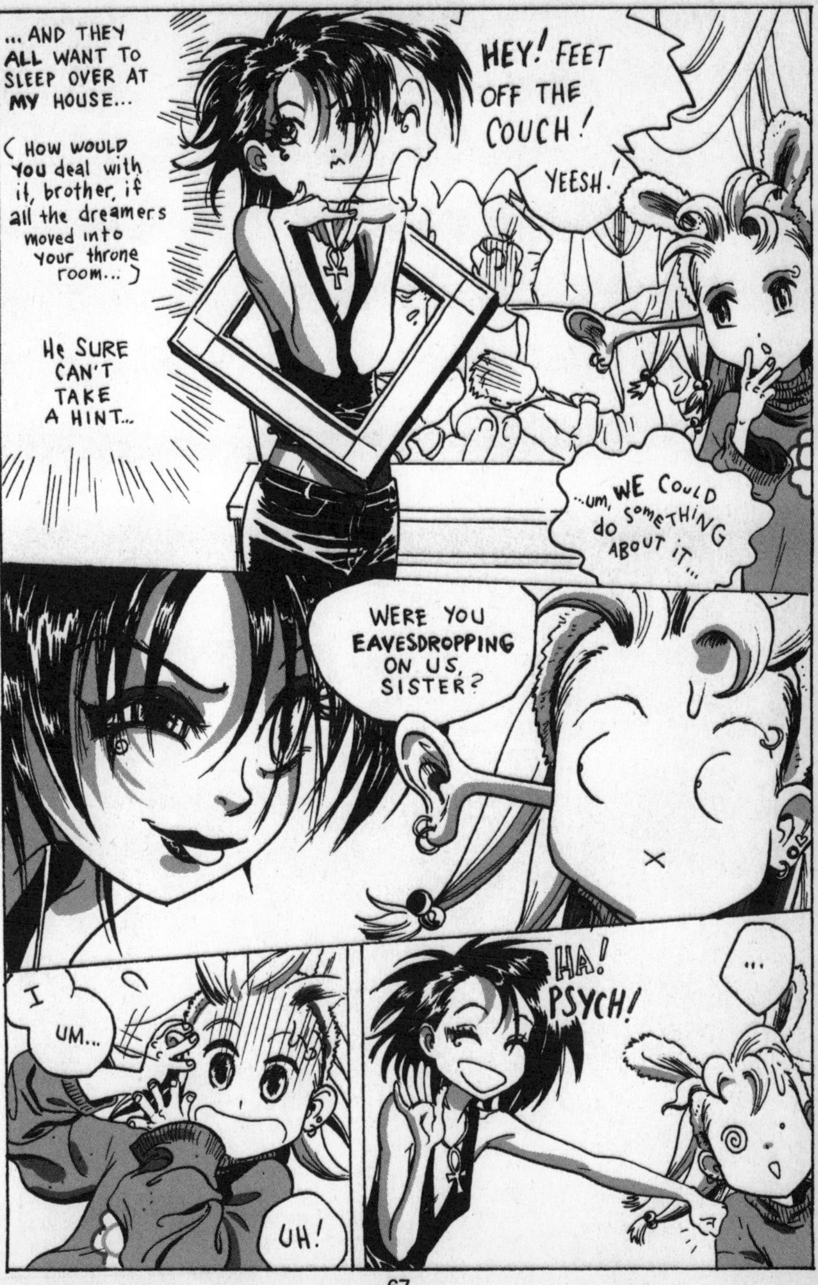
...AND THEY ALL WANT TO SLEEP OVER AT MY HOUSE...
(HOW WOULD YOU deal with it, brother, if all the dreamers moved into your throne room...)
He SURE CAN'T TAKE A HINT...
HEY! FEET OFF THE COUCH!
YEESH!
...um, WE COULD do SOMETHING ABOUT IT...
WERE YOU EAVESDROPPING ON US, SISTER?
I UM...
UH!
HA! PSYCH!
...

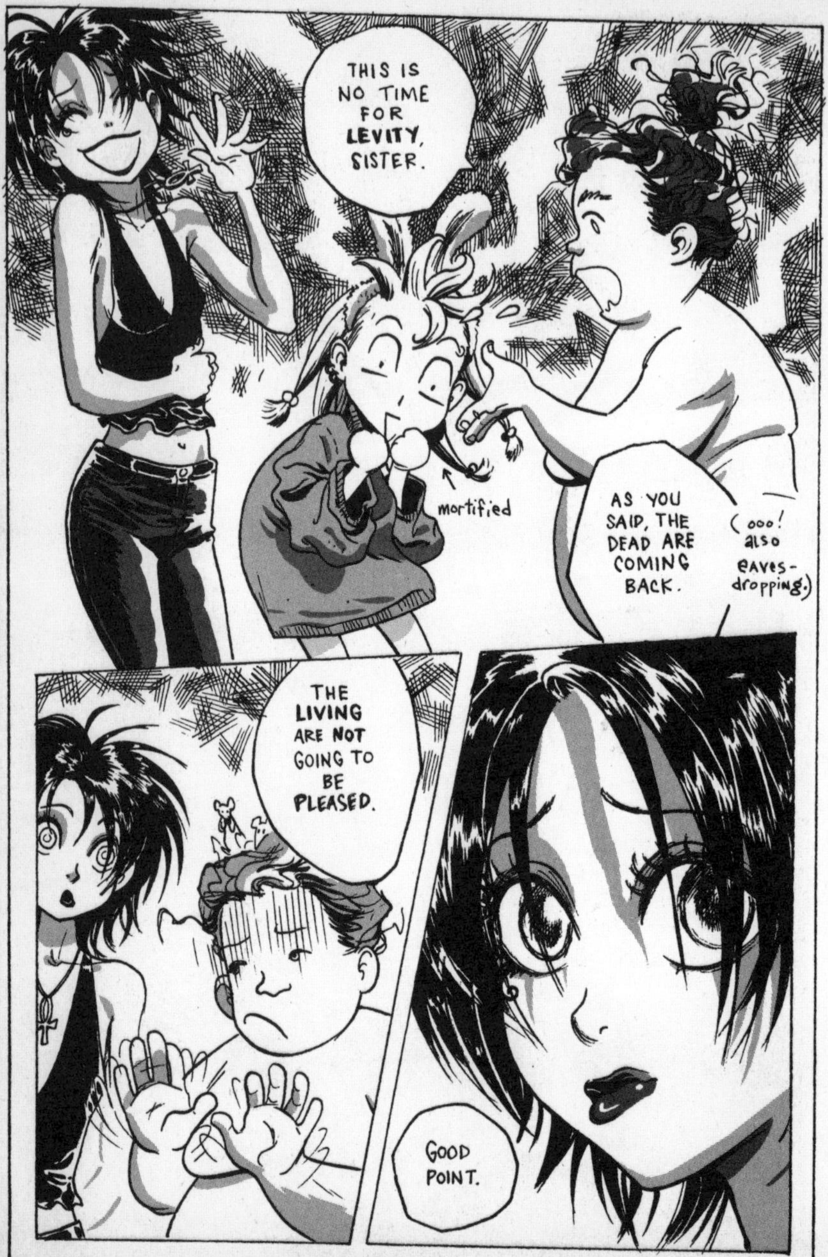
THIS IS NO TIME FOR **LEVITY**, SISTER.
mortified
AS YOU SAID, THE DEAD ARE COMING BACK.
(ooo! also eaves-dropping.)
THE **LIVING** ARE **NOT** GOING TO BE **PLEASED**.
GOOD POINT.

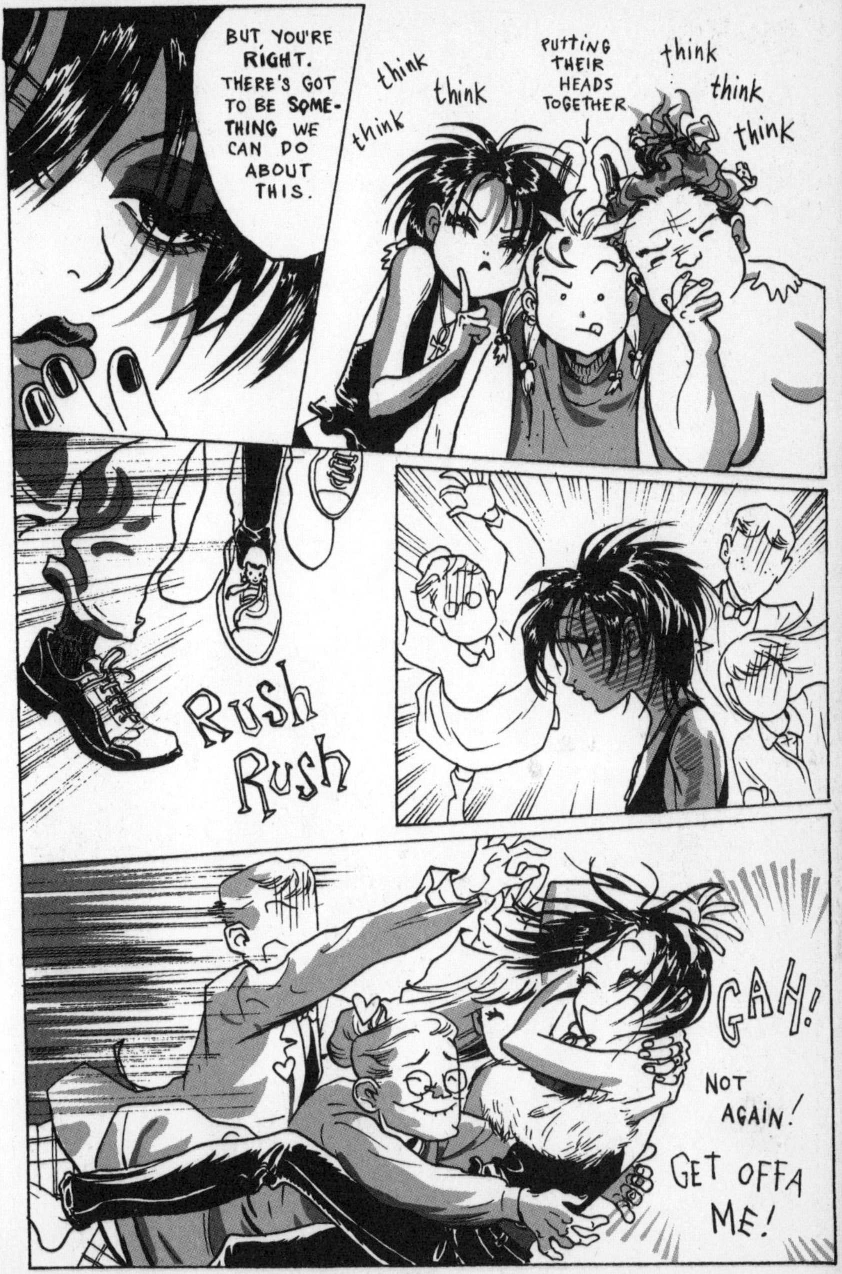
BUT YOU'RE RIGHT. THERE'S GOT TO BE SOMETHING WE CAN DO ABOUT THIS.
think think think
PUTTING THEIR HEADS TOGETHER
think think think
Rush Rush
GAH!
NOT AGAIN!
GET OFFA ME!

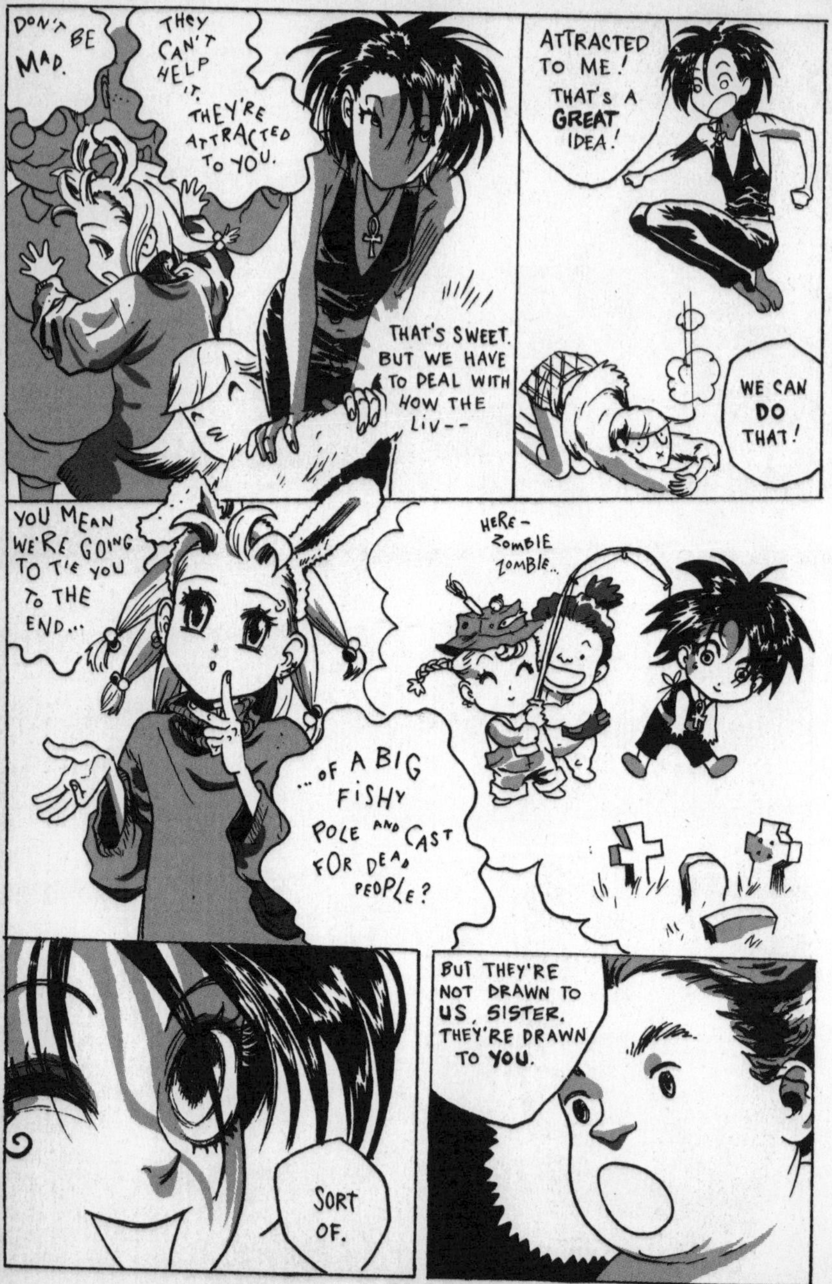

DON'T BE MAD.
THEY CAN'T HELP IT. THEY'RE ATTRACTED TO YOU.
THAT'S SWEET. BUT WE HAVE TO DEAL WITH HOW THE LIV--
ATTRACTED TO ME! THAT'S A GREAT IDEA!
WE CAN DO THAT!
YOU MEAN WE'RE GOING TO TIE YOU TO THE END...
HERE- ZOMBIE ZOMBIE...
...OF A BIG FISHY POLE AND CAST FOR DEAD PEOPLE?
BUT THEY'RE NOT DRAWN TO US, SISTER. THEY'RE DRAWN TO YOU.
SORT OF.

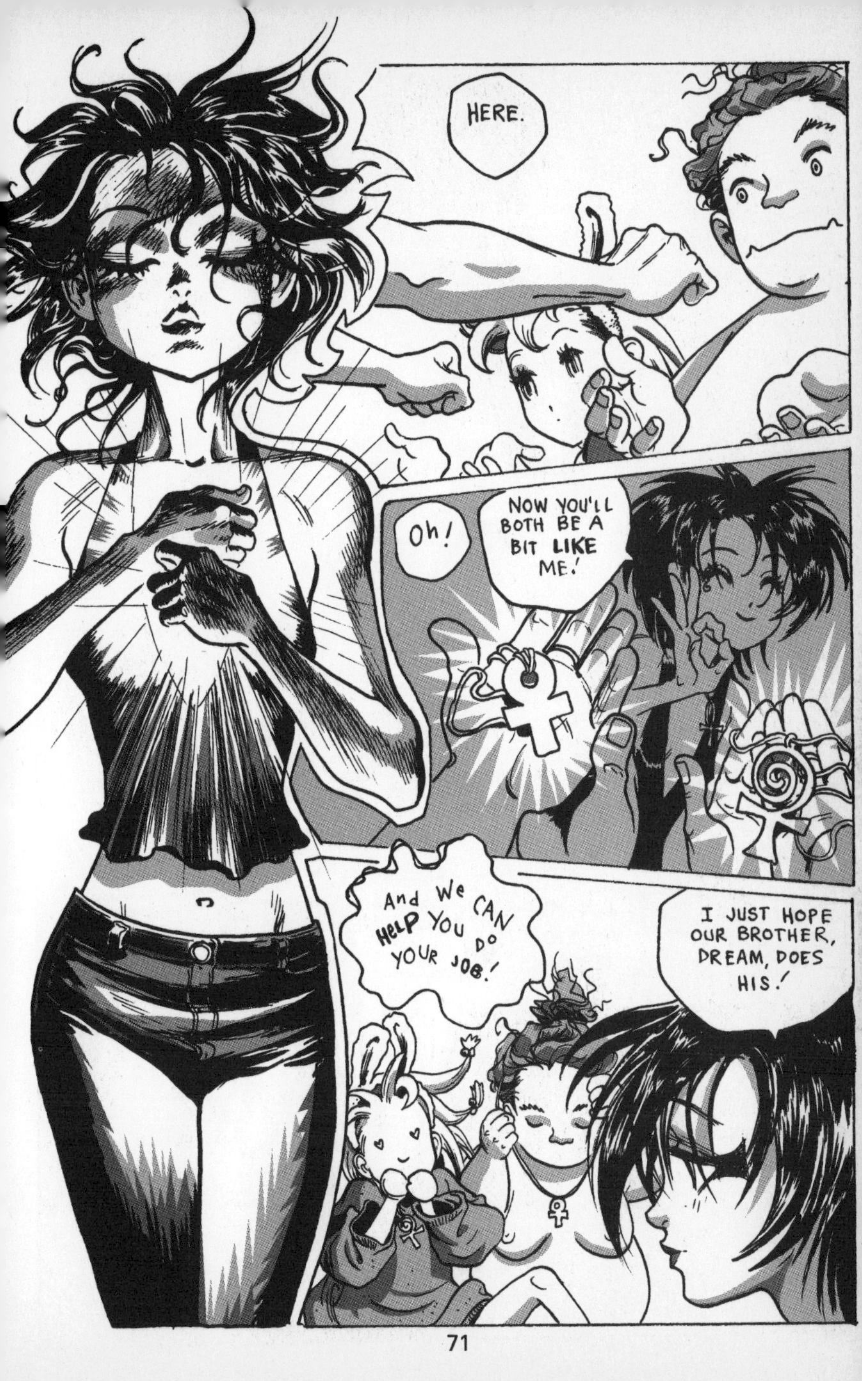
HERE.
Oh!
NOW YOU'LL BOTH BE A BIT LIKE ME!
And We CAN HELP YOU DO YOUR JOB!
I JUST HOPE OUR BROTHER, DREAM, DOES HIS!

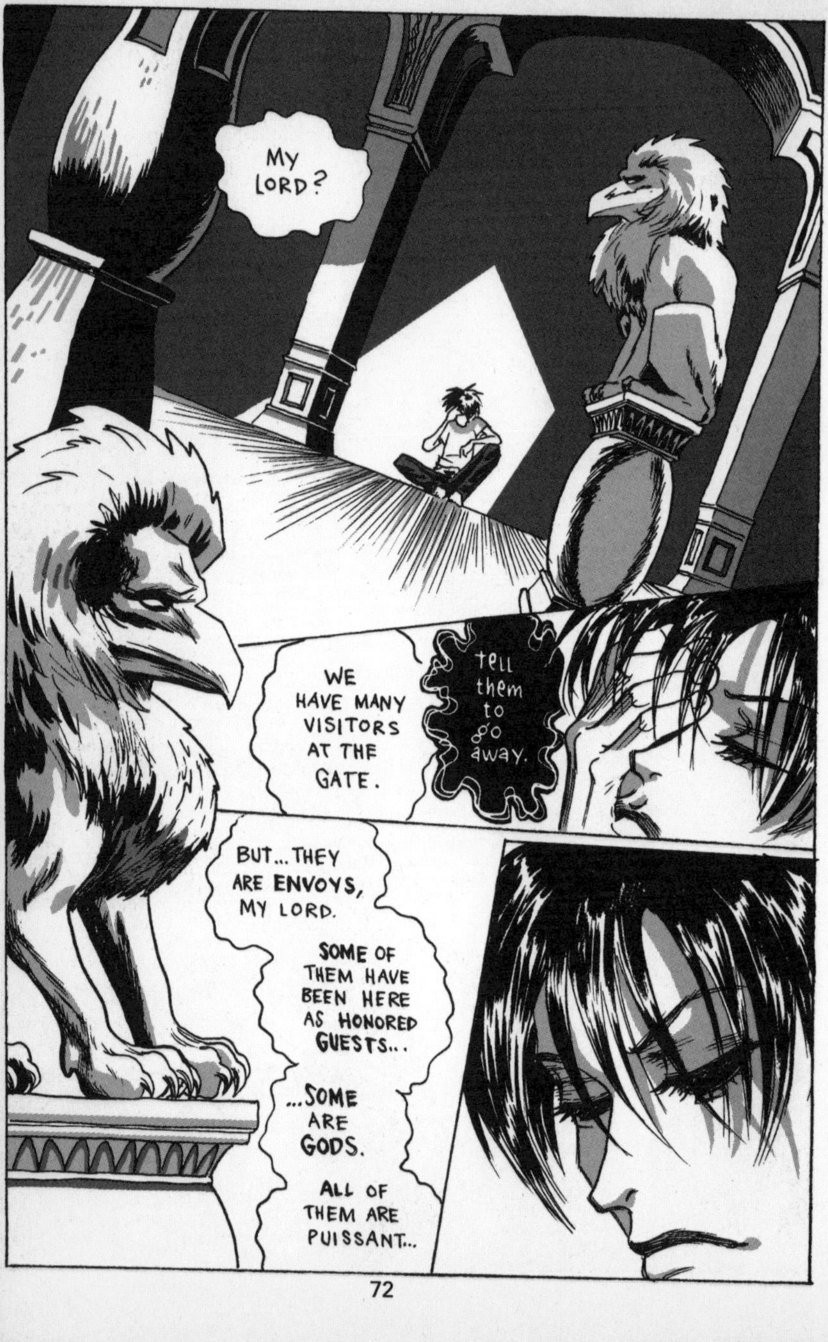
MY LORD?
WE HAVE MANY VISITORS AT THE GATE.
tell them to go away.
BUT... THEY ARE ENVOYS, MY LORD.
SOME OF THEM HAVE BEEN HERE AS HONORED GUESTS...
...SOME ARE GODS.
ALL OF THEM ARE PUISSANT...

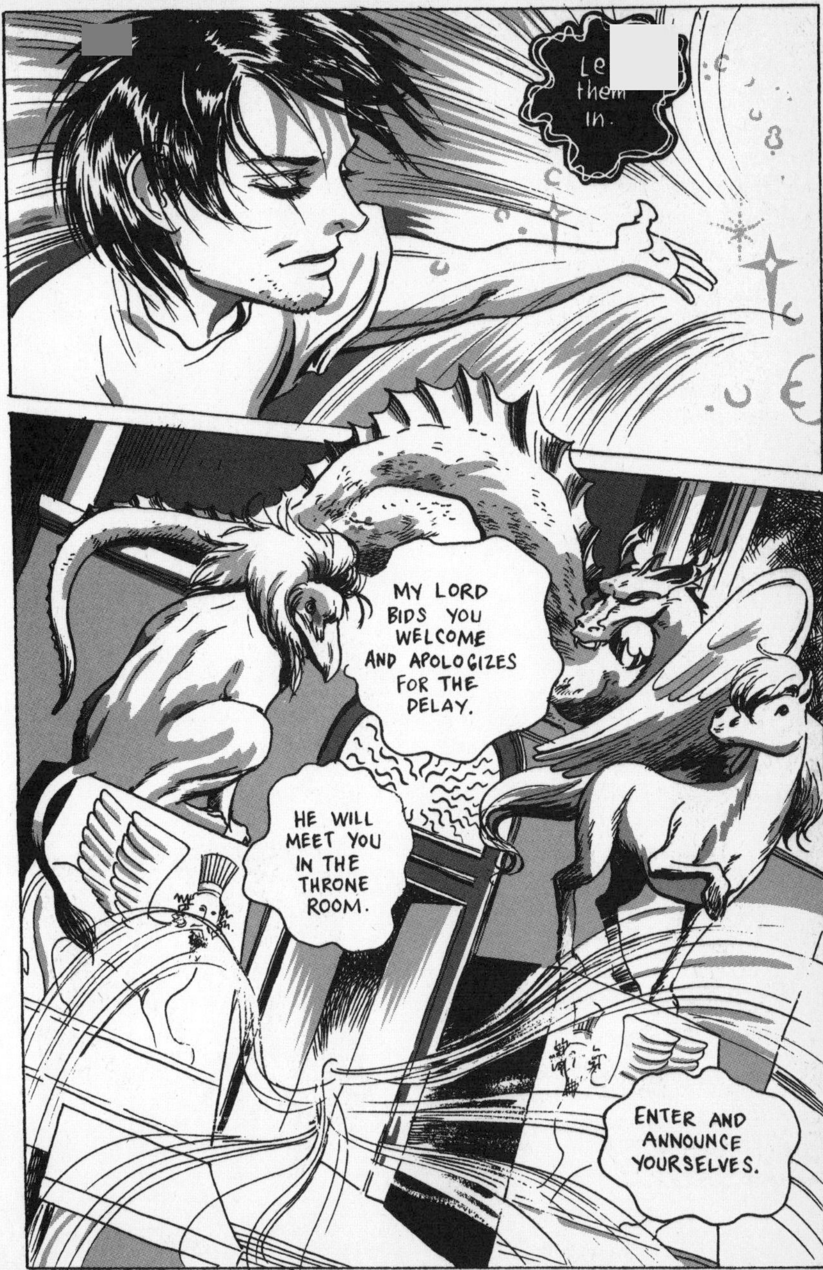
Le them in.
MY LORD BIDS YOU WELCOME AND APOLOGIZES FOR THE DELAY.
HE WILL MEET YOU IN THE THRONE ROOM.
ENTER AND ANNOUNCE YOURSELVES.

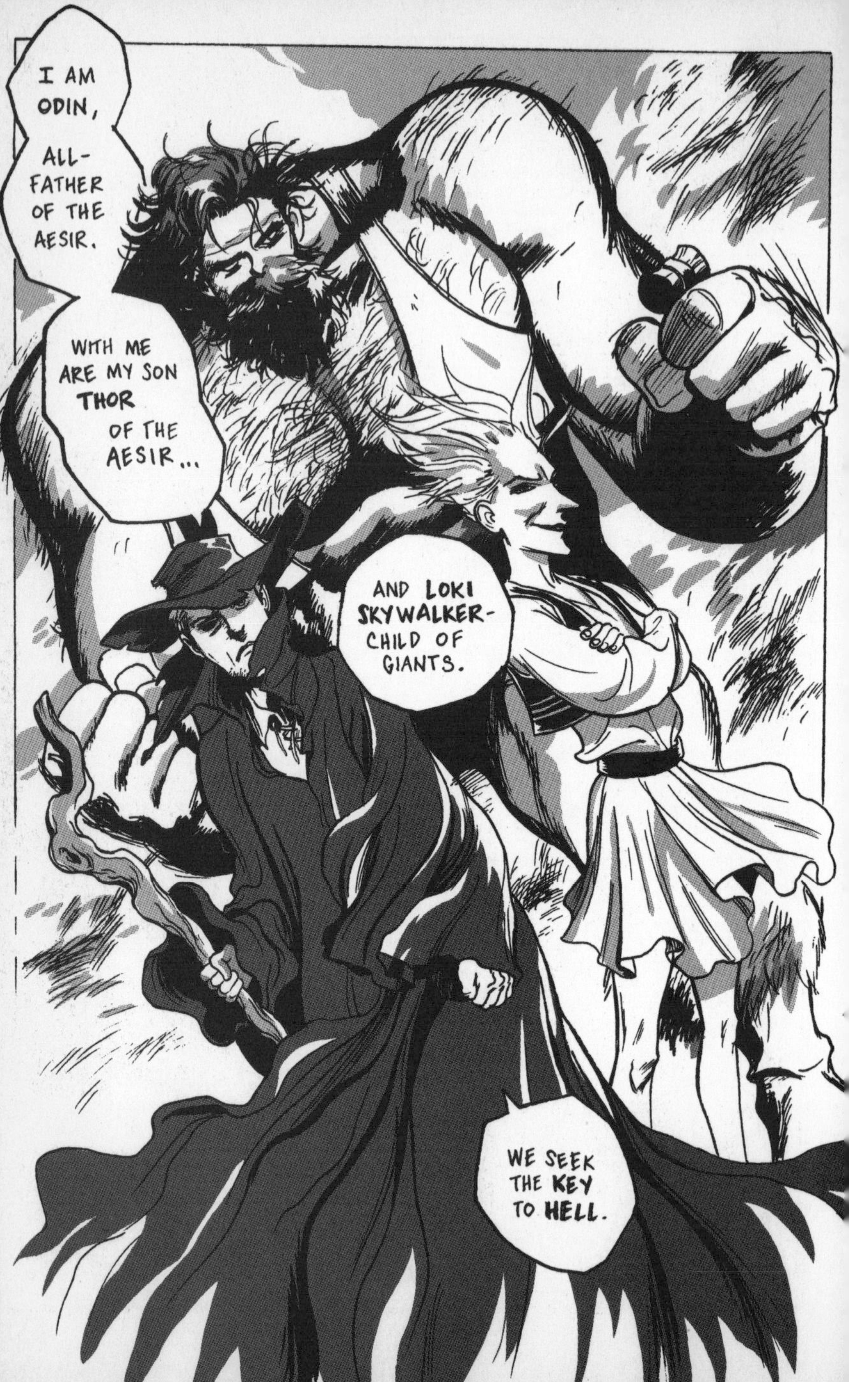

I AM ODIN,
ALL-FATHER OF THE AESIR.
WITH ME ARE MY SON THOR OF THE AESIR...
AND LOKI SKYWALKER-CHILD OF GIANTS.
WE SEEK THE KEY TO HELL.

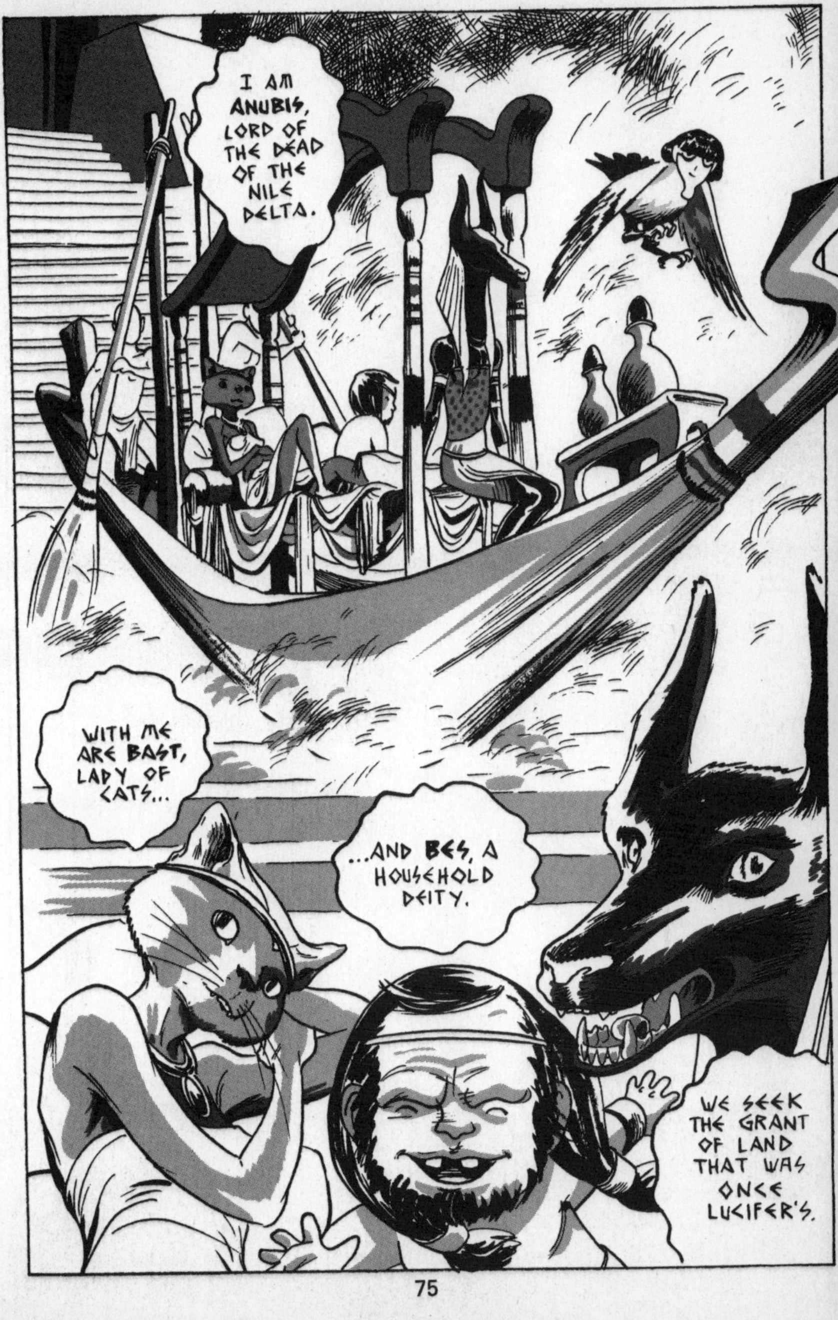
I AM ANUBIS, LORD OF THE DEAD OF THE NILE DELTA.
WITH ME ARE BAST, LADY OF CATS...
...AND BES, A HOUSEHOLD DEITY.
WE SEEK THE GRANT OF LAND THAT WAS ONCE LUCIFER'S.

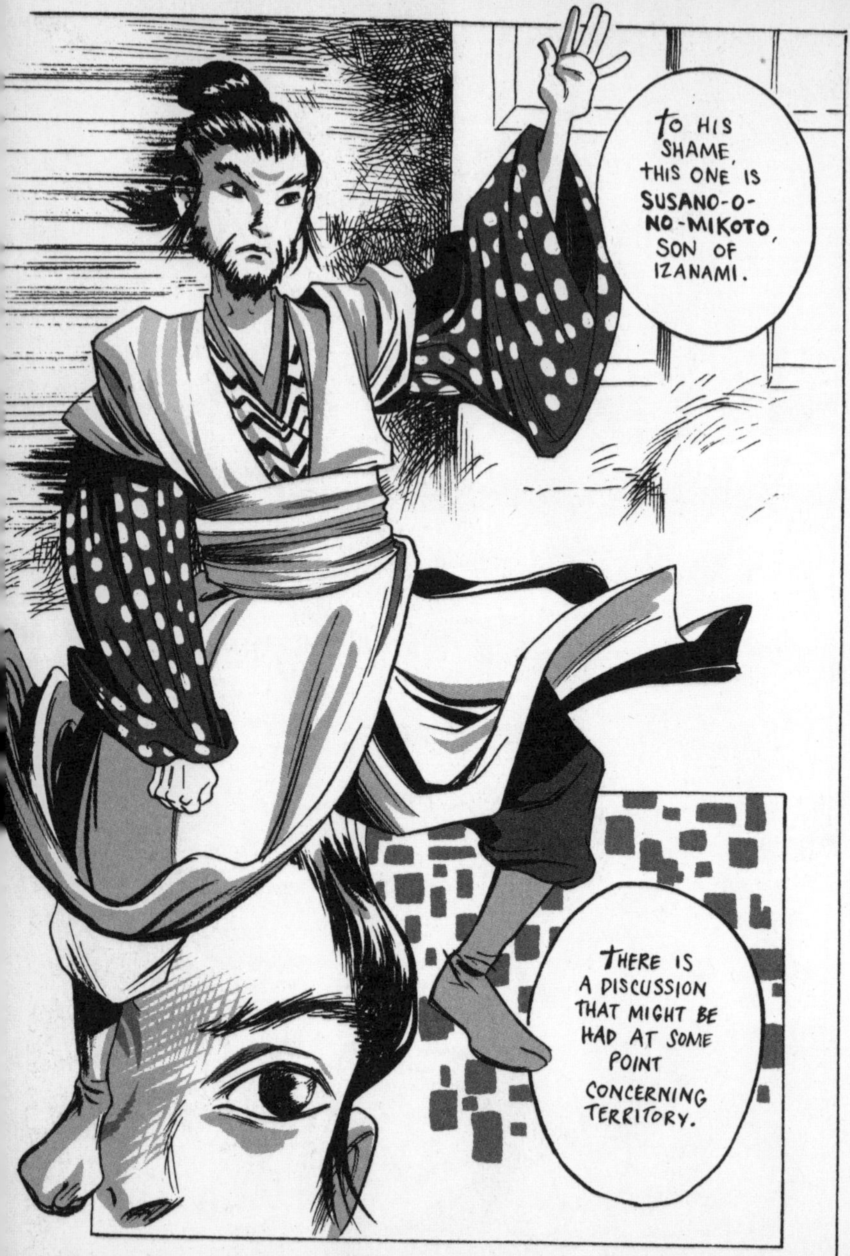
TO HIS SHAME, THIS ONE IS SUSANO-O-NO-MIKOTO, SON OF IZANAMI.
THERE IS A DISCUSSION THAT MIGHT BE HAD AT SOME POINT CONCERNING TERRITORY.

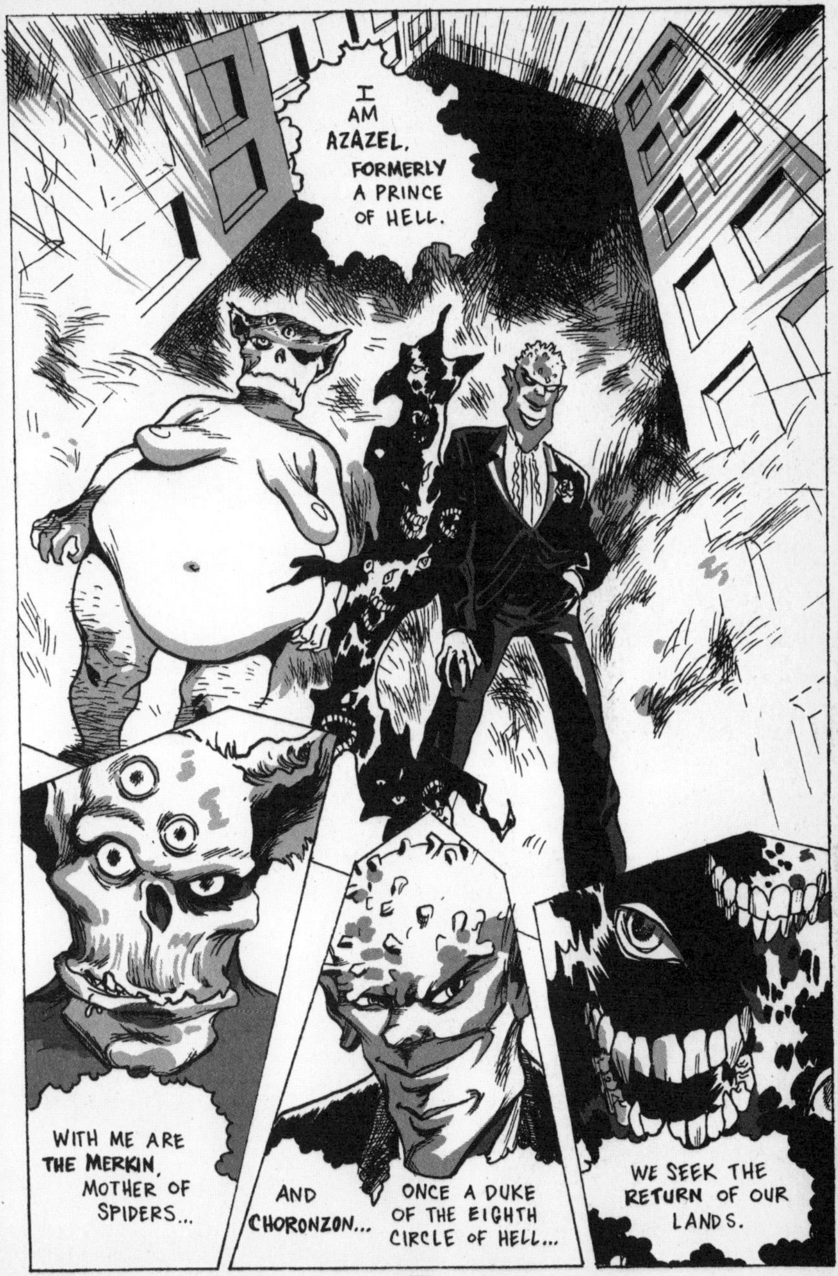
I AM AZAZEL, FORMERLY A PRINCE OF HELL.
WITH ME ARE THE MERKIN, MOTHER OF SPIDERS...
AND CHORONZON...
ONCE A DUKE OF THE EIGHTH CIRCLE OF HELL...
WE SEEK THE RETURN OF OUR LANDS.

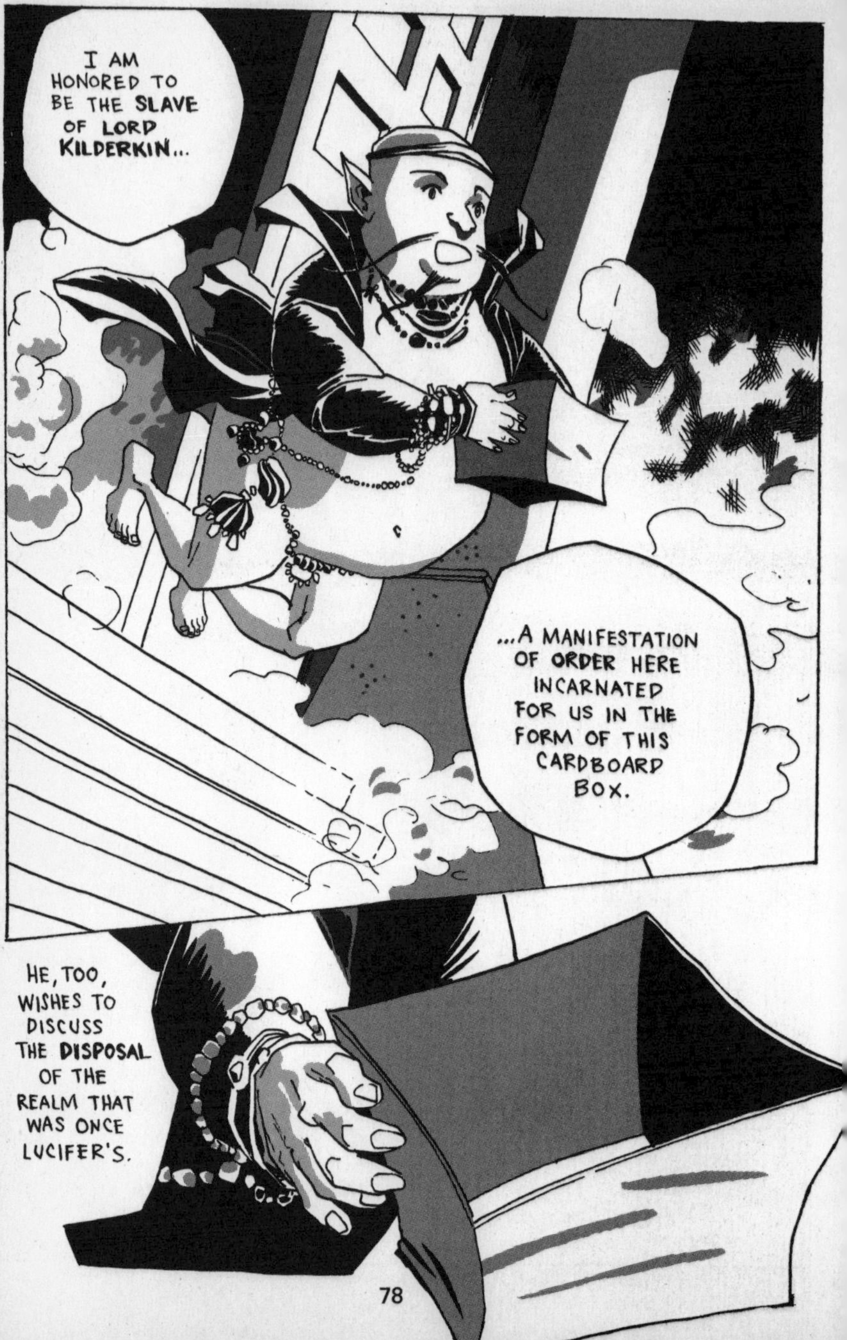
I AM HONORED TO BE THE SLAVE OF LORD KILDERKIN...
...A MANIFESTATION OF ORDER HERE INCARNATED FOR US IN THE FORM OF THIS CARDBOARD BOX.
HE, TOO, WISHES TO DISCUSS THE DISPOSAL OF THE REALM THAT WAS ONCE LUCIFER'S.

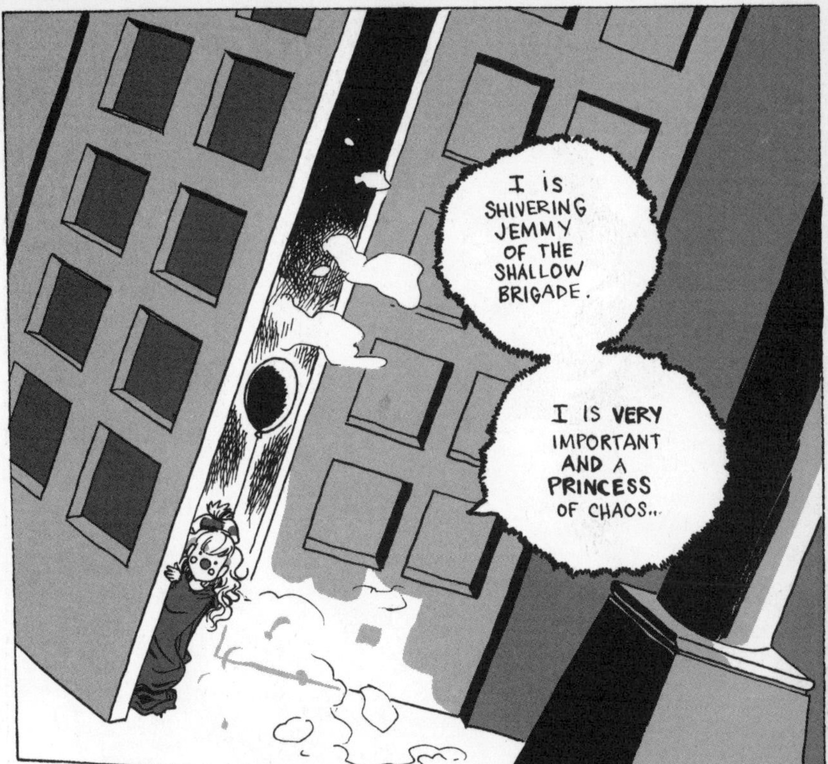
I IS SHIVERING JEMMY OF THE SHALLOW BRIGADE.
I IS VERY IMPORTANT AND A PRINCESS OF CHAOS..

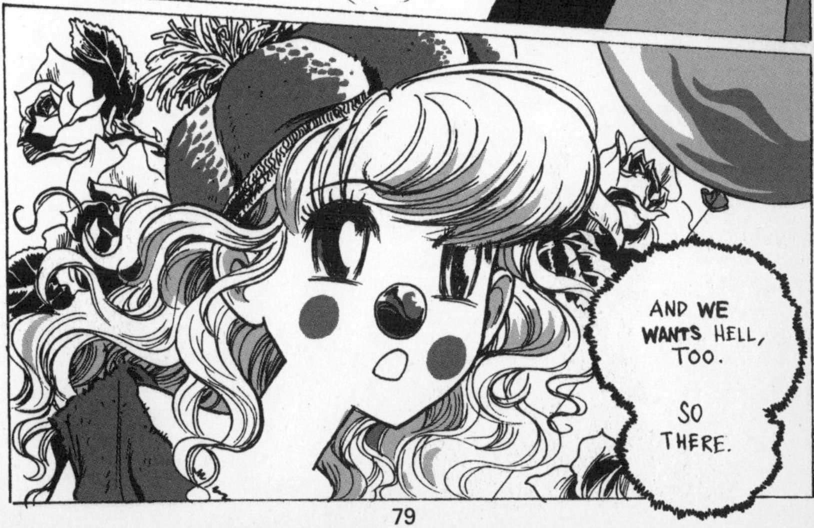
AND WE WANTS HELL, TOO.
SO THERE.

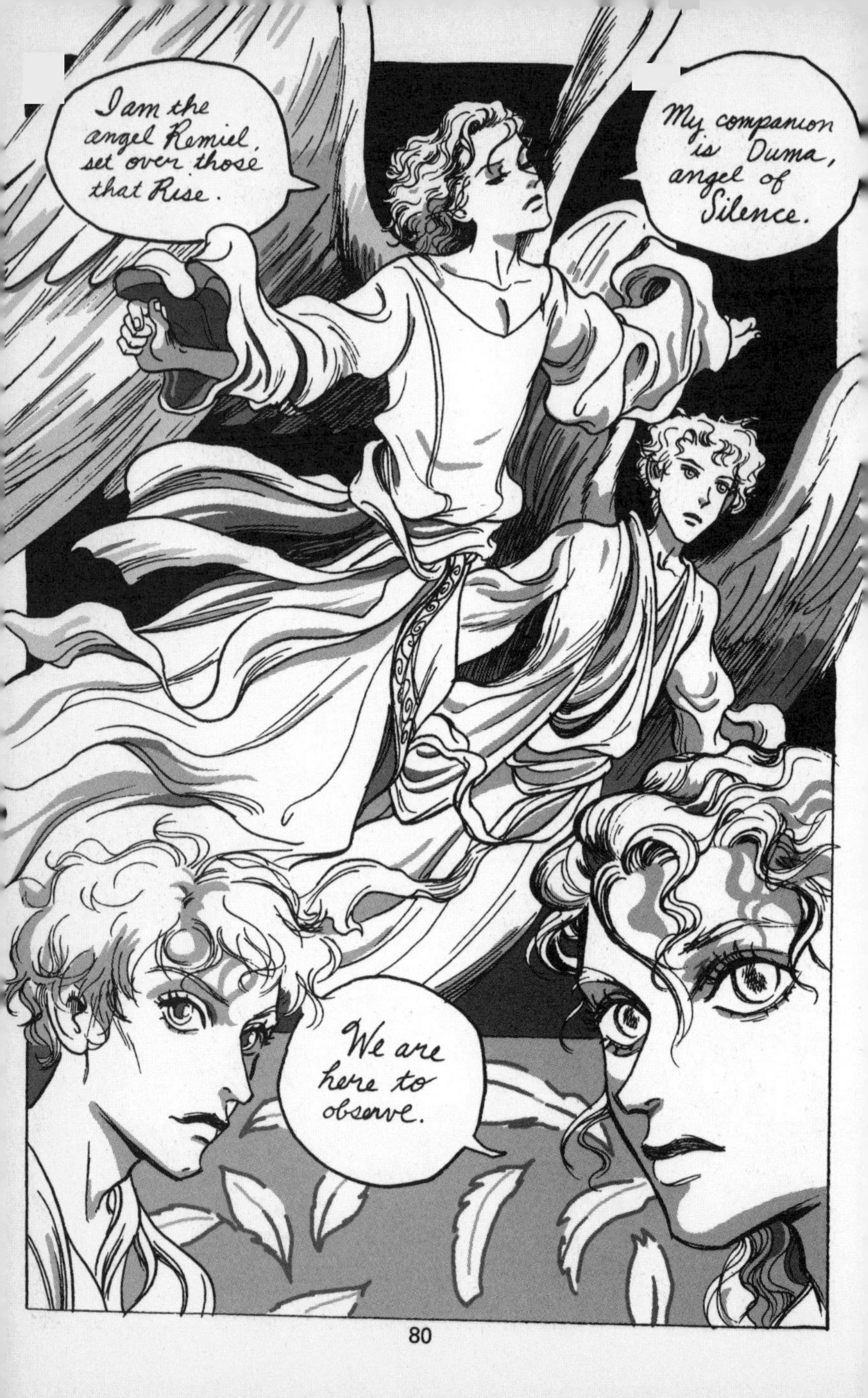
I am the angel Remiel set over those that Rise.
My companion is Duma, angel of Silence.
We are here to observe.

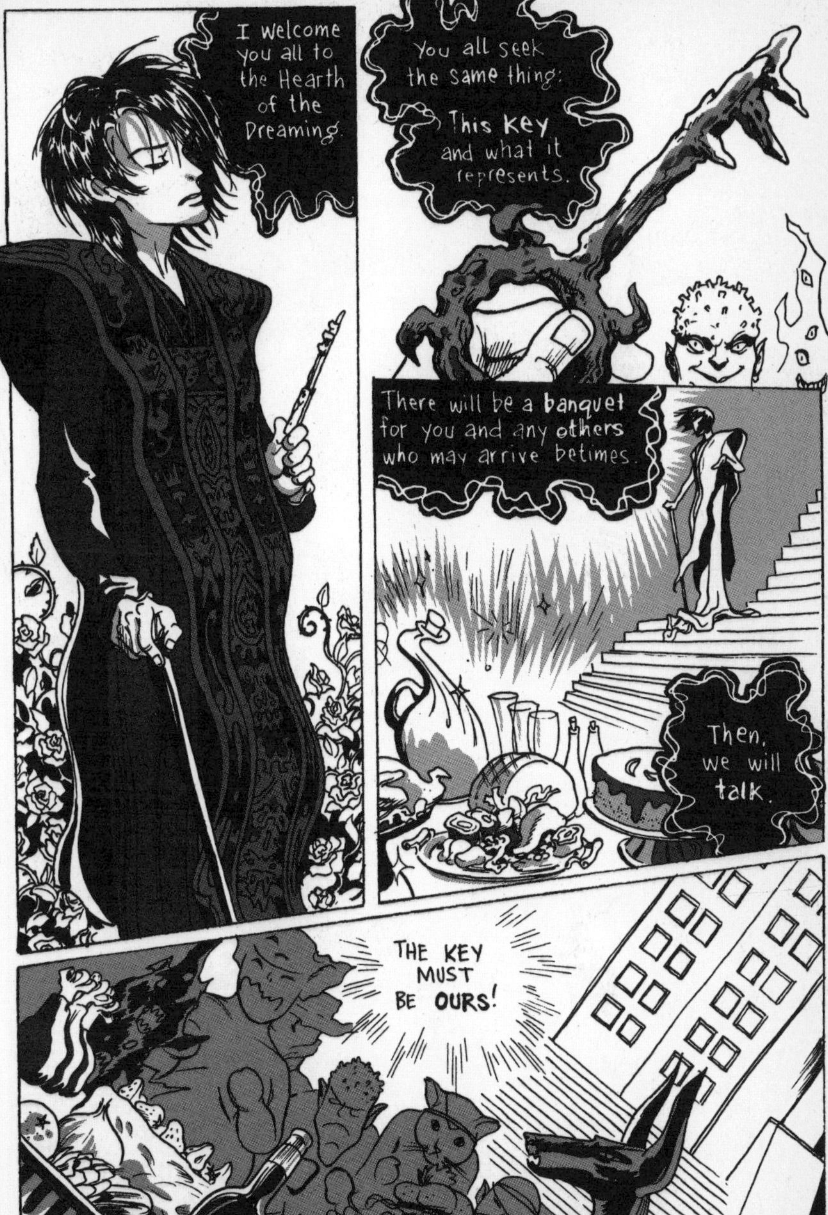
I welcome you all to the Hearth of the Dreaming.
You all seek the same thing:
This key and what it represents.
There will be a banquet for you and any others who may arrive betimes.
Then, we will talk.
THE KEY MUST BE OURS!

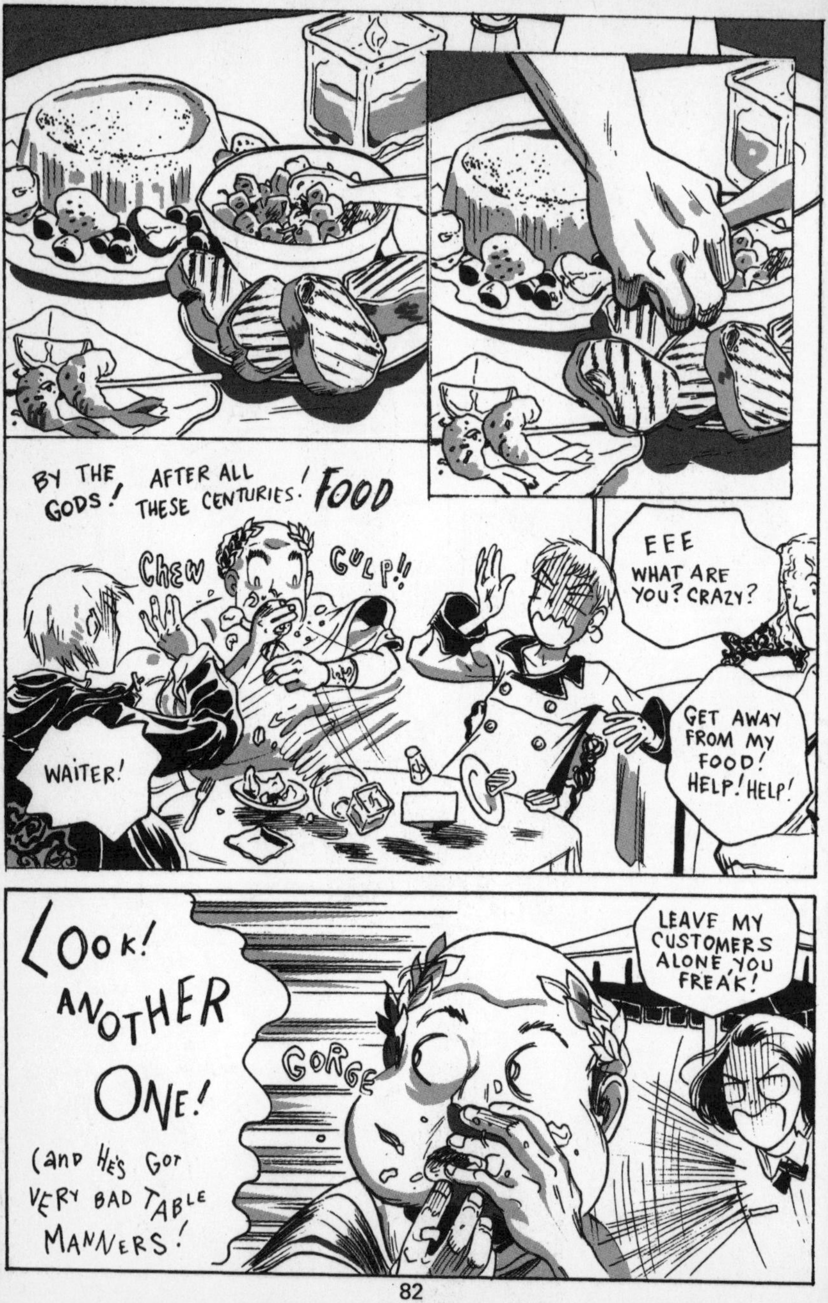
BY THE GODS! AFTER ALL THESE CENTURIES! FOOD
CHEW
GULP!!
EEE WHAT ARE YOU? CRAZY?
WAITER!
GET AWAY FROM MY FOOD! HELP! HELP!
LOOK! ANOTHER ONE!
(AND HE'S GOT VERY BAD TABLE MANNERS!
GORGE
LEAVE MY CUSTOMERS ALONE, YOU FREAK!

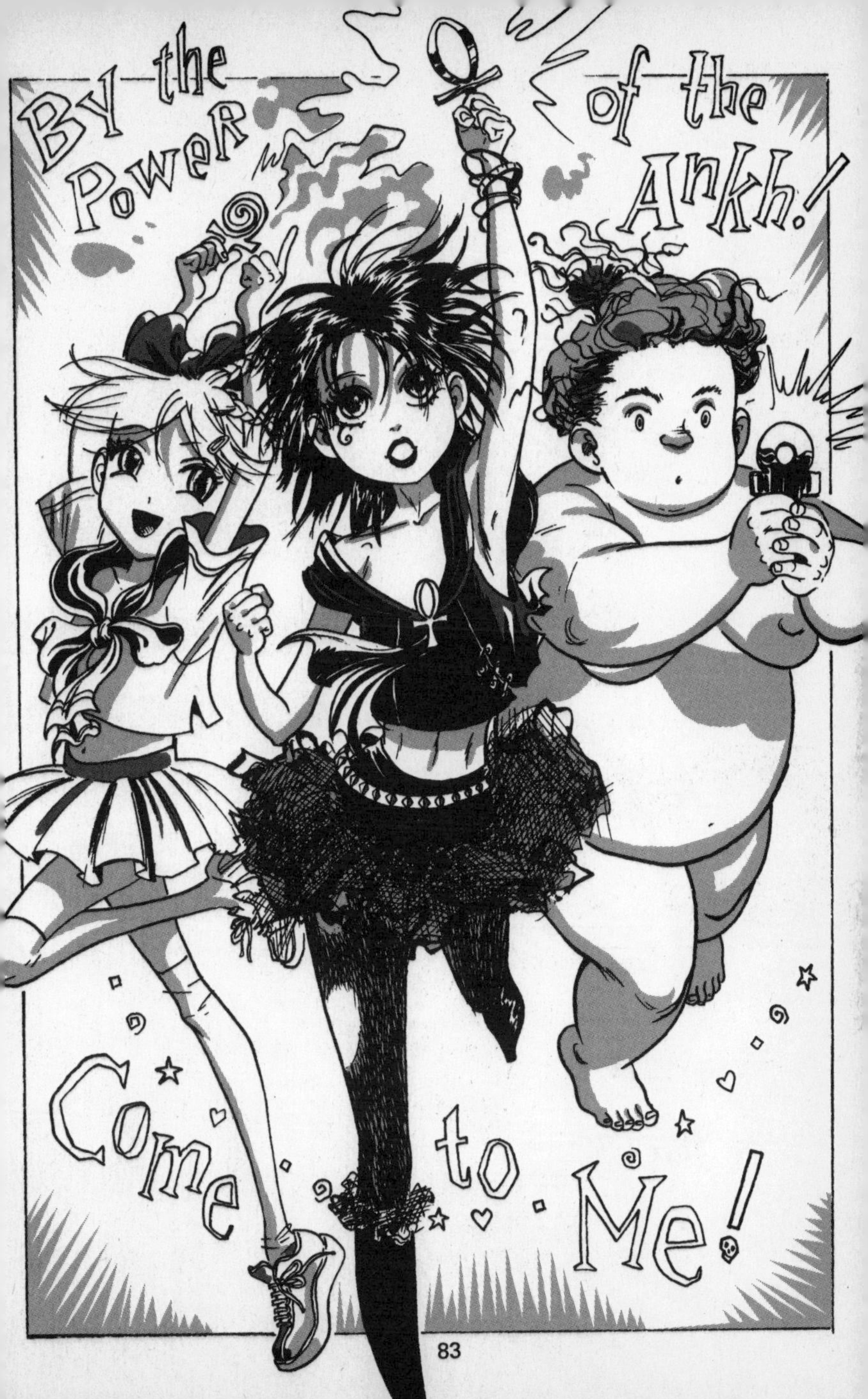
By the Power of the Ankh!
Come to Me!

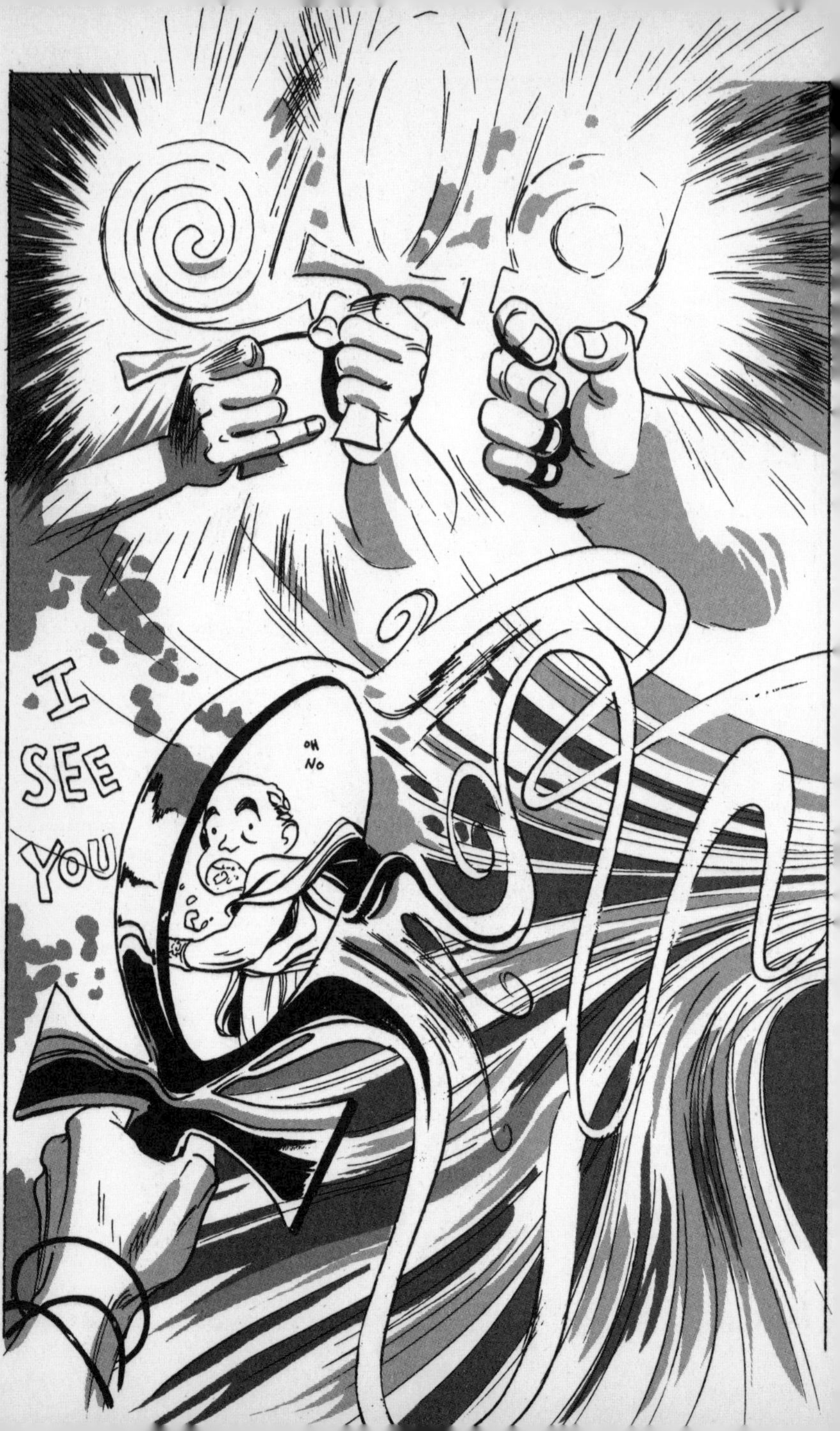
I SEE YOU
OH NO

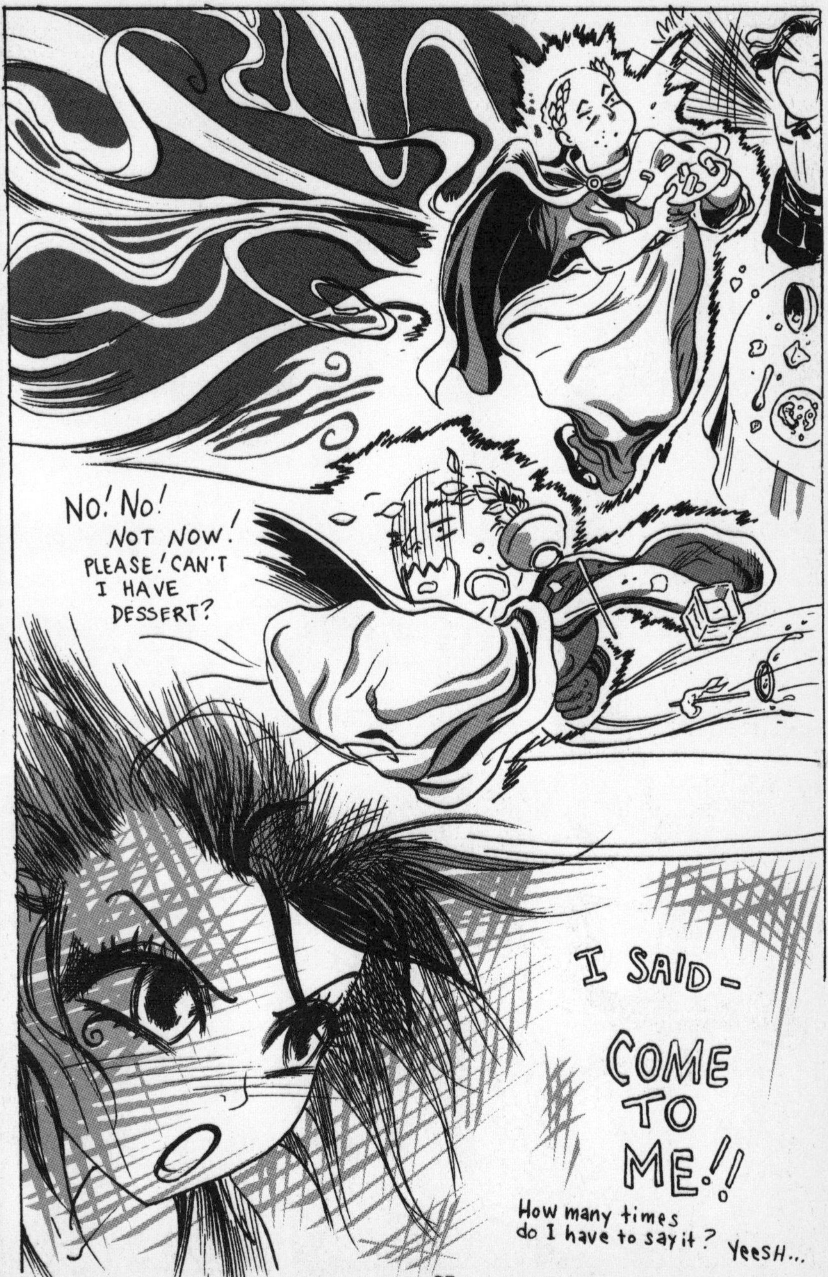
NO! NO! NOT NOW! PLEASE! CAN'T I HAVE DESSERT?
I SAID-
COME TO ME!!
How many times do I have to say it? YEESH...

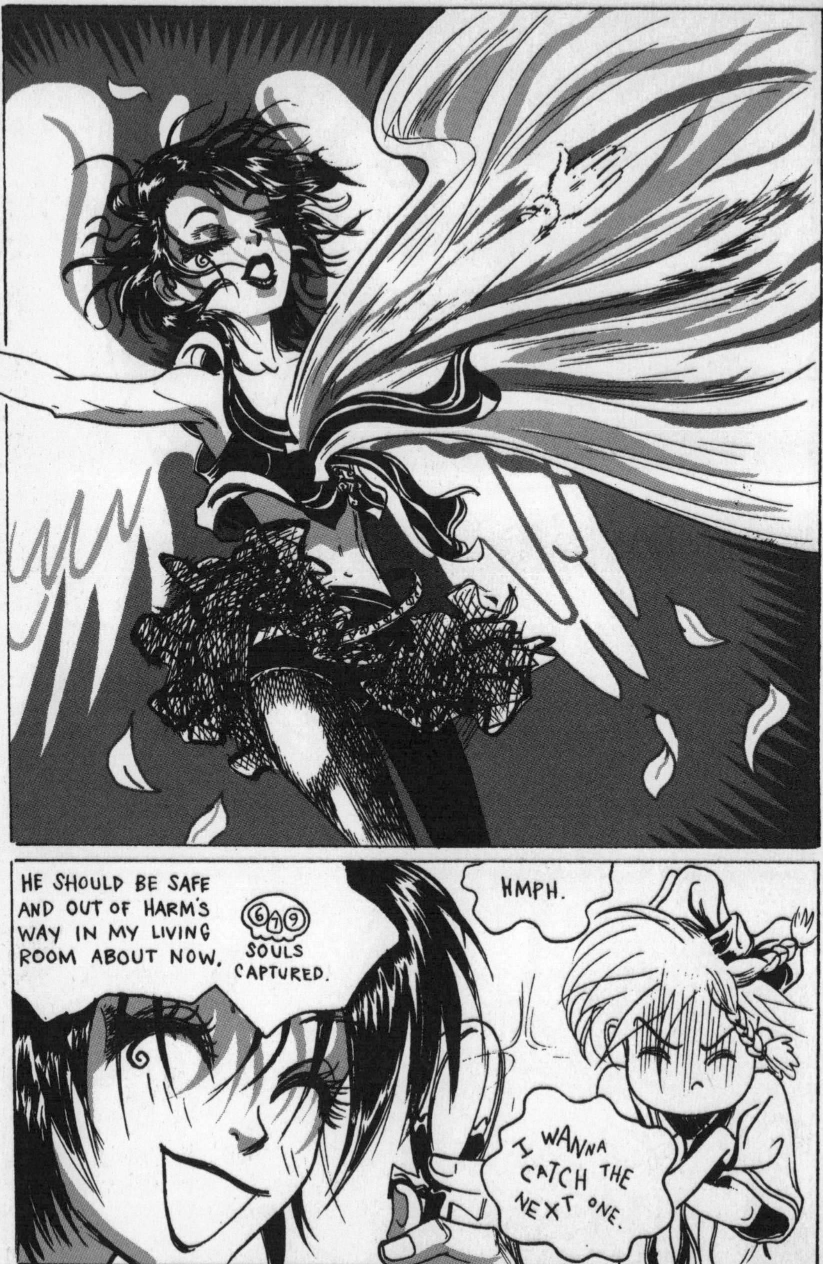

HE SHOULD BE SAFE AND OUT OF HARM'S WAY IN MY LIVING ROOM ABOUT NOW.
679 SOULS CAPTURED.
HMPH.
I WANNA CATCH THE NEXT ONE.

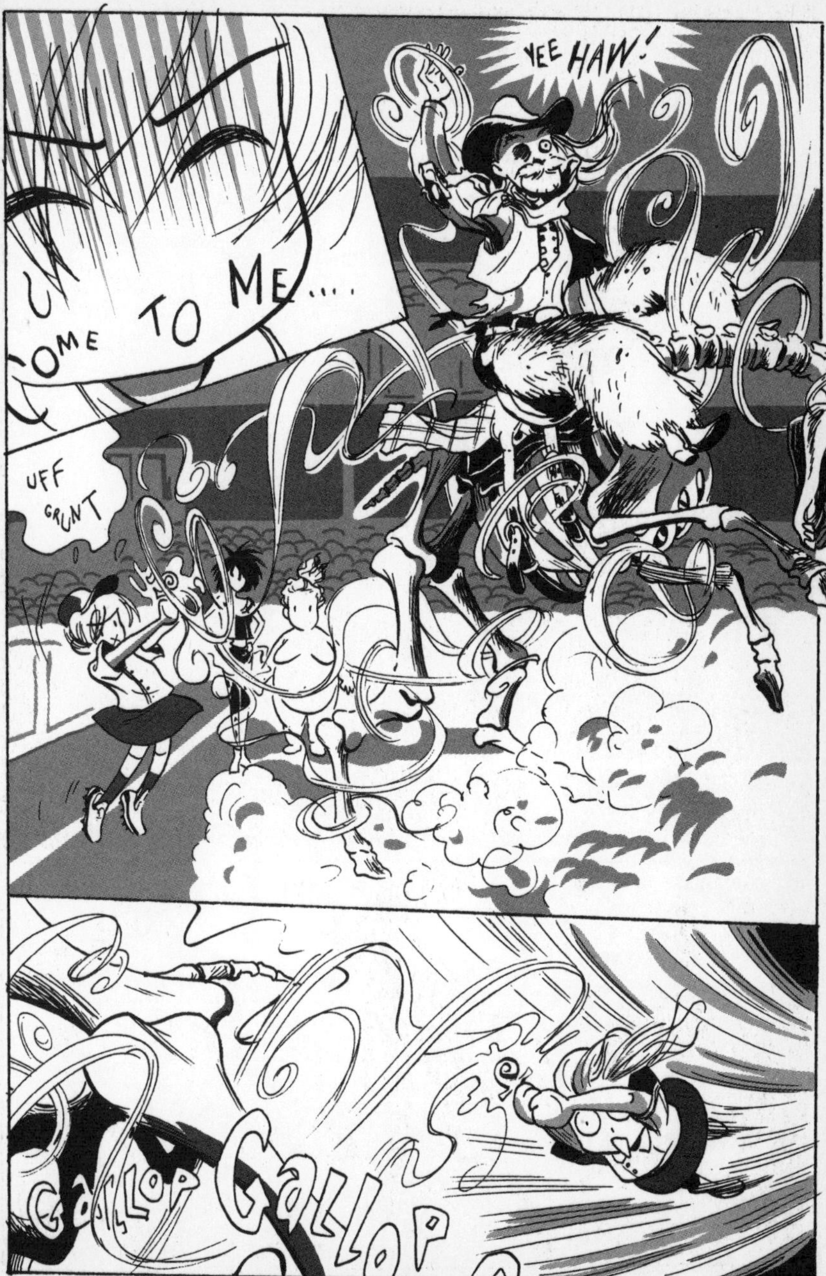

YEE HAW!
COME TO ME....
UFF GRUNT
GALLOP GALLOP

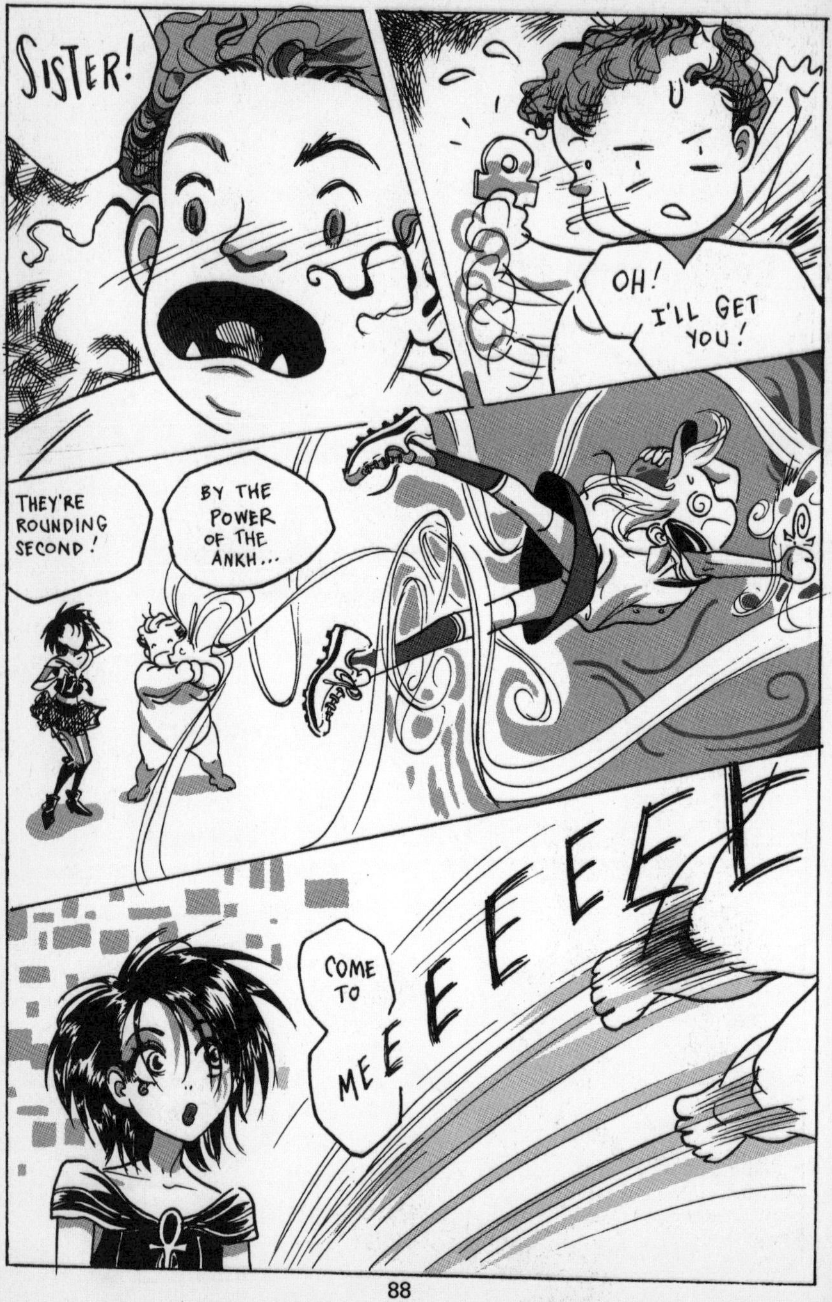
SISTER!
OH! I'LL GET YOU!
THEY'RE ROUNDING SECOND!
BY THE POWER OF THE ANKH...
COME TO MEEEEEEEL

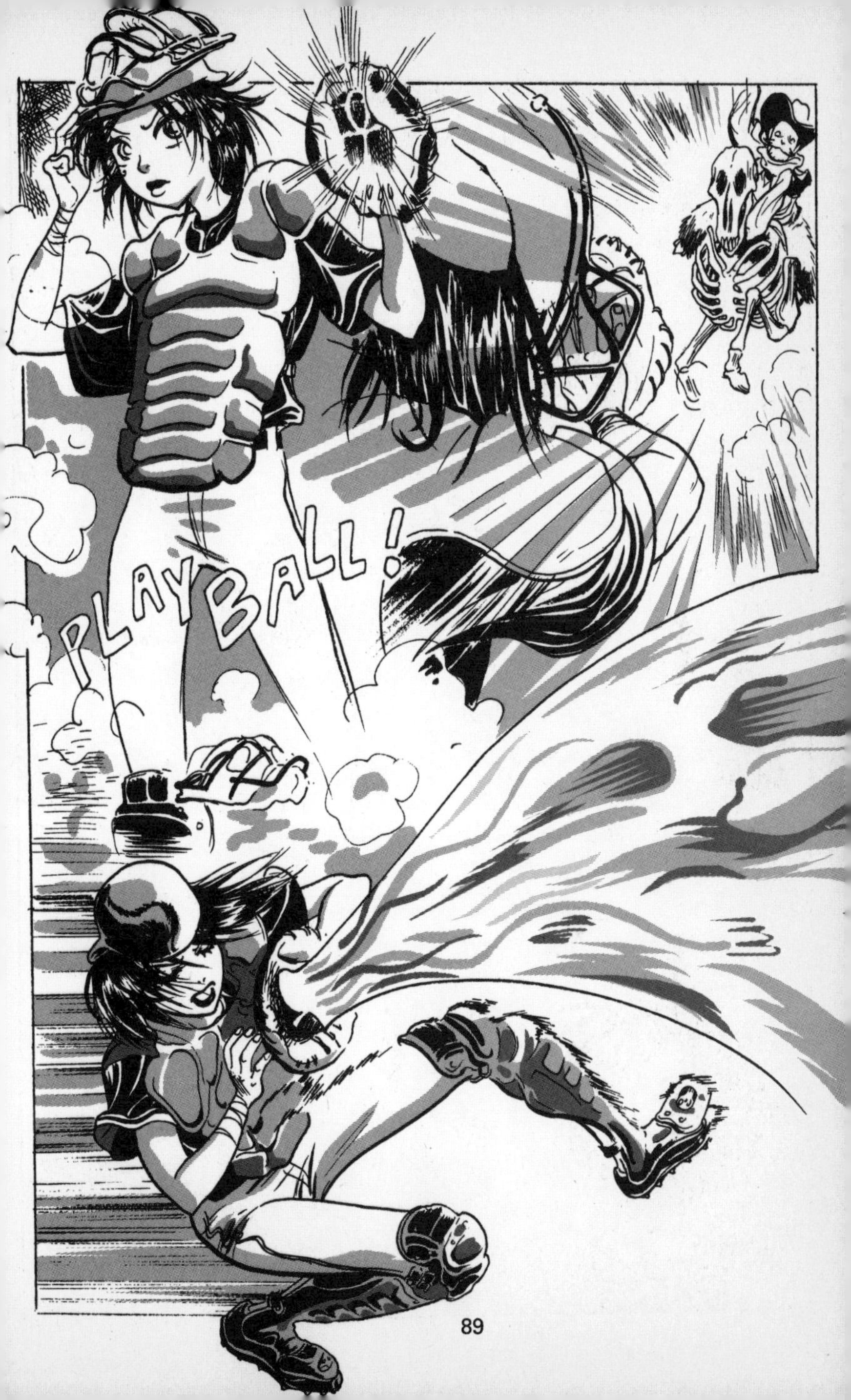
PLAY BALL!

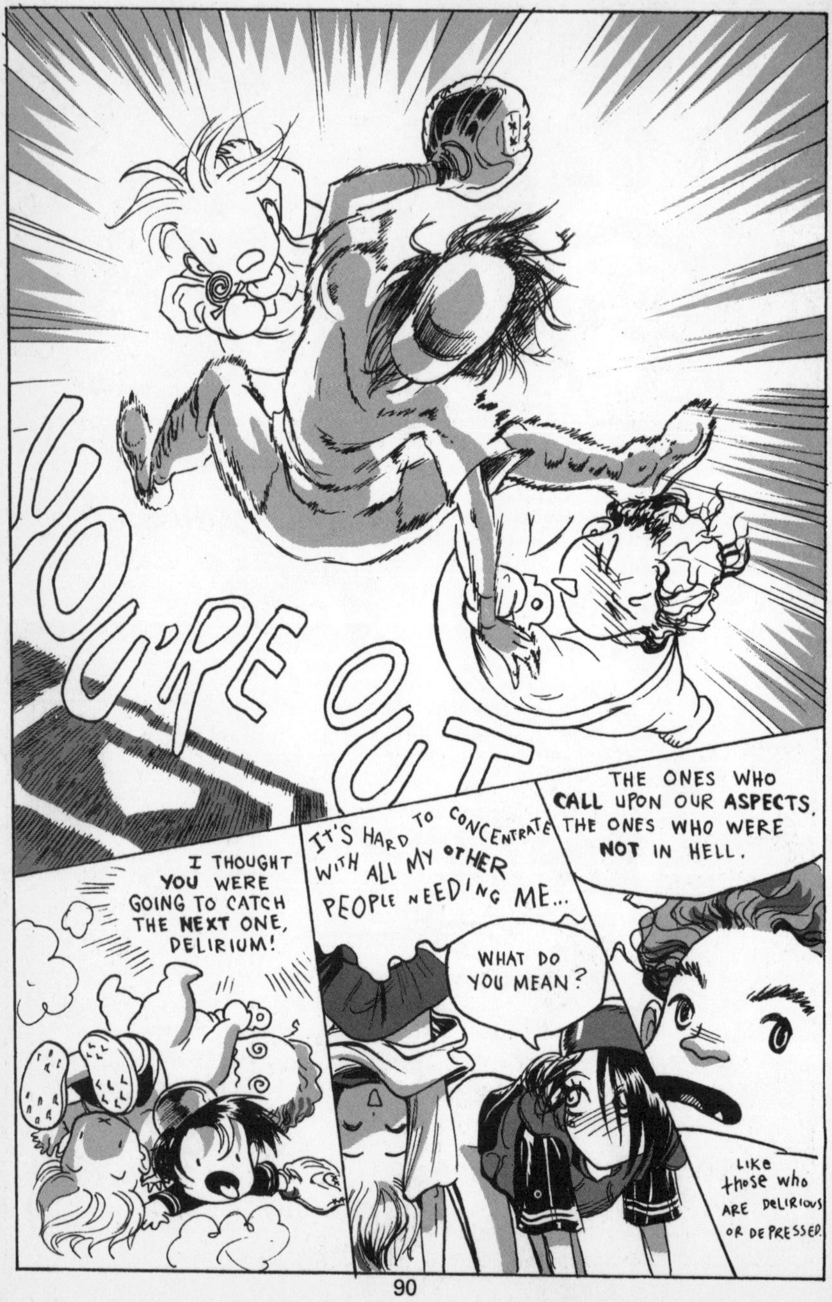
YOU'RE OUT
I THOUGHT YOU WERE GOING TO CATCH THE NEXT ONE, DELIRIUM!
IT'S HARD TO CONCENTRATE WITH ALL MY OTHER PEOPLE NEEDING ME...
WHAT DO YOU MEAN?
THE ONES WHO CALL UPON OUR ASPECTS. THE ONES WHO WERE NOT IN HELL.
Like those who are delirious or depressed.

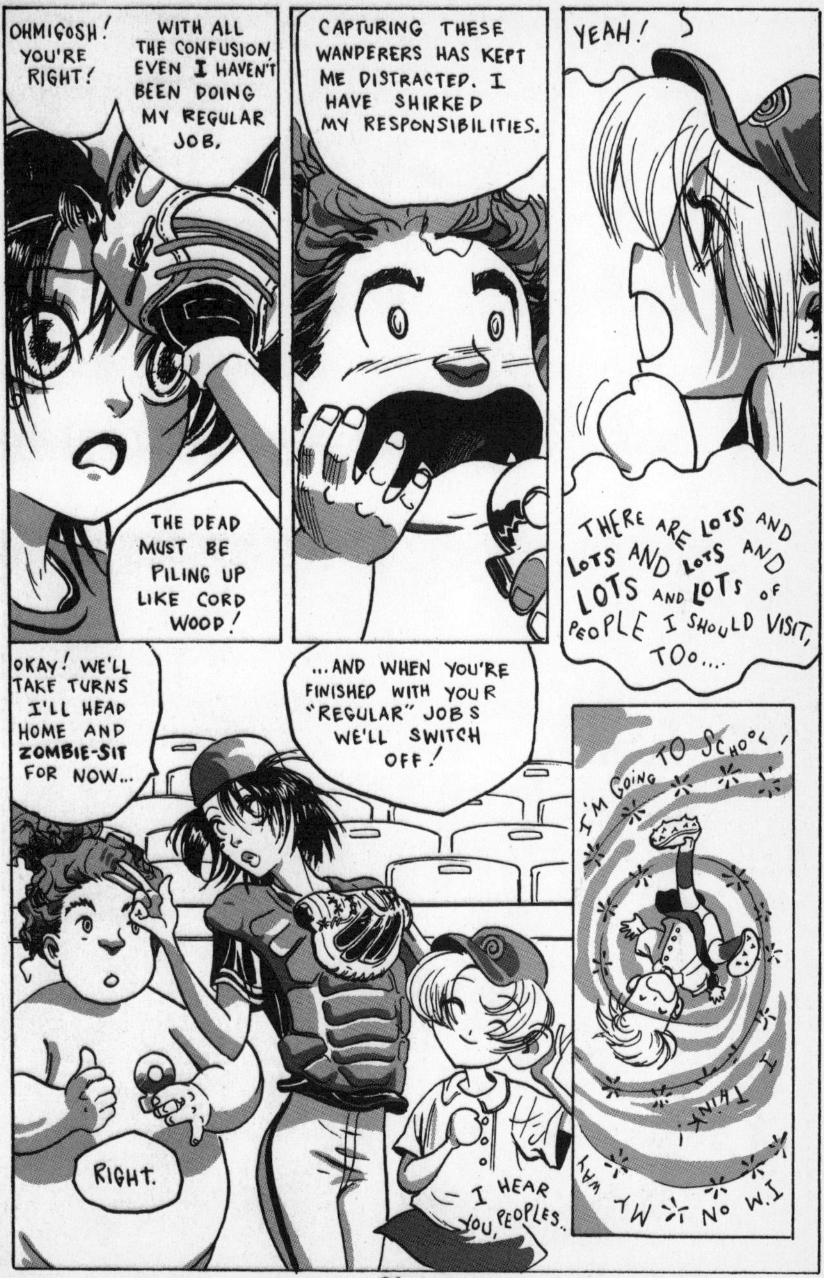
OHMIGOSH! YOU'RE RIGHT!
WITH ALL THE CONFUSION, EVEN I HAVEN'T BEEN DOING MY REGULAR JOB.
THE DEAD MUST BE PILING UP LIKE CORD WOOD!
CAPTURING THESE WANDERERS HAS KEPT ME DISTRACTED. I HAVE SHIRKED MY RESPONSIBILITIES.
YEAH!
THERE ARE LOTS AND LOTS AND LOTS AND LOTS AND LOTS OF PEOPLE I SHOULD VISIT, TOO...
OKAY! WE'LL TAKE TURNS I'LL HEAD HOME AND ZOMBIE-SIT FOR NOW...
...AND WHEN YOU'RE FINISHED WITH YOUR "REGULAR" JOBS WE'LL SWITCH OFF!
RIGHT.
I HEAR YOU, PEOPLES..
I'M GOING TO SCHOOL!
I THINK I KNOW MY WAY

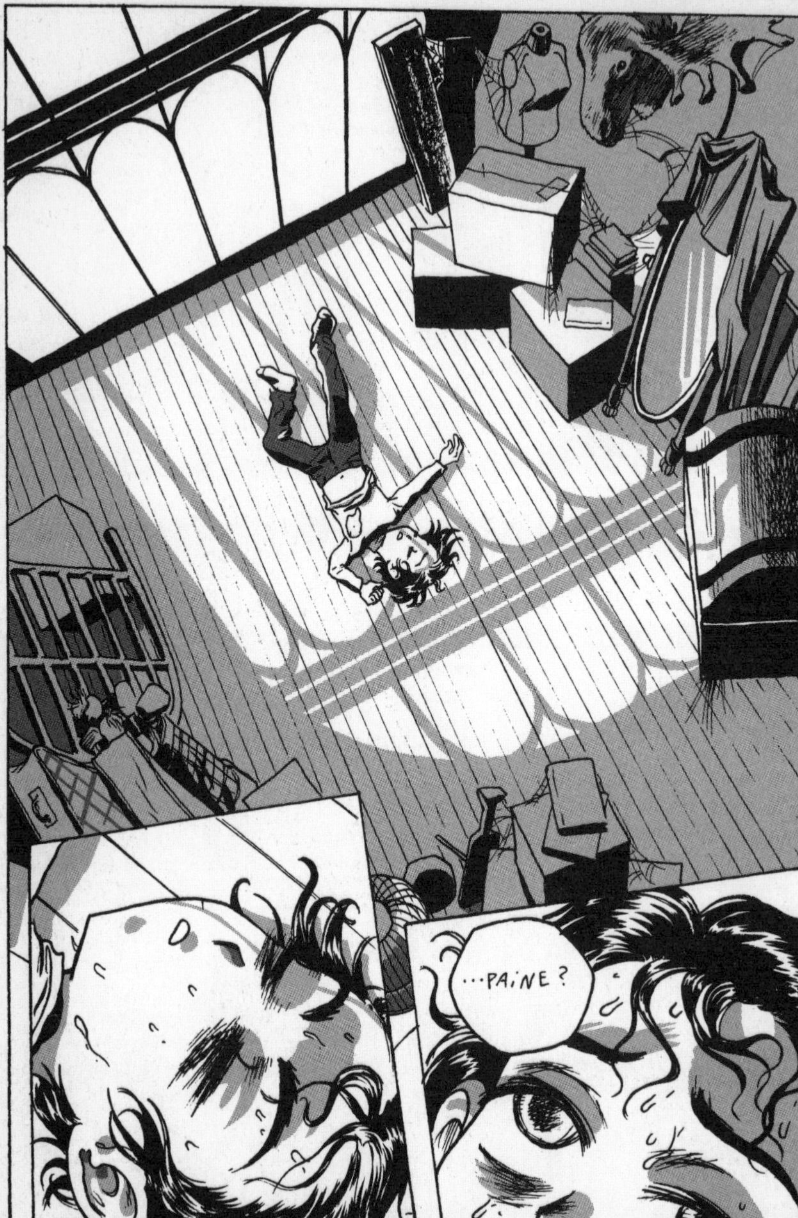
...PAINE?

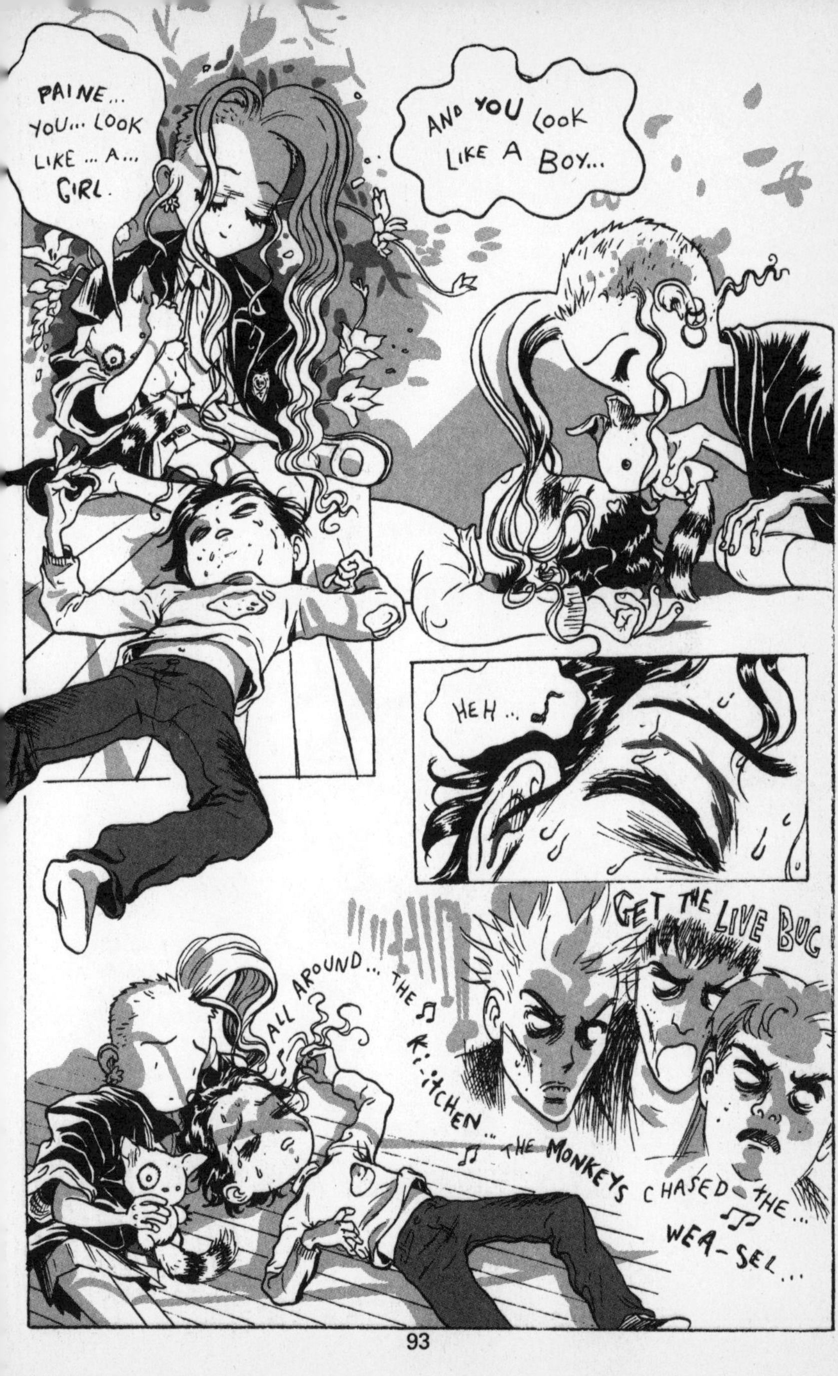
PAINE... YOU... LOOK LIKE ... A... GIRL.
AND YOU LOOK LIKE A BOY...
HEH ...
GET THE LIVE BUG
ALL AROUND... THE KI-ITCHEN... THE MONKEYS CHASED THE... WEA-SEL...

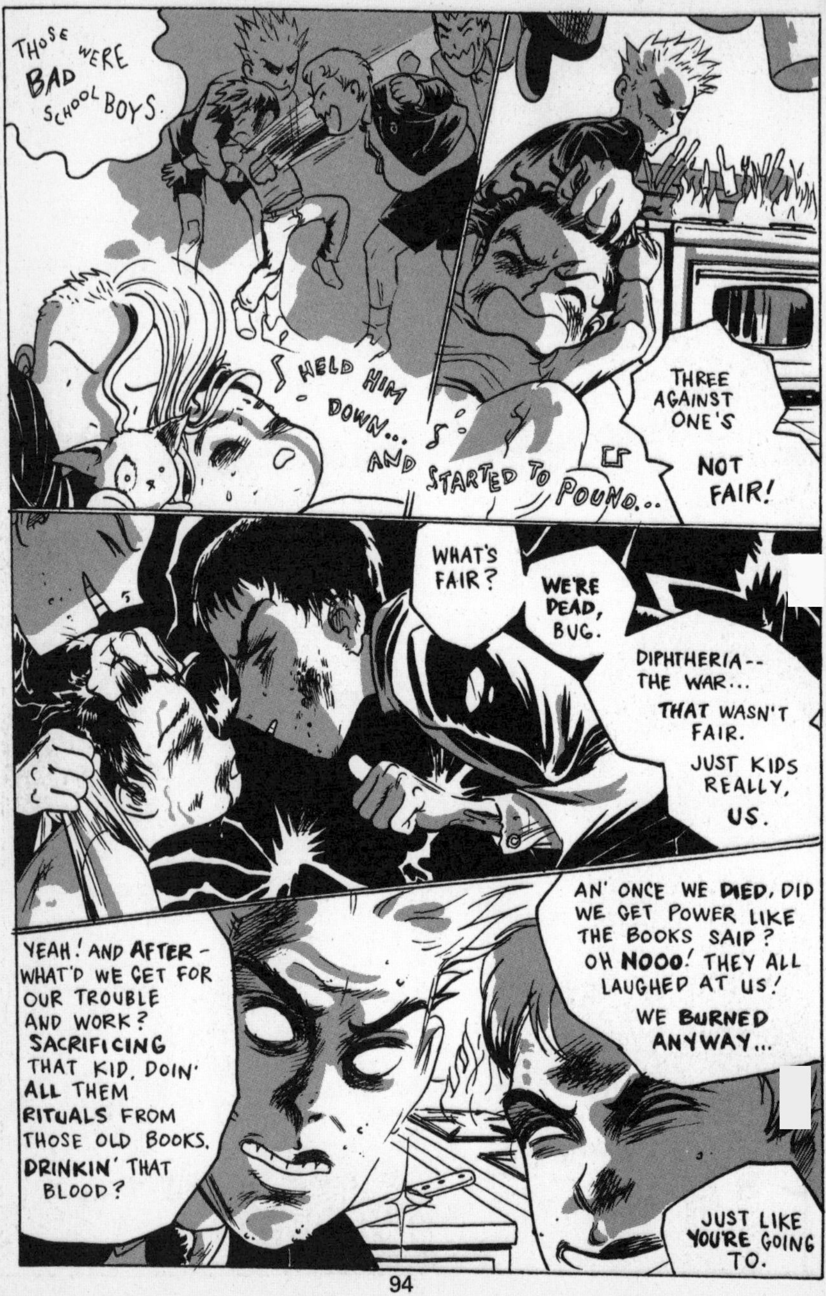
THOSE WERE BAD SCHOOL BOYS.
HELD HIM DOWN...
AND STARTED TO POUND...
THREE AGAINST ONE'S NOT FAIR!
WHAT'S FAIR?
WE'RE DEAD, BUG.
DIPHTHERIA-- THE WAR... THAT WASN'T FAIR. JUST KIDS REALLY, US.
YEAH! AND AFTER - WHAT'D WE GET FOR OUR TROUBLE AND WORK? SACRIFICING THAT KID, DOIN' ALL THEM RITUALS FROM THOSE OLD BOOKS. DRINKIN' THAT BLOOD?
AN' ONCE WE DIED, DID WE GET POWER LIKE THE BOOKS SAID? OH NOOO! THEY ALL LAUGHED AT US! WE BURNED ANYWAY...
JUST LIKE YOU'RE GOING TO.

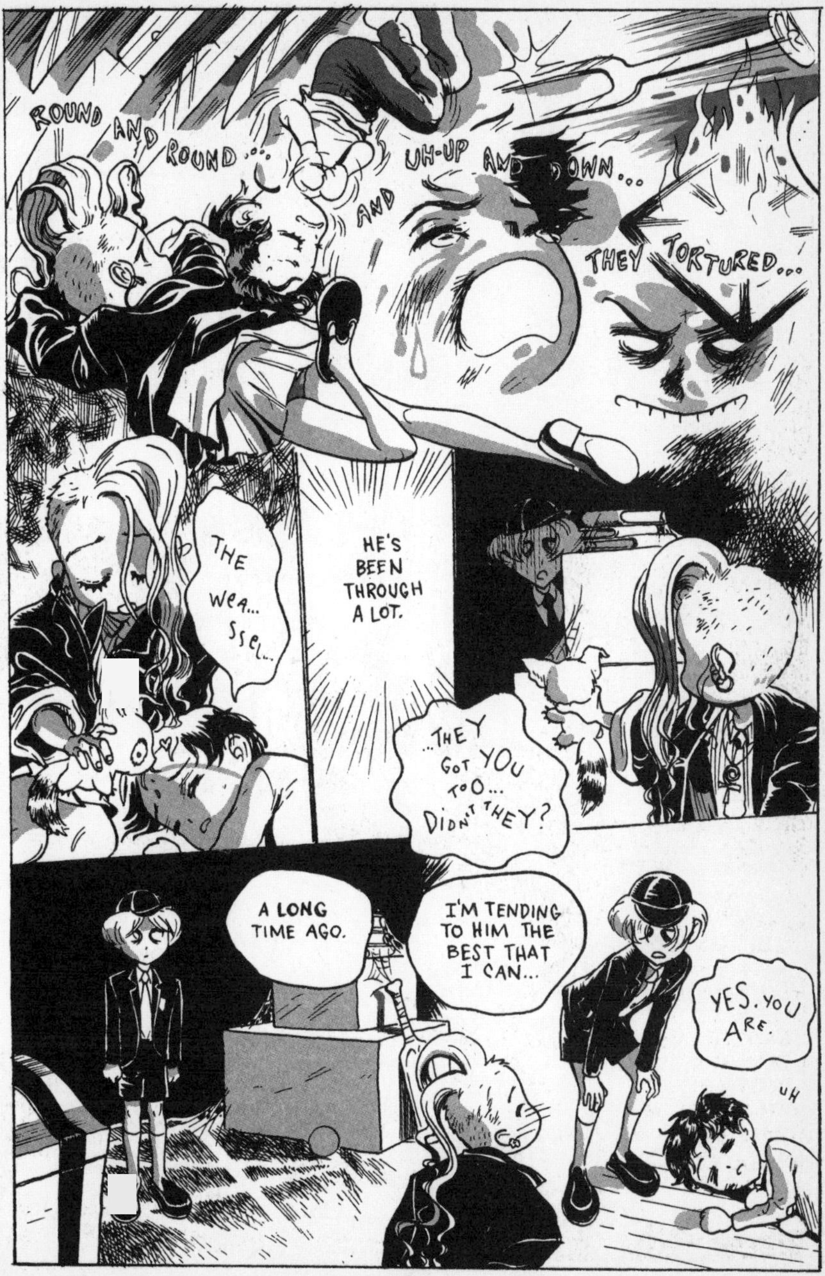
ROUND AND ROUND...
AND UH-UP AND DOWN...
THEY TORTURED...
THE wea... ssel...
HE'S BEEN THROUGH A LOT.
...THEY GOT YOU TOO... DIDN'T THEY?
A LONG TIME AGO.
I'M TENDING TO HIM THE BEST THAT I CAN...
YES. YOU ARE.
UH

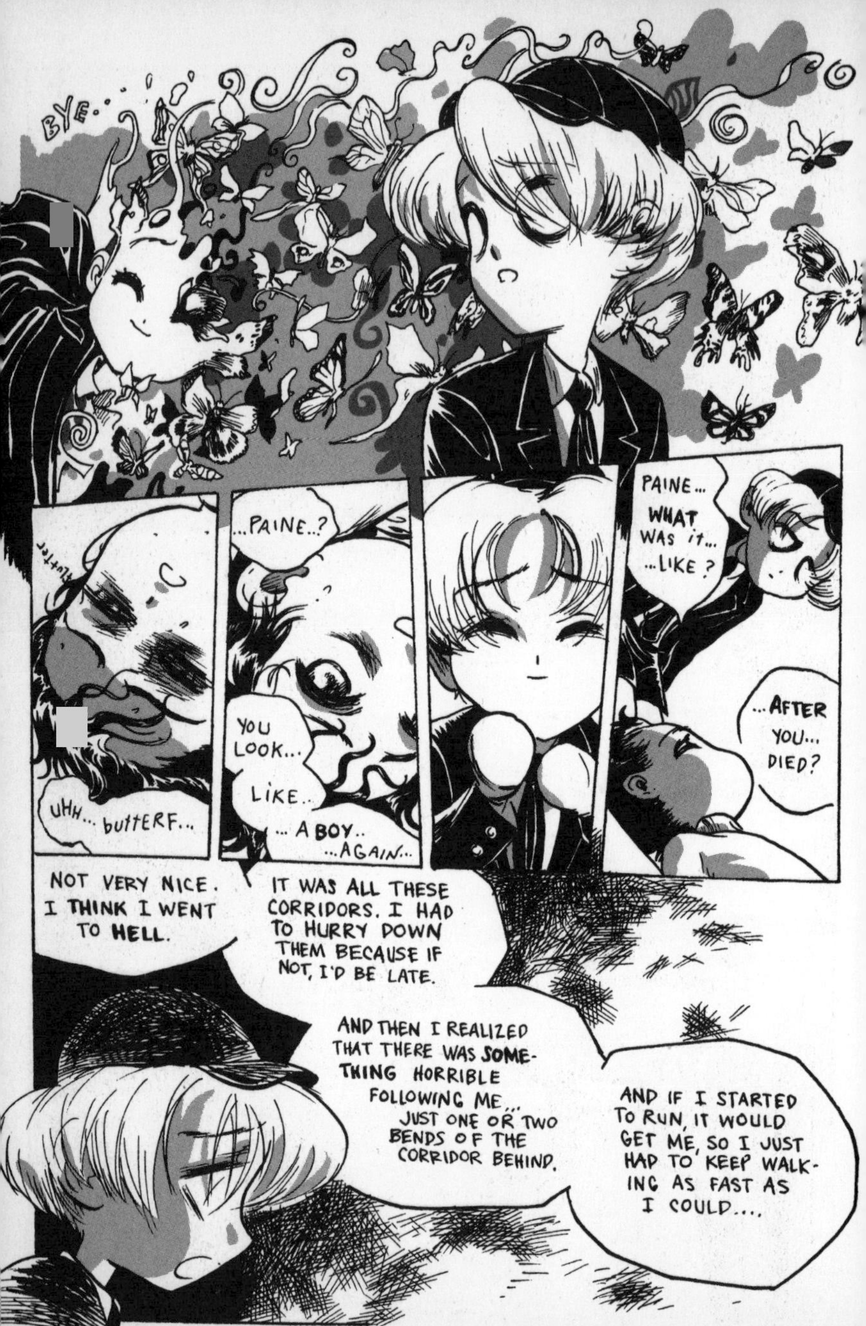

BYE...
flutter
UHH... butterF...
...PAINE..?
YOU LOOK...
LIKE..
...A BOY.. ...AGAIN...
PAINE... WHAT WAS it... ...LIKE?
...AFTER YOU... DIED?
NOT VERY NICE. I THINK I WENT TO HELL.
IT WAS ALL THESE CORRIDORS. I HAD TO HURRY DOWN THEM BECAUSE IF NOT, I'D BE LATE.
AND THEN I REALIZED THAT THERE WAS SOMETHING HORRIBLE FOLLOWING ME... JUST ONE OR TWO BENDS OF THE CORRIDOR BEHIND.
AND IF I STARTED TO RUN, IT WOULD GET ME, SO I JUST HAD TO KEEP WALKING AS FAST AS I COULD....

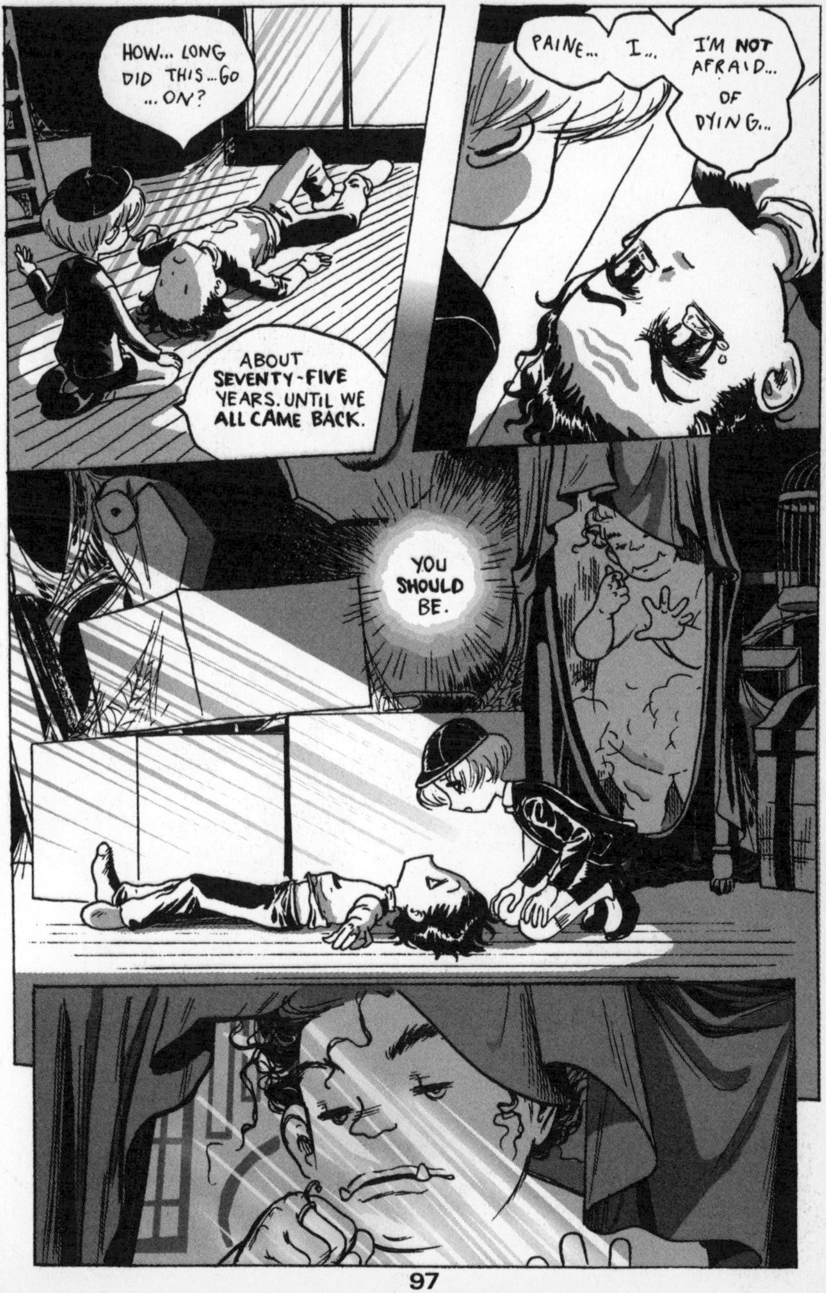
HOW... LONG DID THIS...GO ...ON?
ABOUT SEVENTY-FIVE YEARS. UNTIL WE ALL CAME BACK.
PAINE... I... I'M NOT AFRAID... OF DYING...
YOU SHOULD BE.

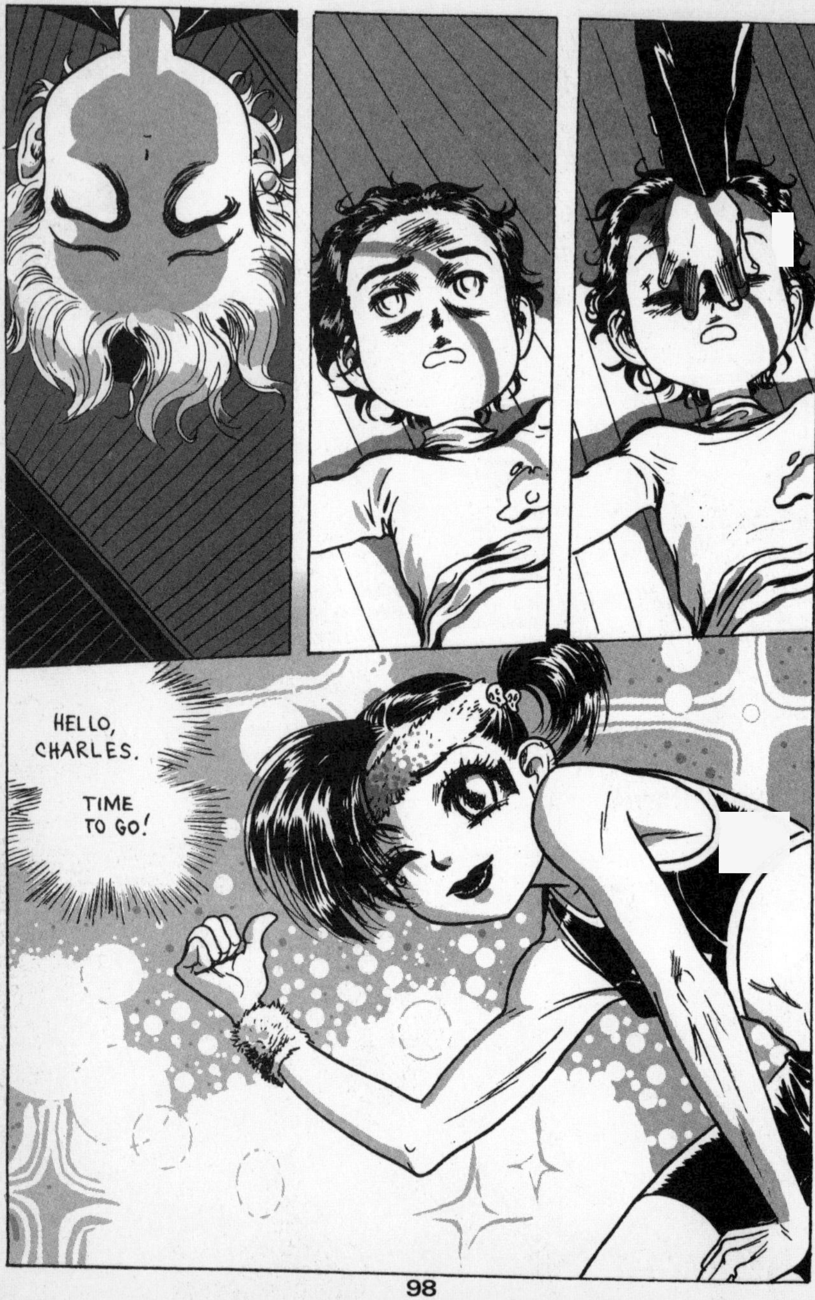
HELLO, CHARLES.
TIME TO GO!

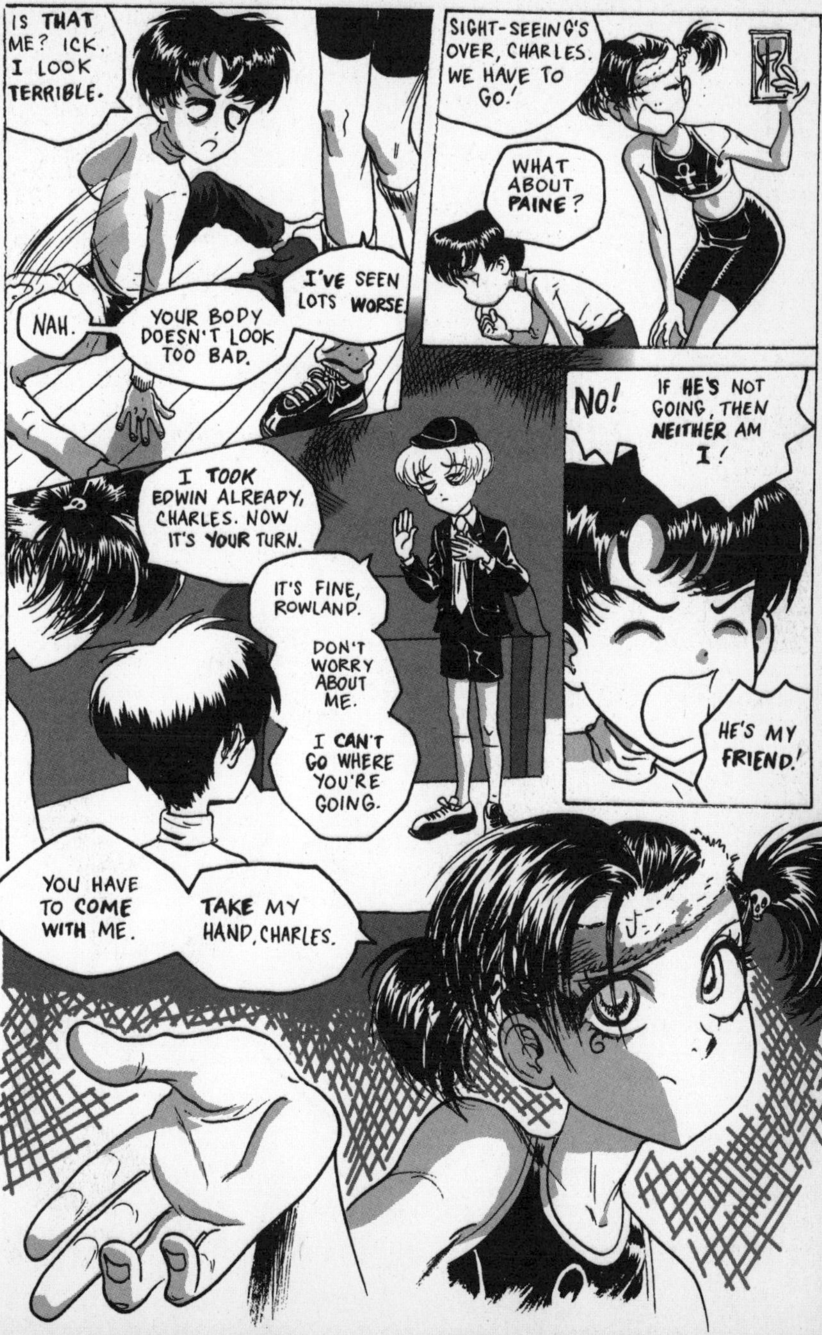

IS THAT ME? ICK. I LOOK TERRIBLE.
NAH.
YOUR BODY DOESN'T LOOK TOO BAD.
I'VE SEEN LOTS WORSE.
SIGHT-SEEING'S OVER, CHARLES. WE HAVE TO GO!
WHAT ABOUT PAINE?
I TOOK EDWIN ALREADY, CHARLES. NOW IT'S YOUR TURN.
IT'S FINE, ROWLAND.
DON'T WORRY ABOUT ME.
I CAN'T GO WHERE YOU'RE GOING.
NO!
IF HE'S NOT GOING, THEN NEITHER AM I!
HE'S MY FRIEND!
YOU HAVE TO COME WITH ME.
TAKE MY HAND, CHARLES.

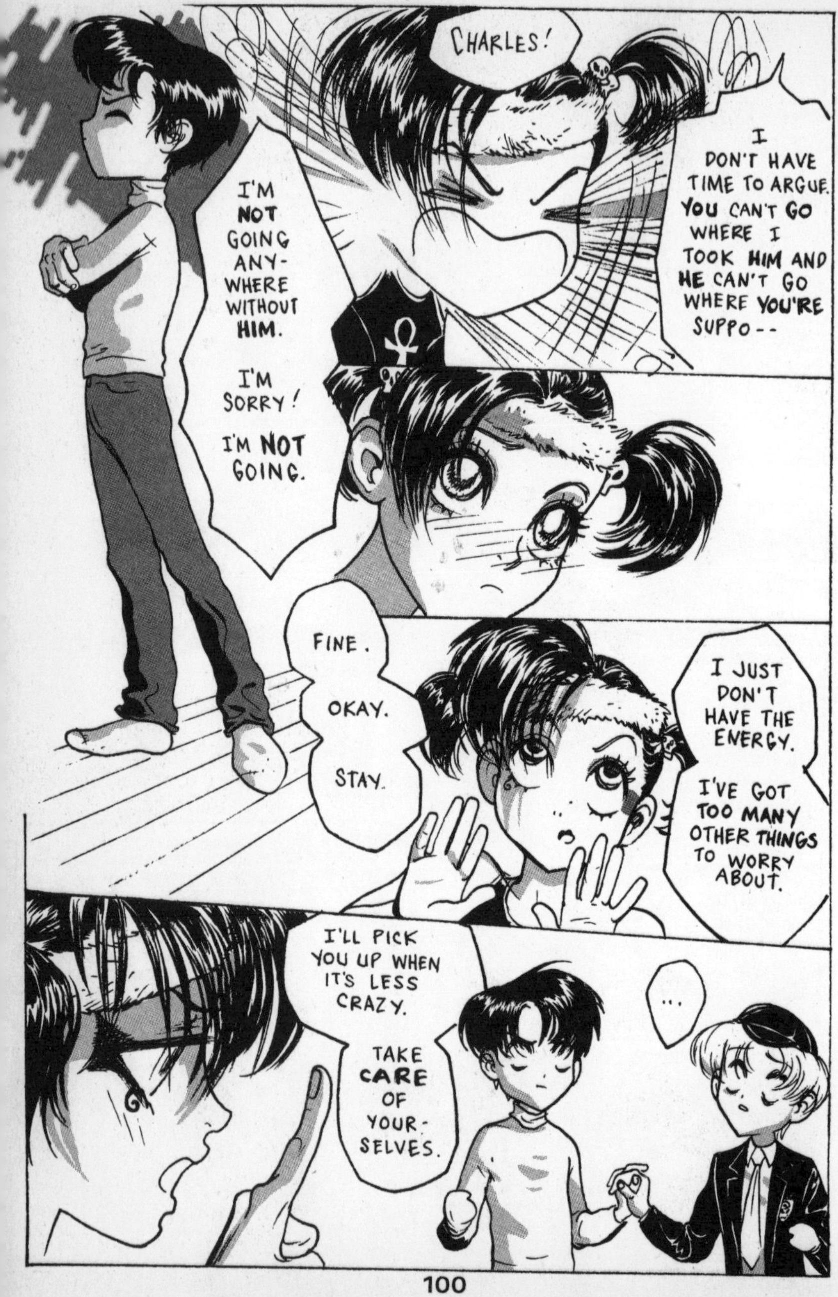
CHARLES!
I'M NOT GOING ANY-WHERE WITHOUT HIM.
I'M SORRY!
I'M NOT GOING.
I DON'T HAVE TIME TO ARGUE. YOU CAN'T GO WHERE I TOOK HIM AND HE CAN'T GO WHERE YOU'RE SUPPO--
FINE.
OKAY.
STAY.
I JUST DON'T HAVE THE ENERGY.
I'VE GOT TOO MANY OTHER THINGS TO WORRY ABOUT.
I'LL PICK YOU UP WHEN IT'S LESS CRAZY.
TAKE CARE OF YOUR-SELVES.
...

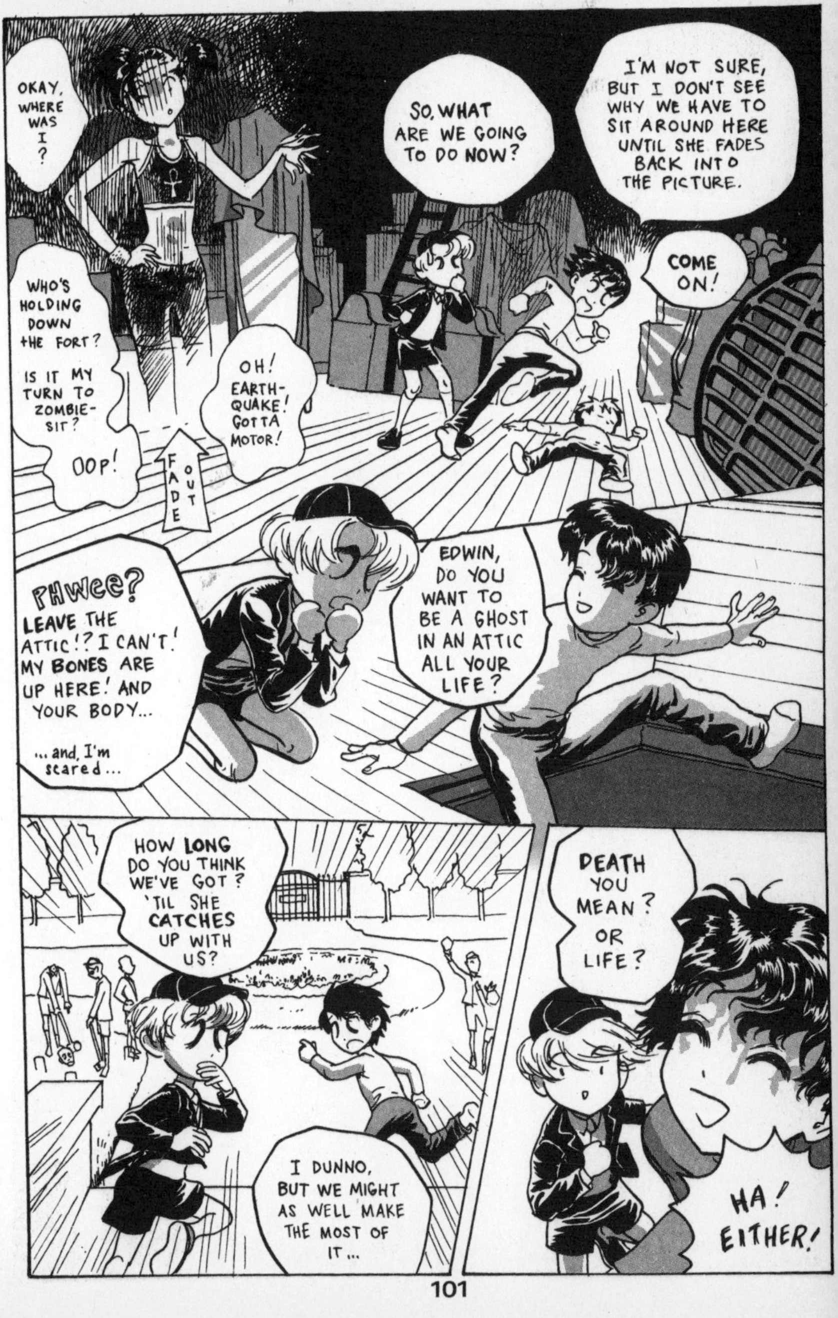
OKAY, WHERE WAS I?
WHO'S HOLDING DOWN THE FORT?
IS IT MY TURN TO ZOMBIE-SIT?
OOP!
FADE OUT
SO, WHAT ARE WE GOING TO DO NOW?
I'M NOT SURE, BUT I DON'T SEE WHY WE HAVE TO SIT AROUND HERE UNTIL SHE FADES BACK INTO THE PICTURE.
COME ON!
OH! EARTH-QUAKE! GOTTA MOTOR!
PHWEE? LEAVE THE ATTIC!? I CAN'T! MY BONES ARE UP HERE! AND YOUR BODY...
... and, I'm scared...
EDWIN, DO YOU WANT TO BE A GHOST IN AN ATTIC ALL YOUR LIFE?
HOW LONG DO YOU THINK WE'VE GOT? 'TIL SHE CATCHES UP WITH US?
I DUNNO, BUT WE MIGHT AS WELL MAKE THE MOST OF IT...
DEATH YOU MEAN? OR LIFE?
HA! EITHER!

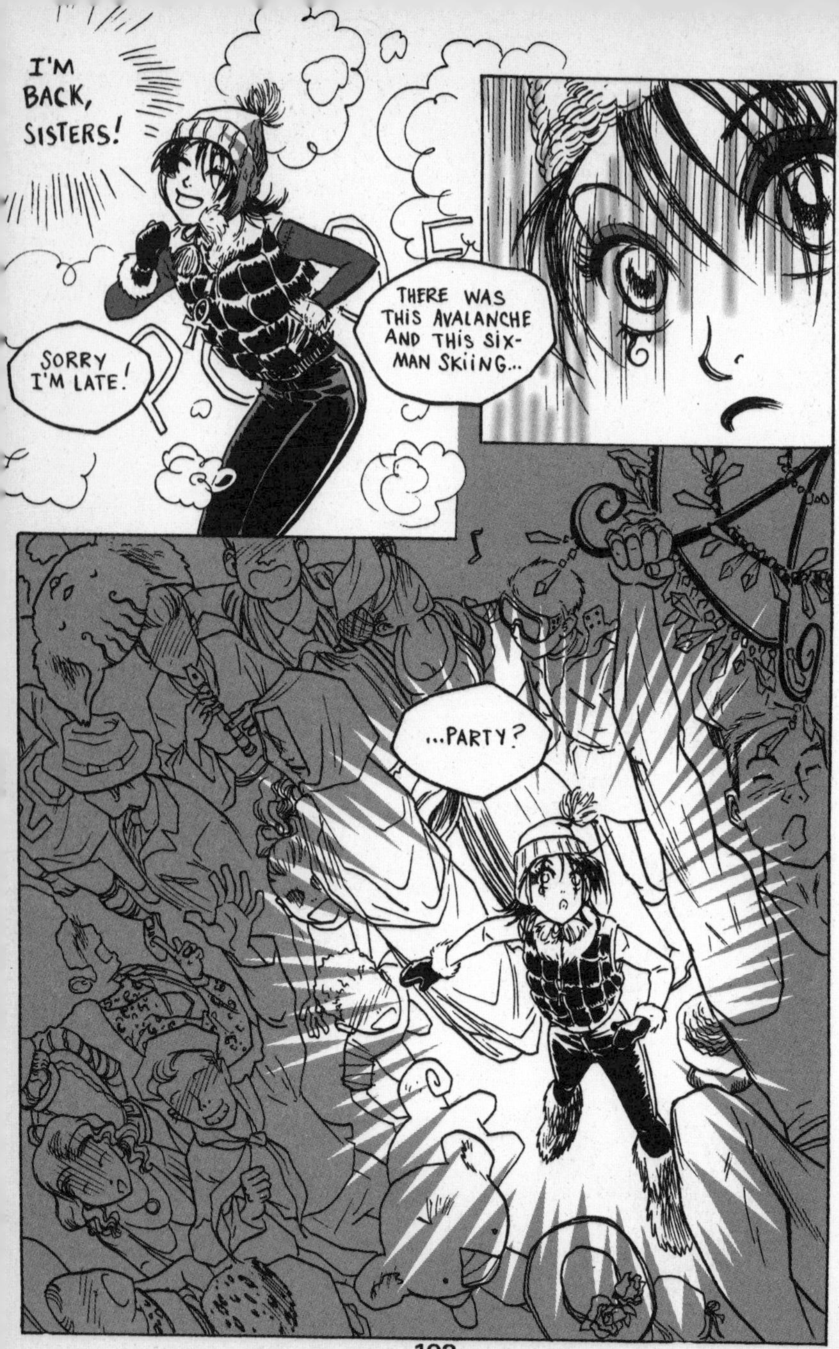
I'M BACK, SISTERS!
SORRY I'M LATE!
THERE WAS THIS AVALANCHE AND THIS SIX-MAN SKIING...
...PARTY?

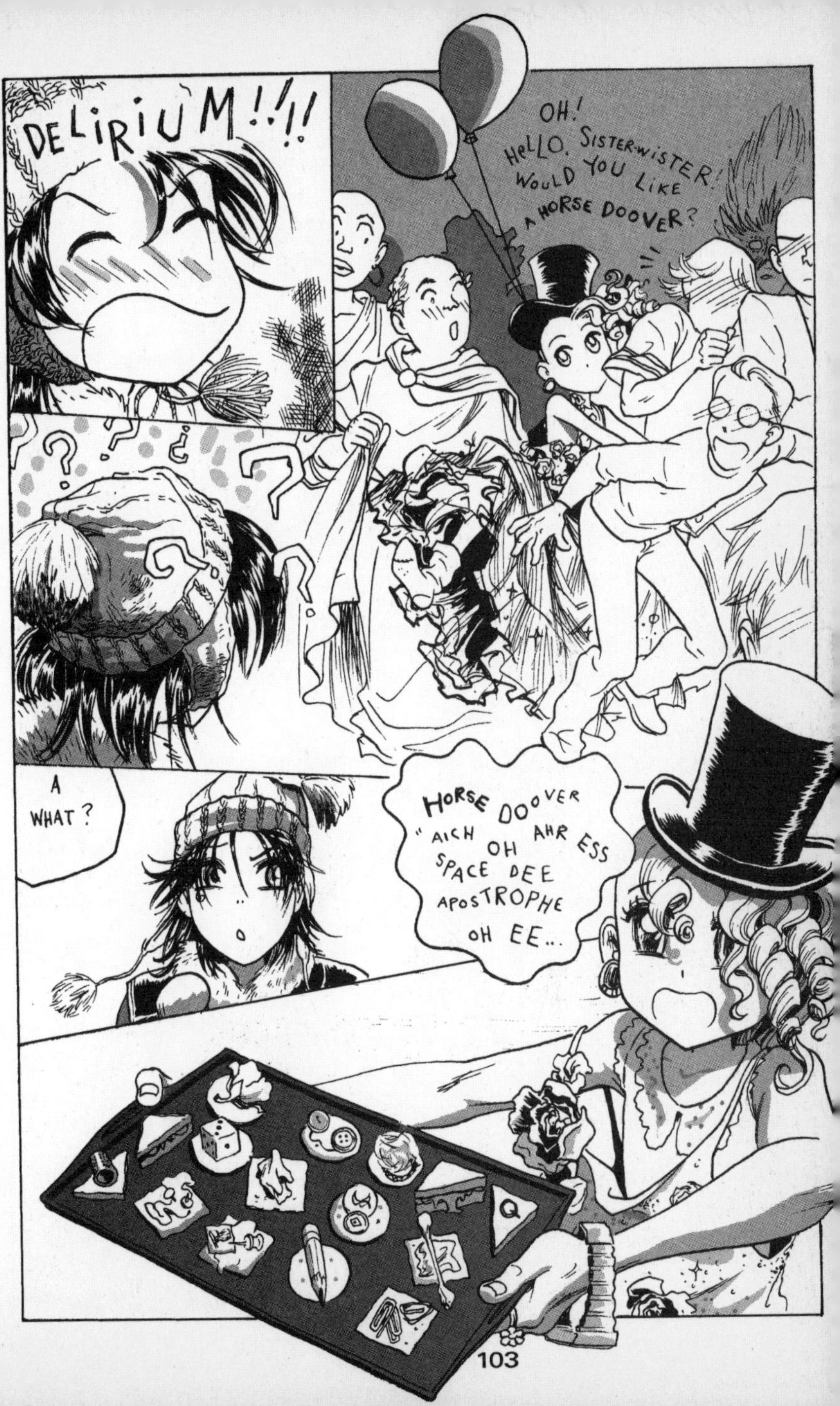
DELIRIUM!!!!!
OH! HELLO, SISTER-WISTER! WOULD YOU LIKE A HORSE DOOVER?
A WHAT?
HORSE DOOVER "AICH OH AHR ESS SPACE DEE APOSTROPHE OH EE...

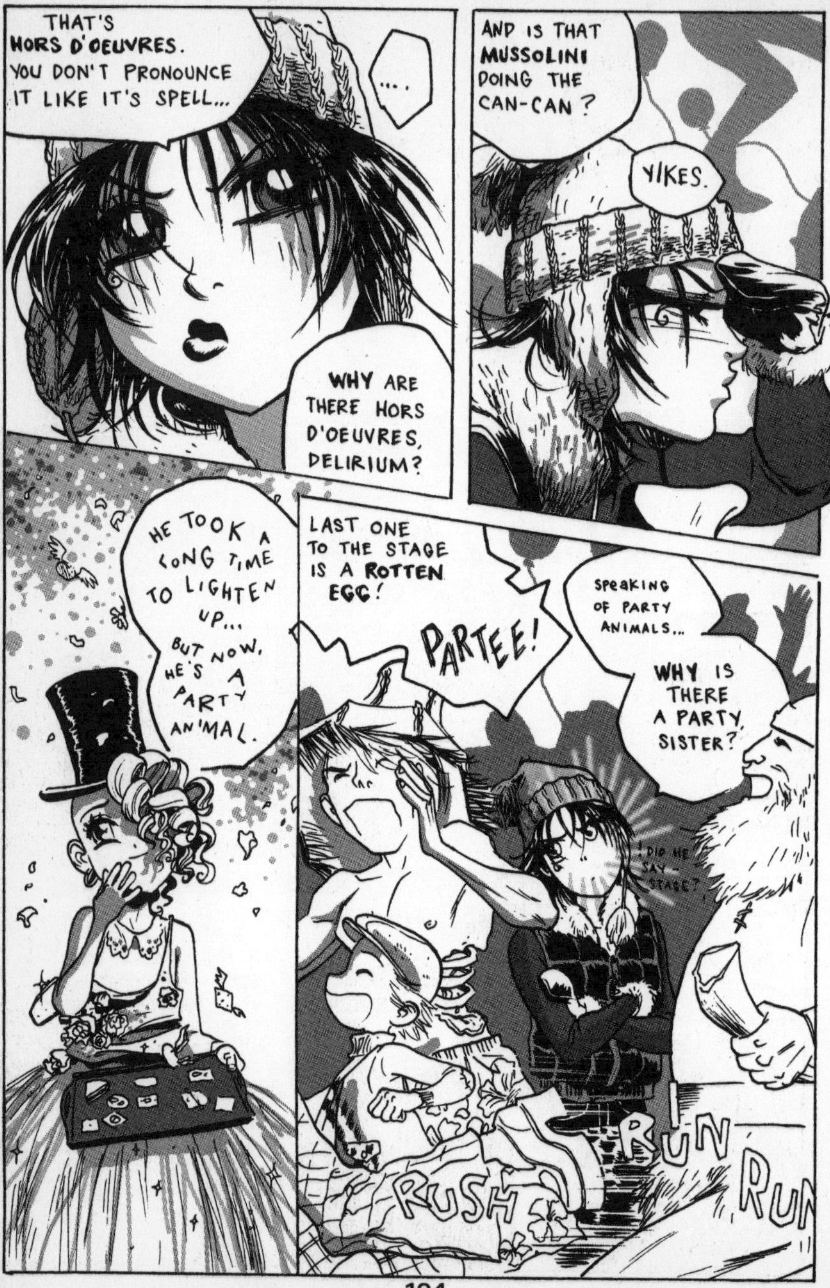
THAT'S HORS D'OEUVRES. YOU DON'T PRONOUNCE IT LIKE IT'S SPELL...
....
AND IS THAT MUSSOLINI DOING THE CAN-CAN?
YIKES.
WHY ARE THERE HORS D'OEUVRES, DELIRIUM?
HE TOOK A LONG TIME TO LIGHTEN UP... BUT NOW, HE'S A PARTY ANIMAL.
LAST ONE TO THE STAGE IS A ROTTEN EGG!
PARTEE!
SPEAKING OF PARTY ANIMALS...
WHY IS THERE A PARTY, SISTER?
DID HE SAY - STAGE?
RUN
RUN
RUSH

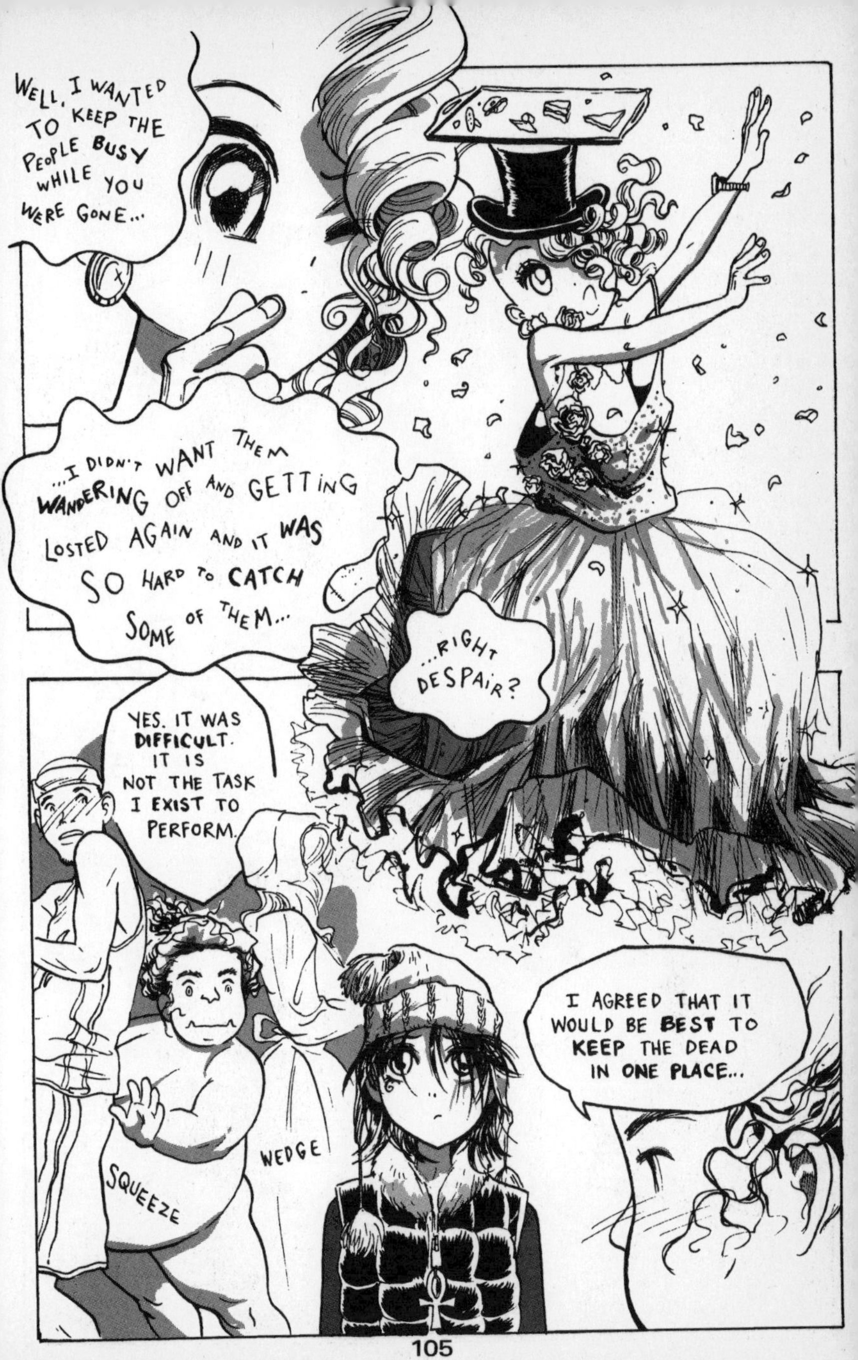
WELL, I WANTED TO KEEP THE PEOPLE BUSY WHILE YOU WERE GONE...
...I DIDN'T WANT THEM WANDERING OFF AND GETTING LOSTED AGAIN AND IT WAS SO HARD TO CATCH SOME OF THEM...
...RIGHT DESPAIR?
YES. IT WAS DIFFICULT. IT IS NOT THE TASK I EXIST TO PERFORM.
I AGREED THAT IT WOULD BE BEST TO KEEP THE DEAD IN ONE PLACE...
WEDGE
SQUEEZE

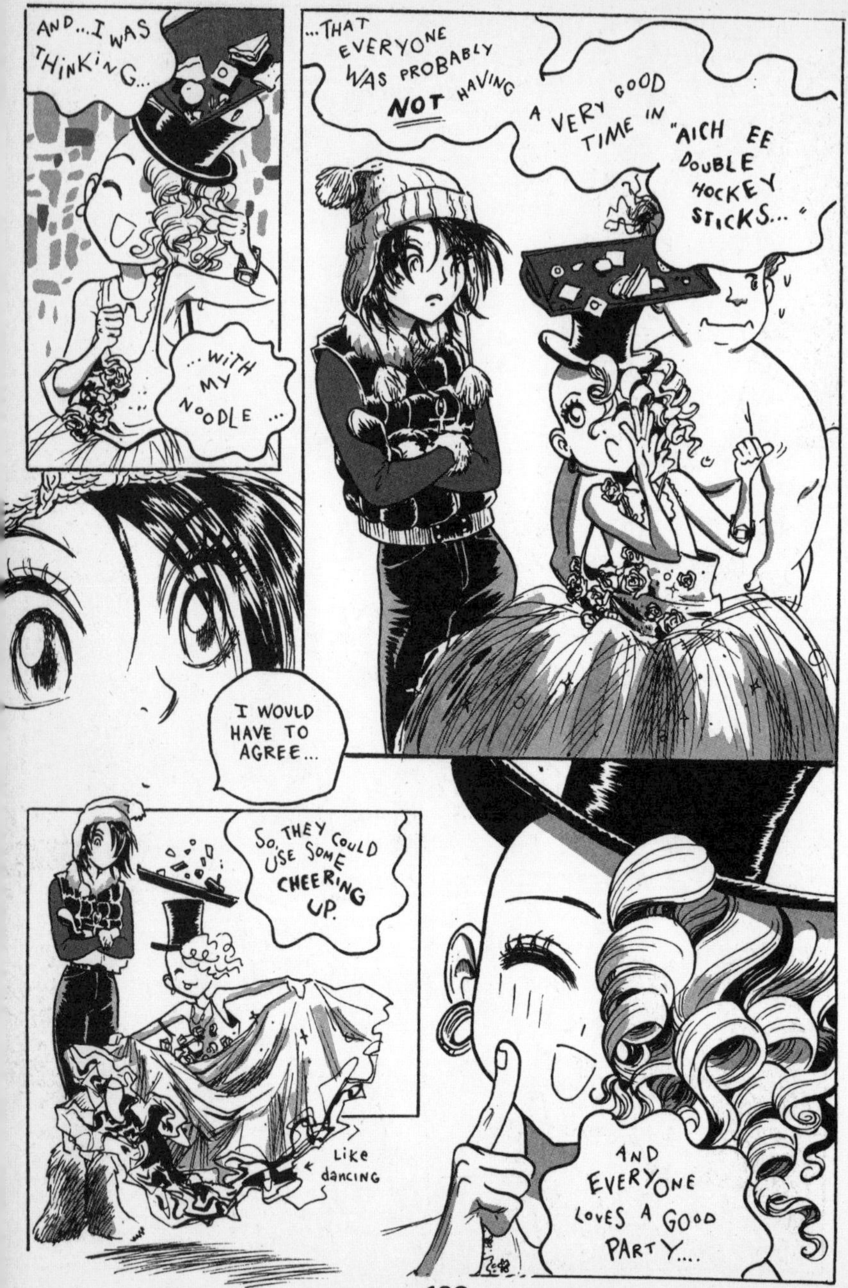
AND... I WAS THINKING...
... WITH MY NOODLE ...
...THAT EVERYONE WAS PROBABLY NOT HAVING A VERY GOOD TIME IN "AICH EE DOUBLE HOCKEY STICKS..."
I WOULD HAVE TO AGREE...
So, THEY COULD USE SOME CHEERING UP.
Like dancing
AND EVERYONE LOVES A GOOD PARTY....

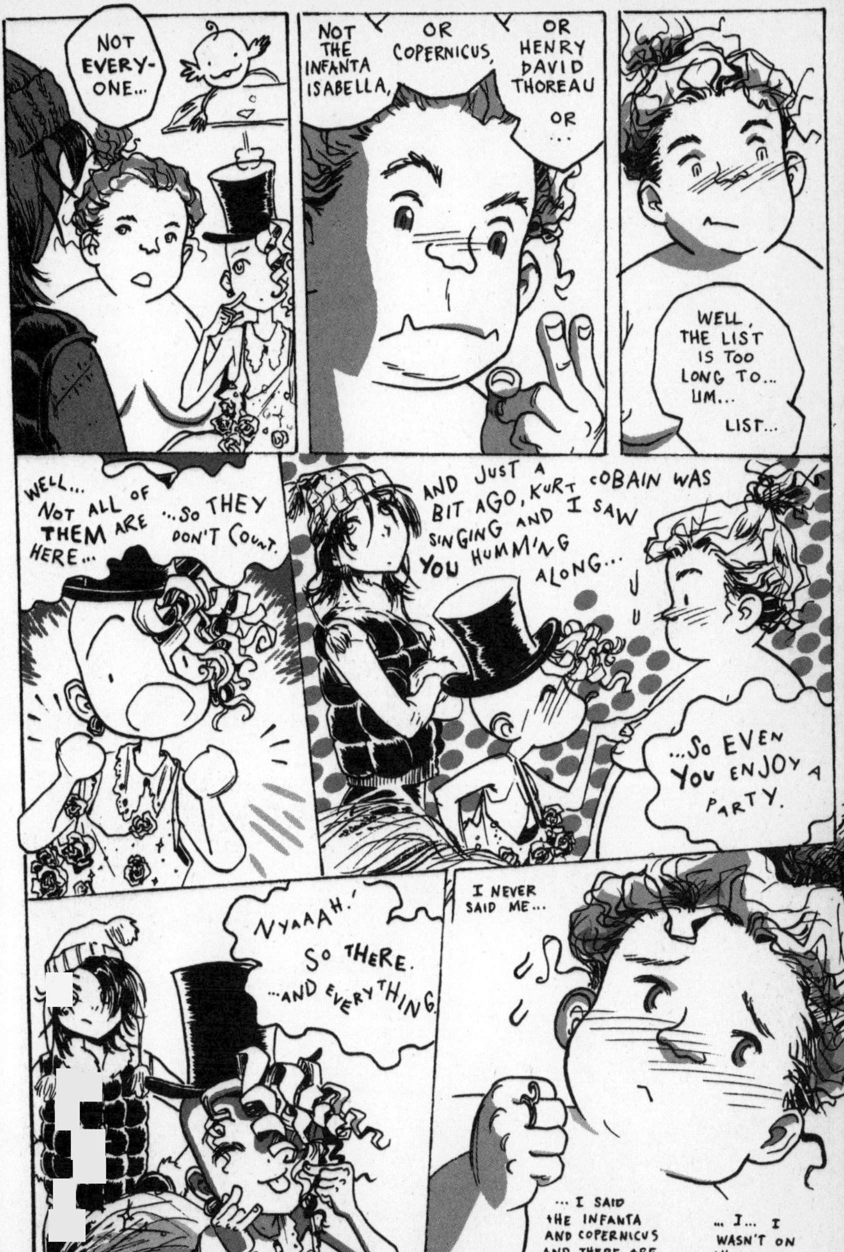
NOT EVERY-ONE...
NOT THE INFANTA ISABELLA,
OR COPERNICUS,
OR HENRY DAVID THOREAU
OR ...
WELL, THE LIST IS TOO LONG TO... UM... LIST...
WELL... NOT ALL OF THEM ARE HERE...
...SO THEY DON'T COUNT.
AND JUST A BIT AGO, KURT COBAIN WAS SINGING AND I SAW YOU HUMMING ALONG...
...SO EVEN YOU ENJOY A PARTY.
NYAAAH!
SO THERE.
...AND EVERYTHING.
I NEVER SAID ME...
... I SAID THE INFANTA AND COPERNICUS AND THERE ARE SCORES OF ....
... I... I WASN'T ON THE LIST...

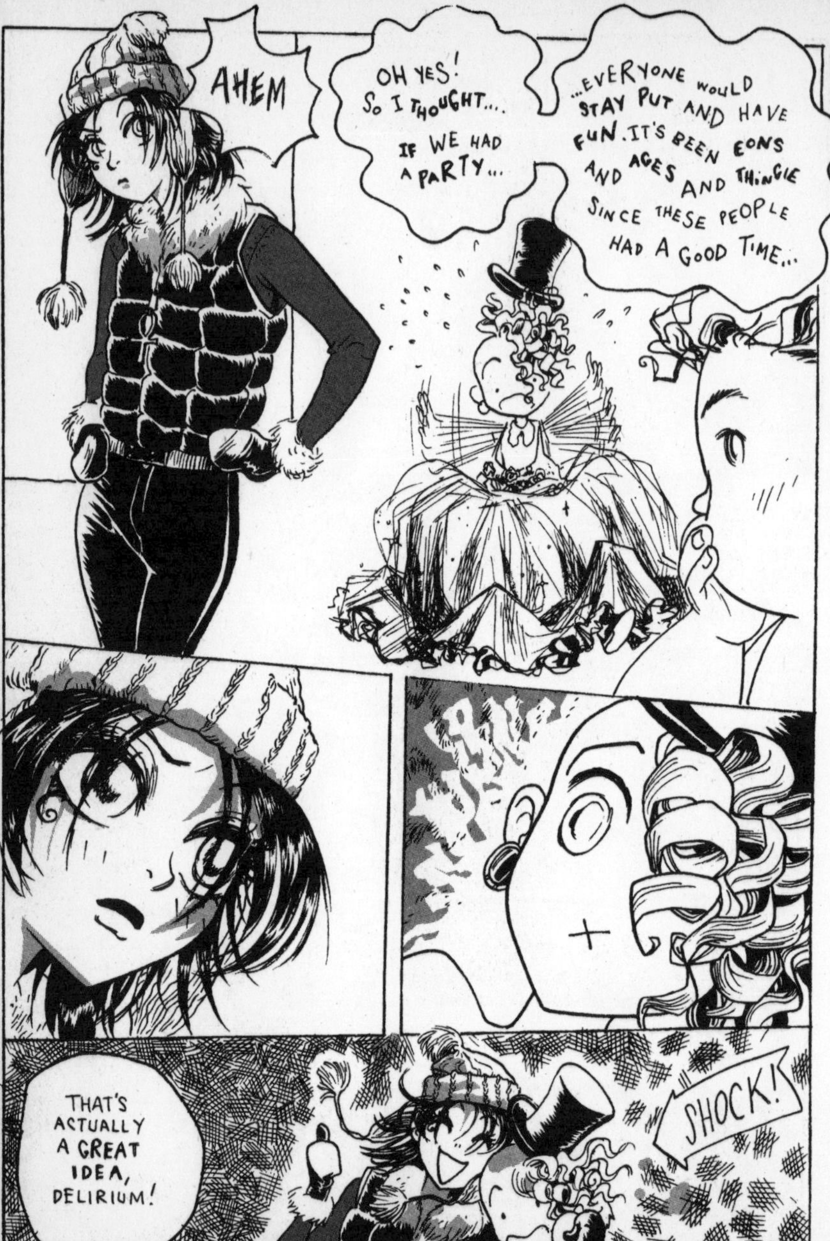
AHEM
OH YES! SO I THOUGHT.... IF WE HAD A PARTY...
...EVERYONE WOULD STAY PUT AND HAVE FUN. IT'S BEEN EONS AND AGES AND THINGIE SINCE THESE PEOPLE HAD A GOOD TIME...
THAT'S ACTUALLY A GREAT IDEA, DELIRIUM!
SHOCK!

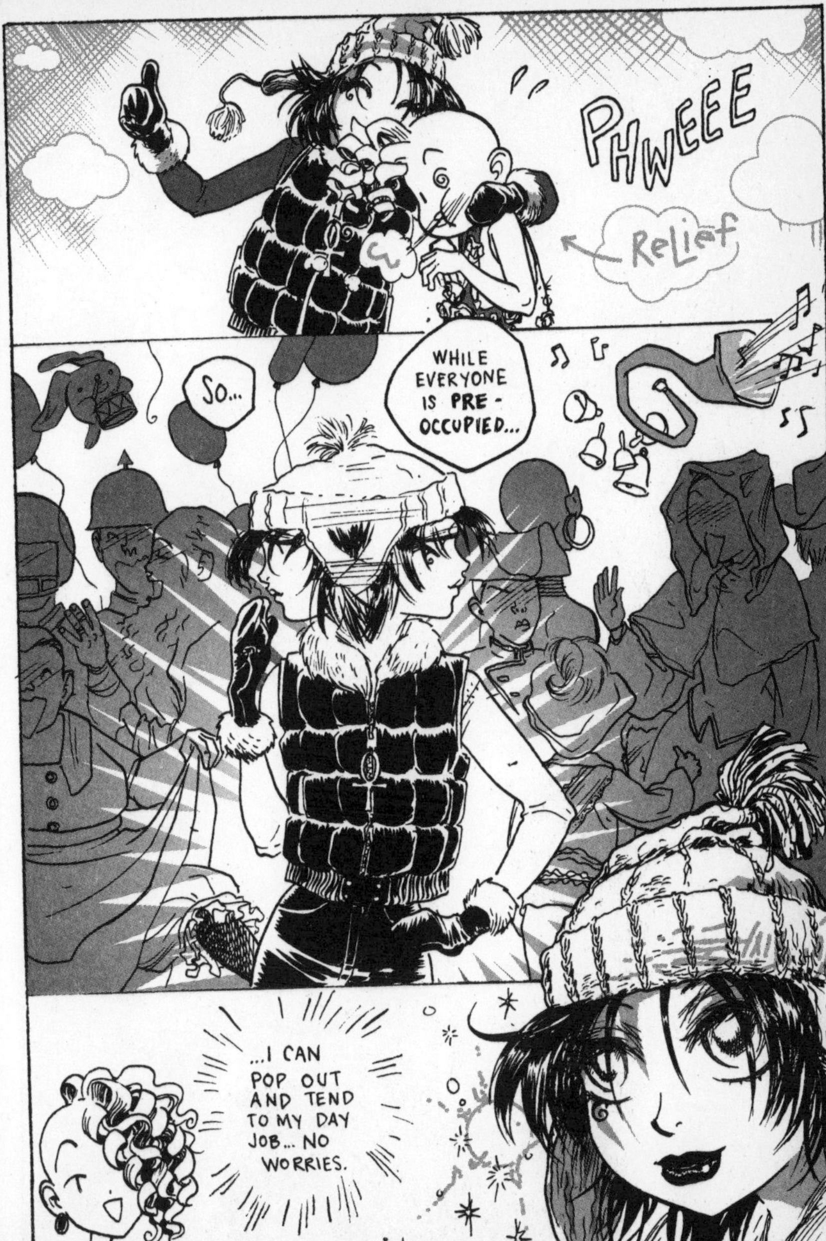
PHWEEE
Relief
SO...
WHILE EVERYONE IS PRE-OCCUPIED...
...I CAN POP OUT AND TEND TO MY DAY JOB... NO WORRIES.

AND THAT'S NOT ALL I CAN DO... WATCH!
WATCH ME! I CAN DO MORE PARTY THINGS.
ZZiiiP!
BALLOONS AND ANIMALS!!
ARR!!
THAT'S A BADGER! OH GOD! WHY
SNAKES
HEE! HEE! KITTY! AN' BAWOOMS
LOOK OUT
MY EYE
NO MORE
NOT AGAIN
UM... THAT'S BALLOON ANIMALS, DELIRIUM.
...animals made out of balloons... No teeth ... or claws...
UH-OH! NOT FUN AT A PARTY?

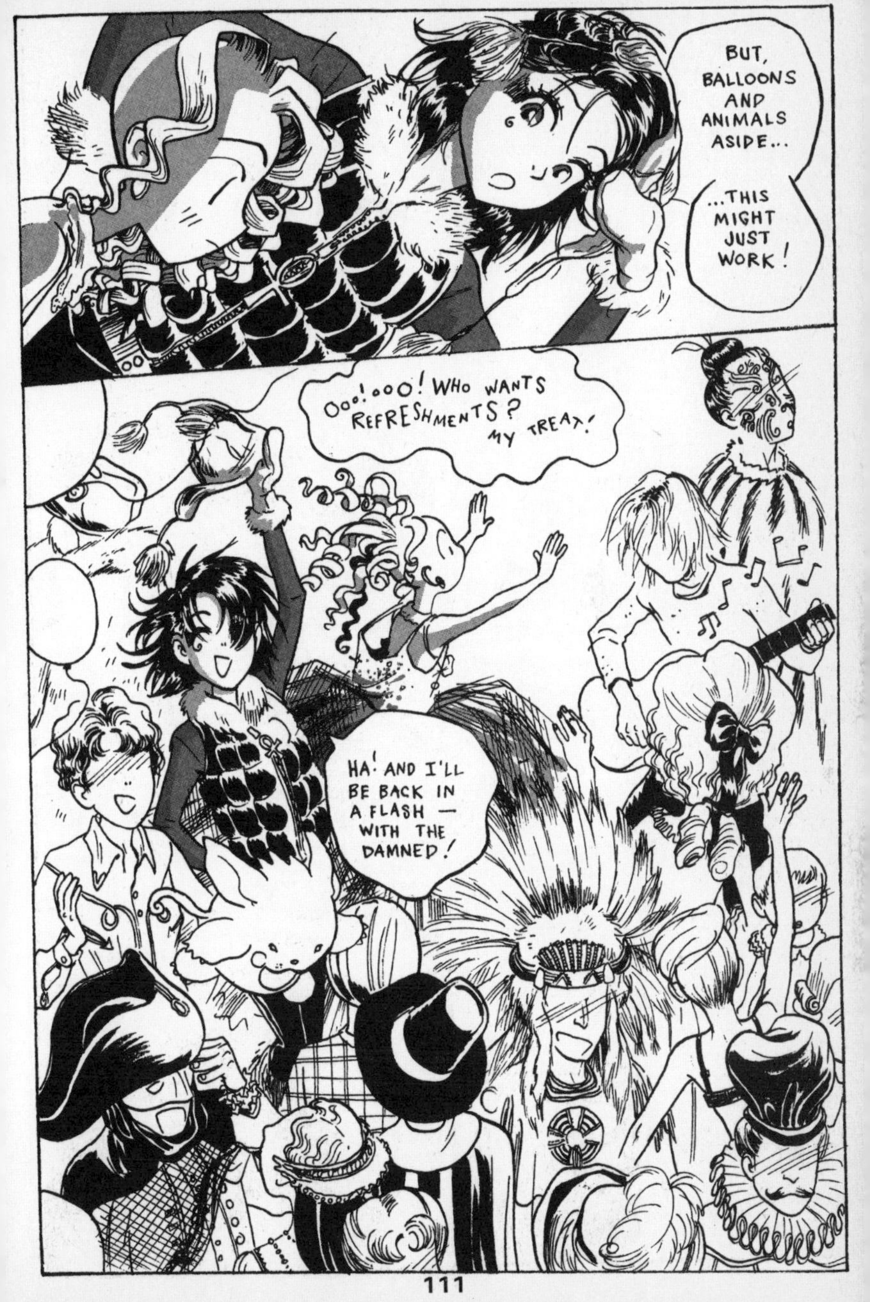
BUT, BALLOONS AND ANIMALS ASIDE...
...THIS MIGHT JUST WORK!
OOO! OOO! WHO WANTS REFRESHMENTS? MY TREAT!
HA! AND I'LL BE BACK IN A FLASH — WITH THE DAMNED!

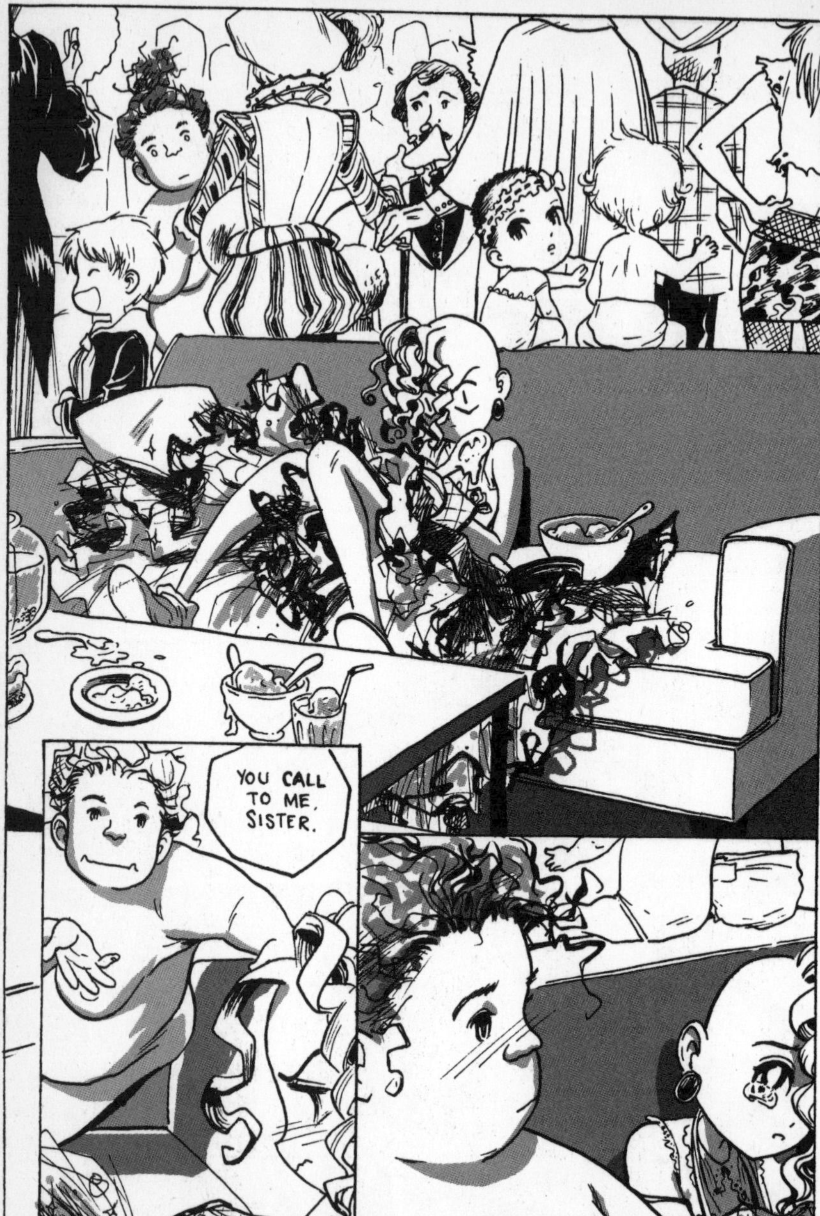
YOU CALL TO ME, SISTER.

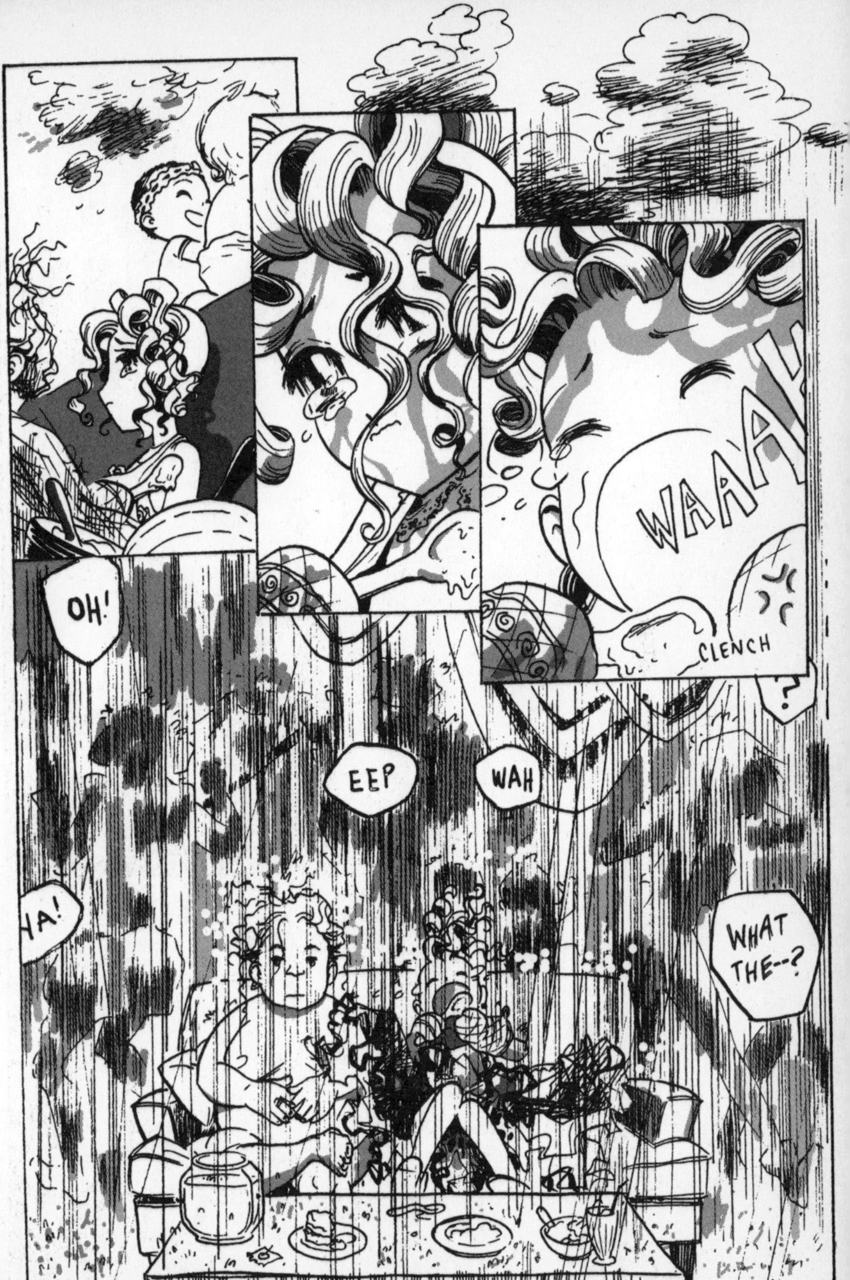
WAAAH
CLENCH
OH!
?
EEP
WAH
HA!
WHAT THE--?

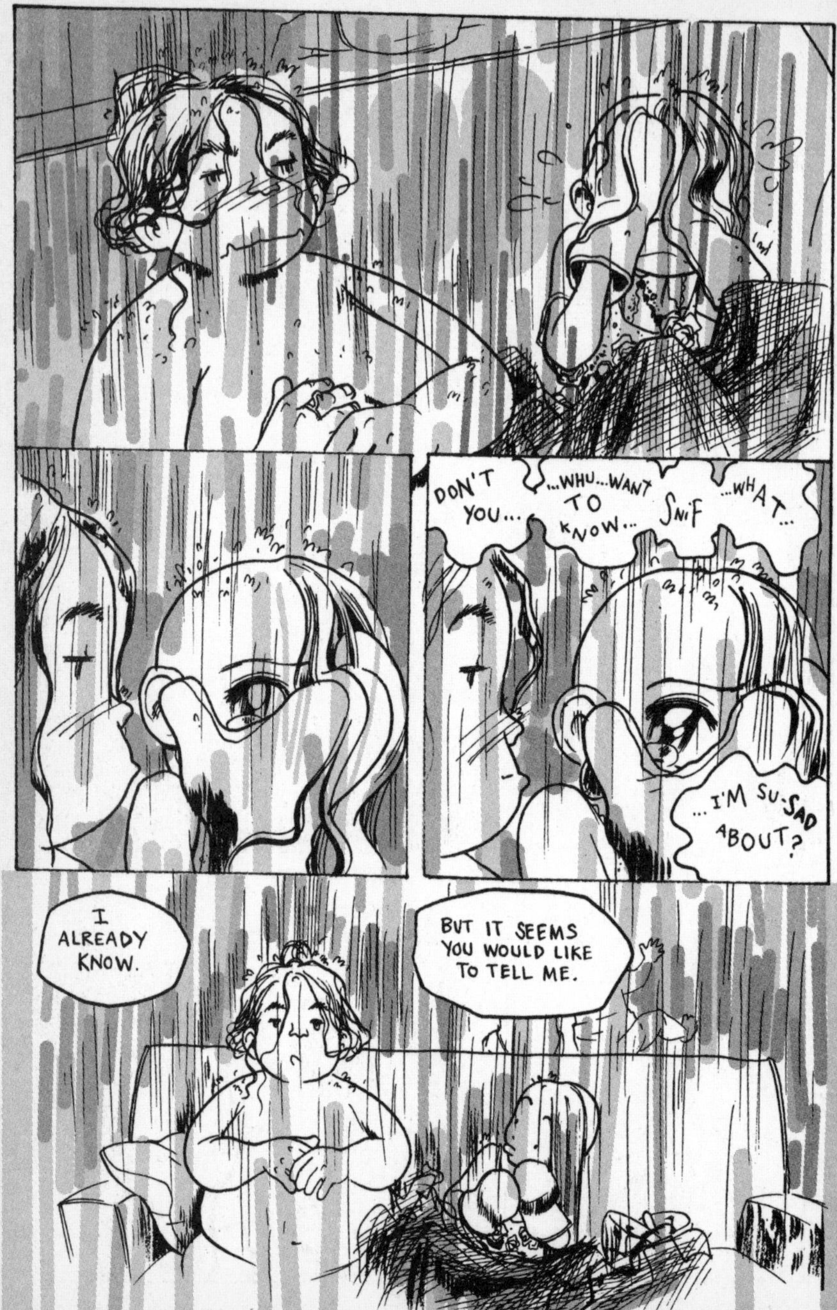

DON'T YOU... ...WHU...WANT TO KNOW... SNIF ...WHAT...
... I'M SU-SAD ABOUT?
I ALREADY KNOW.
BUT IT SEEMS YOU WOULD LIKE TO TELL ME.

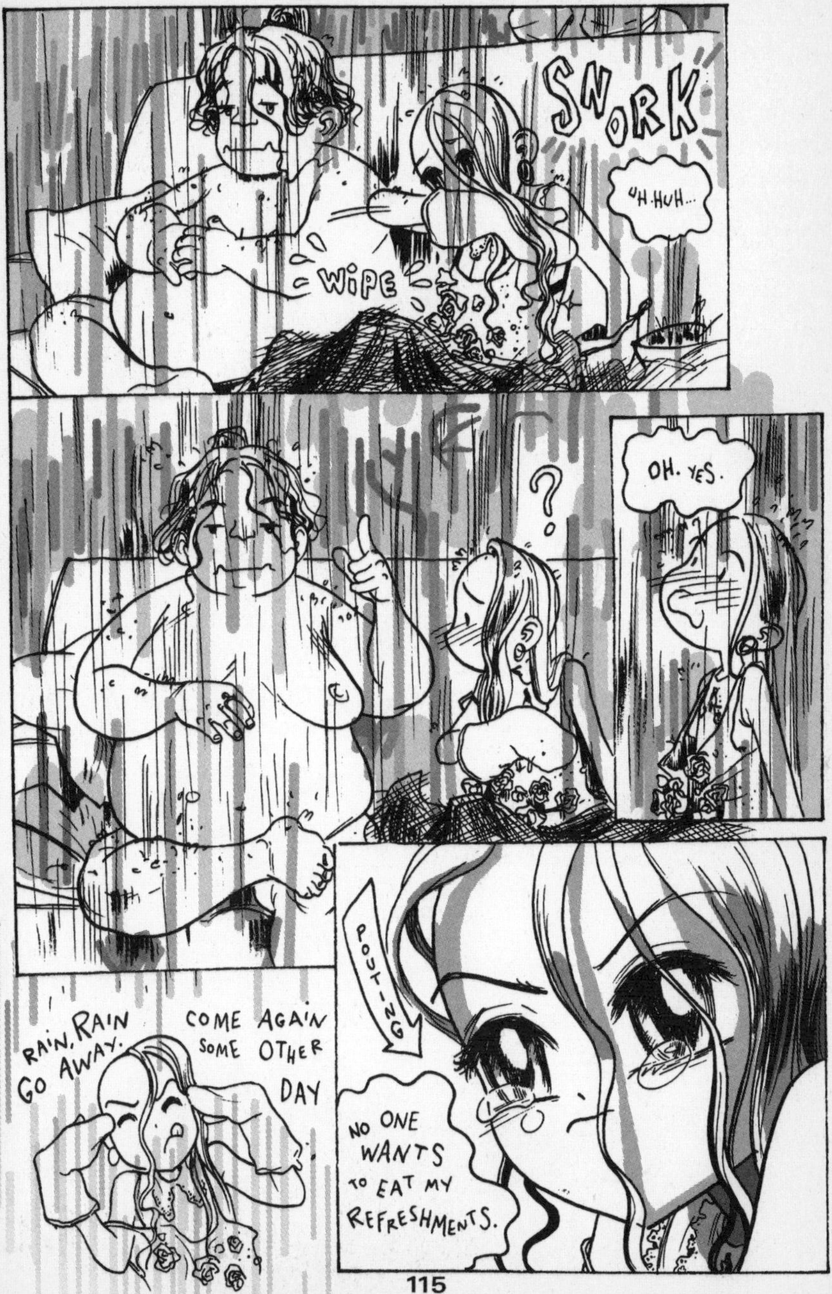
SNORK
UH HUH...
WIPE
?
OH. YES.
POUTING
NO ONE WANTS TO EAT MY REFRESHMENTS.
RAIN, RAIN GO AWAY.
COME AGAIN SOME OTHER DAY

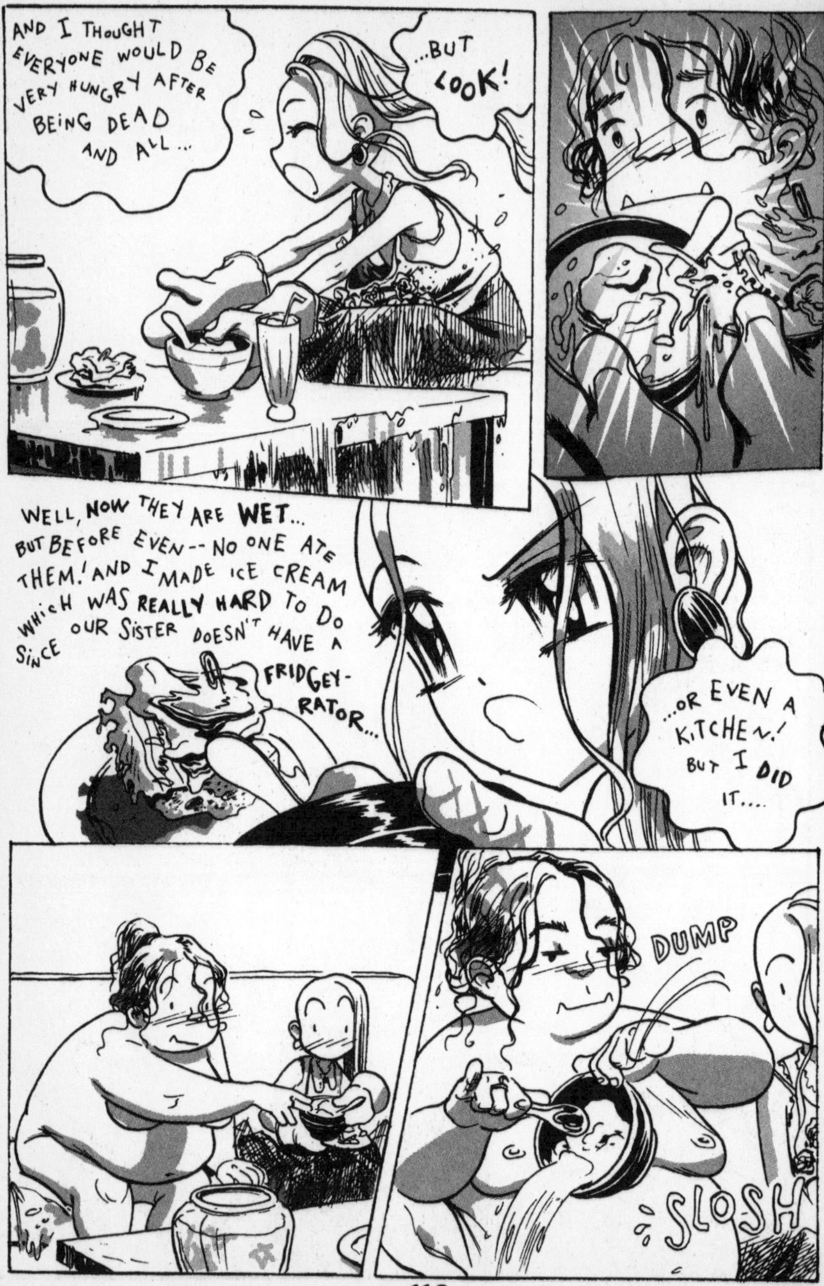
AND I THOUGHT EVERYONE WOULD BE VERY HUNGRY AFTER BEING DEAD AND ALL...
...BUT LOOK!
WELL, NOW THEY ARE WET... BUT BEFORE EVEN-- NO ONE ATE THEM! AND I MADE ICE CREAM WHICH WAS REALLY HARD TO DO SINCE OUR SISTER DOESN'T HAVE A FRIDGEY-RATOR...
...OR EVEN A KITCHEN! BUT I DID IT....
DUMP
SLOSH

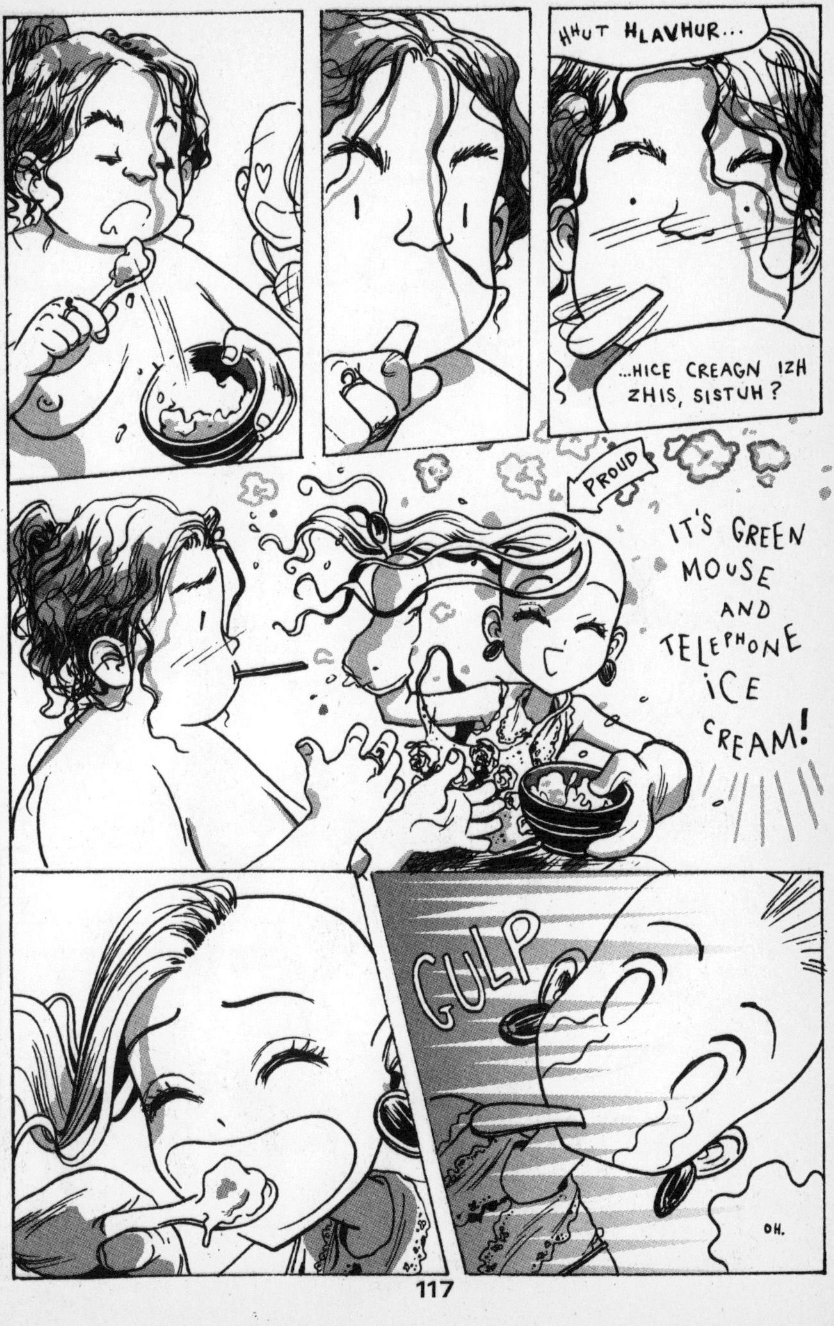
HHUT HLAVHUR...
...HICE CREAGN IZH ZHIS, SISTUH?
PROUD
IT'S GREEN MOUSE AND TELEPHONE ICE CREAM!
GULP
OH.

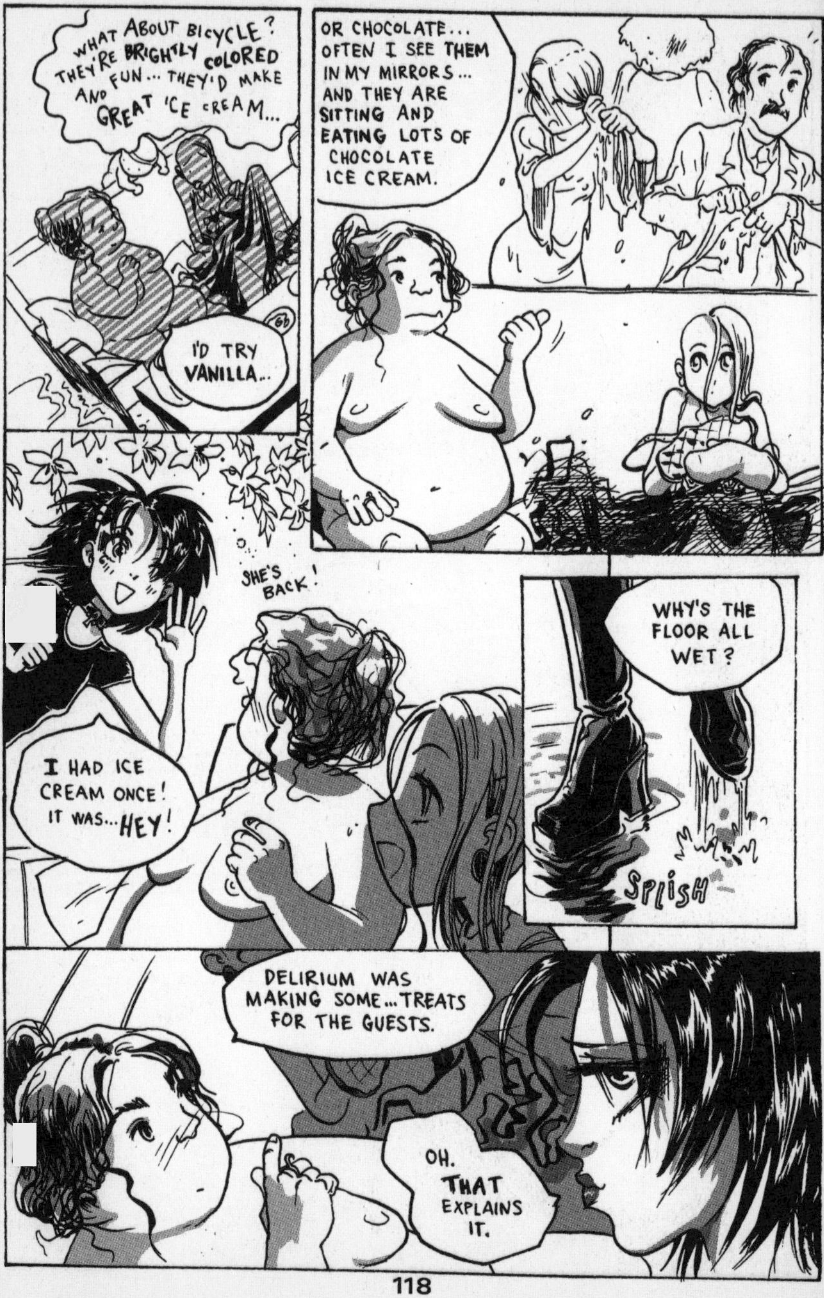
WHAT ABOUT BICYCLE? THEY'RE BRIGHTLY COLORED AND FUN... THEY'D MAKE GREAT ICE CREAM...
I'D TRY VANILLA...
OR CHOCOLATE... OFTEN I SEE THEM IN MY MIRRORS... AND THEY ARE SITTING AND EATING LOTS OF CHOCOLATE ICE CREAM.
SHE'S BACK!
I HAD ICE CREAM ONCE! IT WAS...HEY!
WHY'S THE FLOOR ALL WET?
SPLISH
DELIRIUM WAS MAKING SOME...TREATS FOR THE GUESTS.
OH. THAT EXPLAINS IT.

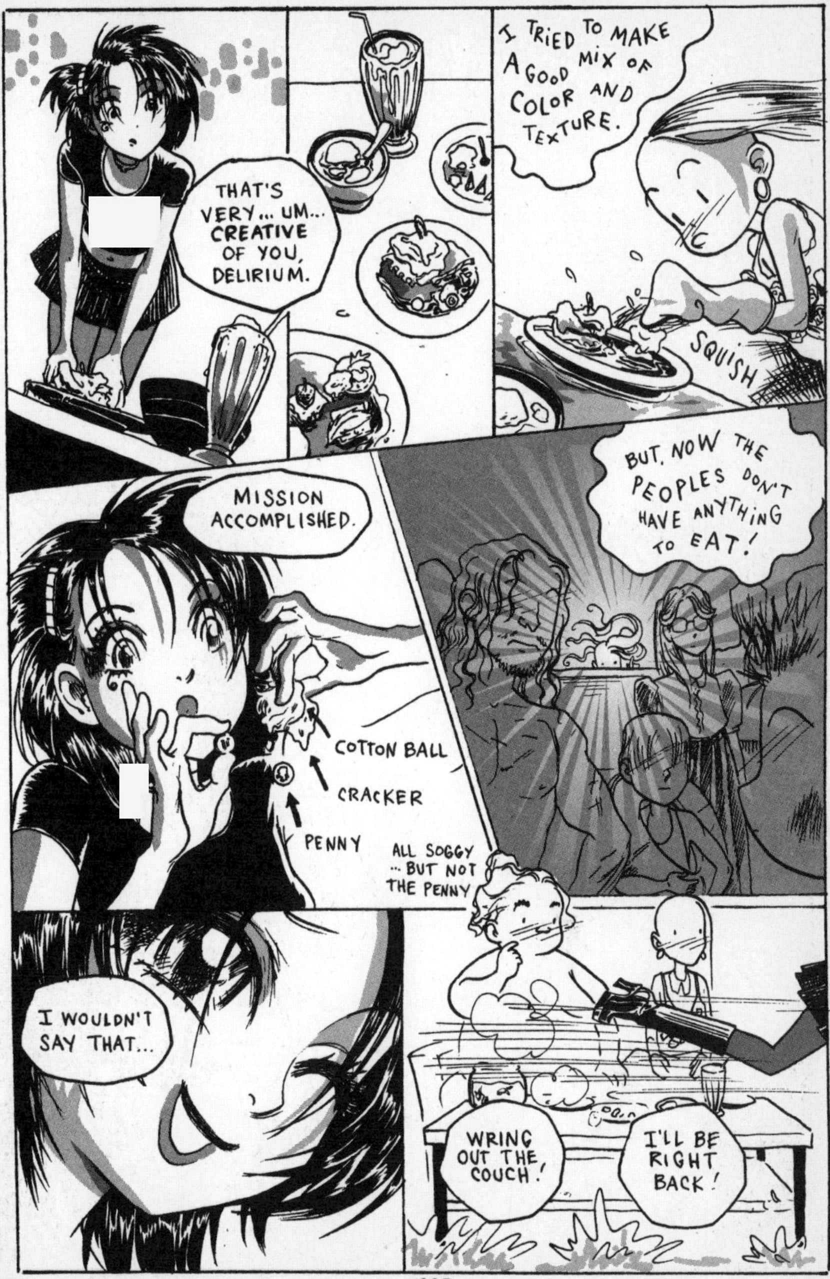
THAT'S VERY... UM... CREATIVE OF YOU, DELIRIUM.
I TRIED TO MAKE A GOOD MIX OF COLOR AND TEXTURE.
SQUISH
MISSION ACCOMPLISHED.
COTTON BALL
CRACKER
PENNY
ALL SOGGY ... BUT NOT THE PENNY
BUT, NOW THE PEOPLES DON'T HAVE ANYTHING TO EAT!
I WOULDN'T SAY THAT...
WRING OUT THE COUCH!
I'LL BE RIGHT BACK!

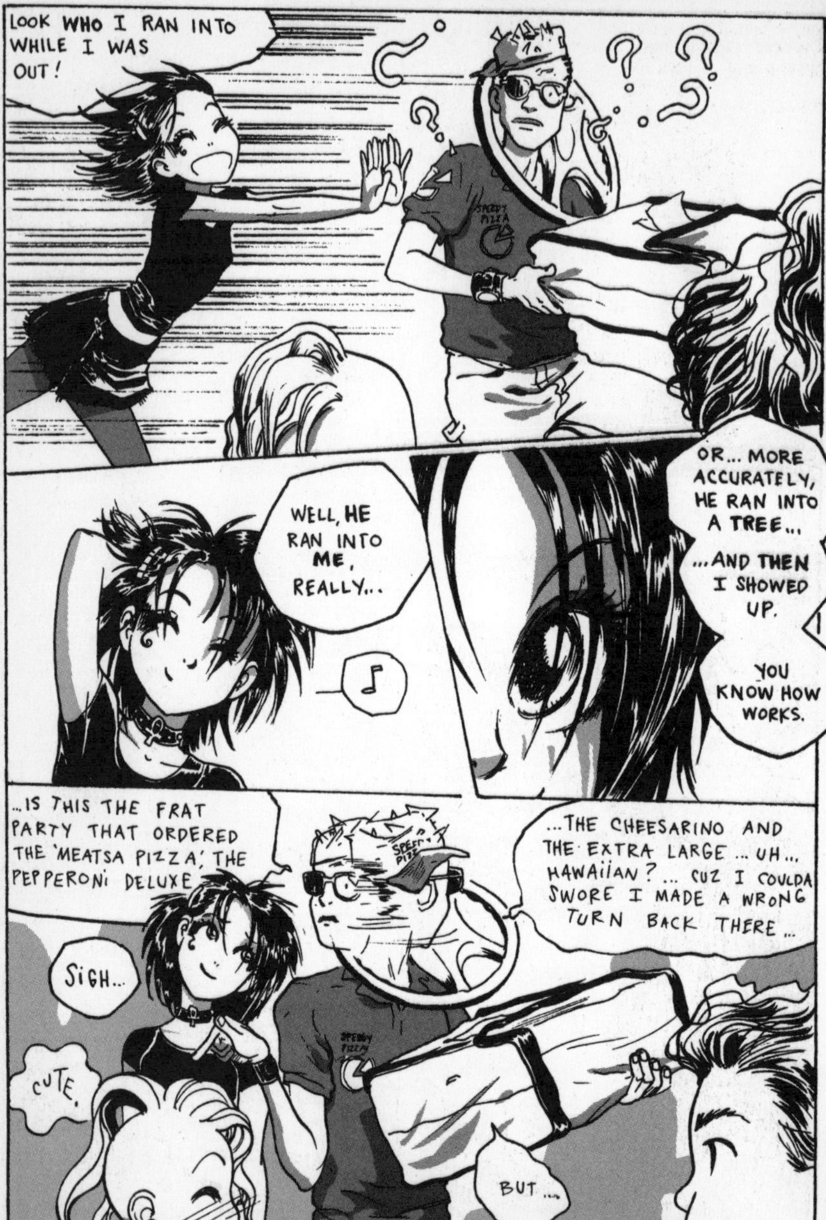

LOOK WHO I RAN INTO WHILE I WAS OUT!
WELL, HE RAN INTO ME, REALLY...
OR... MORE ACCURATELY, HE RAN INTO A TREE...
...AND THEN I SHOWED UP.
YOU KNOW HOW I
WORKS.
...IS THIS THE FRAT PARTY THAT ORDERED THE 'MEATSA PIZZA,' THE PEPPERONI DELUXE
...THE CHEESARINO AND THE EXTRA LARGE ... UH... HAWAIIAN? ... CUZ I COULDA SWORE I MADE A WRONG TURN BACK THERE...
SIGH...
CUTE.
BUT...

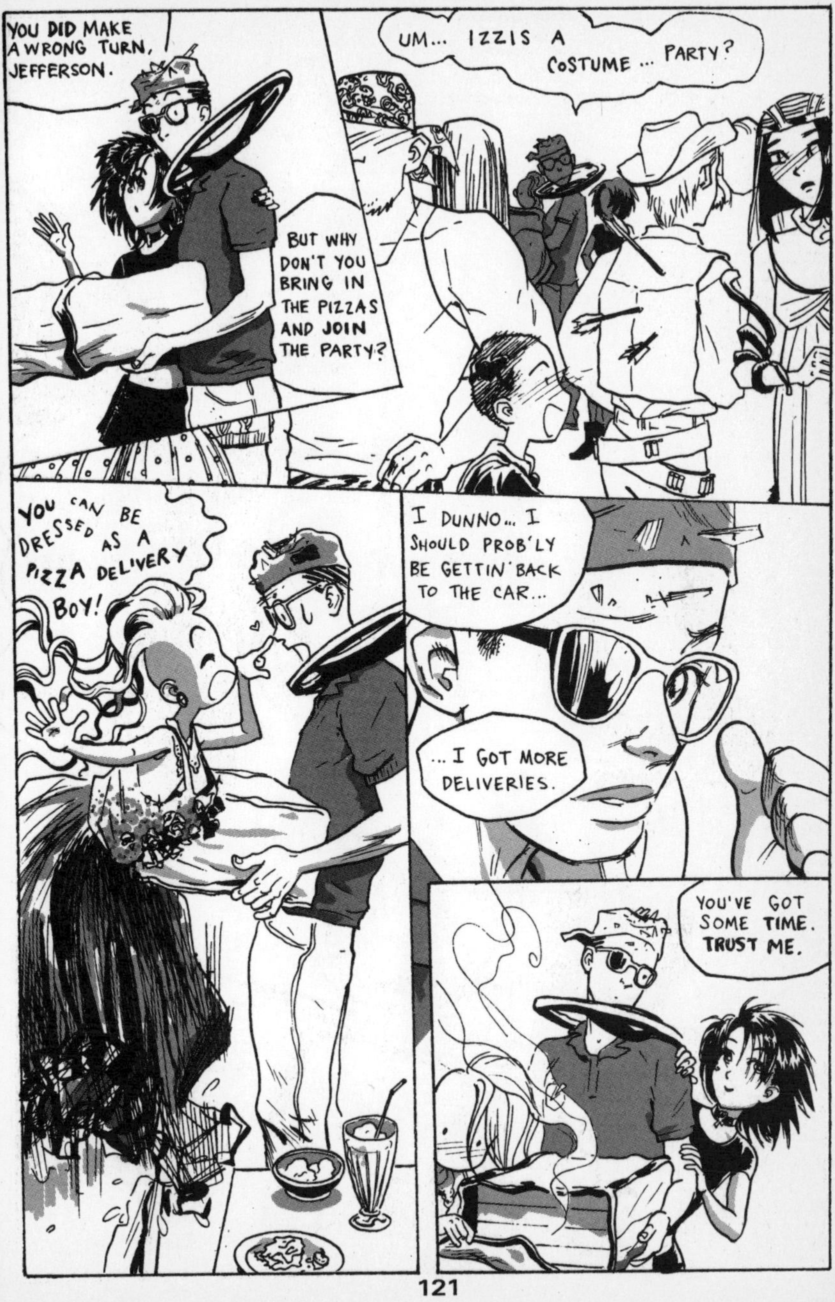
YOU DID MAKE A WRONG TURN, JEFFERSON.
BUT WHY DON'T YOU BRING IN THE PIZZAS AND JOIN THE PARTY?
UM... IZZIS A COSTUME... PARTY?
YOU CAN BE DRESSED AS A PIZZA DELIVERY BOY!
I DUNNO... I SHOULD PROB'LY BE GETTIN' BACK TO THE CAR...
...I GOT MORE DELIVERIES.
YOU'VE GOT SOME TIME. TRUST ME.

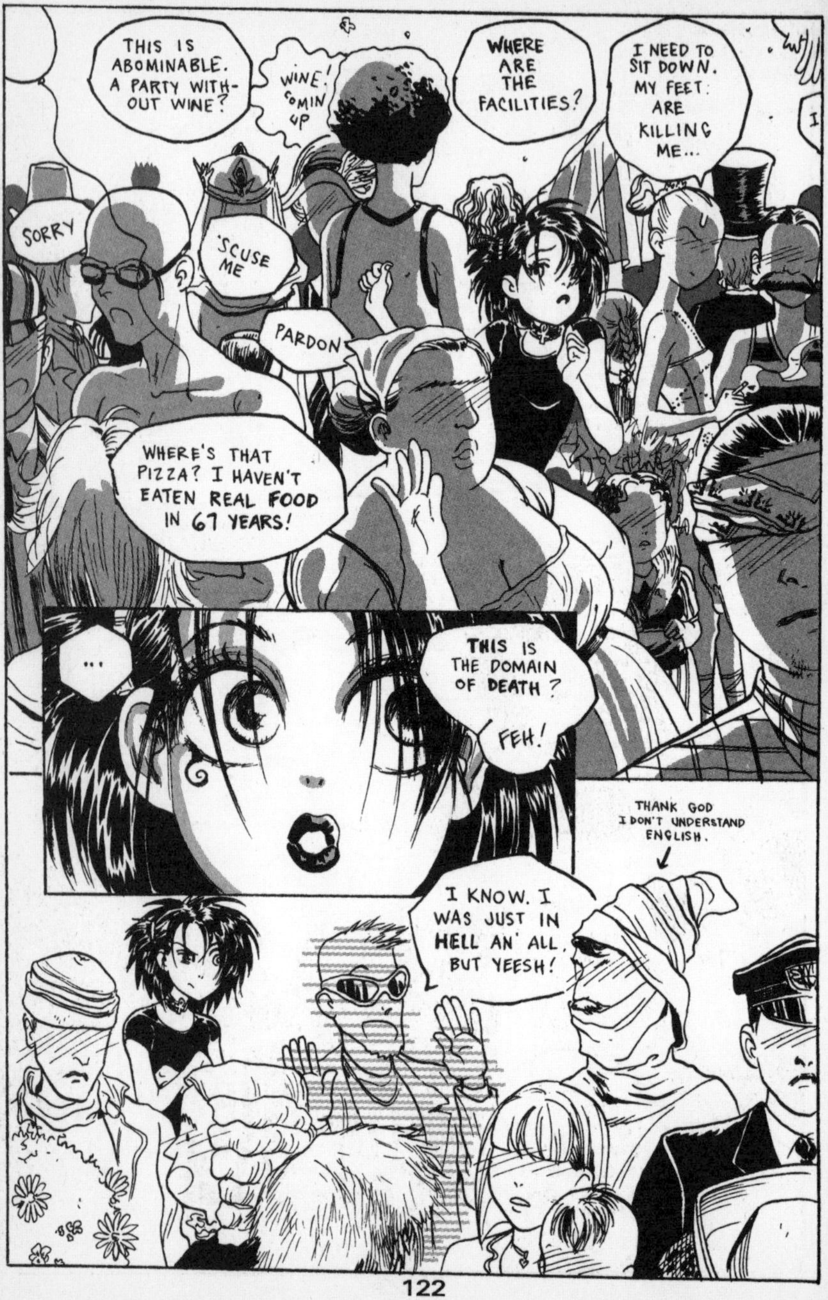
THIS IS ABOMINABLE. A PARTY WITH-OUT WINE?
WINE! COMIN UP
WHERE ARE THE FACILITIES?
I NEED TO SIT DOWN. MY FEET ARE KILLING ME...
SORRY
'SCUSE ME
PARDON
WHERE'S THAT PIZZA? I HAVEN'T EATEN REAL FOOD IN 67 YEARS!
...
THIS IS THE DOMAIN OF DEATH?
FEH!
THANK GOD I DON'T UNDERSTAND ENGLISH.
I KNOW. I WAS JUST IN HELL AN' ALL, BUT YEESH!

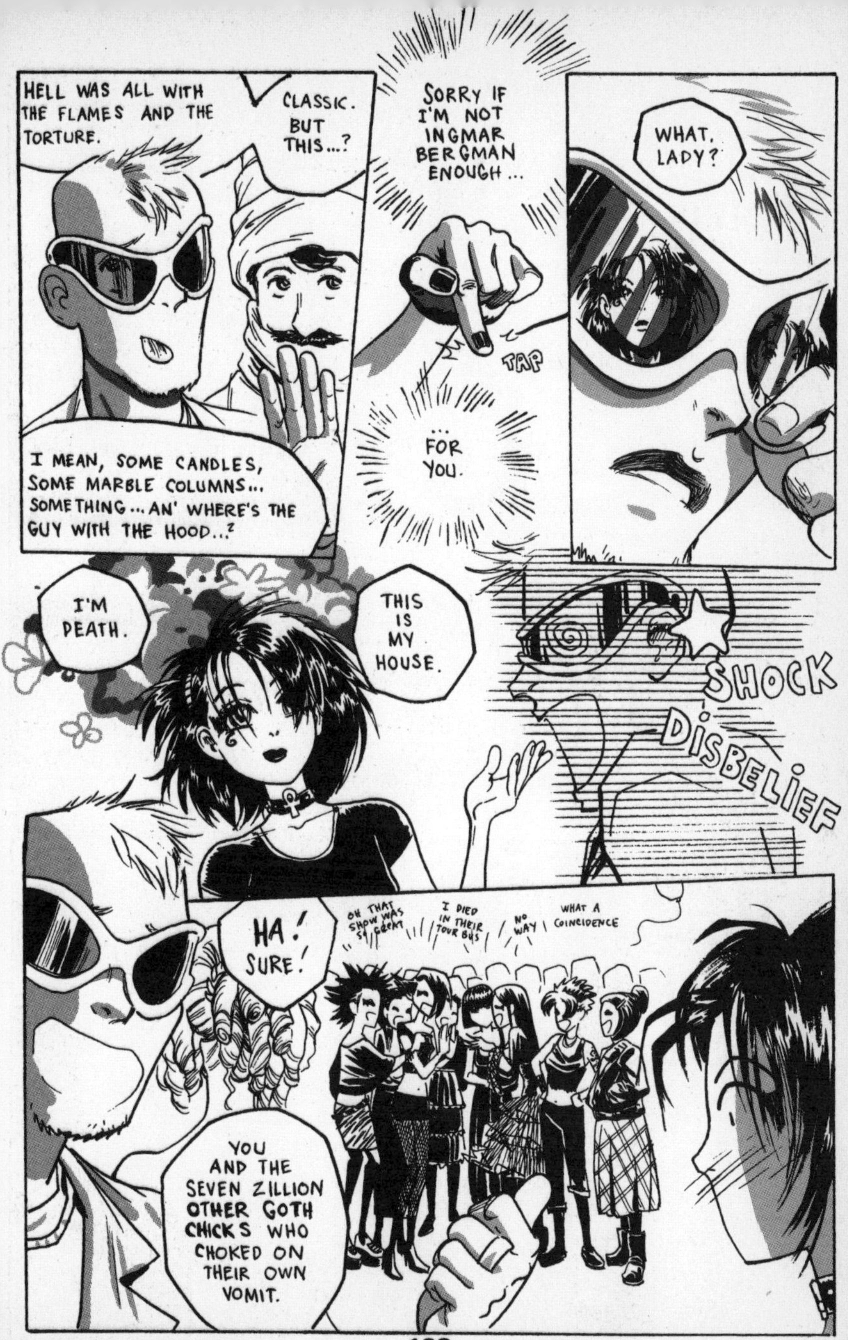
HELL WAS ALL WITH THE FLAMES AND THE TORTURE.
CLASSIC. BUT THIS...?
I MEAN, SOME CANDLES, SOME MARBLE COLUMNS... SOMETHING... AN' WHERE'S THE GUY WITH THE HOOD...?
SORRY IF I'M NOT INGMAR BERGMAN ENOUGH...
TAP
... FOR YOU.
WHAT, LADY?
I'M DEATH.
THIS IS MY HOUSE.
SHOCK
DISBELIEF
HA! SURE!
OH THAT SHOW WAS SO GREAT
I DIED IN THEIR TOUR BUS
NO WAY
WHAT A COINCIDENCE
YOU AND THE SEVEN ZILLION OTHER GOTH CHICKS WHO CHOKED ON THEIR OWN VOMIT.

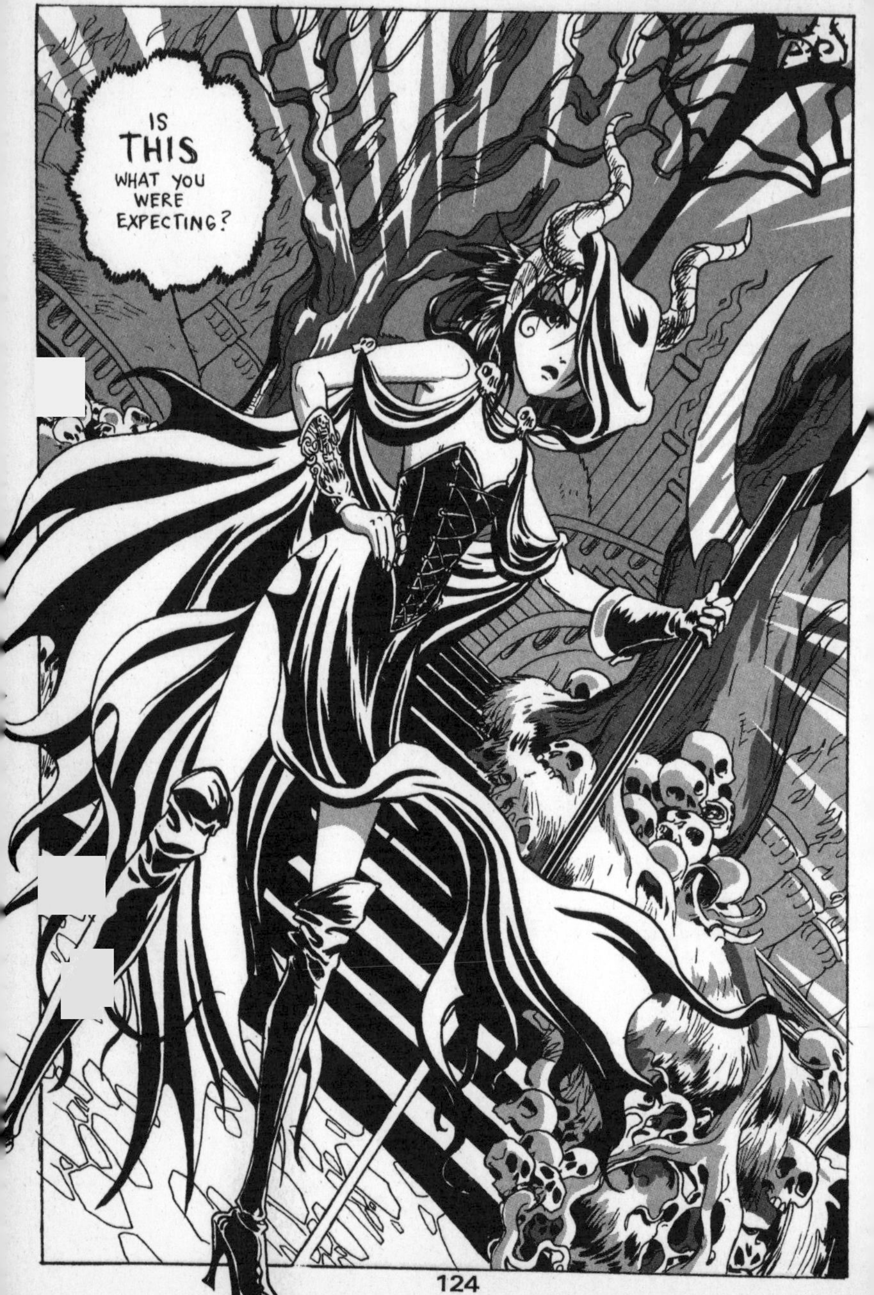
IS THIS WHAT YOU WERE EXPECTING?

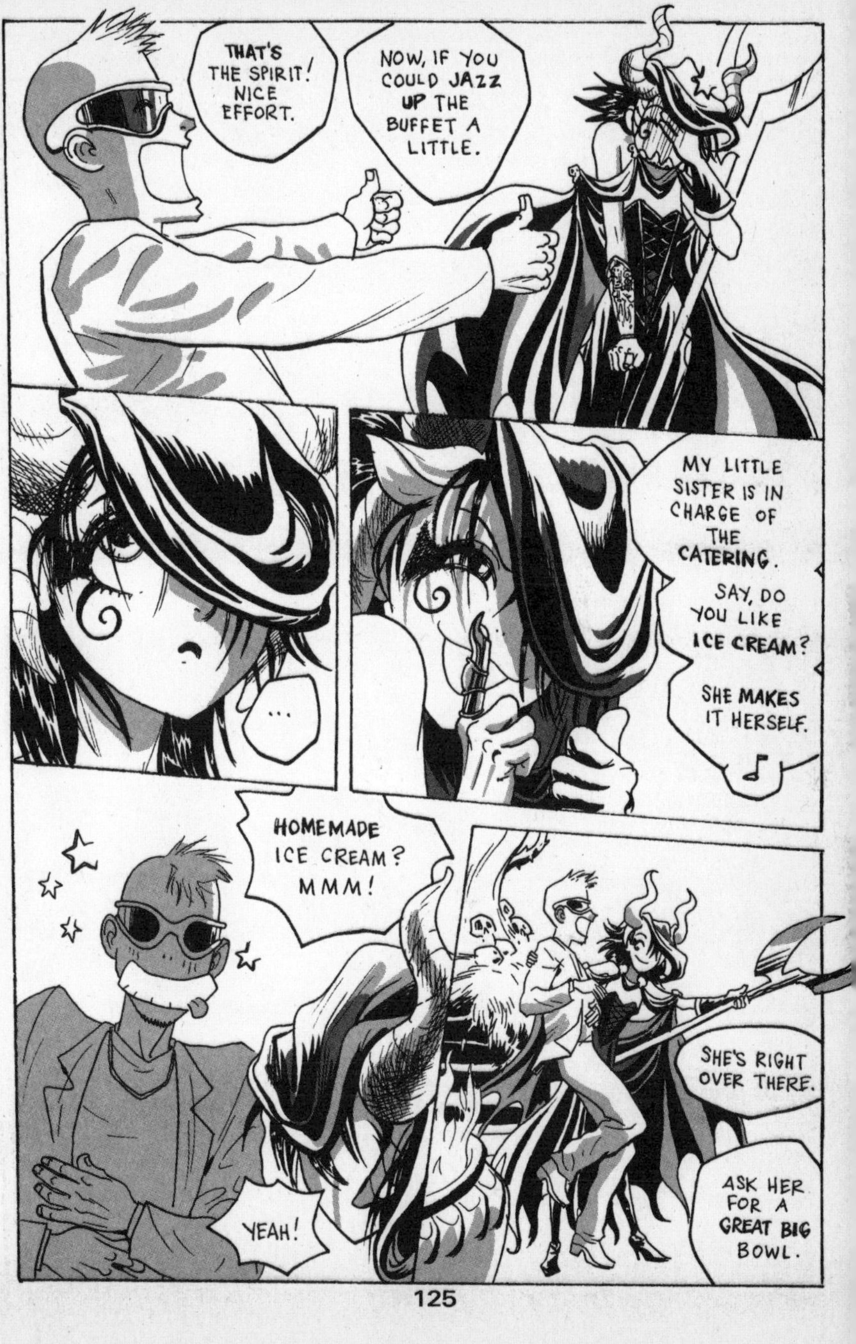
THAT'S THE SPIRIT! NICE EFFORT.
NOW, IF YOU COULD JAZZ UP THE BUFFET A LITTLE.
...
MY LITTLE SISTER IS IN CHARGE OF THE CATERING.
SAY, DO YOU LIKE ICE CREAM?
SHE MAKES IT HERSELF.
HOMEMADE ICE CREAM? MMM!
YEAH!
SHE'S RIGHT OVER THERE.
ASK HER FOR A GREAT BIG BOWL.

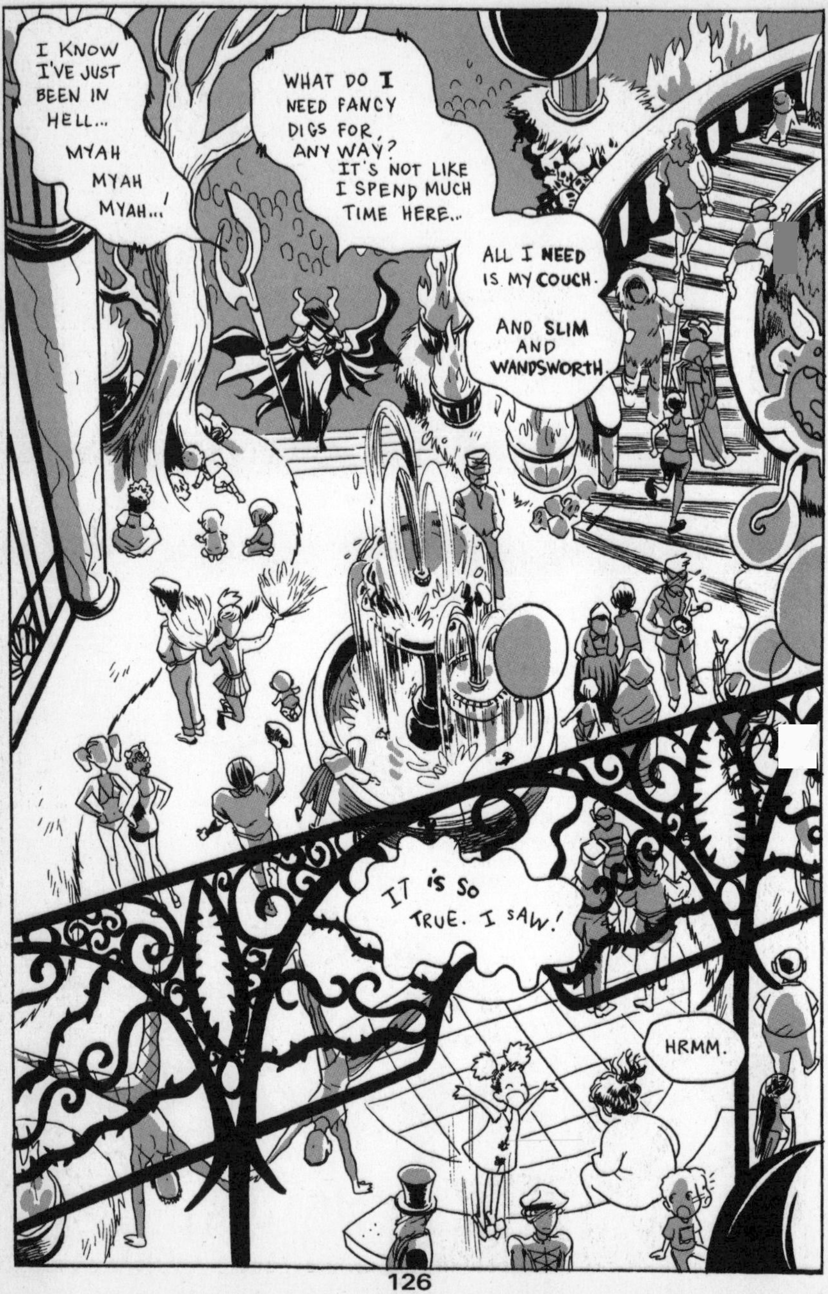
I KNOW I'VE JUST BEEN IN HELL... MYAH MYAH MYAH...!
WHAT DO I NEED FANCY DIGS FOR, ANY WAY? IT'S NOT LIKE I SPEND MUCH TIME HERE...
ALL I NEED IS MY COUCH.
AND SLIM AND WANDSWORTH.
IT IS SO TRUE. I SAW!
HRMM.

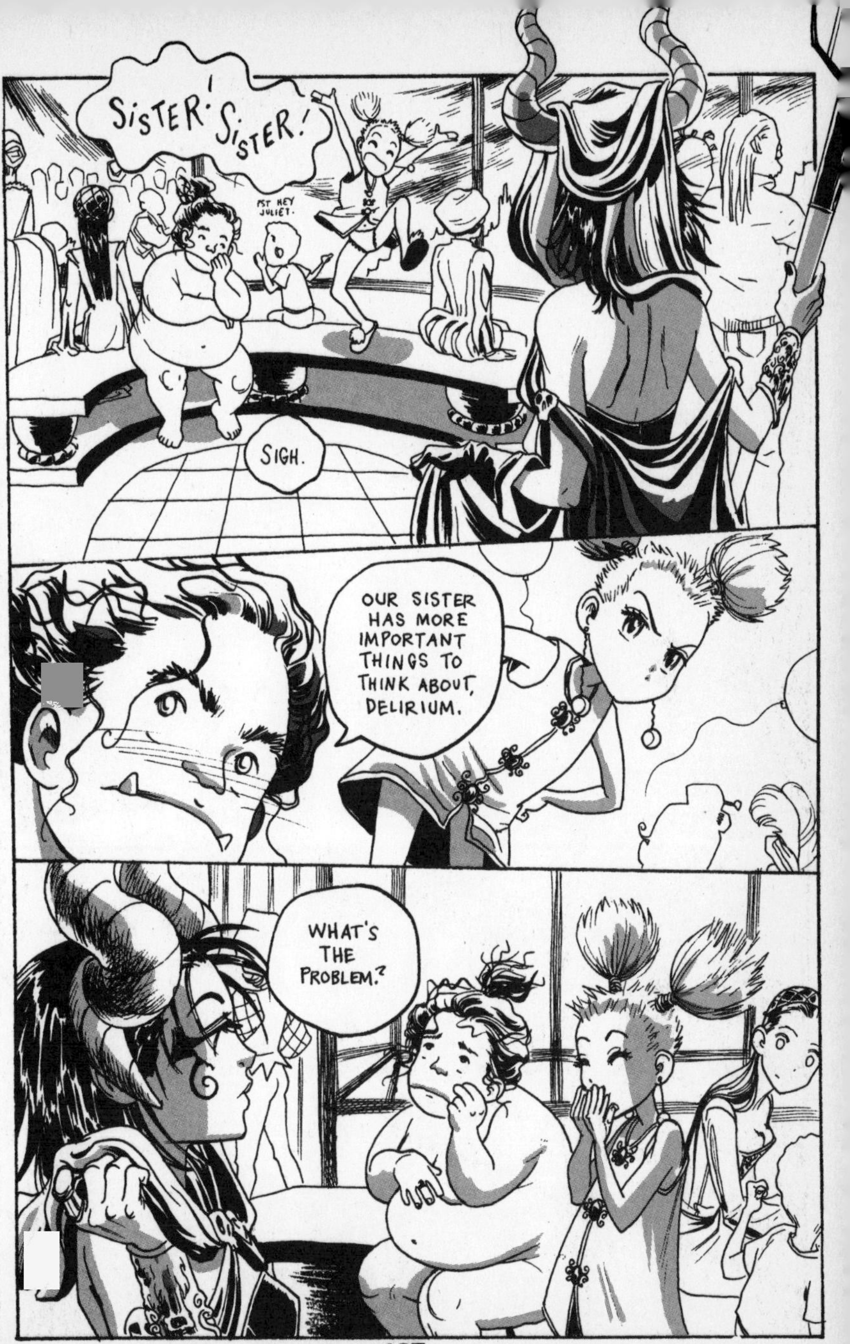
SISTER! SISTER!
PST HEY JULIET.
SIGH.
OUR SISTER HAS MORE IMPORTANT THINGS TO THINK ABOUT, DELIRIUM.
WHAT'S THE PROBLEM?

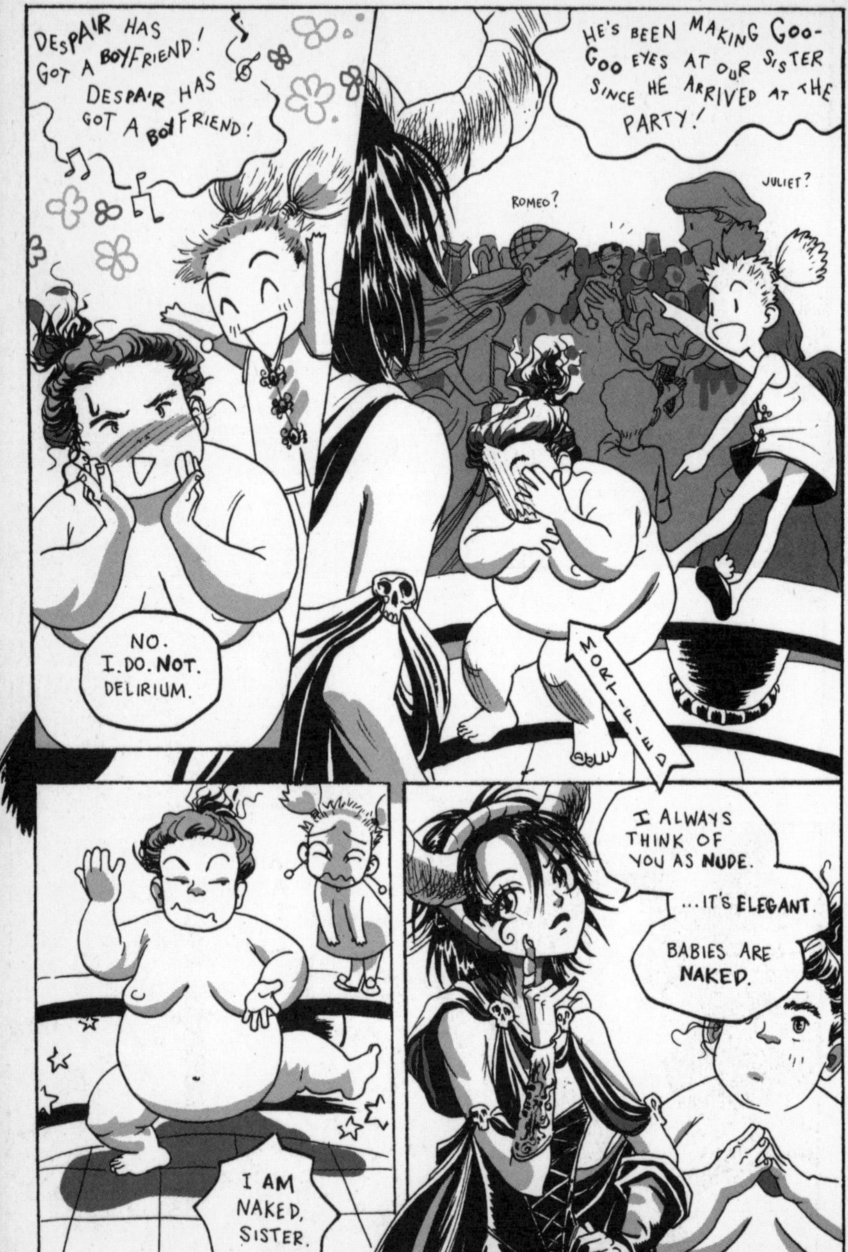
DESPAIR HAS GOT A BOYFRIEND! DESPAIR HAS GOT A BOYFRIEND!
HE'S BEEN MAKING GOO-GOO EYES AT OUR SISTER SINCE HE ARRIVED AT THE PARTY!
ROMEO?
JULIET?
NO. I. DO. NOT. DELIRIUM.
MORTIFIED
I AM NAKED, SISTER.
I ALWAYS THINK OF YOU AS NUDE.
...IT'S ELEGANT.
BABIES ARE NAKED.

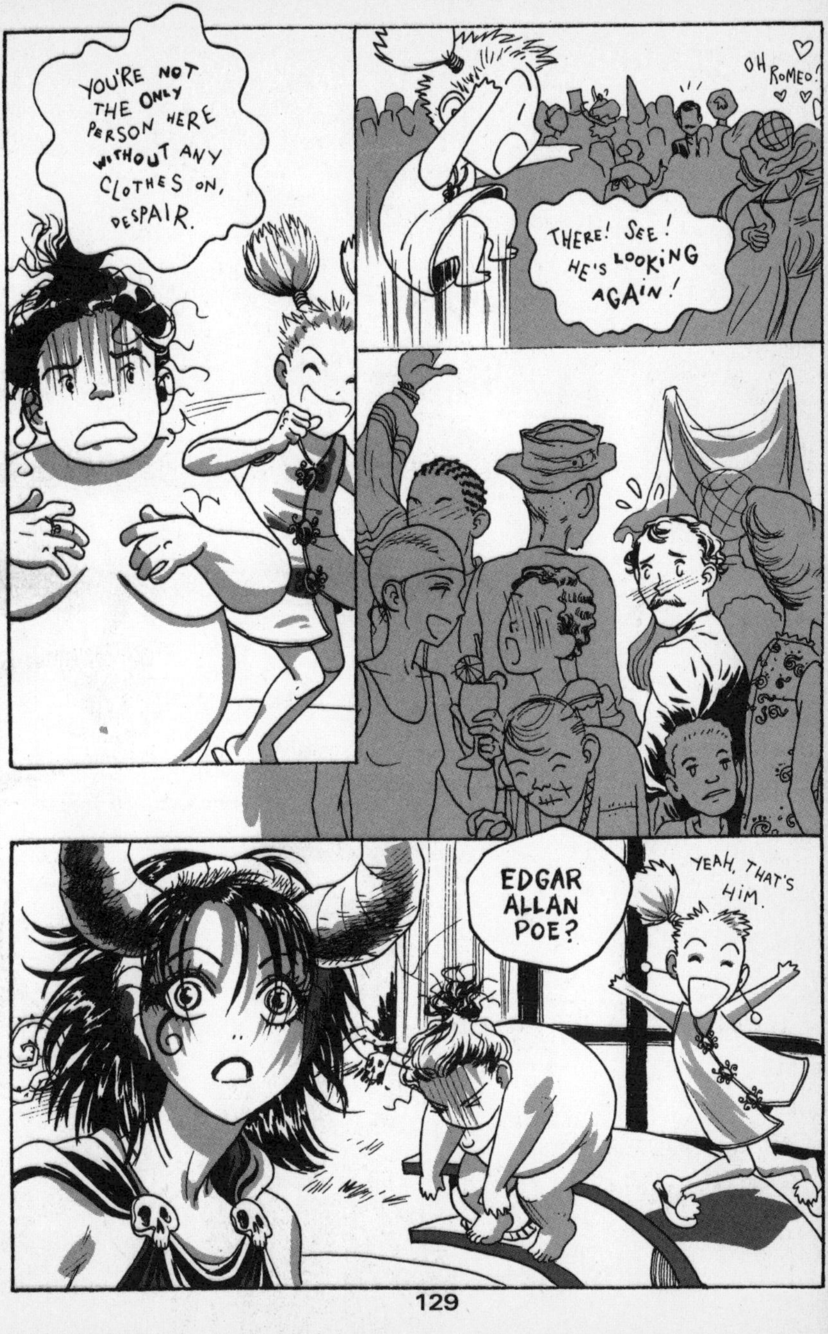
YOU'RE NOT THE ONLY PERSON HERE WITHOUT ANY CLOTHES ON, DESPAIR.
OH ROMEO!
THERE! SEE! HE'S LOOKING AGAIN!
EDGAR ALLAN POE?
YEAH, THAT'S HIM.

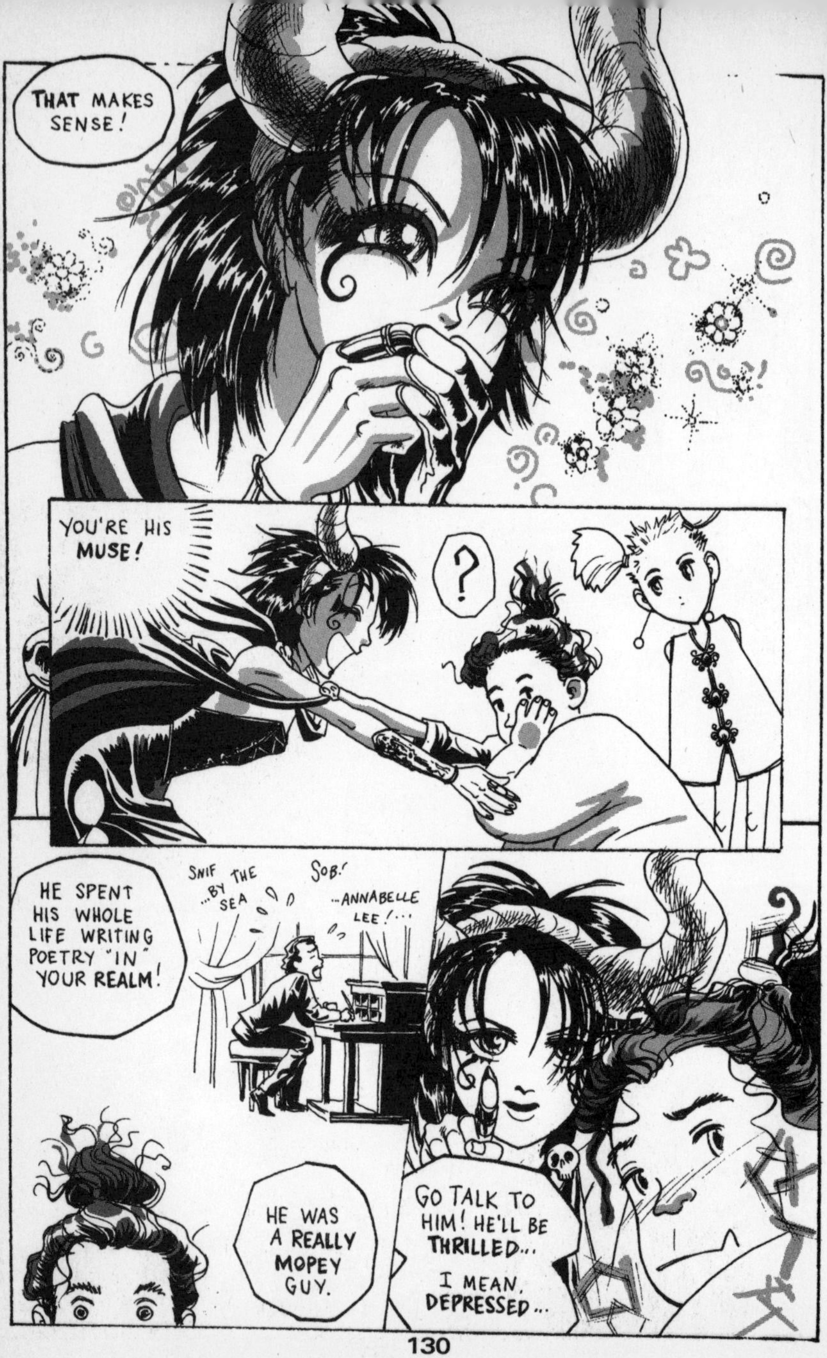
THAT MAKES SENSE!
YOU'RE HIS MUSE!
?
HE SPENT HIS WHOLE LIFE WRITING POETRY "IN" YOUR REALM!
SNIF ...BY THE SEA
SOB!
...ANNABELLE LEE!...
HE WAS A REALLY MOPEY GUY.
GO TALK TO HIM! HE'LL BE THRILLED...
I MEAN, DEPRESSED...

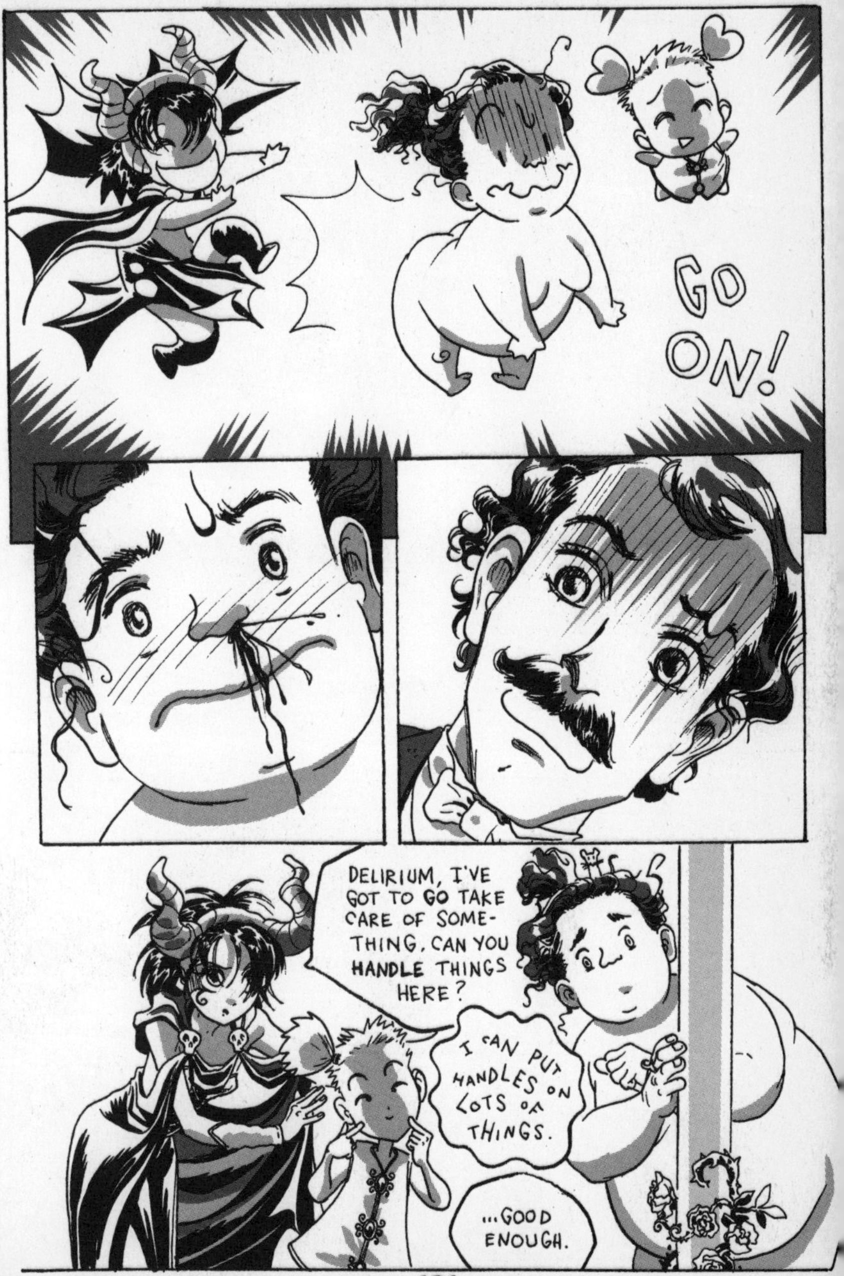
GO ON!
DELIRIUM, I'VE GOT TO GO TAKE CARE OF SOME-THING. CAN YOU HANDLE THINGS HERE?
I CAN PUT HANDLES ON LOTS OF THINGS.
...GOOD ENOUGH.

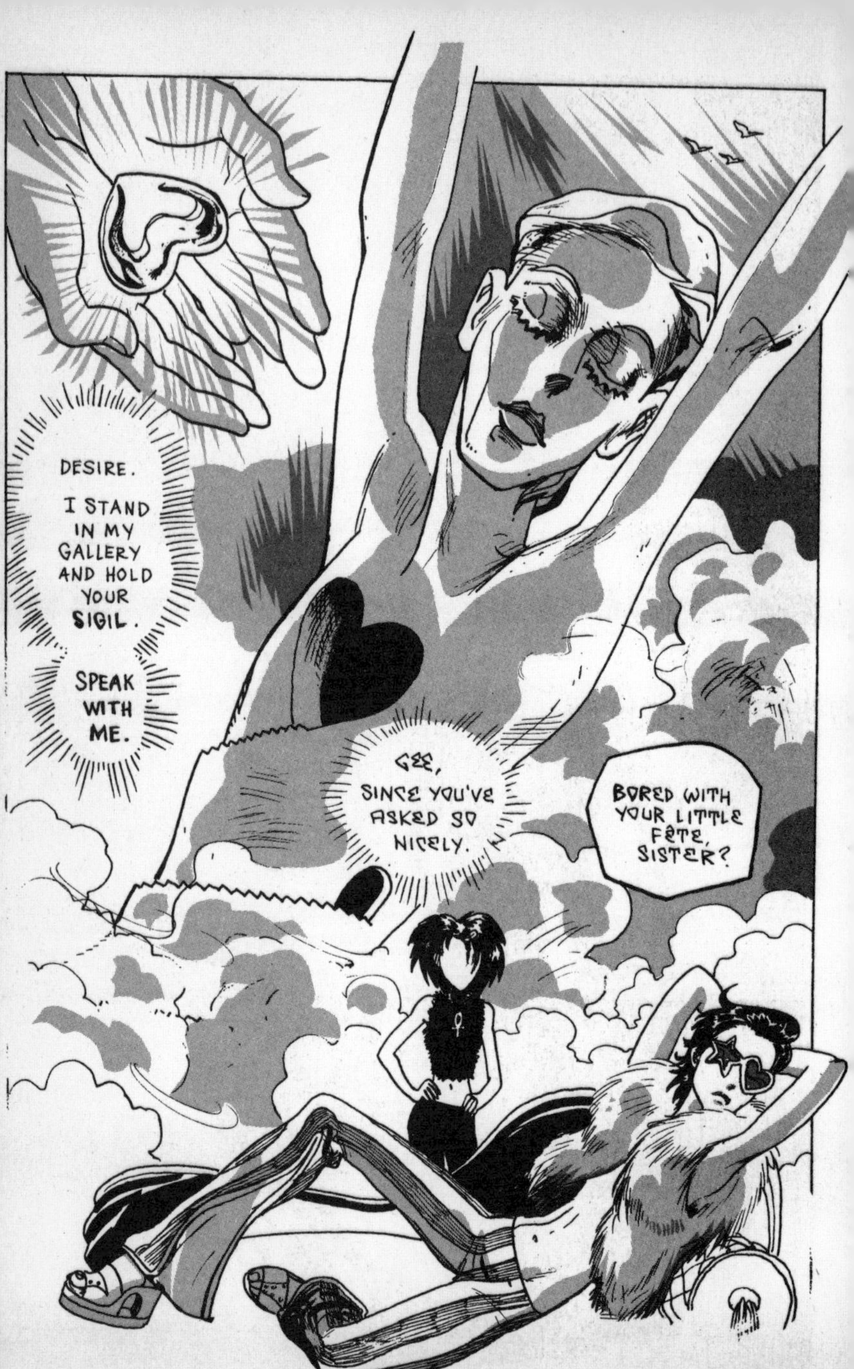
DESIRE.
I STAND IN MY GALLERY AND HOLD YOUR SIGIL.
SPEAK WITH ME.
GEE, SINCE YOU'VE ASKED SO NICELY.
BORED WITH YOUR LITTLE FÊTE, SISTER?

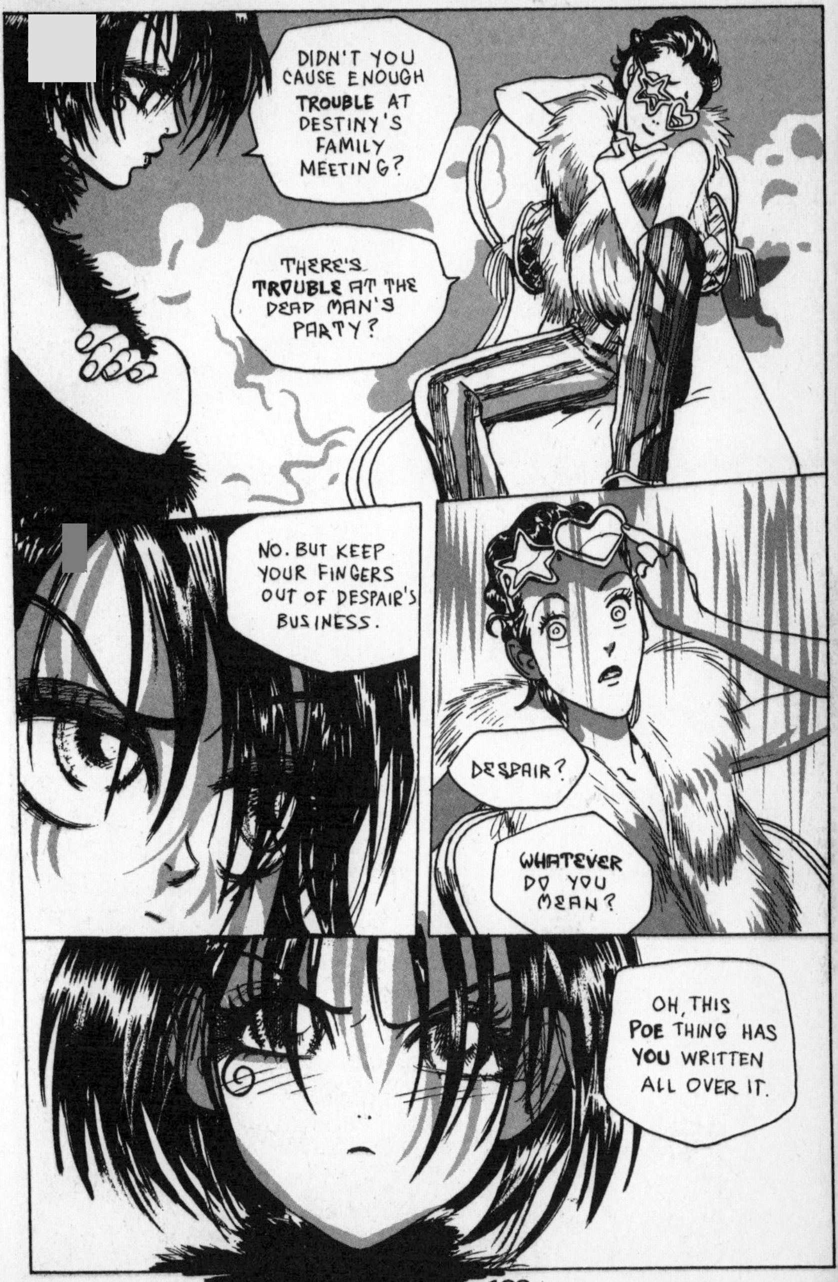

DIDN'T YOU CAUSE ENOUGH TROUBLE AT DESTINY'S FAMILY MEETING?
THERE'S TROUBLE AT THE DEAD MAN'S PARTY?
NO. BUT KEEP YOUR FINGERS OUT OF DESPAIR'S BUSINESS.
DESPAIR?
WHATEVER DO YOU MEAN?
OH, THIS POE THING HAS YOU WRITTEN ALL OVER IT.

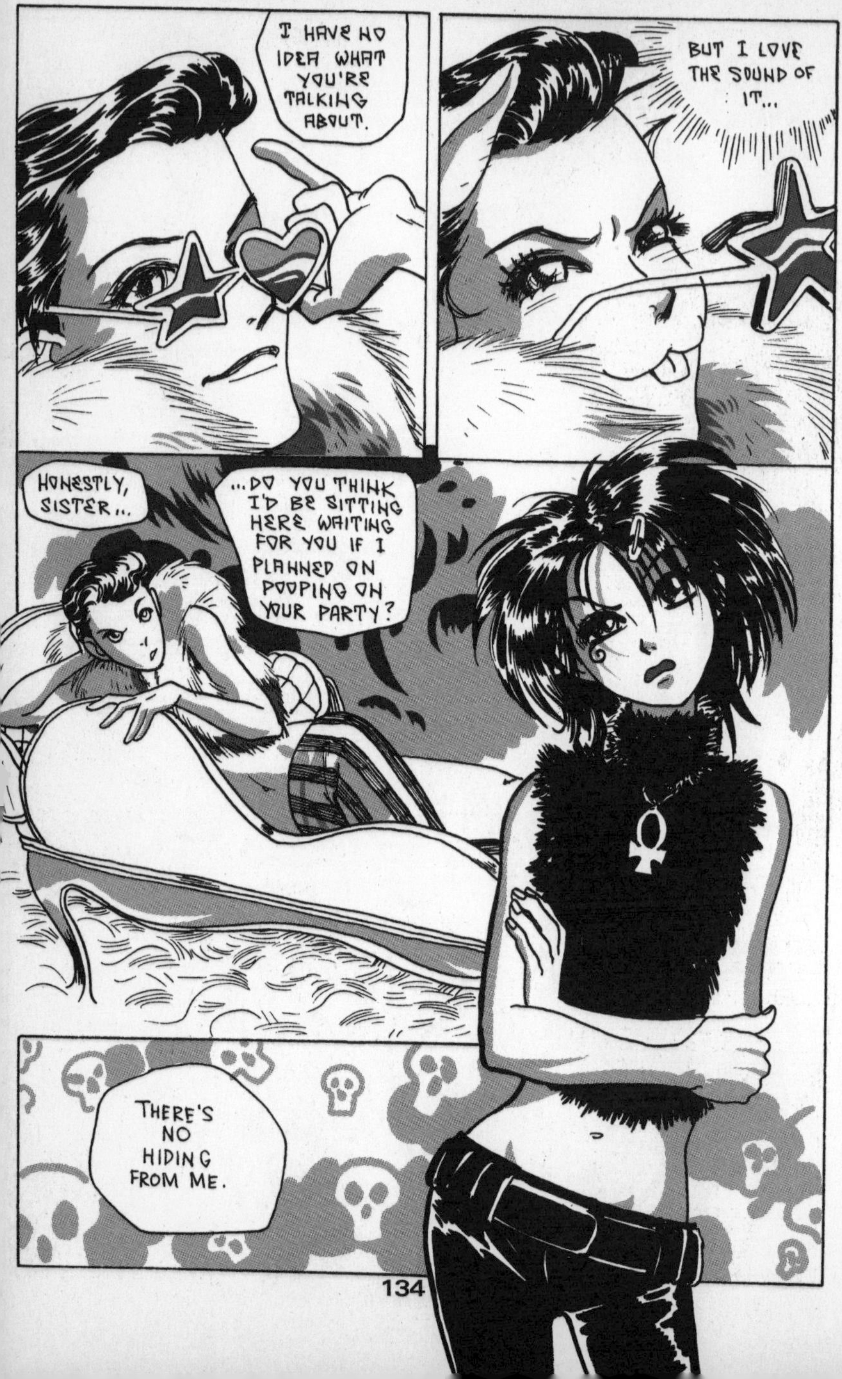
I HAVE NO IDEA WHAT YOU'RE TALKING ABOUT.
BUT I LOVE THE SOUND OF IT...
HONESTLY, SISTER...
...DO YOU THINK I'D BE SITTING HERE WAITING FOR YOU IF I PLANNED ON POOPING ON YOUR PARTY?
THERE'S NO HIDING FROM ME.

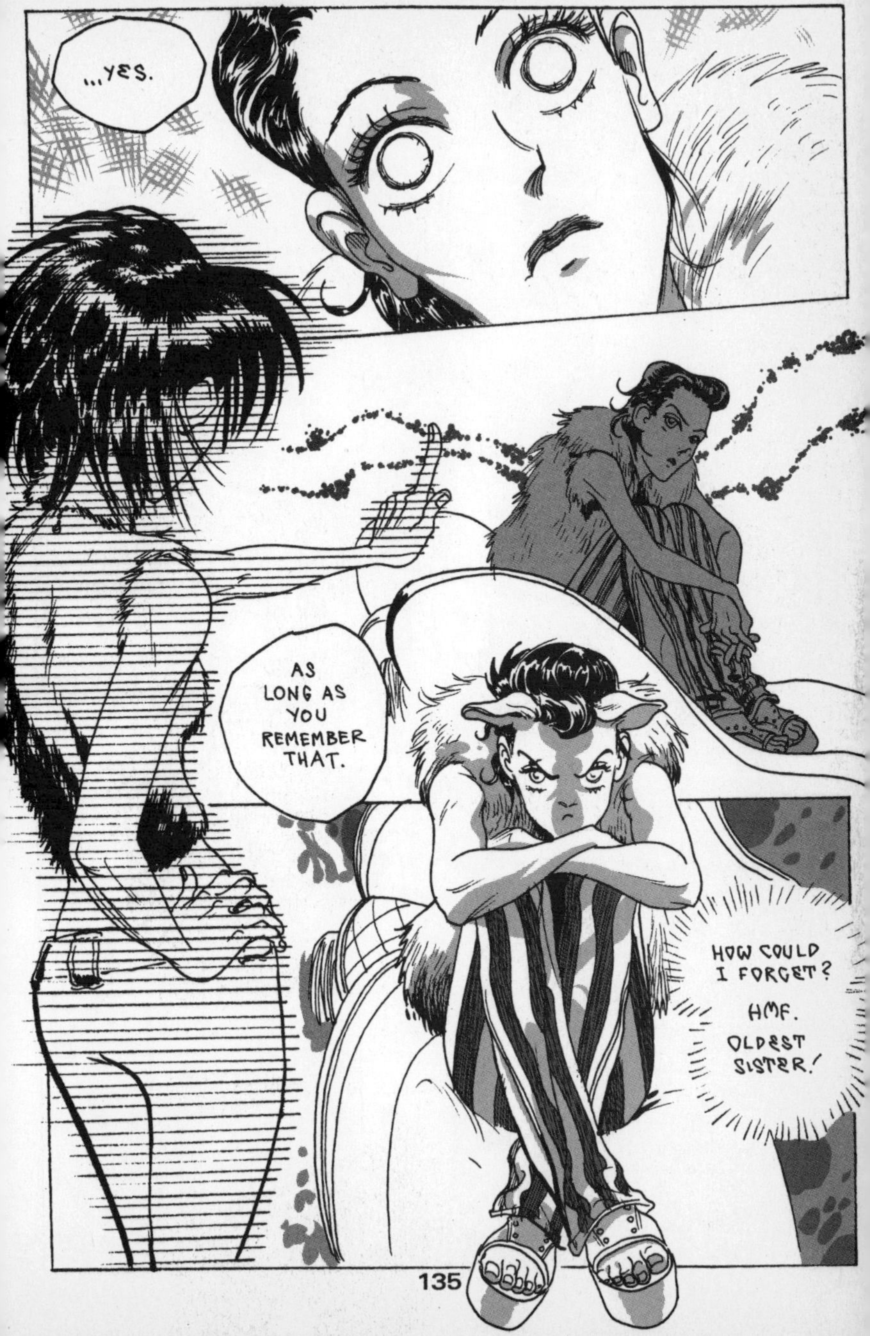
...YES.
AS LONG AS YOU REMEMBER THAT.
HOW COULD I FORGET? HMF. OLDEST SISTER!

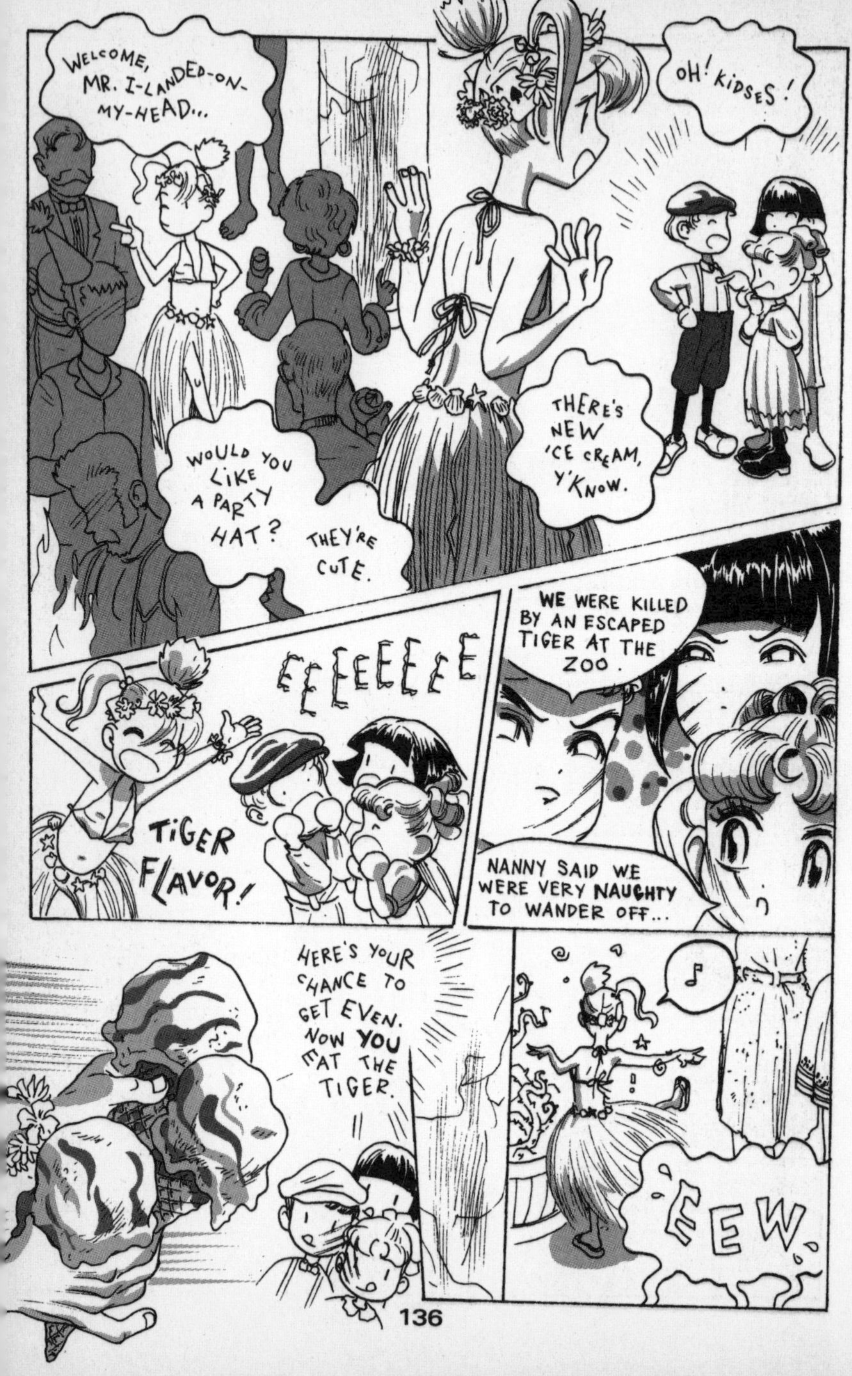

WELCOME, MR. I-LANDED-ON-MY-HEAD...
OH! KIDSES!
WOULD YOU LIKE A PARTY HAT?
THEY'RE CUTE.
THERE'S NEW ICE CREAM, Y'KNOW.
EEEEEEEE
TIGER FLAVOR!
WE WERE KILLED BY AN ESCAPED TIGER AT THE ZOO.
NANNY SAID WE WERE VERY NAUGHTY TO WANDER OFF...
HERE'S YOUR CHANCE TO GET EVEN. NOW YOU EAT THE TIGER.
EEW

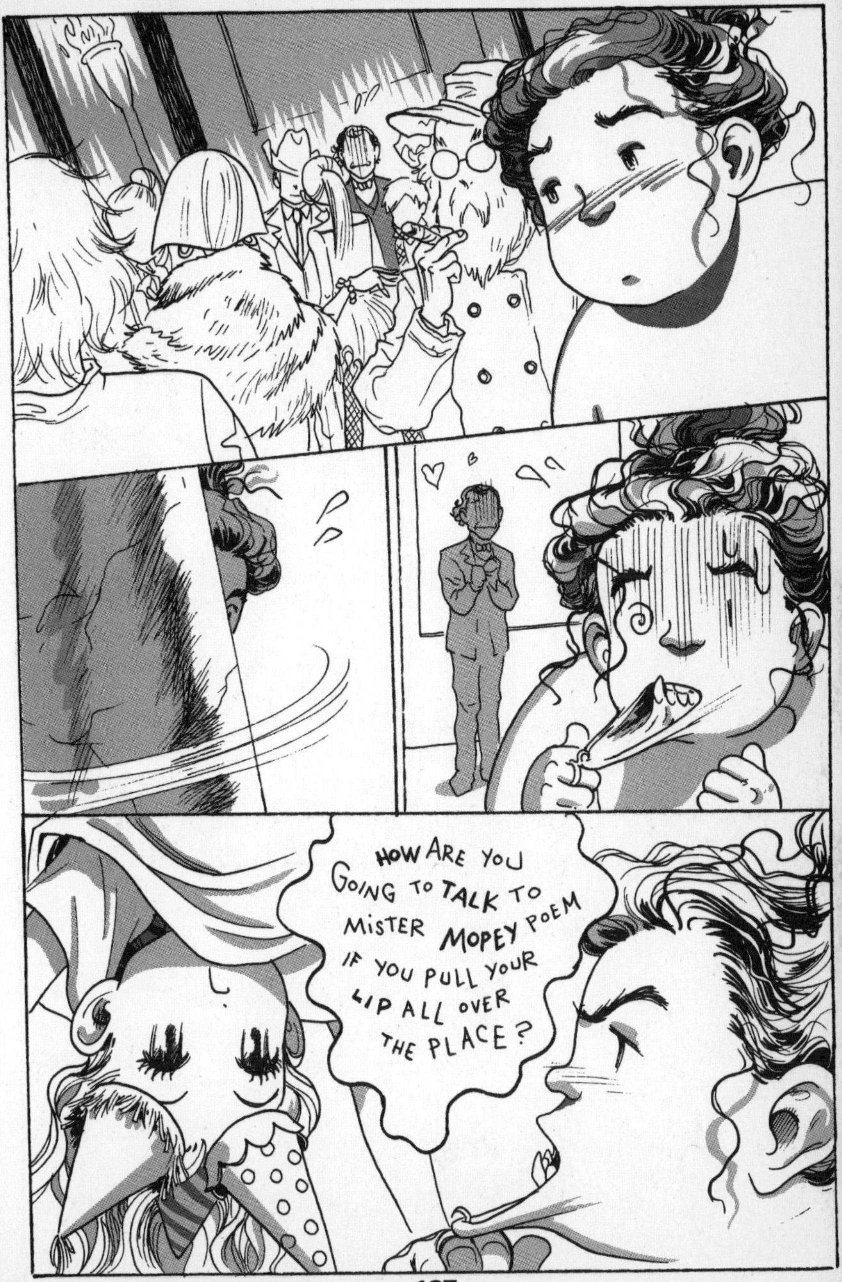
HOW ARE YOU GOING TO TALK TO MISTER MOPEY POEM IF YOU PULL YOUR LIP ALL OVER THE PLACE?

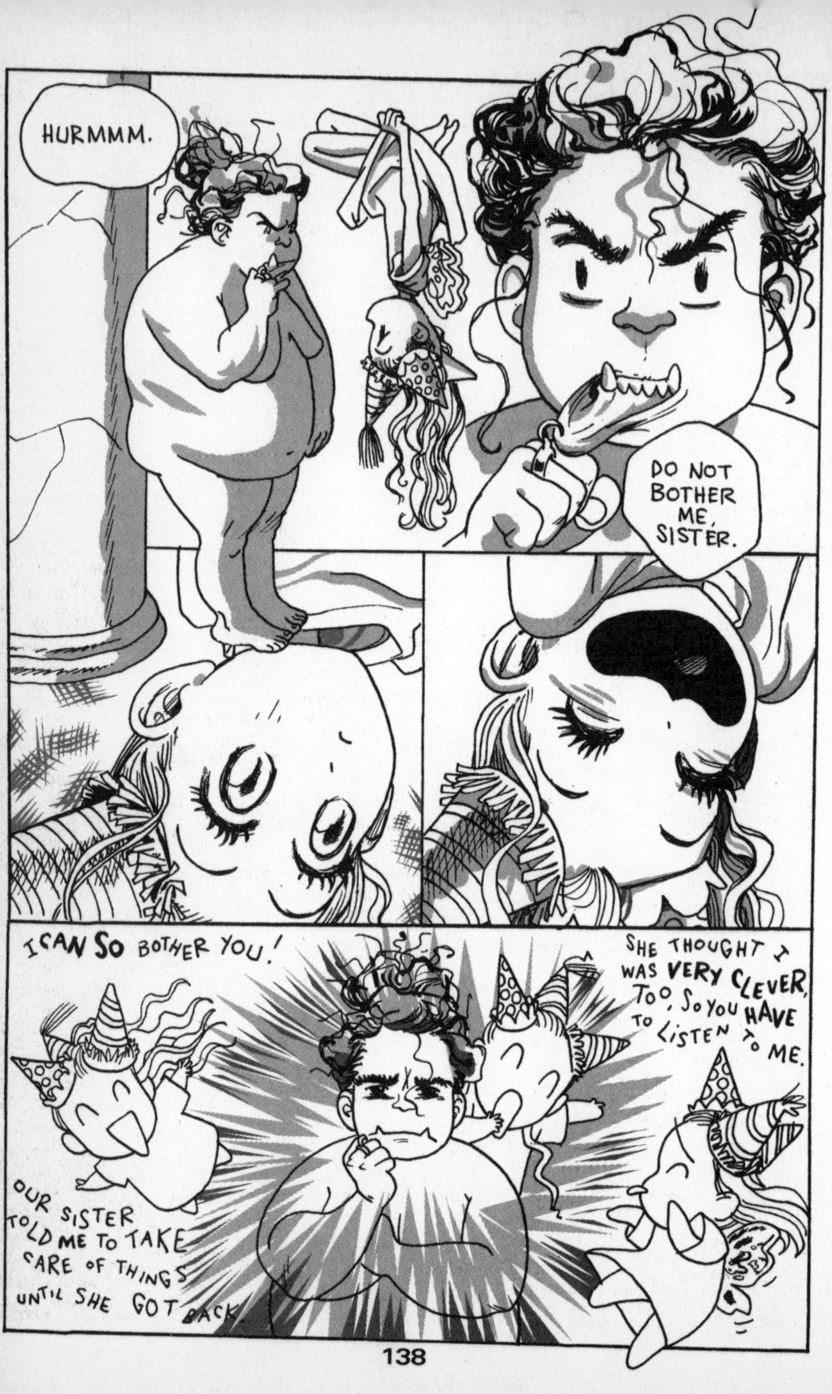
HURMMM.
DO NOT BOTHER ME, SISTER.
I CAN SO BOTHER YOU!
SHE THOUGHT I WAS VERY CLEVER, TOO, SO YOU HAVE TO LISTEN TO ME.
OUR SISTER TOLD ME TO TAKE CARE OF THINGS UNTIL SHE GOT BACK.

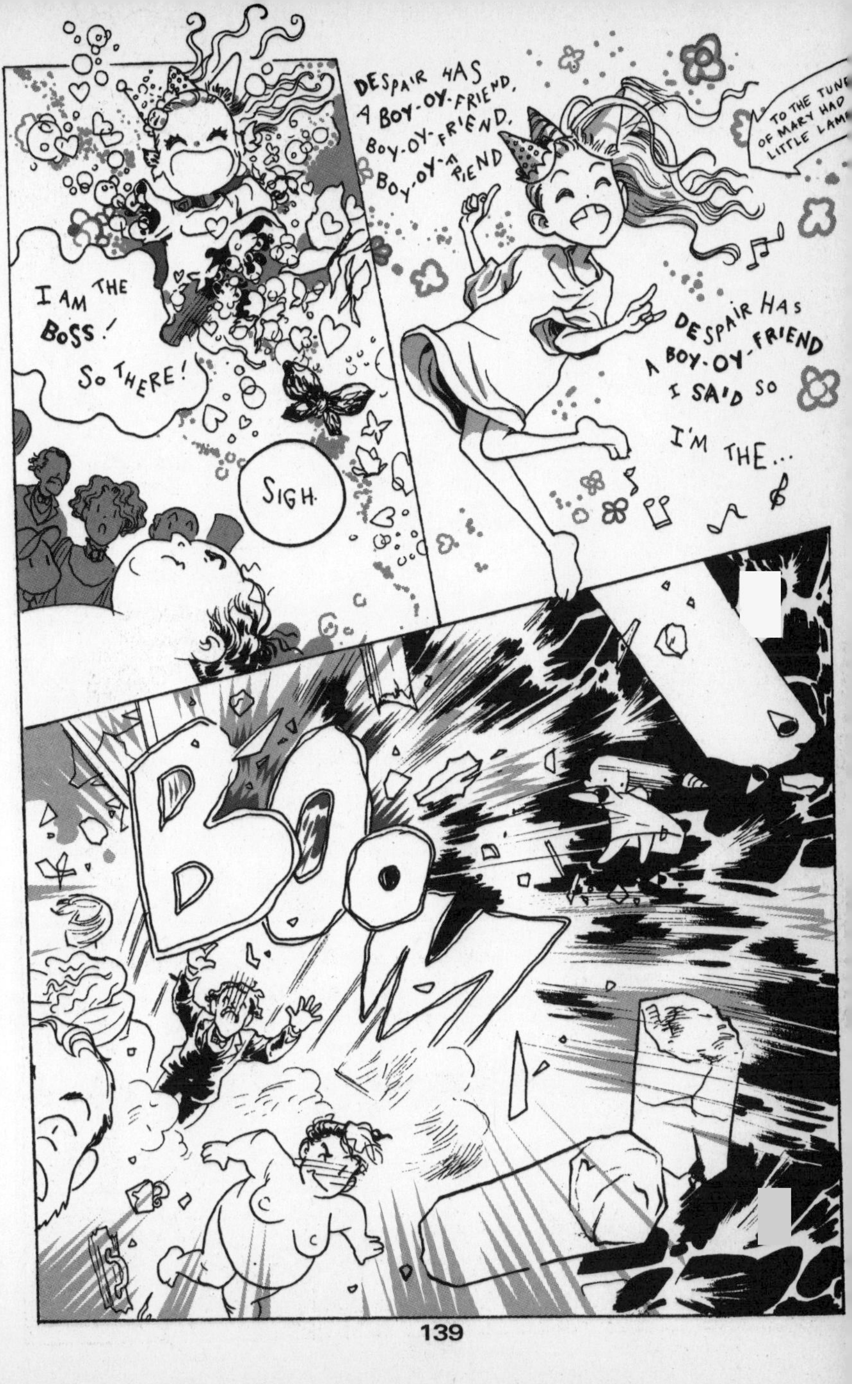
I AM THE BOSS! SO THERE!
SIGH.
DESPAIR HAS A BOY-OY-FRIEND, BOY-OY-FRIEND, BOY-OY-A FRIEND
TO THE TUN OF MARY HAD LITTLE LAM
DESPAIR HAS A BOY-OY-FRIEND I SAID SO
I'M THE...
BOOM

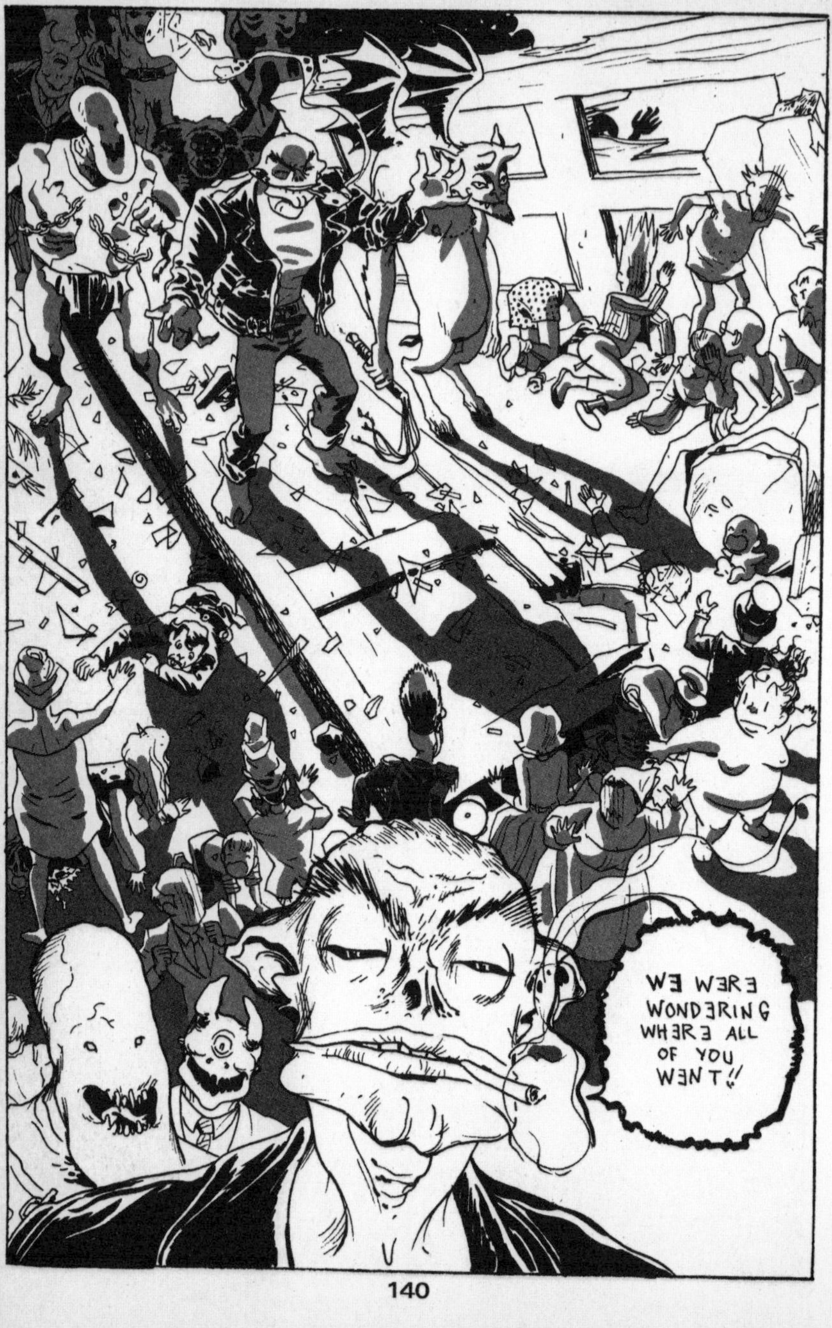
WE WERE WONDERING WHERE ALL OF YOU WENT!!

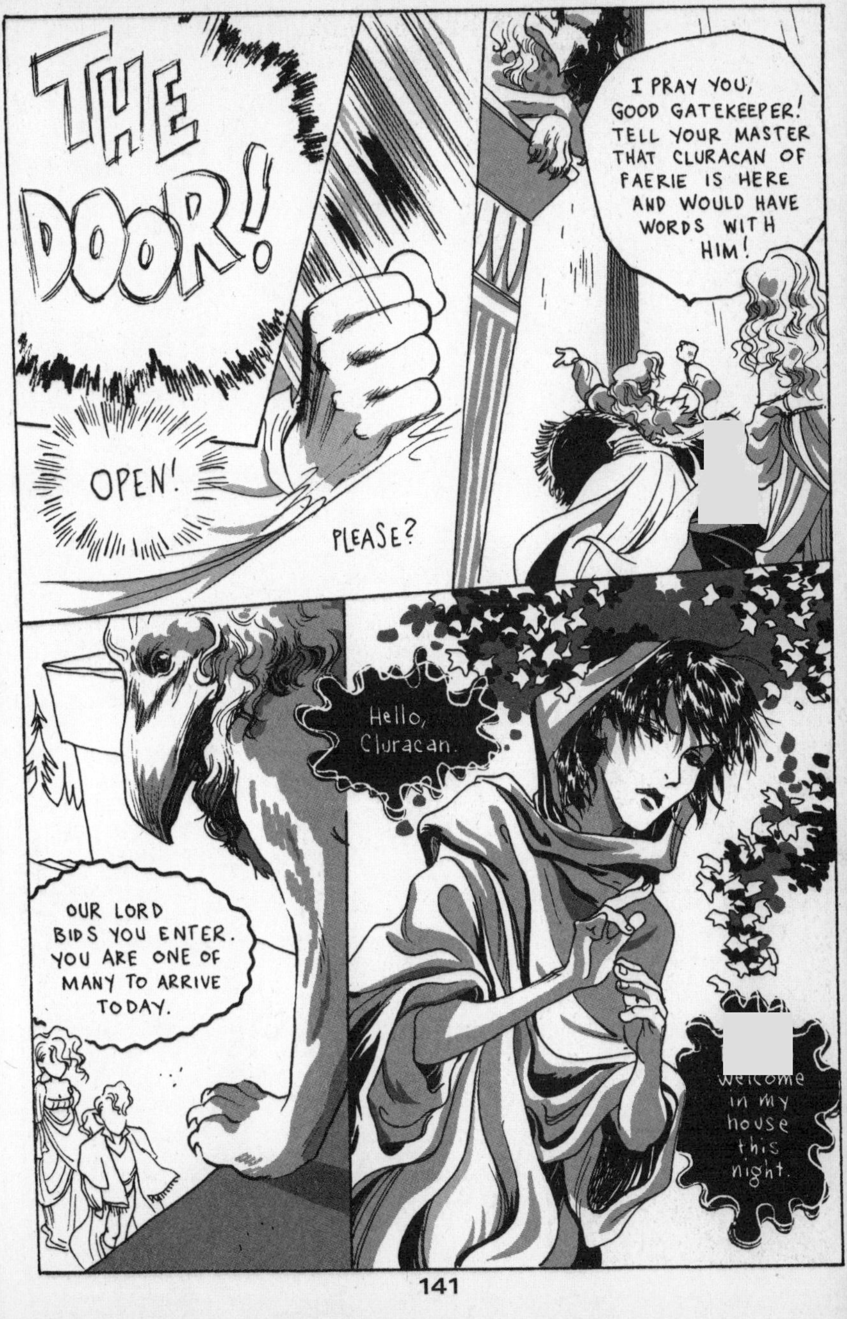
THE DOOR!
OPEN!
PLEASE?
I PRAY YOU, GOOD GATEKEEPER! TELL YOUR MASTER THAT CLURACAN OF FAERIE IS HERE AND WOULD HAVE WORDS WITH HIM!
OUR LORD BIDS YOU ENTER. YOU ARE ONE OF MANY TO ARRIVE TODAY.
Hello, Cluracan.
welcome in my house this night.

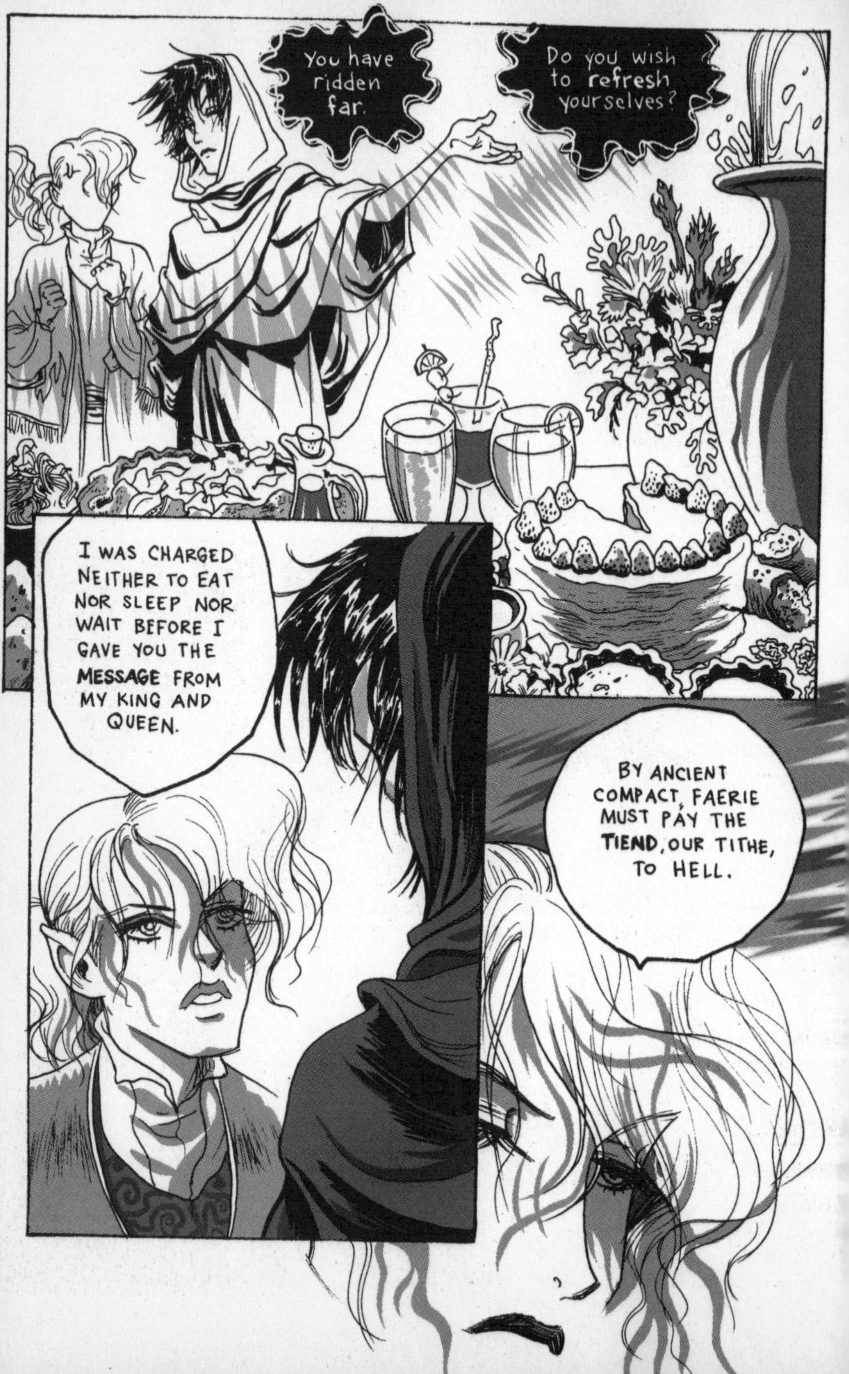
You have ridden far.
Do you wish to refresh yourselves?
I WAS CHARGED NEITHER TO EAT NOR SLEEP NOR WAIT BEFORE I GAVE YOU THE MESSAGE FROM MY KING AND QUEEN.
BY ANCIENT COMPACT, FAERIE MUST PAY THE TIEND, OUR TITHE, TO HELL.

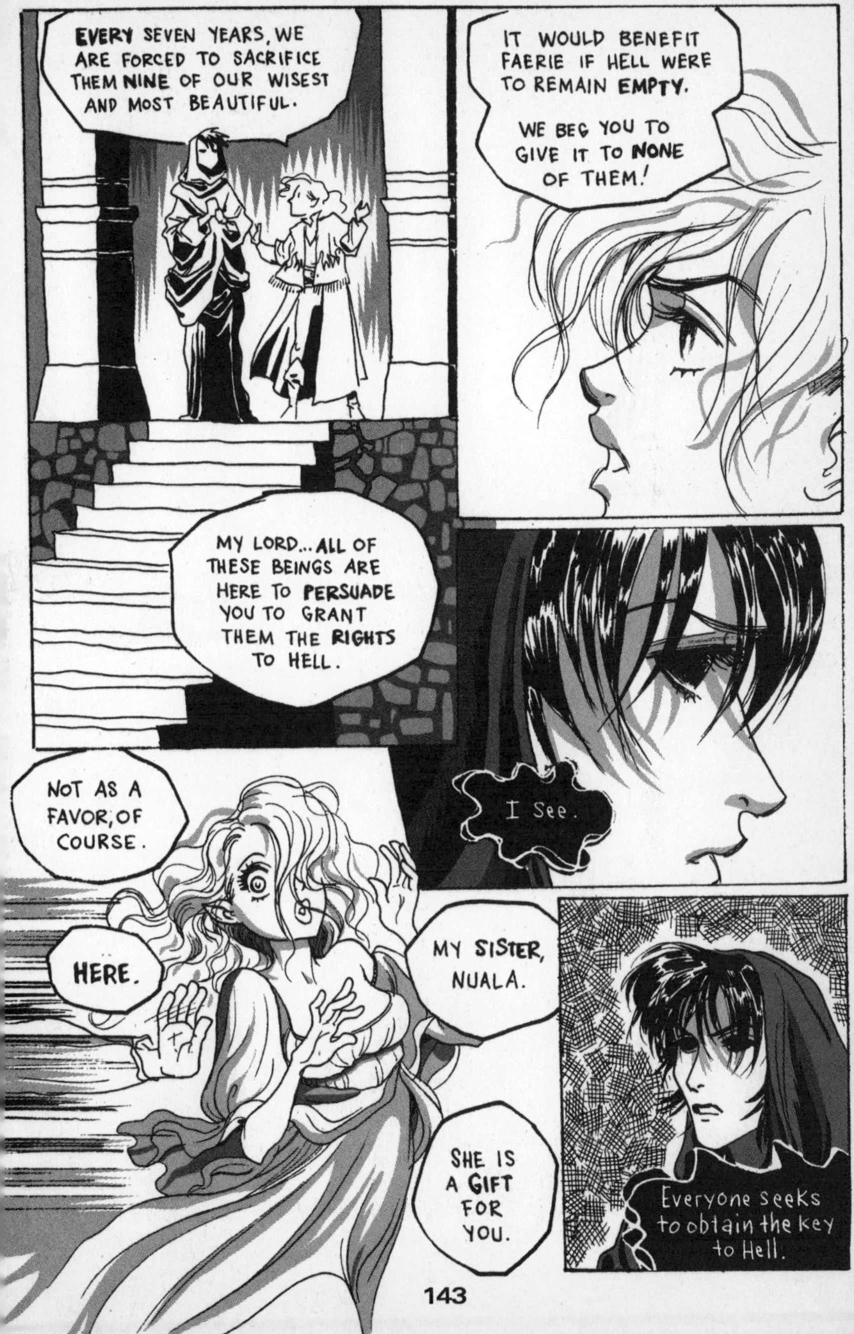
EVERY SEVEN YEARS, WE ARE FORCED TO SACRIFICE THEM NINE OF OUR WISEST AND MOST BEAUTIFUL.
IT WOULD BENEFIT FAERIE IF HELL WERE TO REMAIN EMPTY.
WE BEG YOU TO GIVE IT TO NONE OF THEM!
MY LORD... ALL OF THESE BEINGS ARE HERE TO PERSUADE YOU TO GRANT THEM THE RIGHTS TO HELL.
I See.
NOT AS A FAVOR, OF COURSE.
HERE.
MY SISTER, NUALA.
SHE IS A GIFT FOR YOU.
Everyone seeks to obtain the key to Hell.

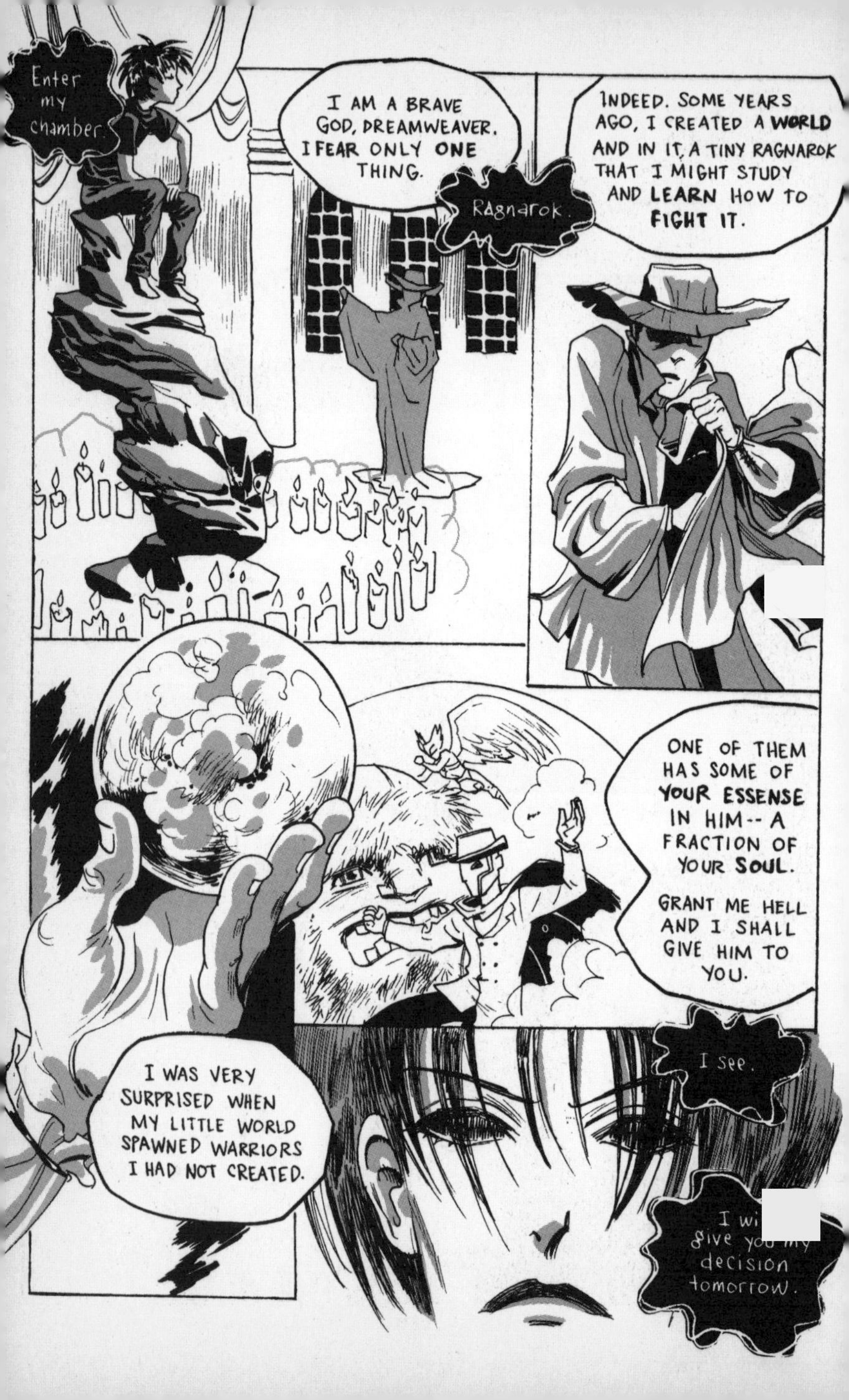
Enter my chamber.
I AM A BRAVE GOD, DREAMWEAVER. I FEAR ONLY ONE THING.
Ragnarok.
INDEED. SOME YEARS AGO, I CREATED A WORLD AND IN IT, A TINY RAGNAROK THAT I MIGHT STUDY AND LEARN HOW TO FIGHT IT.
ONE OF THEM HAS SOME OF YOUR ESSENSE IN HIM-- A FRACTION OF YOUR SOUL.
GRANT ME HELL AND I SHALL GIVE HIM TO YOU.
I WAS VERY SURPRISED WHEN MY LITTLE WORLD SPAWNED WARRIORS I HAD NOT CREATED.
I see.
I wi give you decision tomorrow.

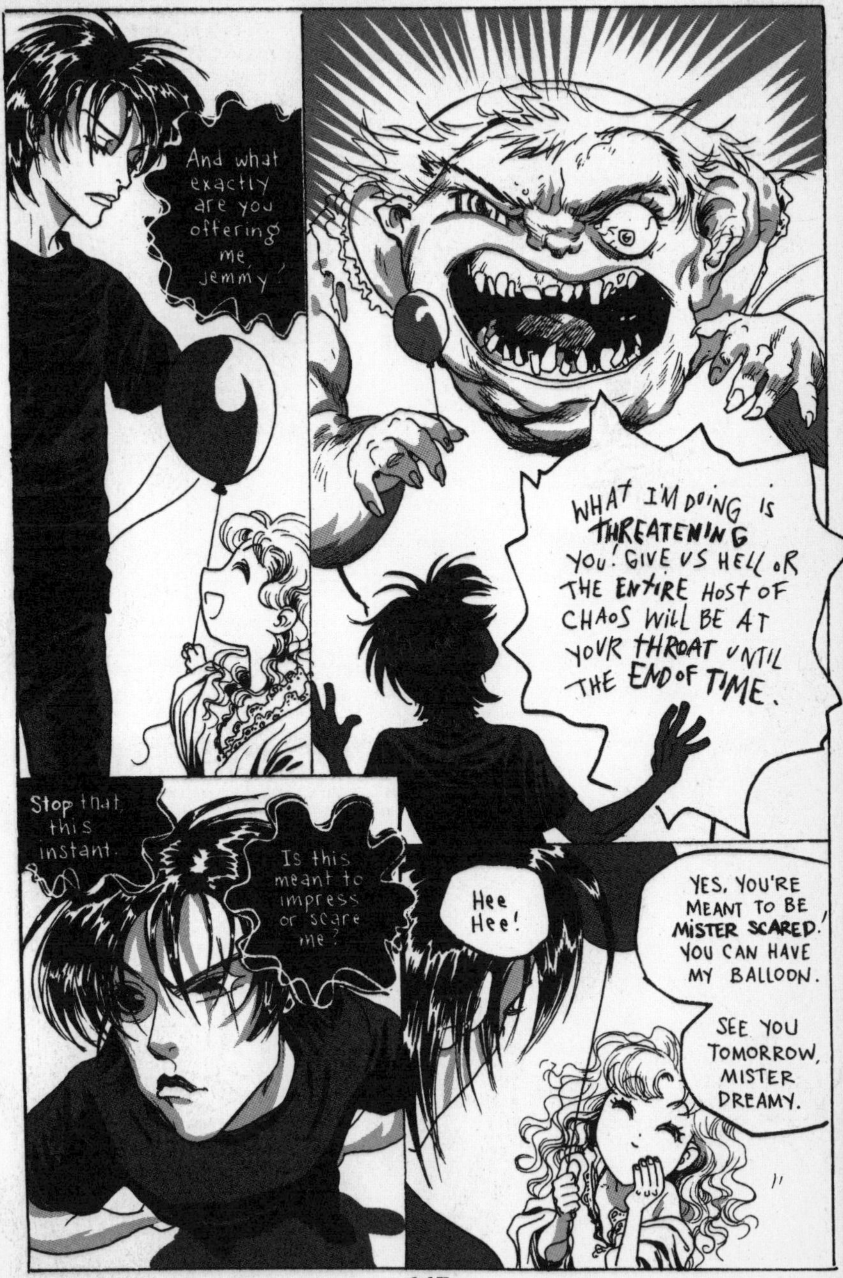
And what exactly are you offering me, jemmy?
WHAT I'M DOING IS THREATENING YOU! GIVE US HELL OR THE ENTIRE HOST OF CHAOS WILL BE AT YOUR THROAT UNTIL THE END OF TIME.
Stop that, this instant.
Is this meant to impress or scare me?
Hee Hee!
YES, YOU'RE MEANT TO BE MISTER SCARED! YOU CAN HAVE MY BALLOON.
SEE YOU TOMORROW, MISTER DREAMY.

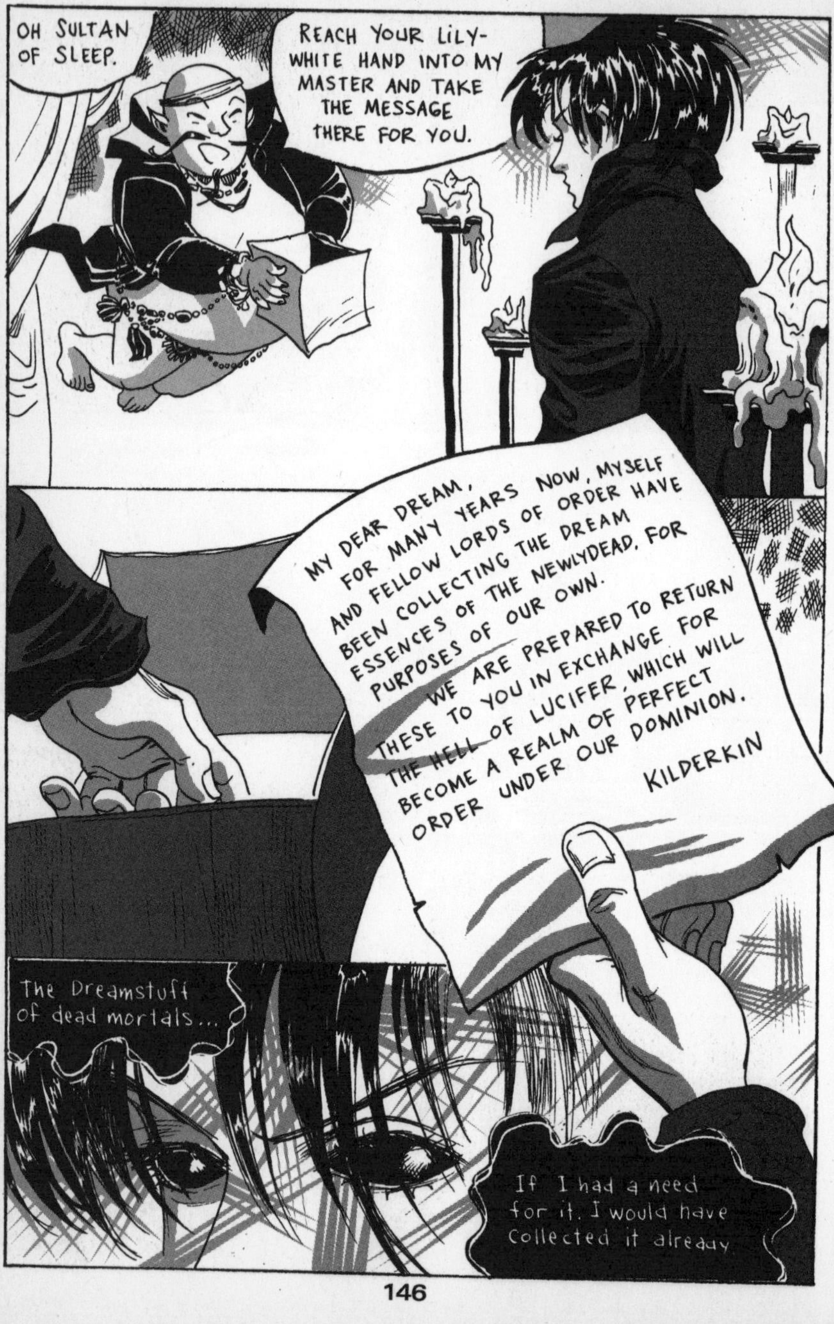
OH SULTAN OF SLEEP.
REACH YOUR LILY-WHITE HAND INTO MY MASTER AND TAKE THE MESSAGE THERE FOR YOU.
MY DEAR DREAM,
FOR MANY YEARS NOW, MYSELF AND FELLOW LORDS OF ORDER HAVE BEEN COLLECTING THE DREAM ESSENCES OF THE NEWLYDEAD, FOR PURPOSES OF OUR OWN.
WE ARE PREPARED TO RETURN THESE TO YOU IN EXCHANGE FOR THE HELL OF LUCIFER, WHICH WILL BECOME A REALM OF PERFECT ORDER UNDER OUR DOMINION.
KILDERKIN
The Dreamstuff of dead mortals...
If I had a need for it, I would have collected it already.

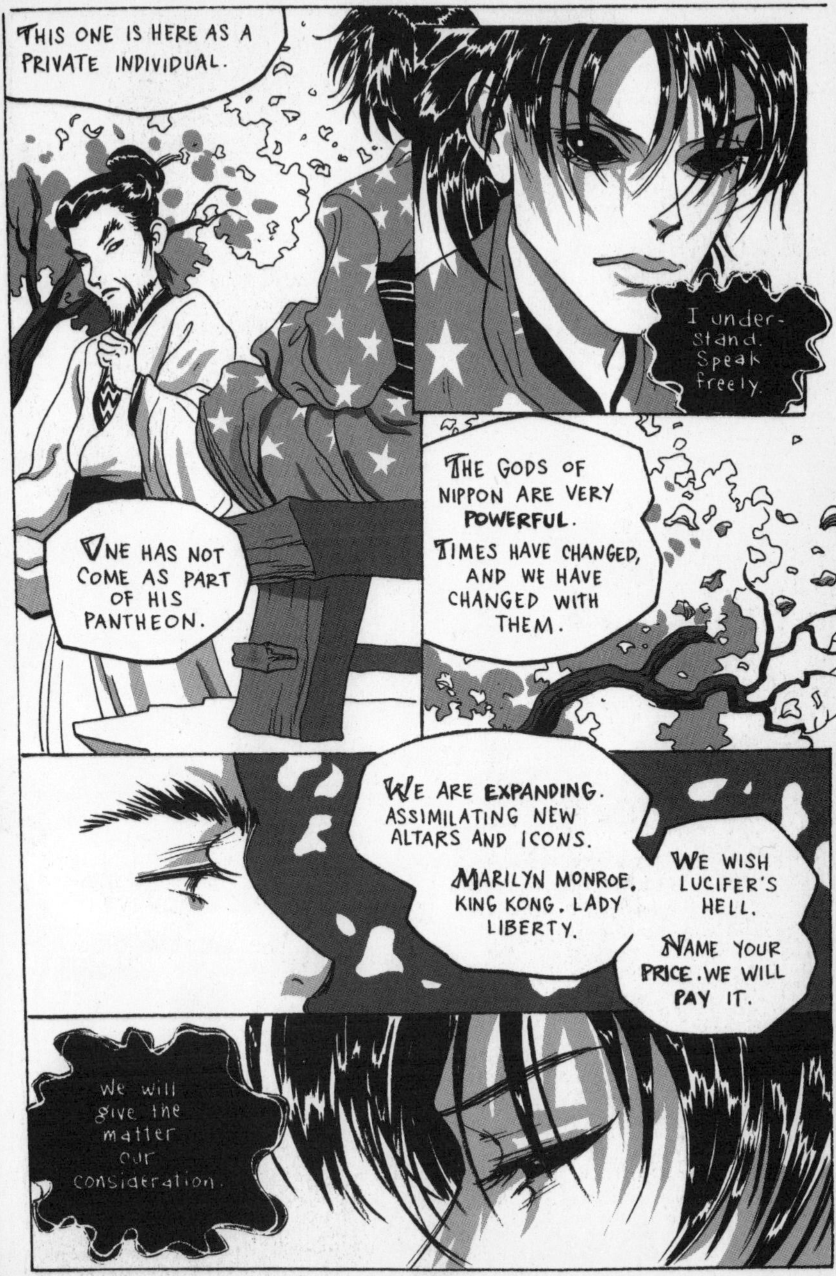
THIS ONE IS HERE AS A PRIVATE INDIVIDUAL.
I understand. Speak freely.
ONE HAS NOT COME AS PART OF HIS PANTHEON.
THE GODS OF NIPPON ARE VERY POWERFUL.
TIMES HAVE CHANGED, AND WE HAVE CHANGED WITH THEM.
WE ARE EXPANDING. ASSIMILATING NEW ALTARS AND ICONS.
MARILYN MONROE. KING KONG. LADY LIBERTY.
WE WISH LUCIFER'S HELL.
NAME YOUR PRICE. WE WILL PAY IT.
We will give the matter our consideration.

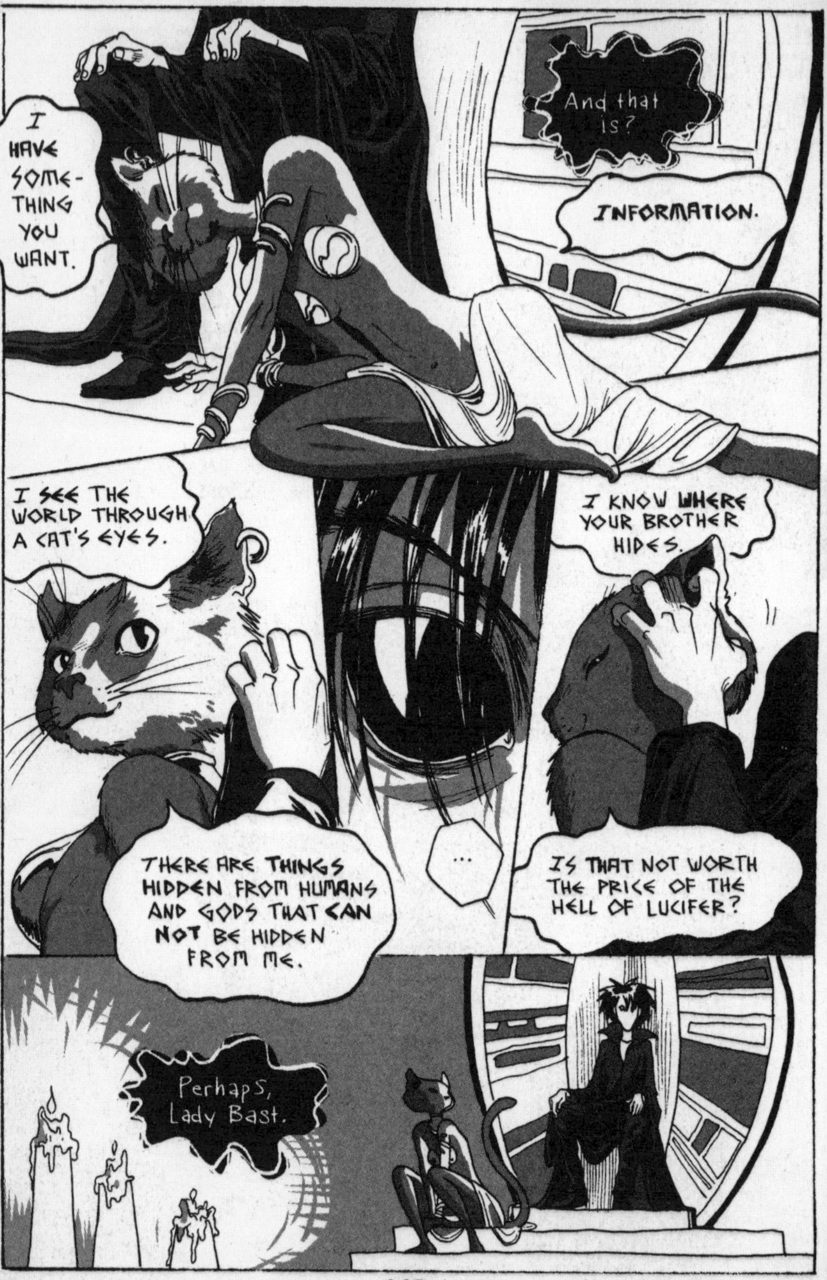
I HAVE SOMETHING YOU WANT.
And that is?
INFORMATION.
I SEE THE WORLD THROUGH A CAT'S EYES.
THERE ARE THINGS HIDDEN FROM HUMANS AND GODS THAT CAN NOT BE HIDDEN FROM ME.
...
I KNOW WHERE YOUR BROTHER HIDES.
IS THAT NOT WORTH THE PRICE OF THE HELL OF LUCIFER?
Perhaps, Lady Bast.

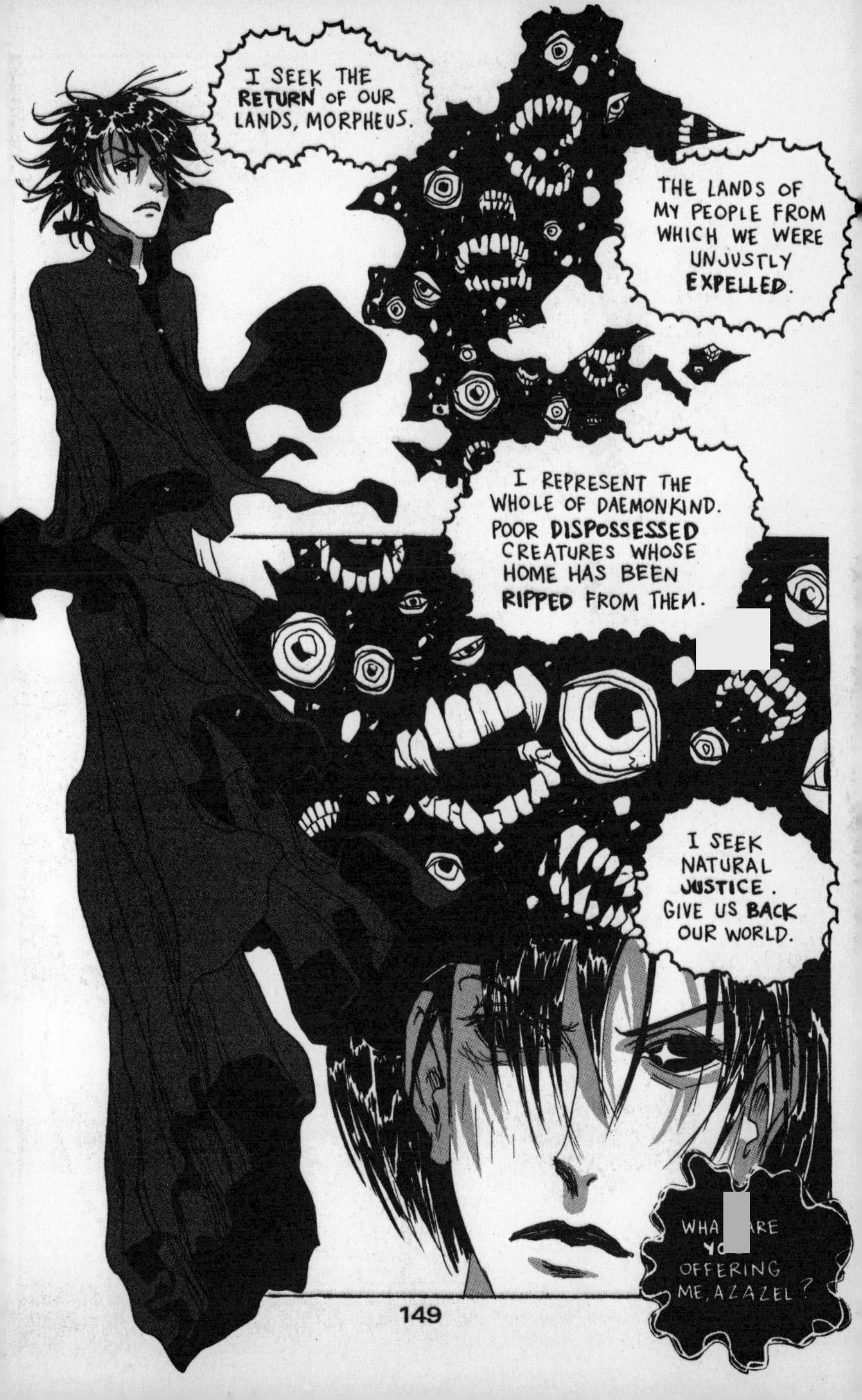
I SEEK THE RETURN OF OUR LANDS, MORPHEUS.
THE LANDS OF MY PEOPLE FROM WHICH WE WERE UNJUSTLY EXPELLED.
I REPRESENT THE WHOLE OF DAEMONKIND. POOR DISPOSSESSED CREATURES WHOSE HOME HAS BEEN RIPPED FROM THEM.
I SEEK NATURAL JUSTICE. GIVE US BACK OUR WORLD.
WHA ARE YO OFFERING ME, AZAZEL?

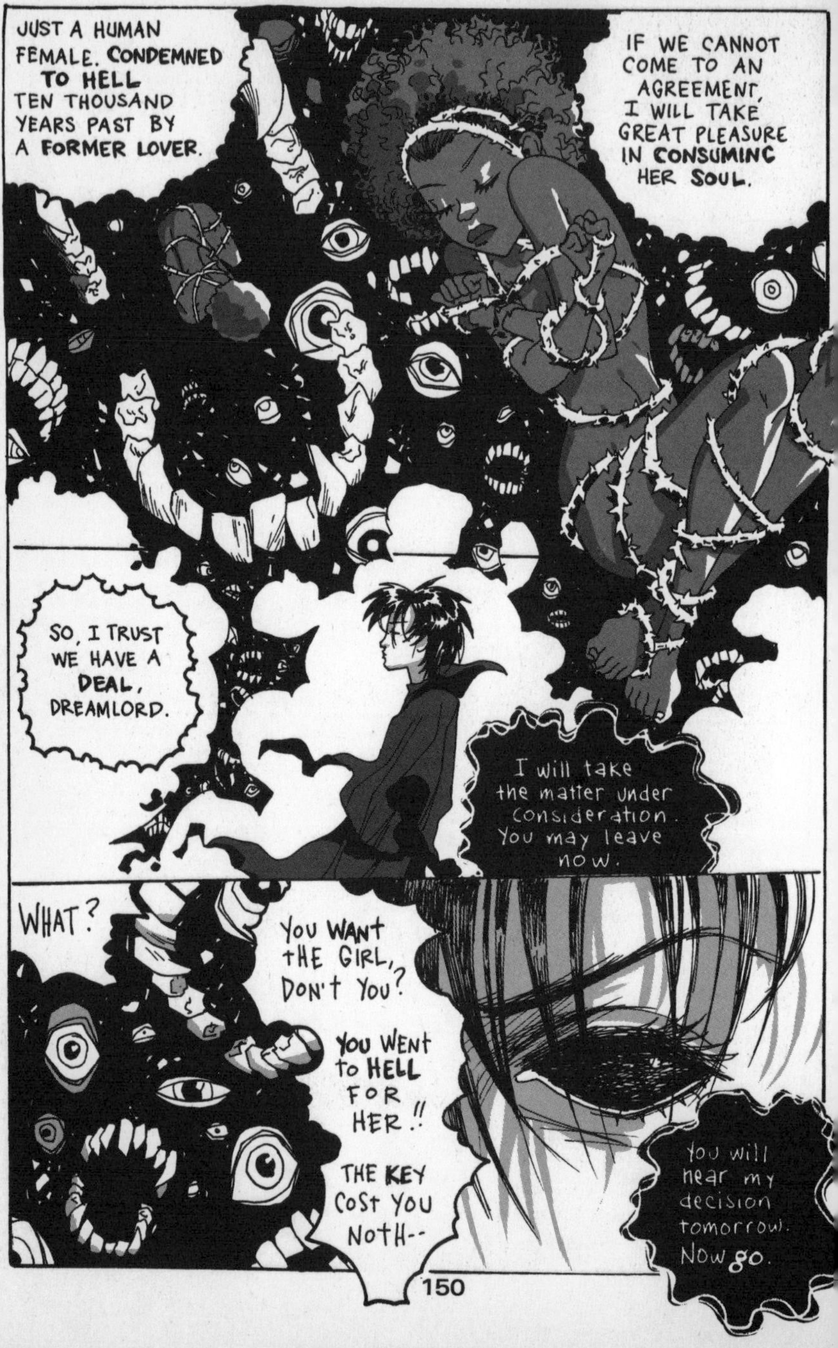
JUST A HUMAN FEMALE. CONDEMNED TO HELL TEN THOUSAND YEARS PAST BY A FORMER LOVER.
IF WE CANNOT COME TO AN AGREEMENT, I WILL TAKE GREAT PLEASURE IN CONSUMING HER SOUL.
SO, I TRUST WE HAVE A DEAL, DREAMLORD.
I will take the matter under consideration. You may leave now.
WHAT?
YOU WANT THE GIRL, DON'T YOU?
YOU WENT to HELL FOR HER!!
THE KEY COST YOU NOTH--
You will hear my decision tomorrow. Now go.

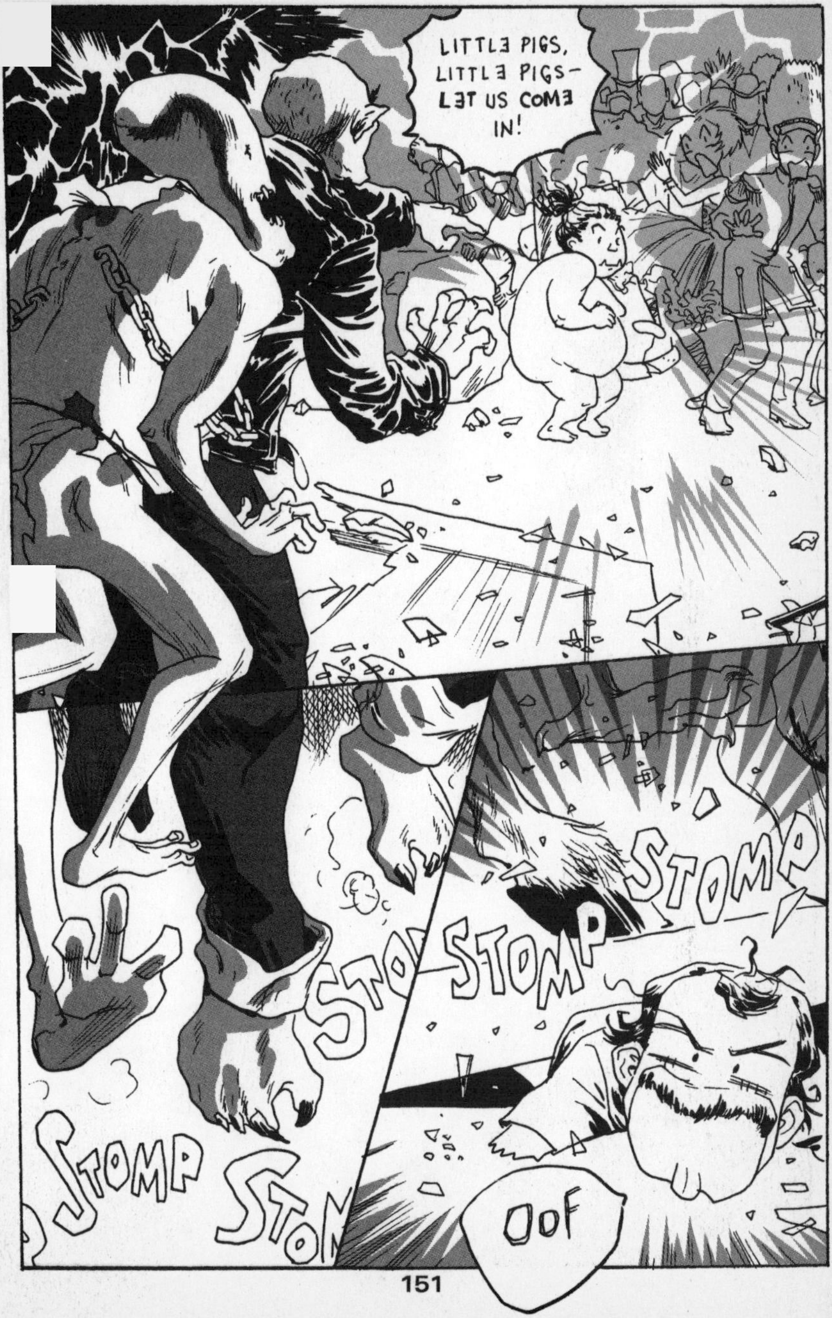
LITTLE PIGS, LITTLE PIGS- LET US COME IN!
STOMP
STOMP
STOMP
STOMP
STOM
STOM
OOF

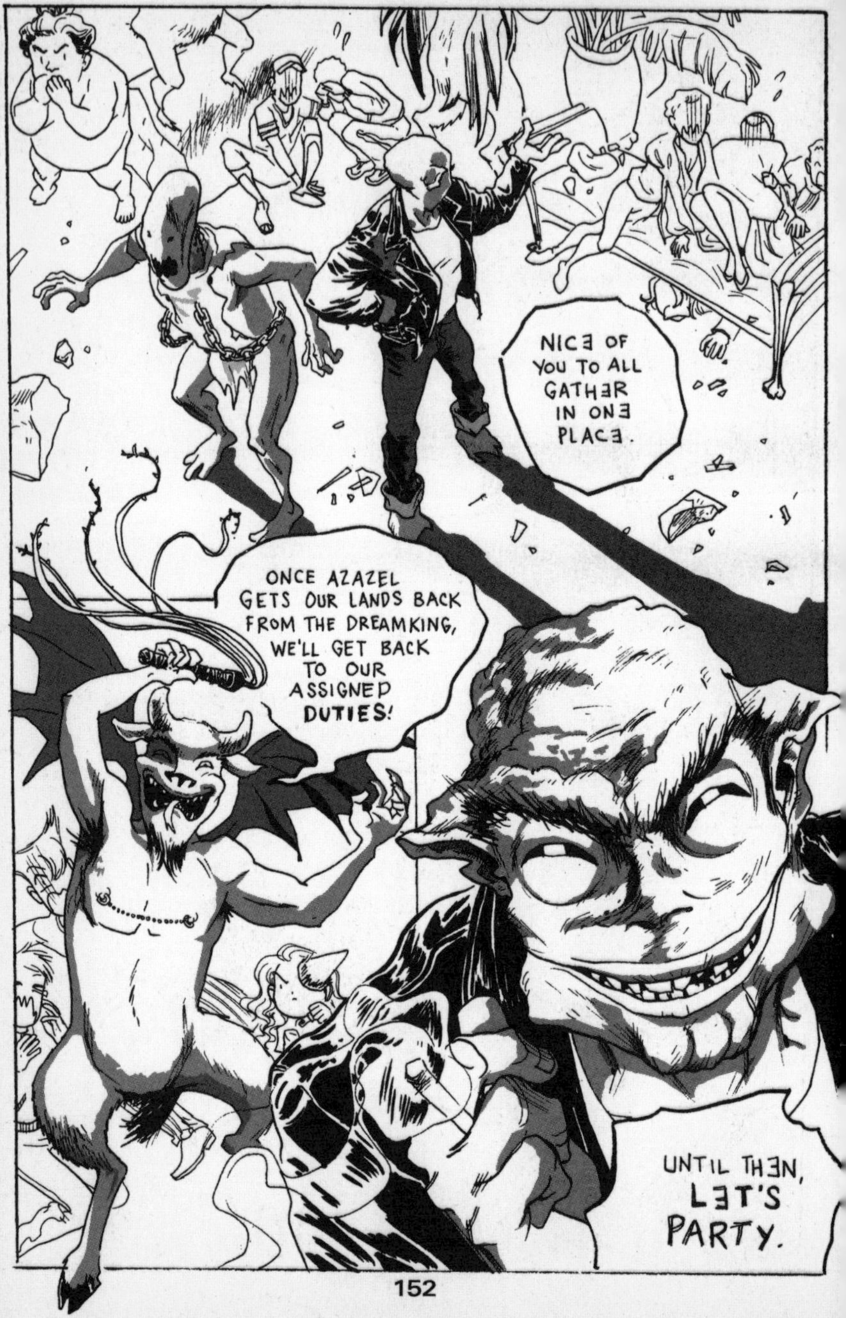
NICE OF YOU TO ALL GATHER IN ONE PLACE.
ONCE AZAZEL GETS OUR LANDS BACK FROM THE DREAMKING, WE'LL GET BACK TO OUR ASSIGNED DUTIES!
UNTIL THEN, LET'S PARTY.

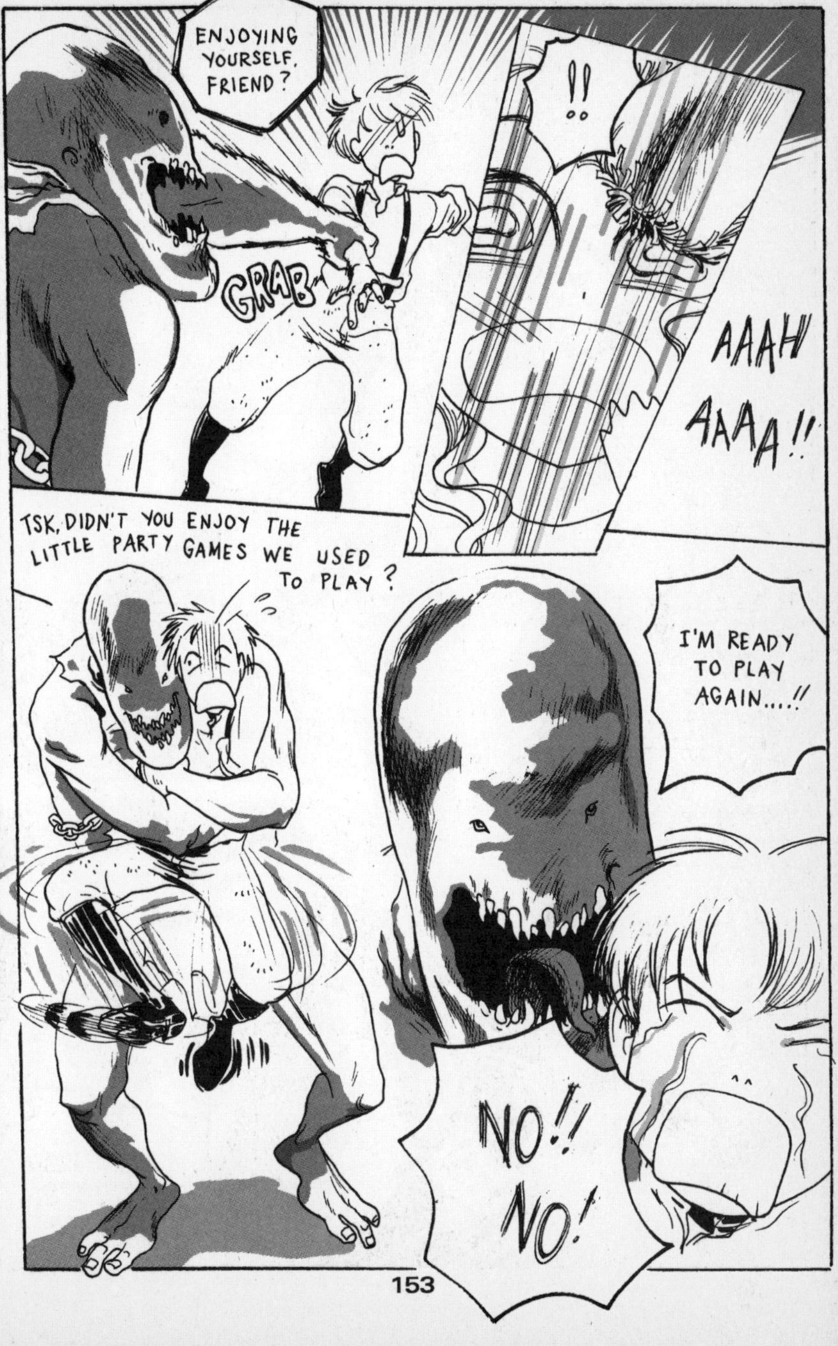
ENJOYING YOURSELF, FRIEND?
GRAB
!!
AAAH AAAA!!
TSK, DIDN'T YOU ENJOY THE LITTLE PARTY GAMES WE USED TO PLAY?
I'M READY TO PLAY AGAIN....!!
NO!! NO!

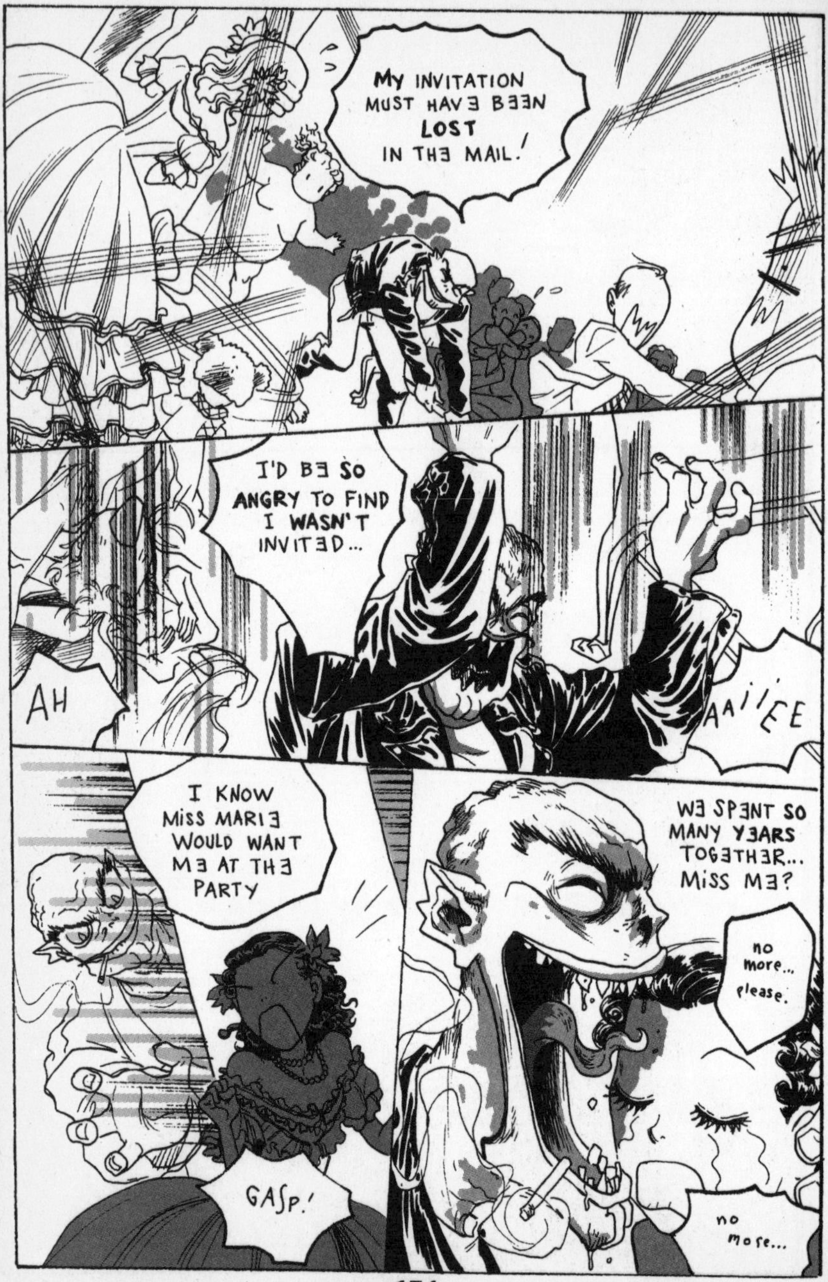
MY INVITATION MUST HAVE BEEN LOST IN THE MAIL!
I'D BE SO ANGRY TO FIND I WASN'T INVITED...
AH
AAIIEE
I KNOW MISS MARIE WOULD WANT ME AT THE PARTY
GASP!
WE SPENT SO MANY YEARS TOGETHER... MISS ME?
no more... please.
no more...

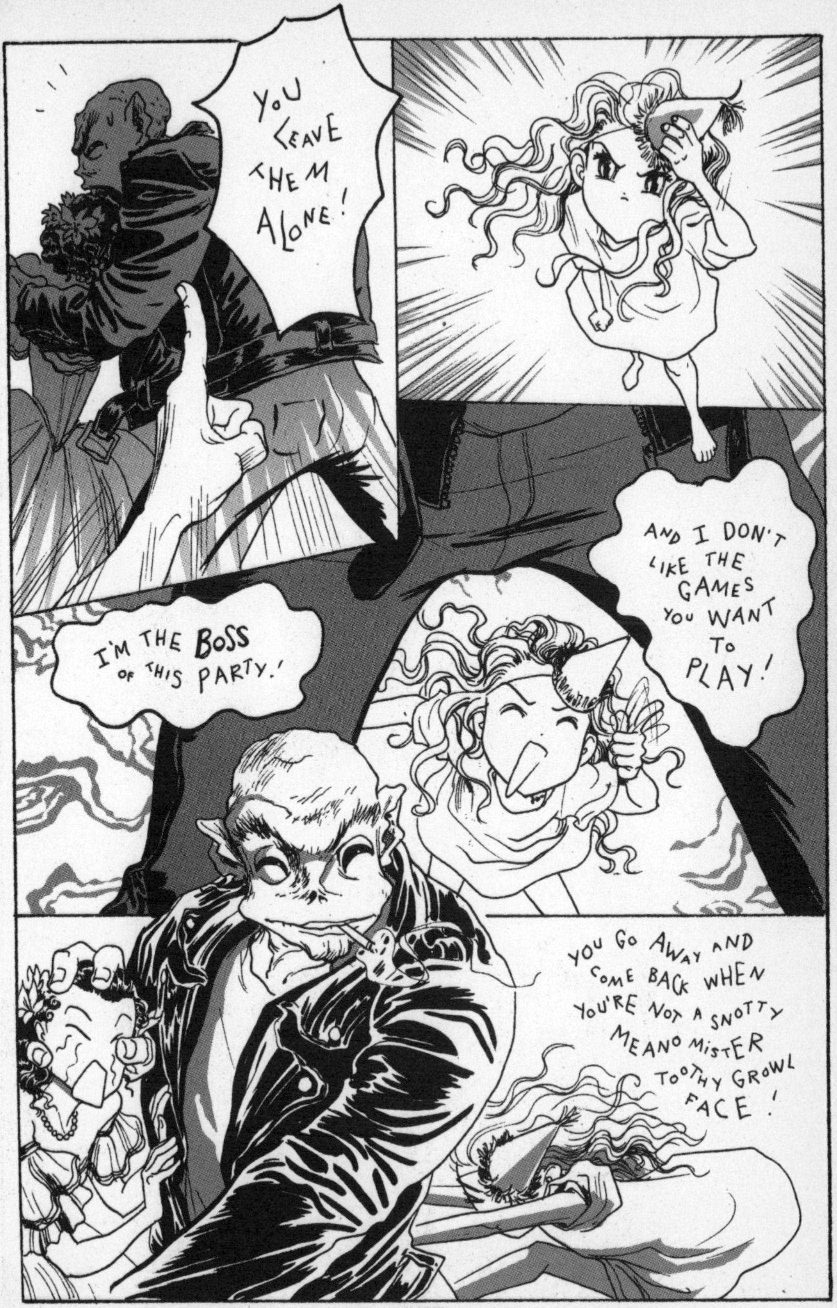
YOU LEAVE THEM ALONE!
AND I DON'T LIKE THE GAMES YOU WANT TO PLAY!
I'M THE BOSS OF THIS PARTY!
YOU GO AWAY AND COME BACK WHEN YOU'RE NOT A SNOTTY MEANO MISTER TOOTHY GROWL FACE!

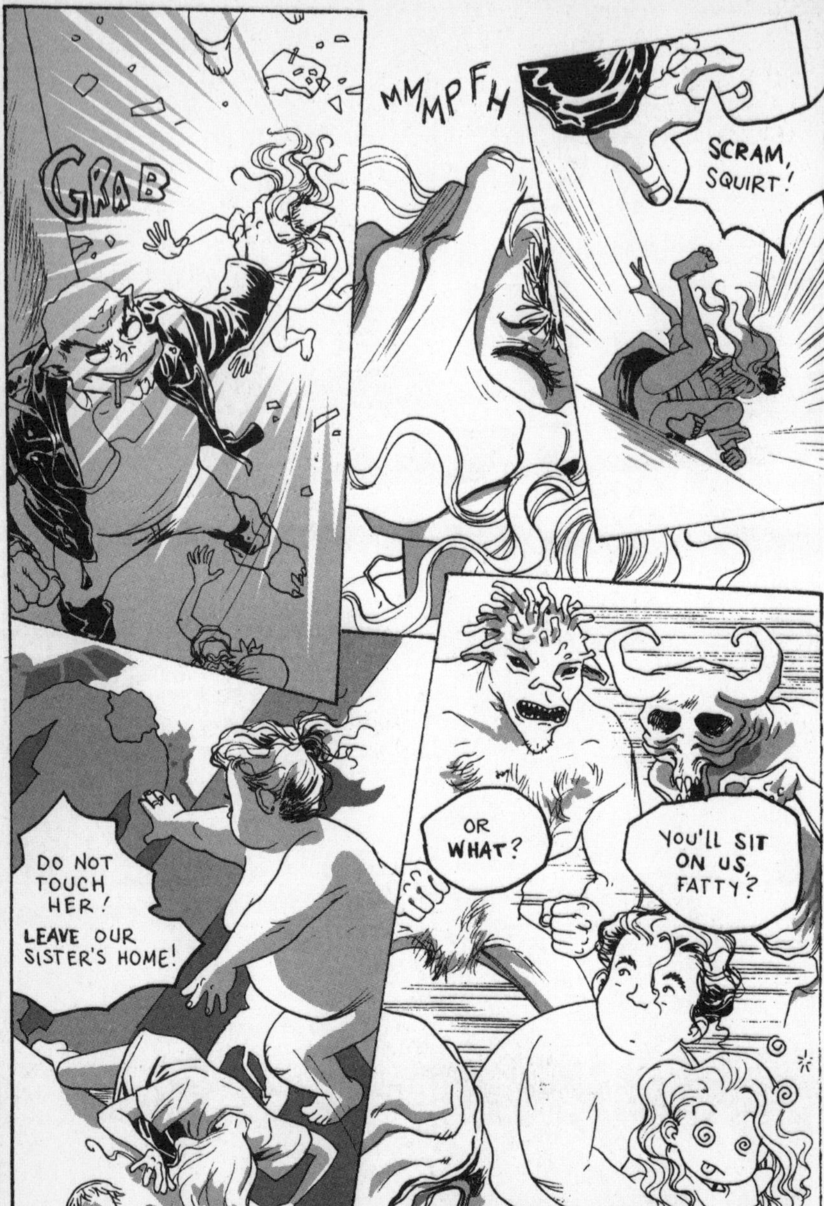
GRAB
MMMPFH
SCRAM, SQUIRT!
DO NOT TOUCH HER!
LEAVE OUR SISTER'S HOME!
OR WHAT?
YOU'LL SIT ON US, FATTY?

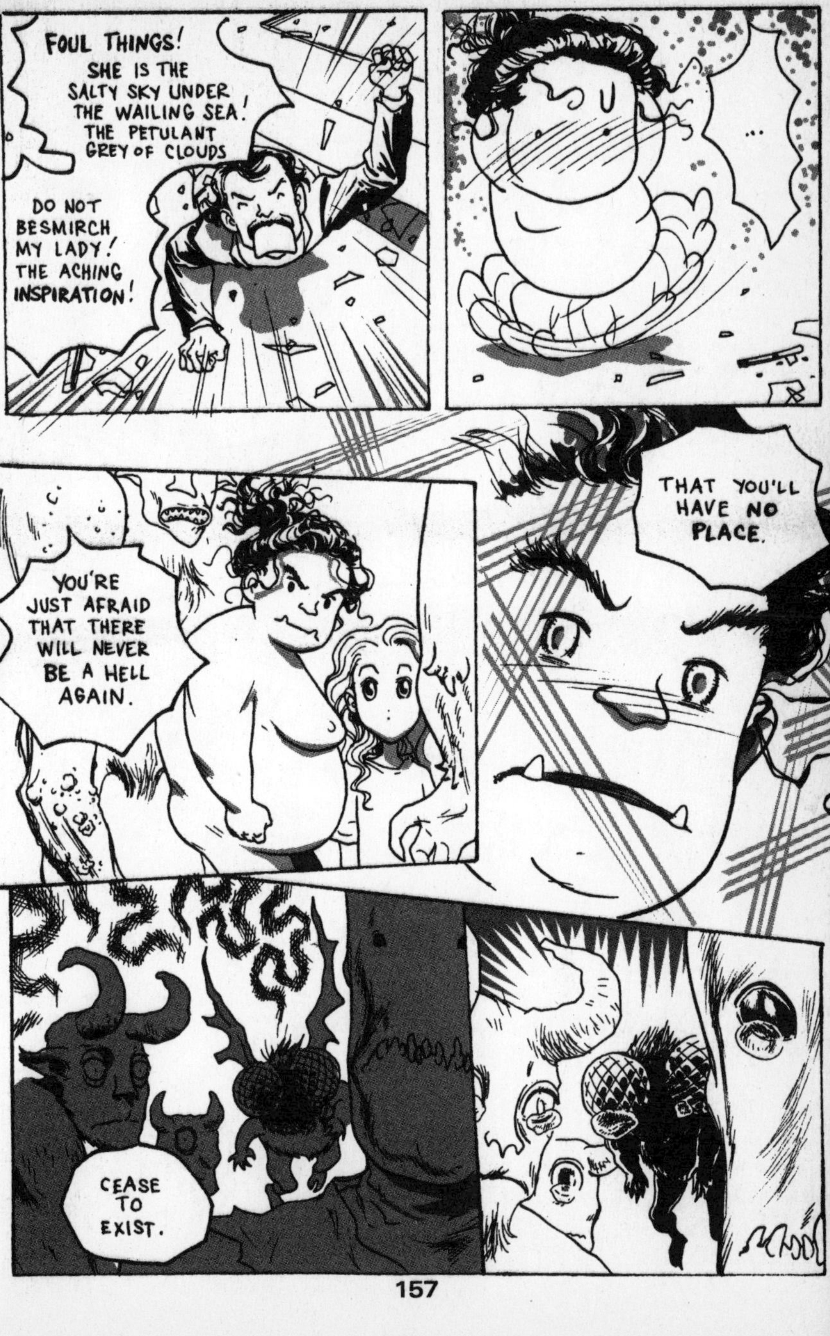
FOUL THINGS! SHE IS THE SALTY SKY UNDER THE WAILING SEA! THE PETULANT GREY OF CLOUDS
DO NOT BESMIRCH MY LADY! THE ACHING INSPIRATION!
...
YOU'RE JUST AFRAID THAT THERE WILL NEVER BE A HELL AGAIN.
THAT YOU'LL HAVE NO PLACE.
CEASE TO EXIST.

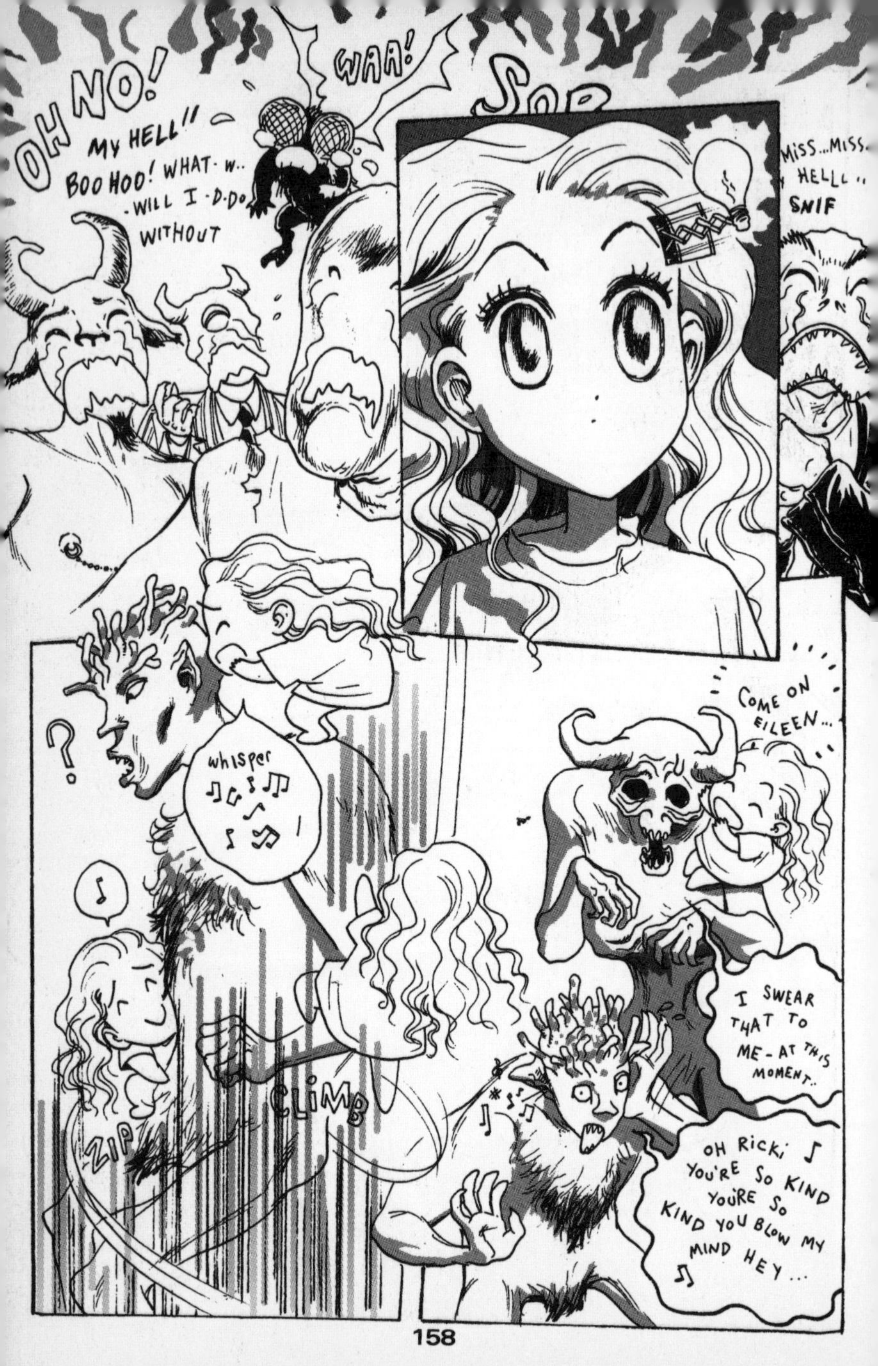
OH NO!
MY HELL"
BOO HOO! WHAT- W.. -WILL I -D-DO WITHOUT
WAA!
SOB
MISS...MISS HELLL.. SNIF
?
whisper
COME ON EILEEN...
I SWEAR THAT TO ME- AT THIS MOMENT..
ZIP
CLIMB
OH RICKI YOU'RE SO KIND YOU'RE SO KIND YOU BLOW MY MIND HEY...

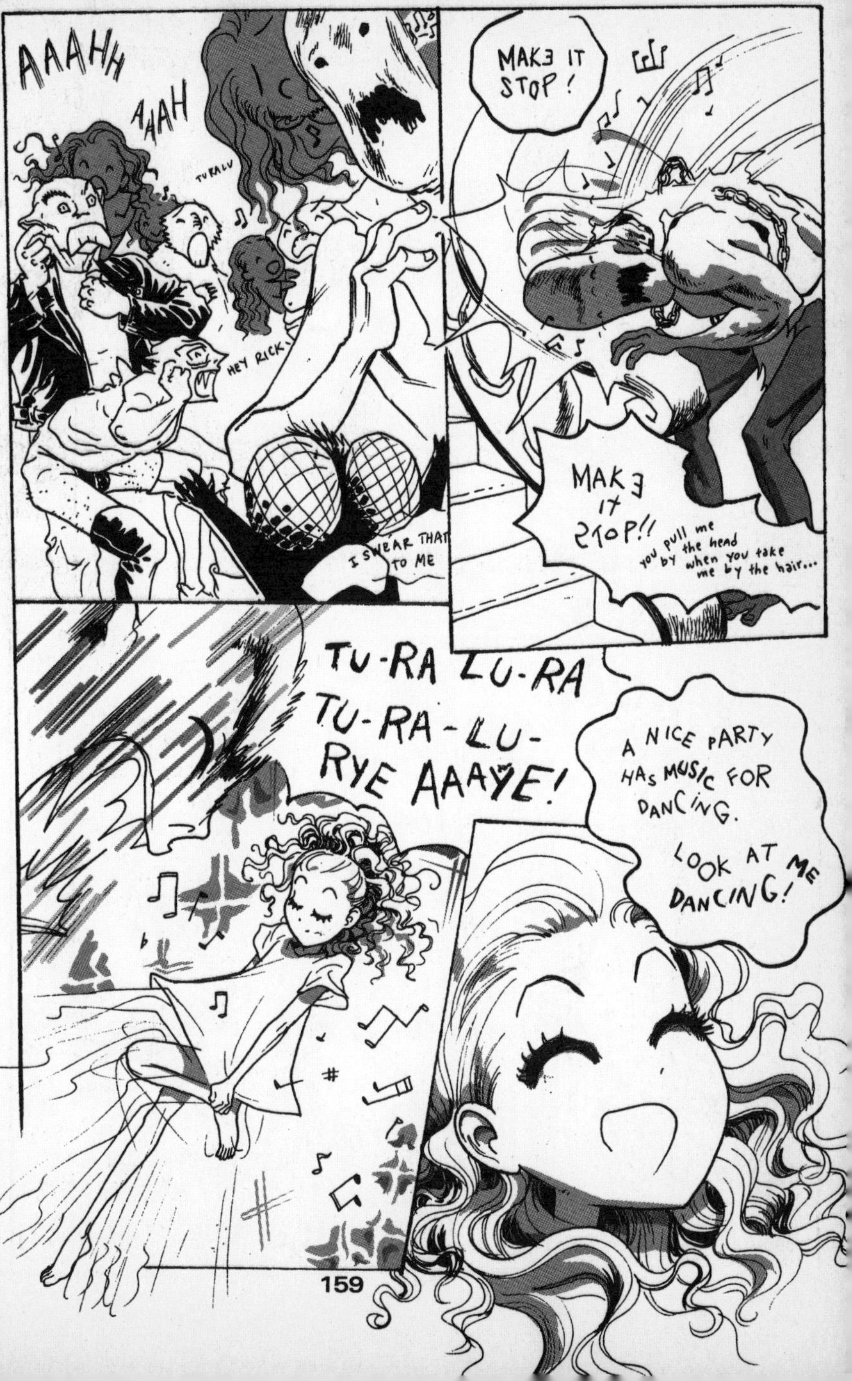
AAAHH
AAAH
TURALU
HEY RICK
I SWEAR THAT TO ME
MAKE IT STOP!
MAKE IT STOP!!
you pull me by the head when you take me by the hair...
TU-RA LU-RA TU-RA-LU-RYE AAAYE!
A NICE PARTY HAS MUSIC FOR DANCING.
LOOK AT ME DANCING!

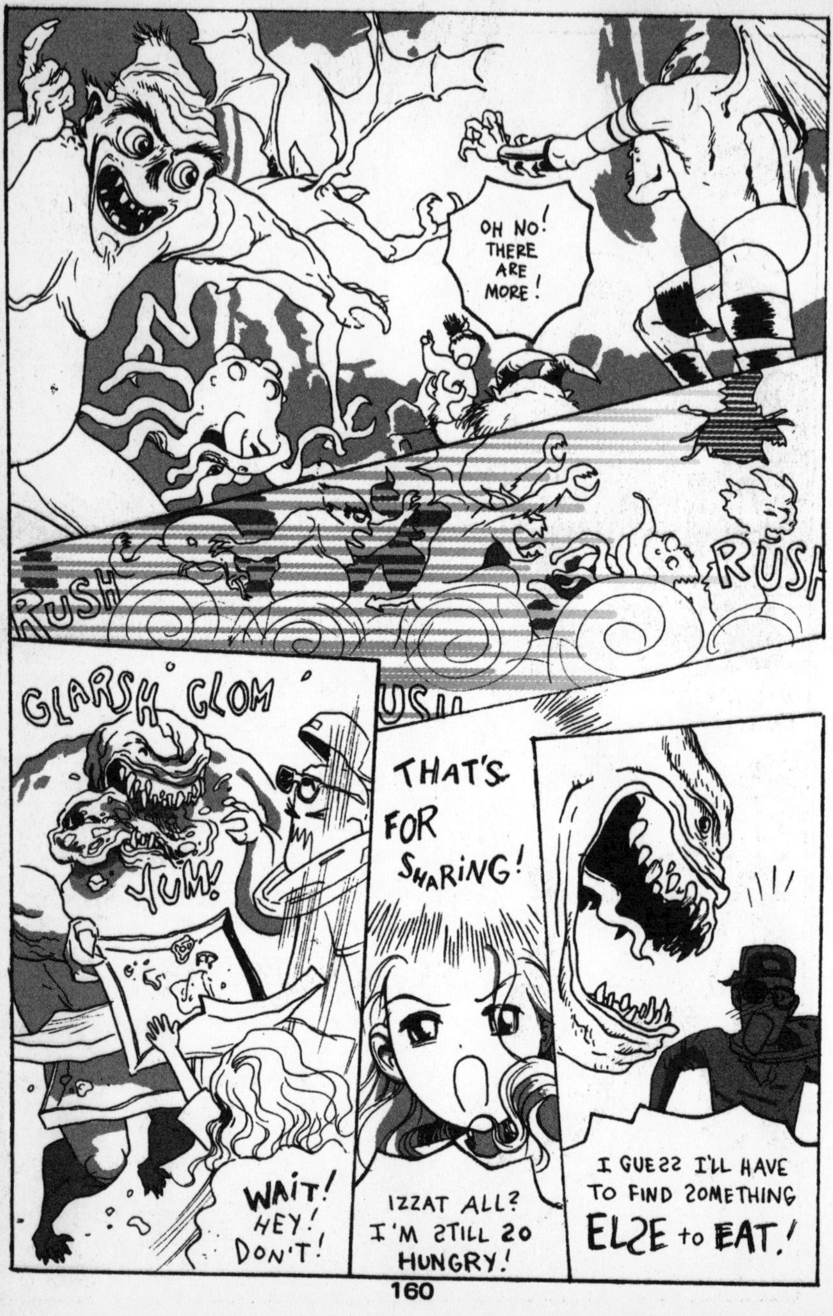
OH NO! THERE ARE MORE!
RUSH
RUSH
GLARSH GLOM
YUM!
WAIT! HEY! DON'T!
THAT'S FOR SHARING!
IZZAT ALL? I'M STILL SO HUNGRY!
I GUESS I'LL HAVE TO FIND SOMETHING ELSE to EAT!

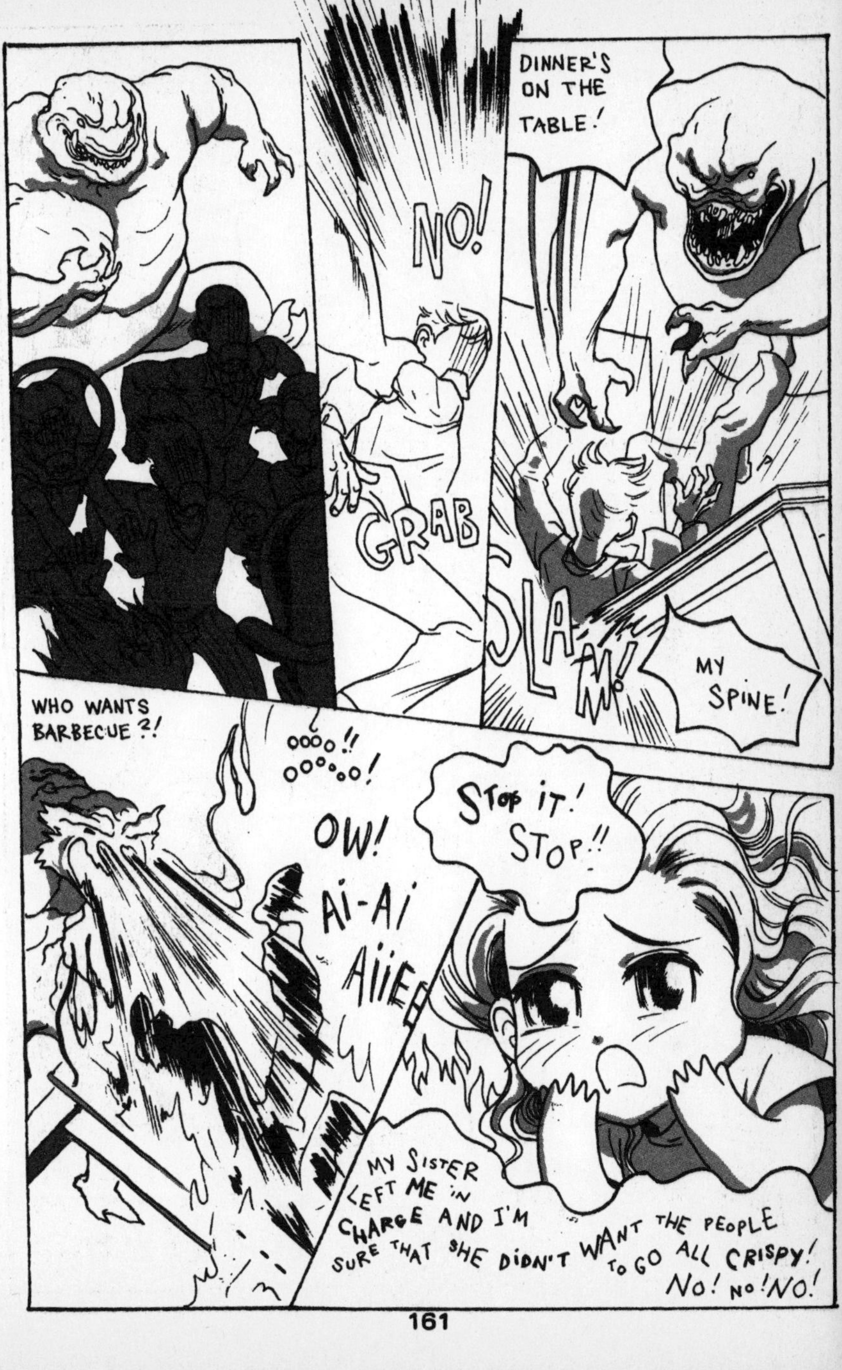

NO!
GRAB
DINNER'S ON THE TABLE!
SLA-M!
MY SPINE!
WHO WANTS BARBECUE ?!
oooo !! ooo°°o!
OW!
Ai-Ai
AiiEE
STOP IT! STOP!!
MY SISTER LEFT ME IN CHARGE AND I'M SURE THAT SHE DIDN'T WANT THE PEOPLE TO GO ALL CRISPY!
NO! NO! NO!

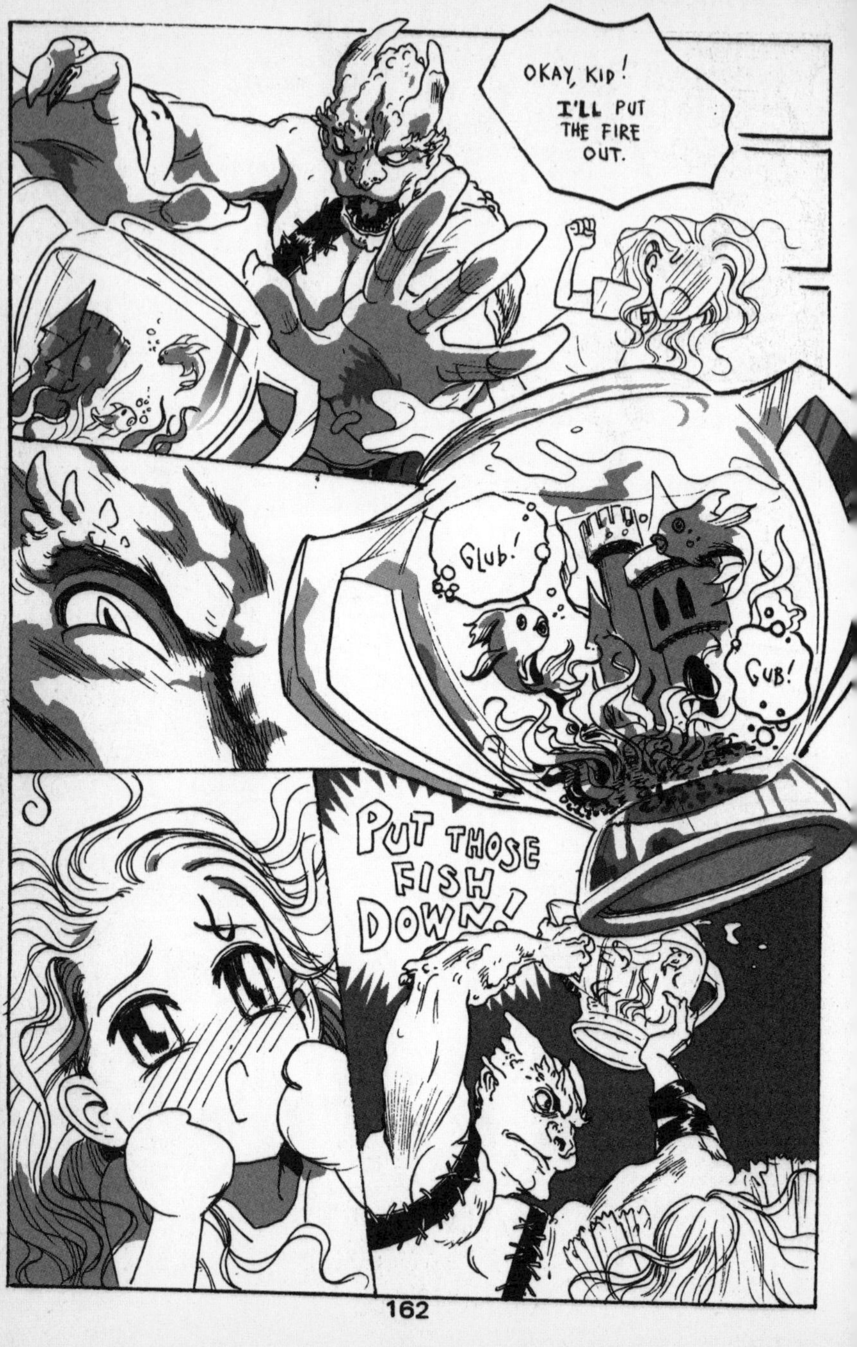
OKAY, KID!
I'LL PUT THE FIRE OUT.
GLUB!
GUB!
PUT THOSE FISH DOWN!

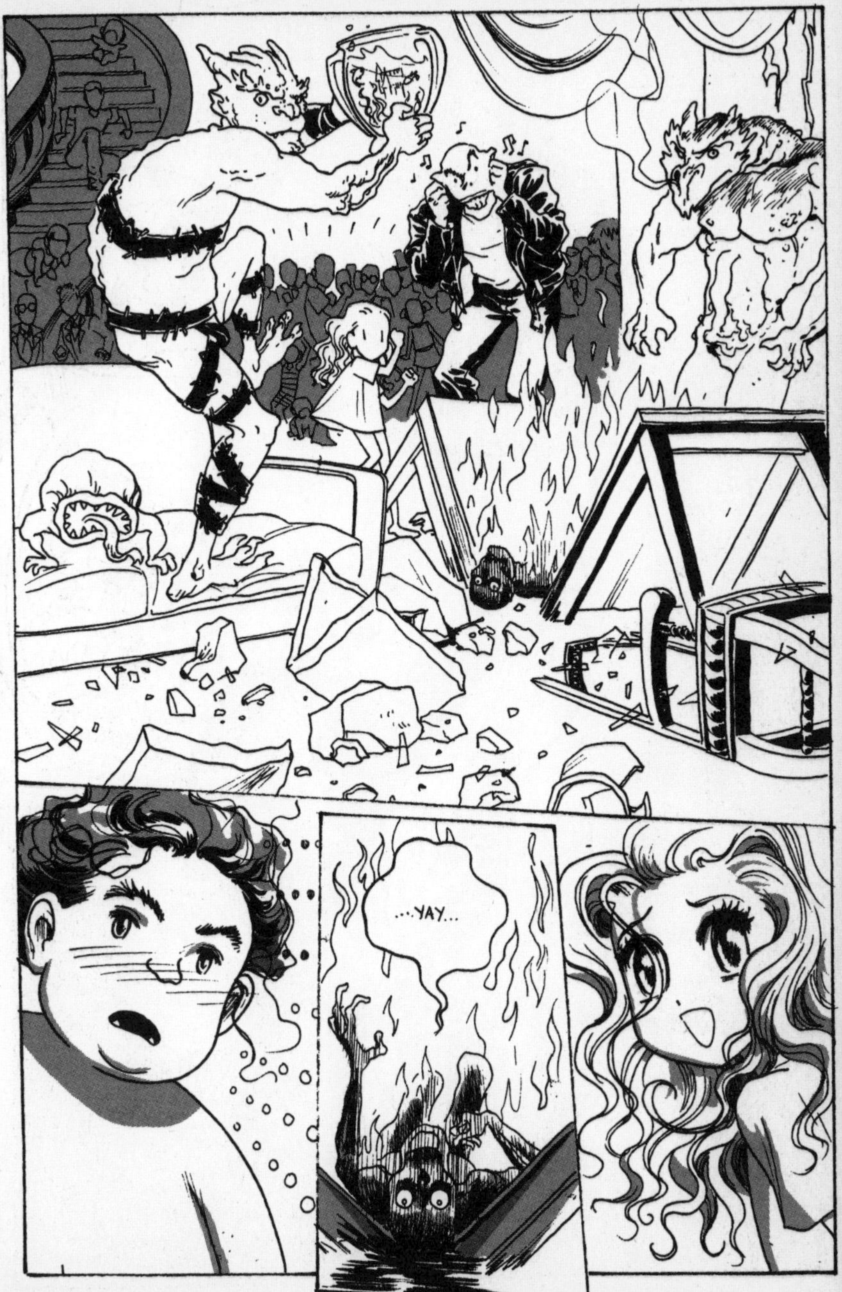
...YAY...

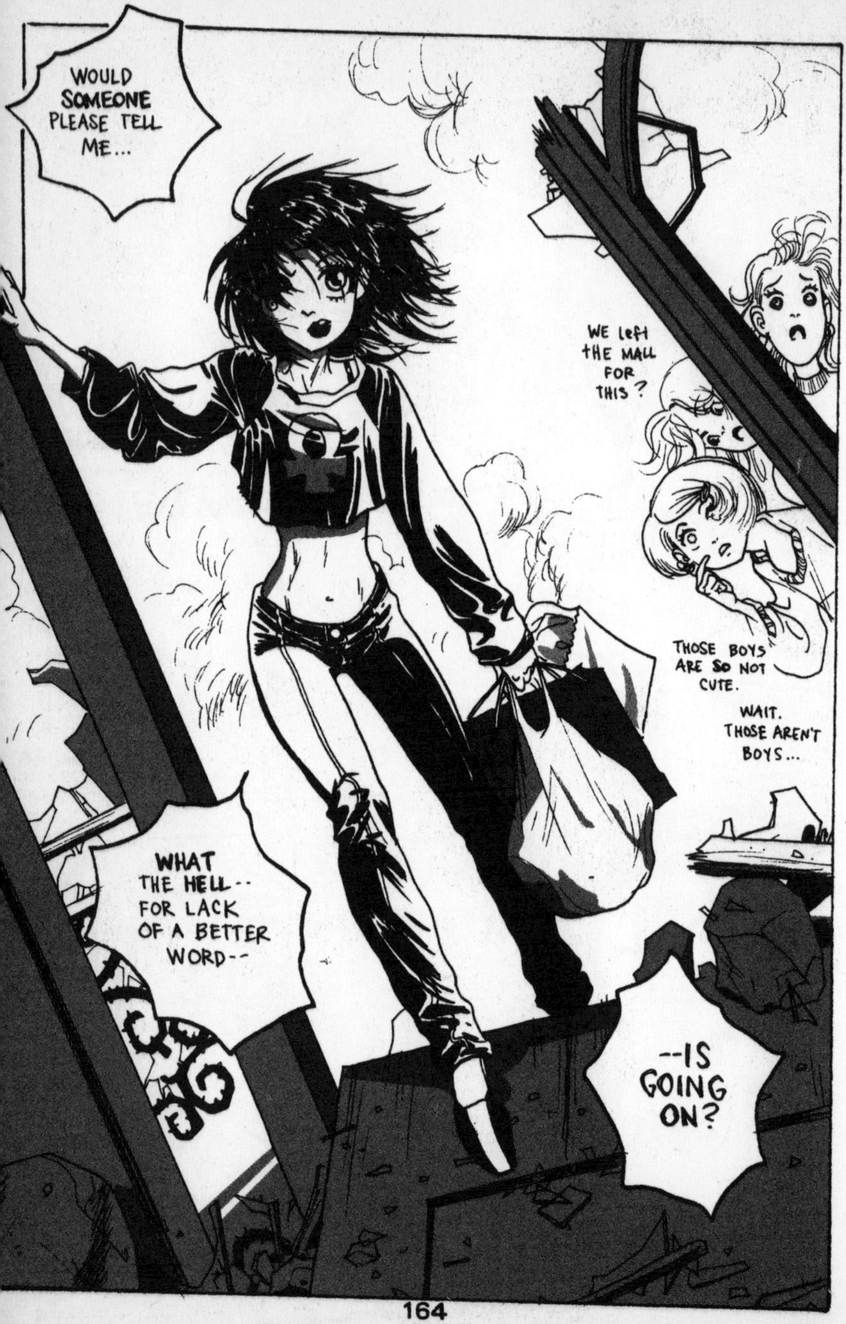
WOULD SOMEONE PLEASE TELL ME...
WE left THE MALL FOR THIS?
THOSE BOYS ARE SO NOT CUTE.
WAIT. THOSE AREN'T BOYS...
WHAT THE HELL-- FOR LACK OF A BETTER WORD--
--IS GOING ON?

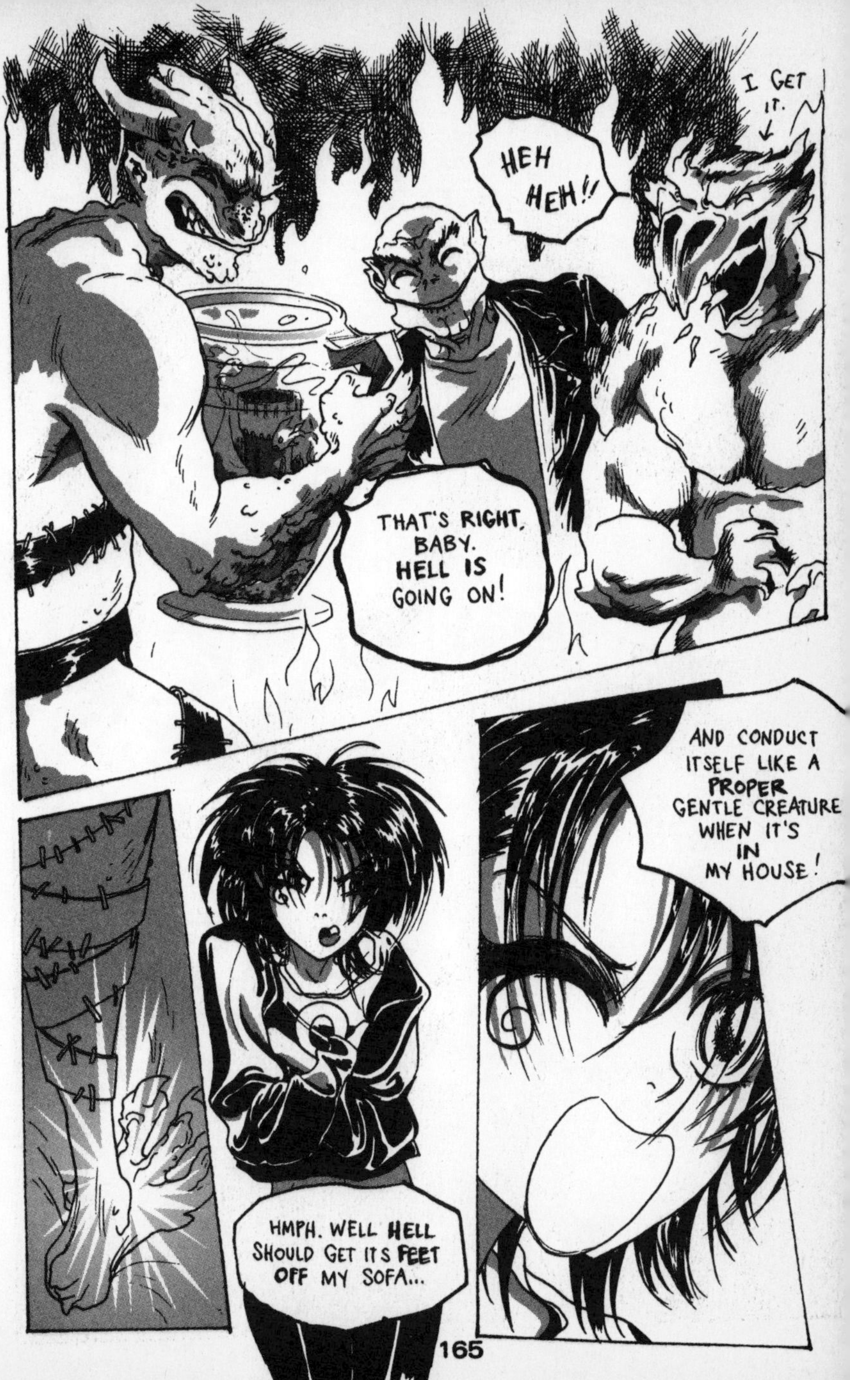
HEH HEH!!
I GET IT.
THAT'S RIGHT, BABY. HELL IS GOING ON!
HMPH. WELL HELL SHOULD GET ITS FEET OFF MY SOFA...
AND CONDUCT ITSELF LIKE A PROPER GENTLE CREATURE WHEN IT'S IN MY HOUSE!

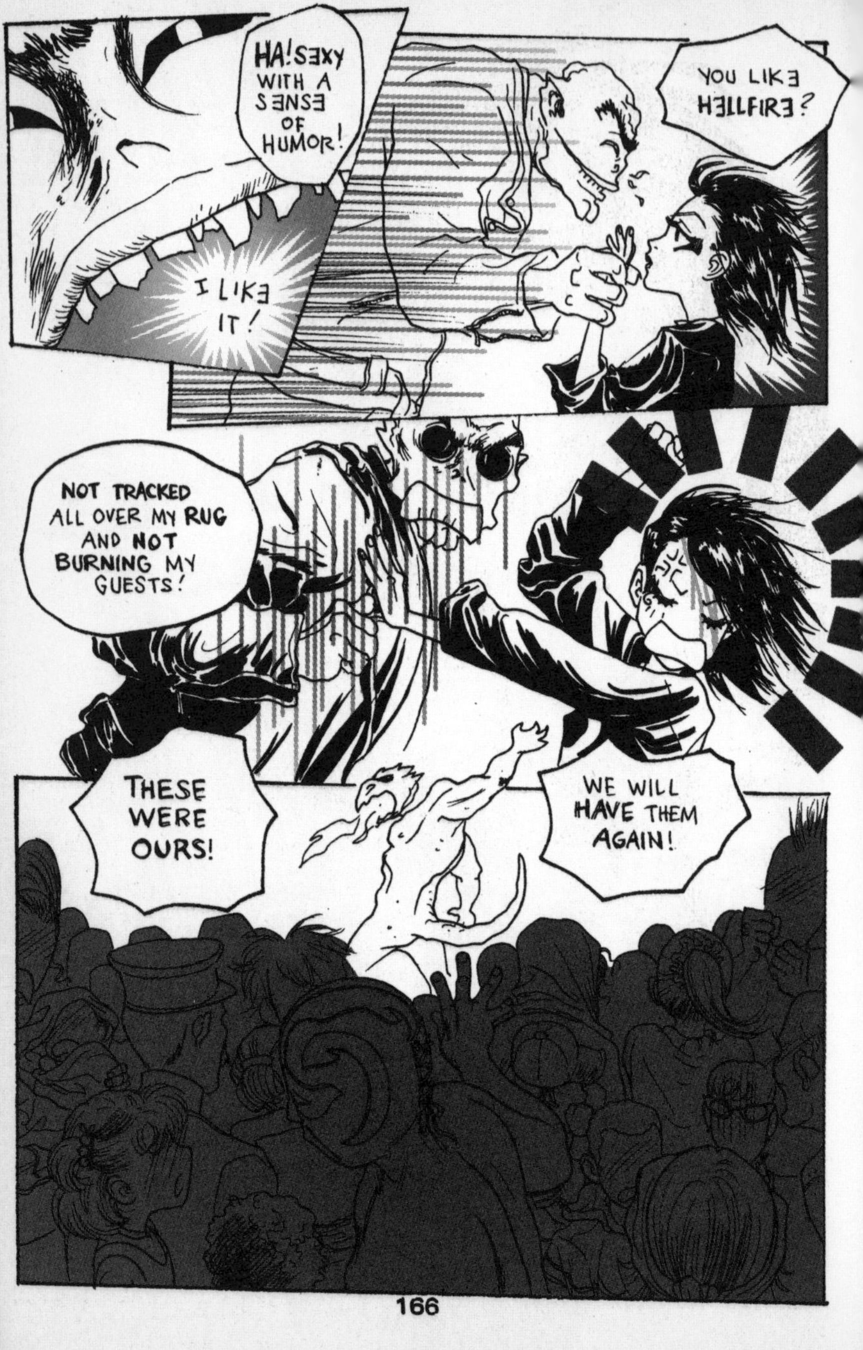
HA! SEXY WITH A SENSE OF HUMOR!
I LIKE IT!
YOU LIKE HELLFIRE?
NOT TRACKED ALL OVER MY RUG AND NOT BURNING MY GUESTS!
THESE WERE OURS!
WE WILL HAVE THEM AGAIN!

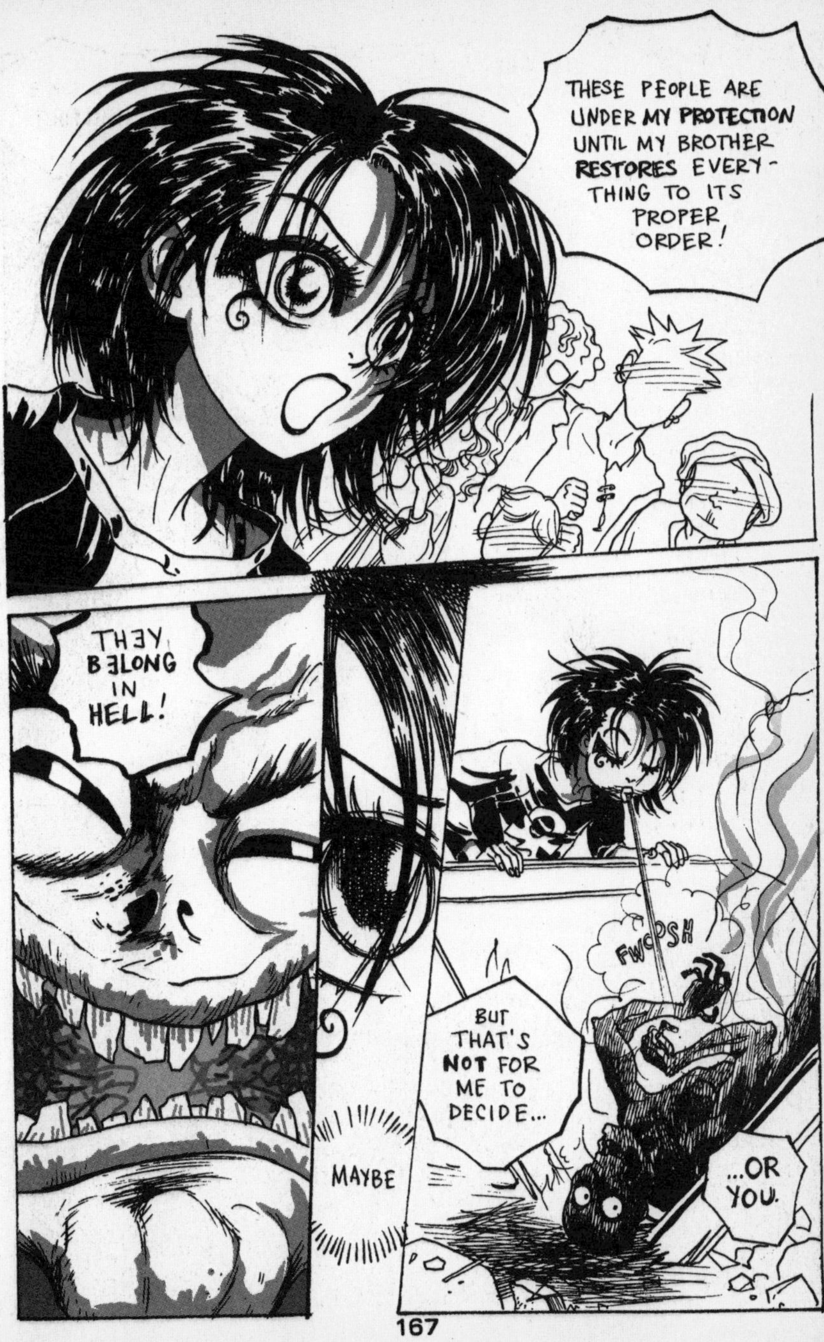
THESE PEOPLE ARE UNDER MY PROTECTION UNTIL MY BROTHER RESTORES EVERY-THING TO ITS PROPER ORDER!
THEY BELONG IN HELL!
FWOOSH
BUT THAT'S NOT FOR ME TO DECIDE...
MAYBE
...OR YOU.

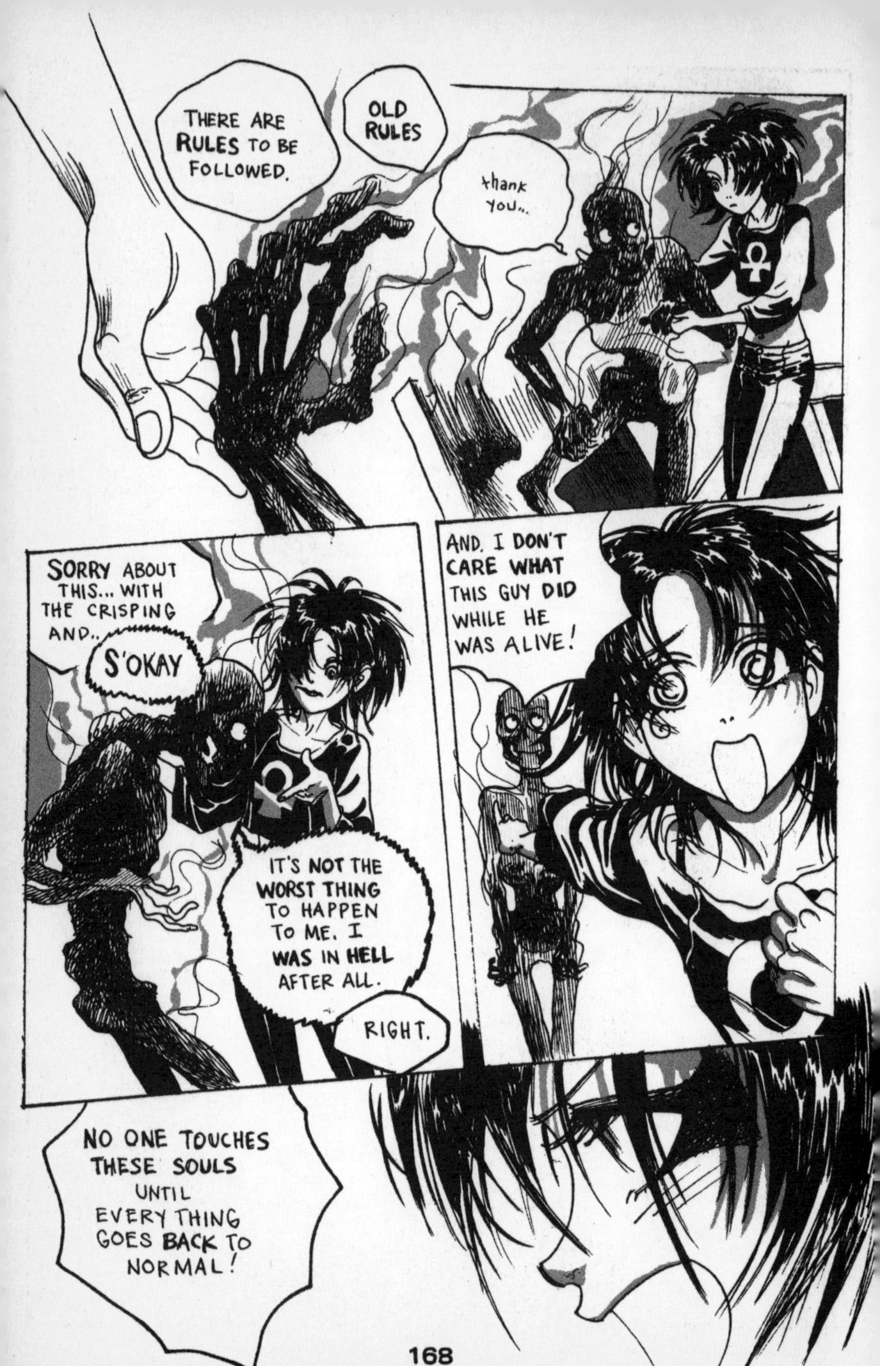
THERE ARE RULES TO BE FOLLOWED.
OLD RULES
thank you..
SORRY ABOUT THIS... WITH THE CRISPING AND..
S'OKAY
IT'S NOT THE WORST THING TO HAPPEN TO ME. I WAS IN HELL AFTER ALL.
RIGHT.
AND, I DON'T CARE WHAT THIS GUY DID WHILE HE WAS ALIVE!
NO ONE TOUCHES THESE SOULS UNTIL EVERY THING GOES BACK TO NORMAL!

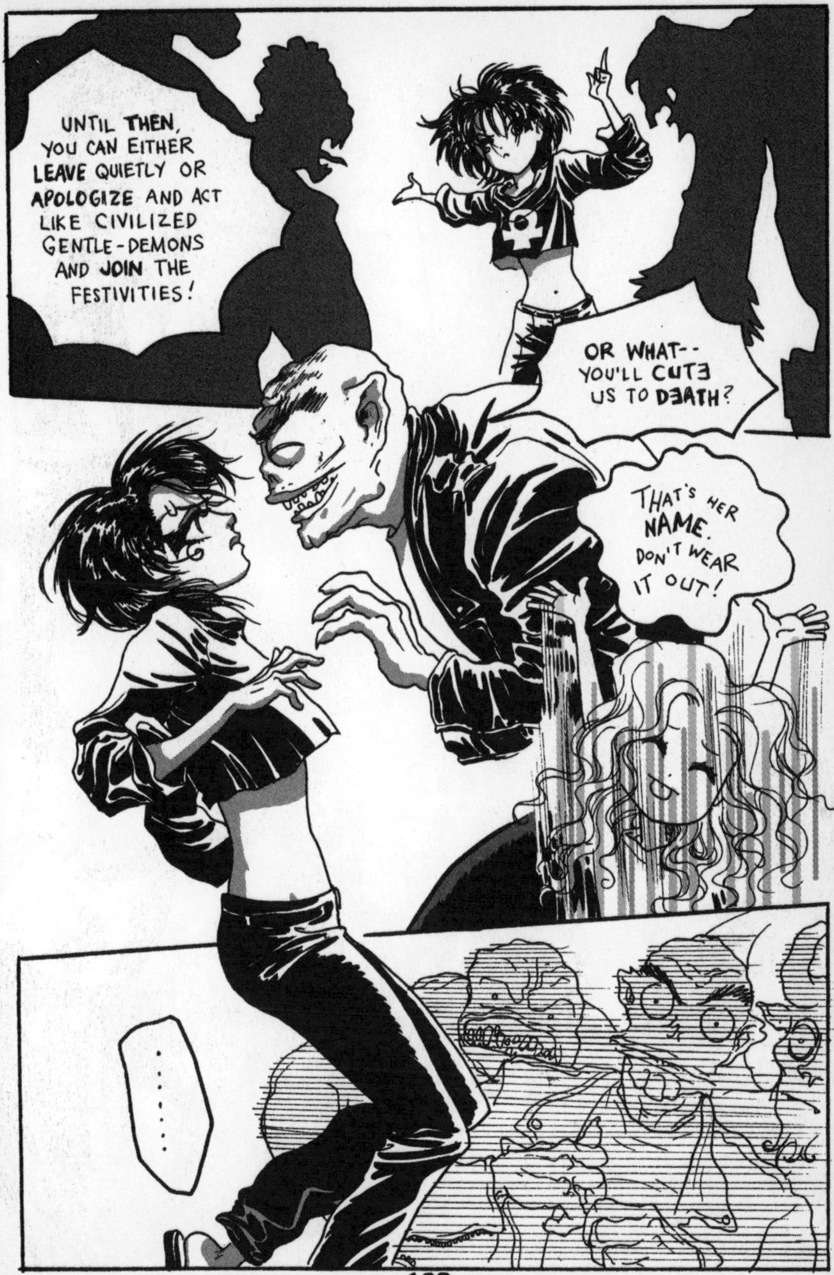
UNTIL THEN, YOU CAN EITHER LEAVE QUIETLY OR APOLOGIZE AND ACT LIKE CIVILIZED GENTLE-DEMONS AND JOIN THE FESTIVITIES!
OR WHAT-- YOU'LL CUTE US TO DEATH?
THAT'S HER NAME. DON'T WEAR IT OUT!
......

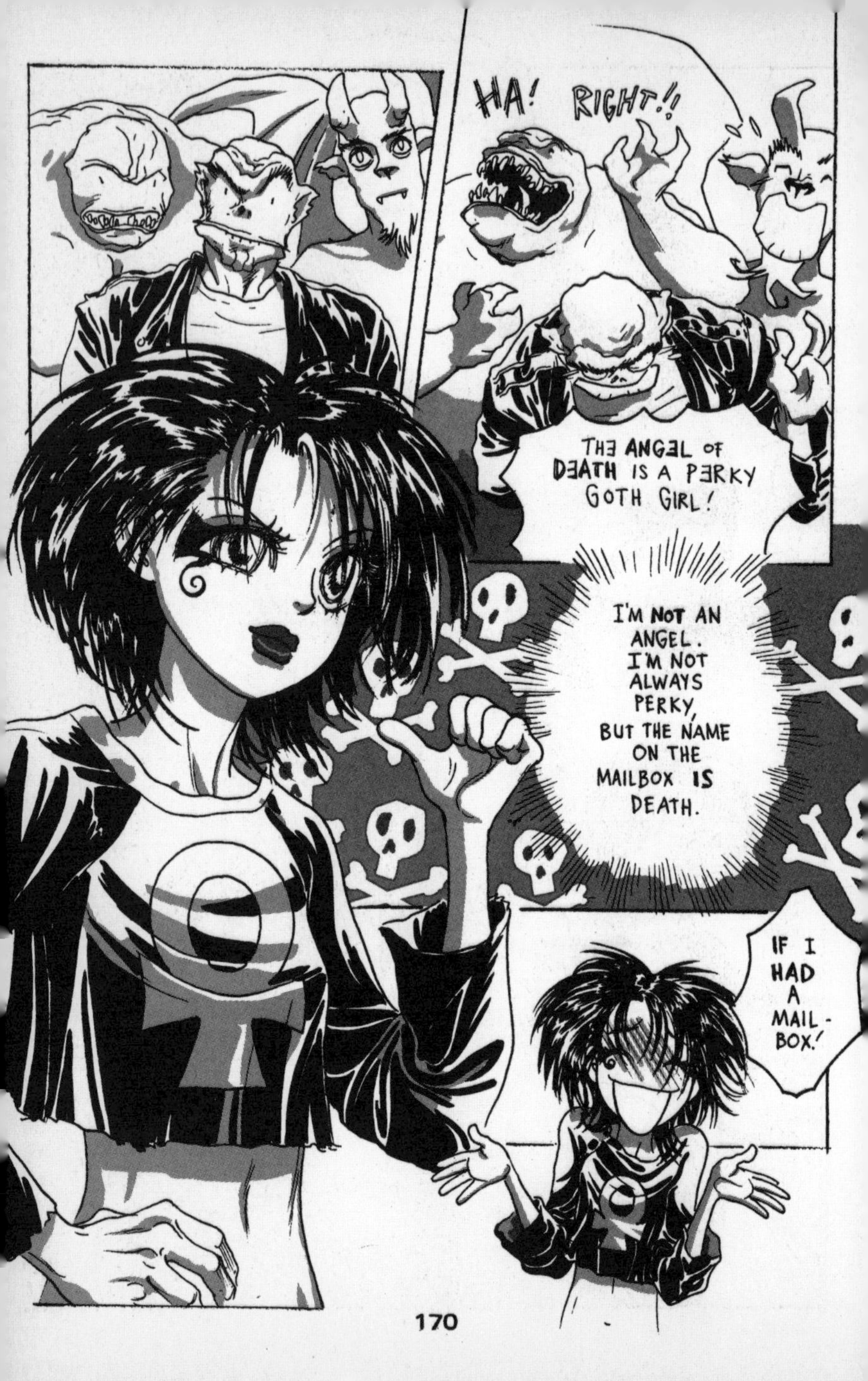
HA! RIGHT!!
THE ANGEL OF DEATH IS A PERKY GOTH GIRL!
I'M NOT AN ANGEL. I'M NOT ALWAYS PERKY, BUT THE NAME ON THE MAILBOX IS DEATH.
IF I HAD A MAIL-BOX!

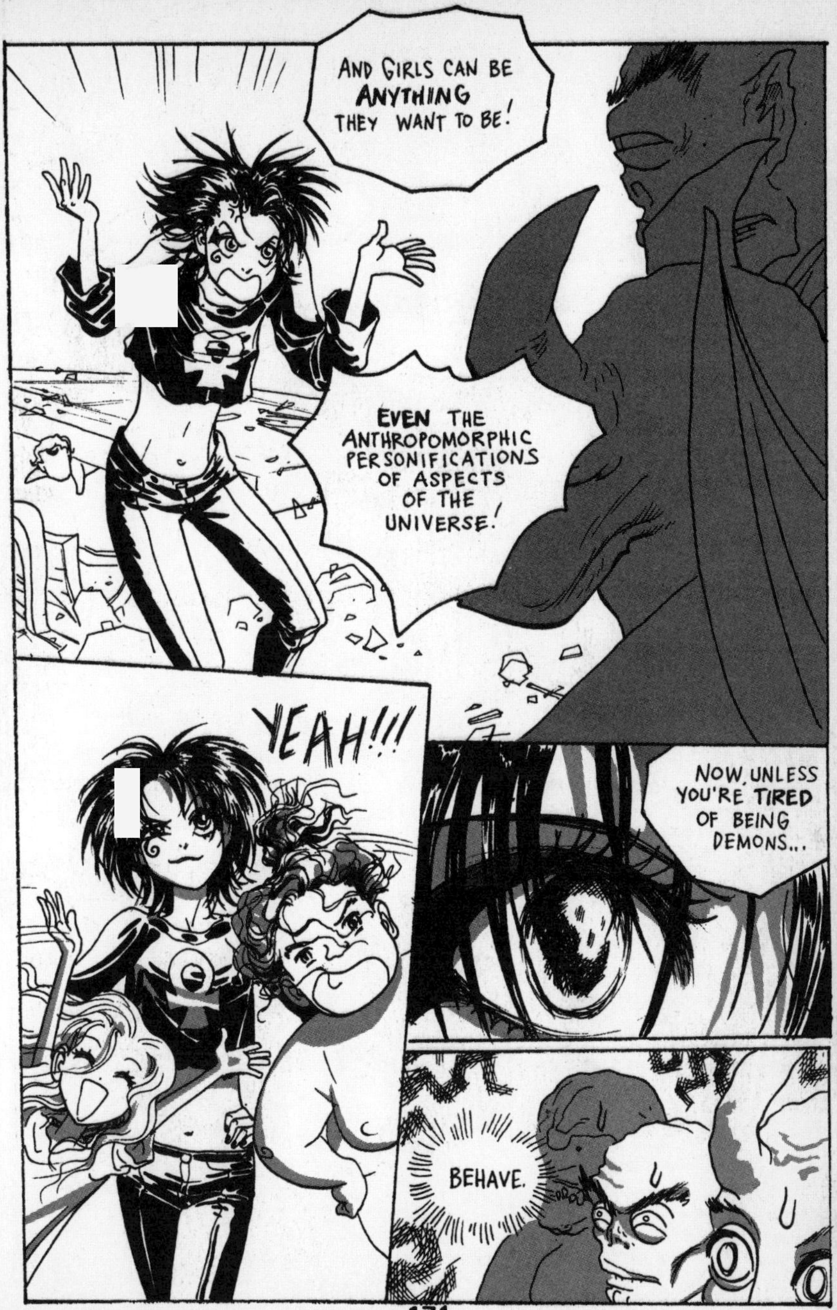
AND GIRLS CAN BE ANYTHING THEY WANT TO BE!
EVEN THE ANTHROPOMORPHIC PERSONIFICATIONS OF ASPECTS OF THE UNIVERSE!
YEAH!!!
NOW, UNLESS YOU'RE TIRED OF BEING DEMONS...
BEHAVE.

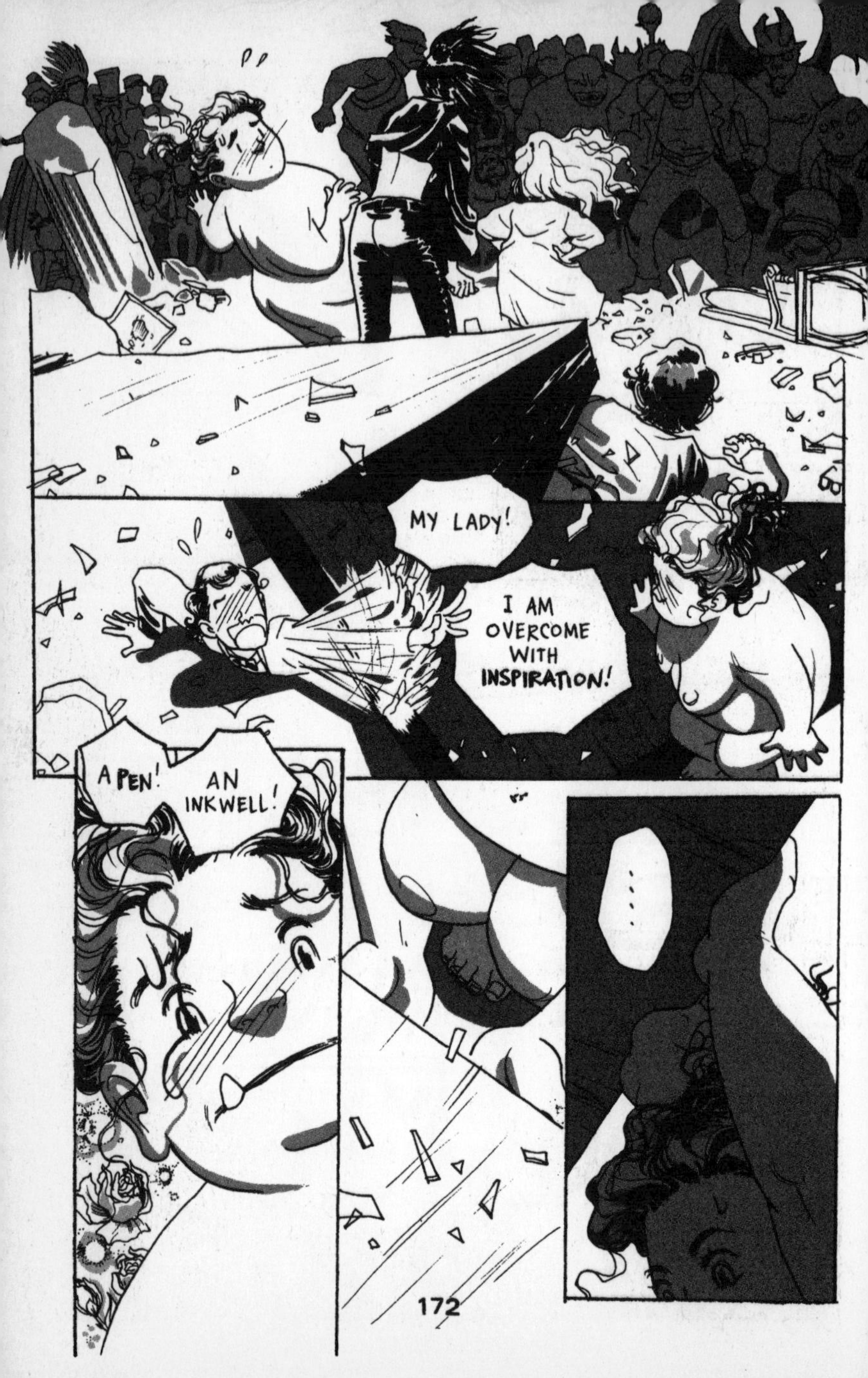
MY LADY!
I AM OVERCOME WITH INSPIRATION!
A PEN! AN INKWELL!
....

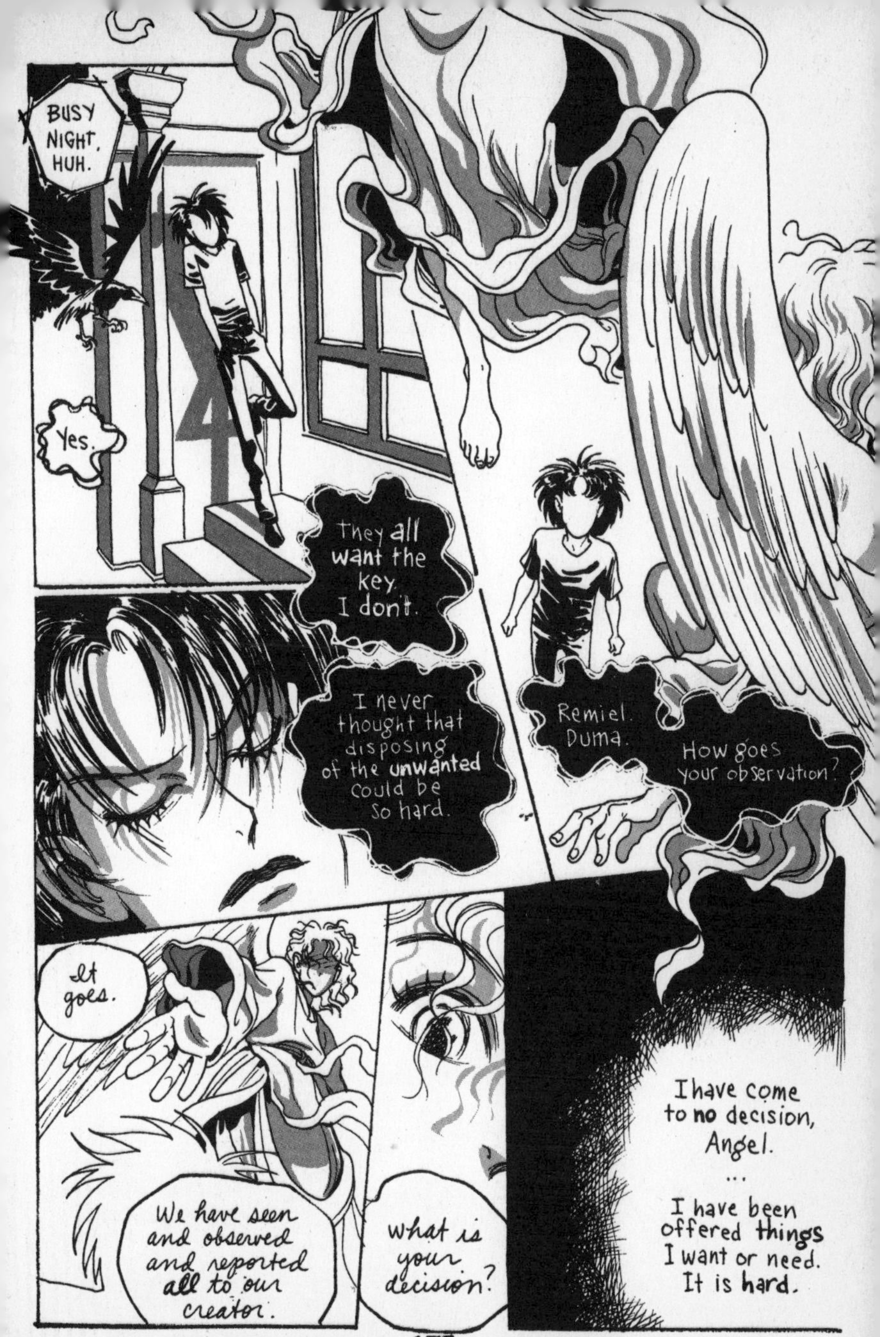

BUSY NIGHT, HUH.
Yes.
they all want the key. I don't.
I never thought that disposing of the unwanted could be so hard.
Remiel. Duma.
How goes your observation?
It goes.
We have seen and observed and reported all to our creator.
what is your decision?
I have come to no decision, Angel.
...
I have been offered things I want or need. It is hard.

Perhaps I should accede to the faeries' wishes and leave Hell empty.
It serves no good purpose...
I have a message for you.
There must be a Hell. A place for demons. A place for the damned.
Hell is Heaven's reflection. Heaven's shadow.
They define each other.
There must be a Hell, for without Hell, Heaven has no meaning.

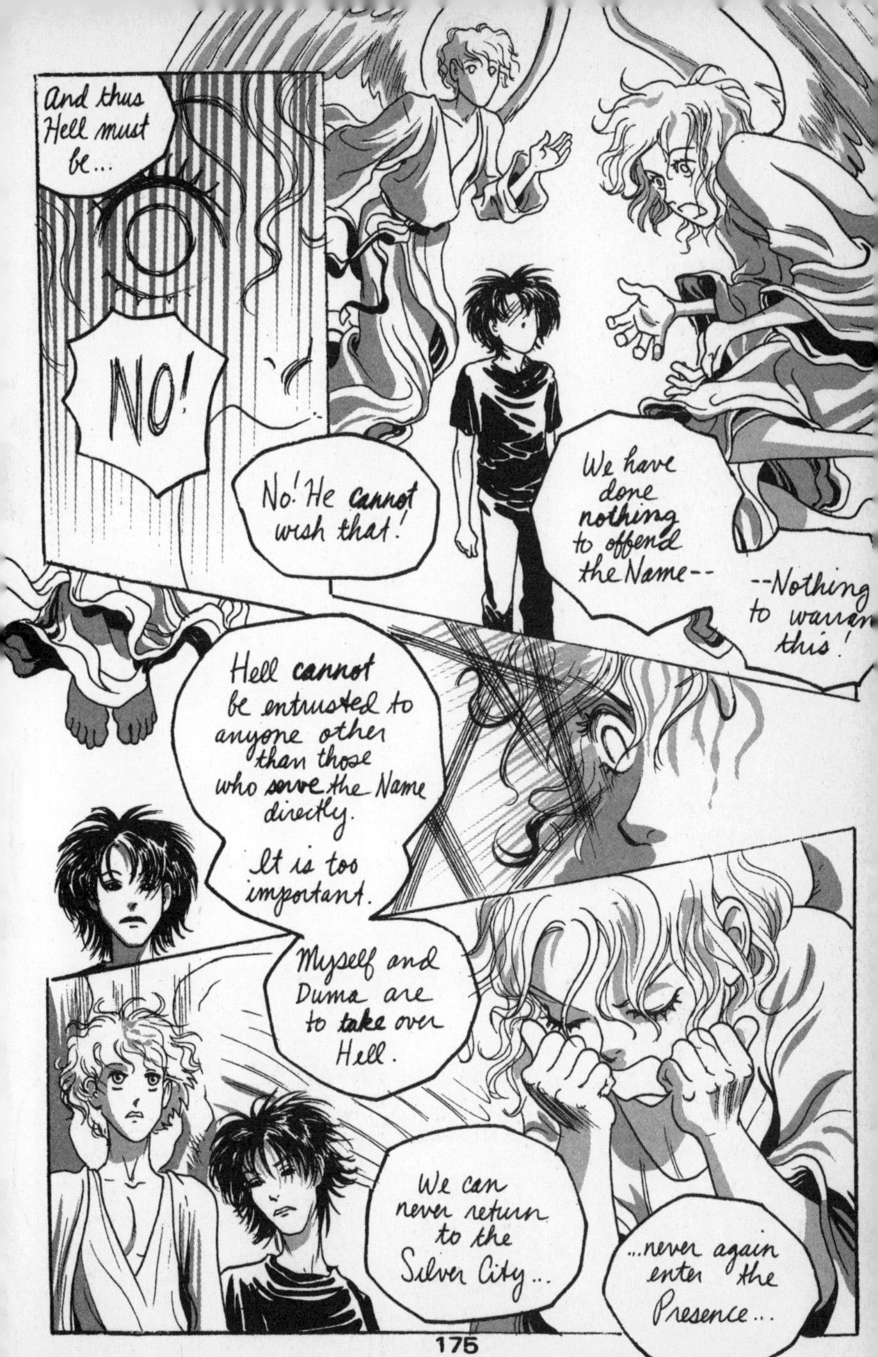
And thus Hell must be...
NO!
No! He **cannot** wish that!
We have done **nothing** to offend the Name--
--Nothing to warrant this!
Hell **cannot** be entrusted to anyone other than those who **serve** the Name directly.
It is too important.
Myself and Duma are to **take** over Hell.
We can never return to the Silver City...
...never again enter the Presence...

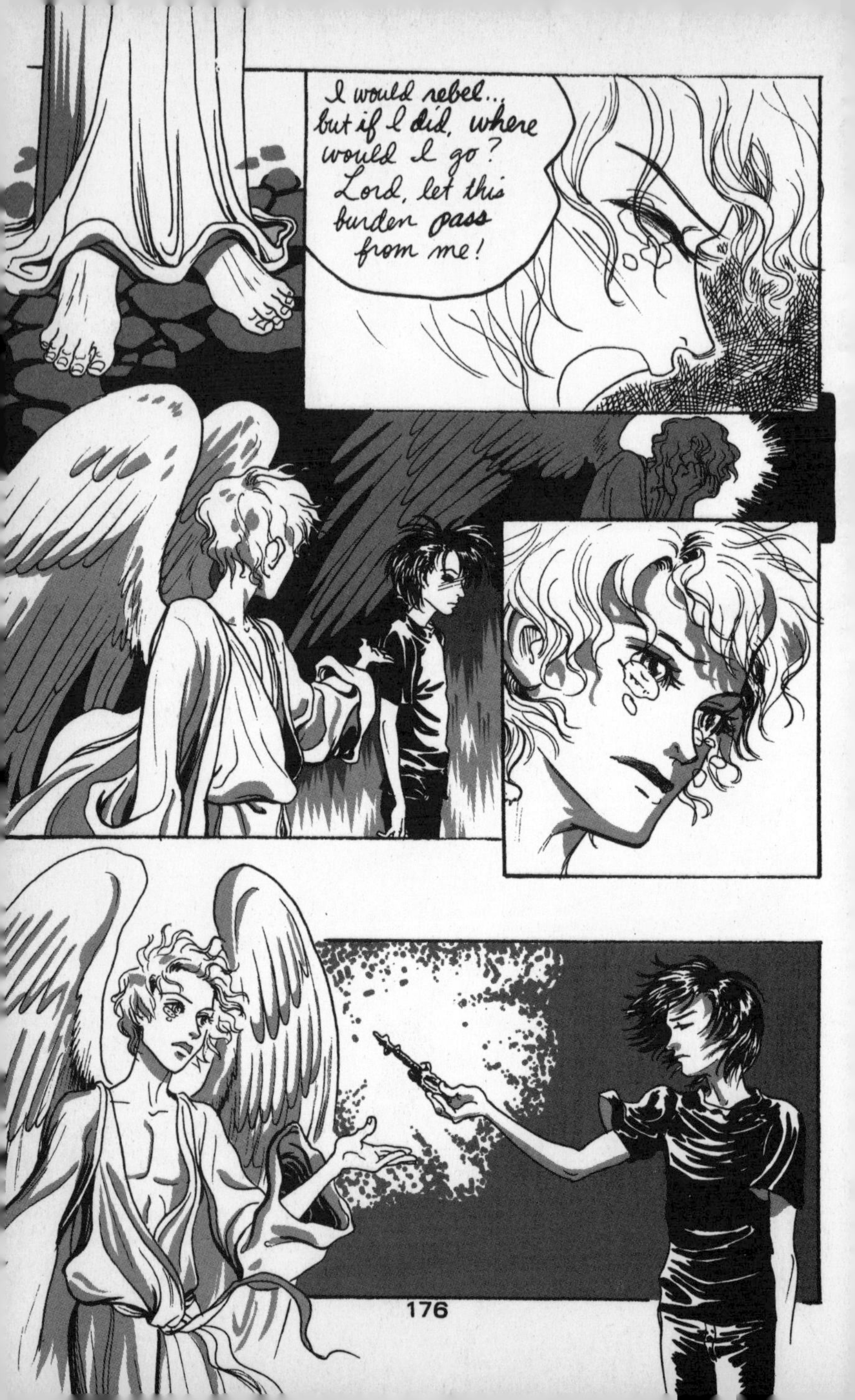
I would rebel... but if I did, where would I go? Lord, let this burden pass from me!

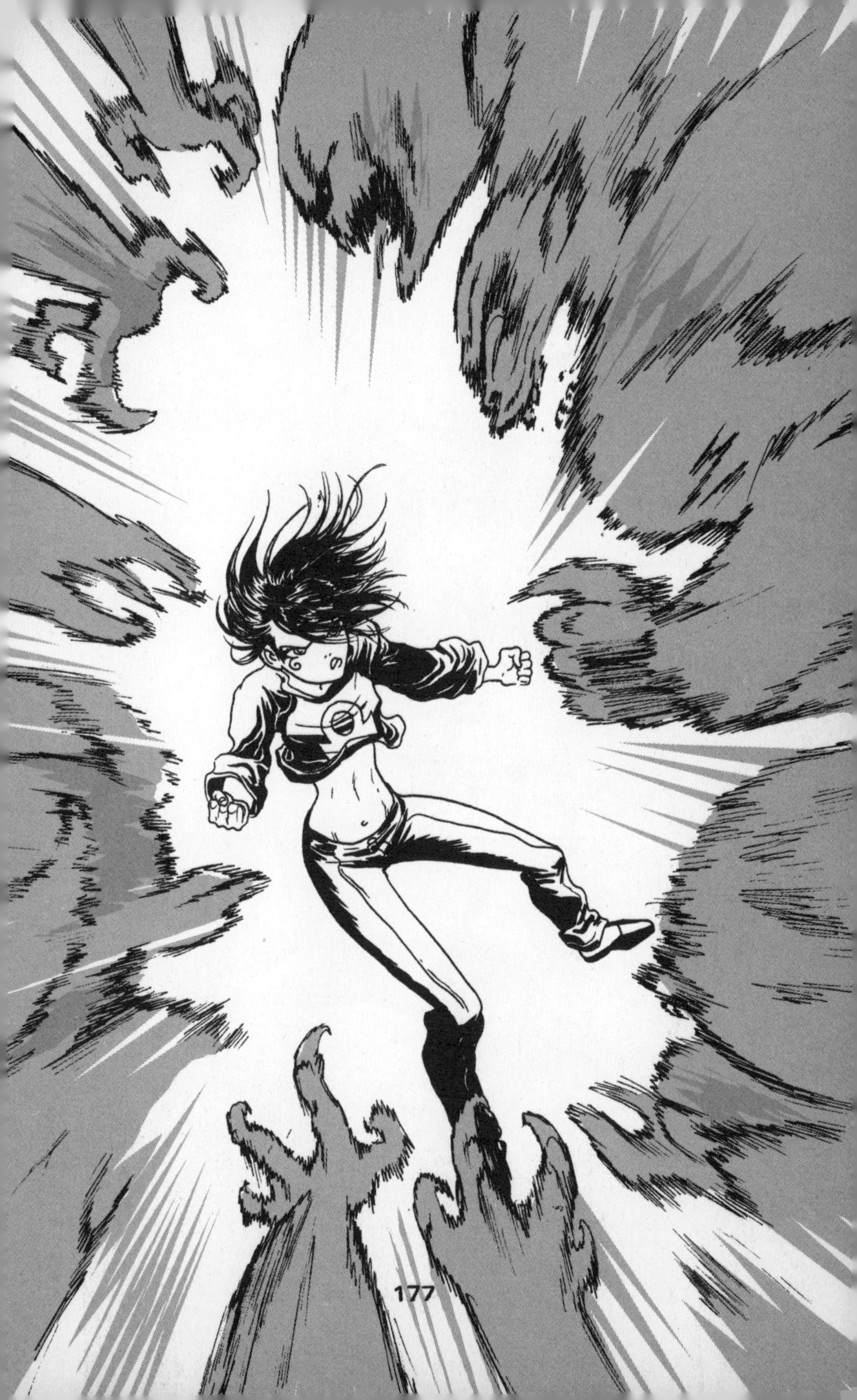

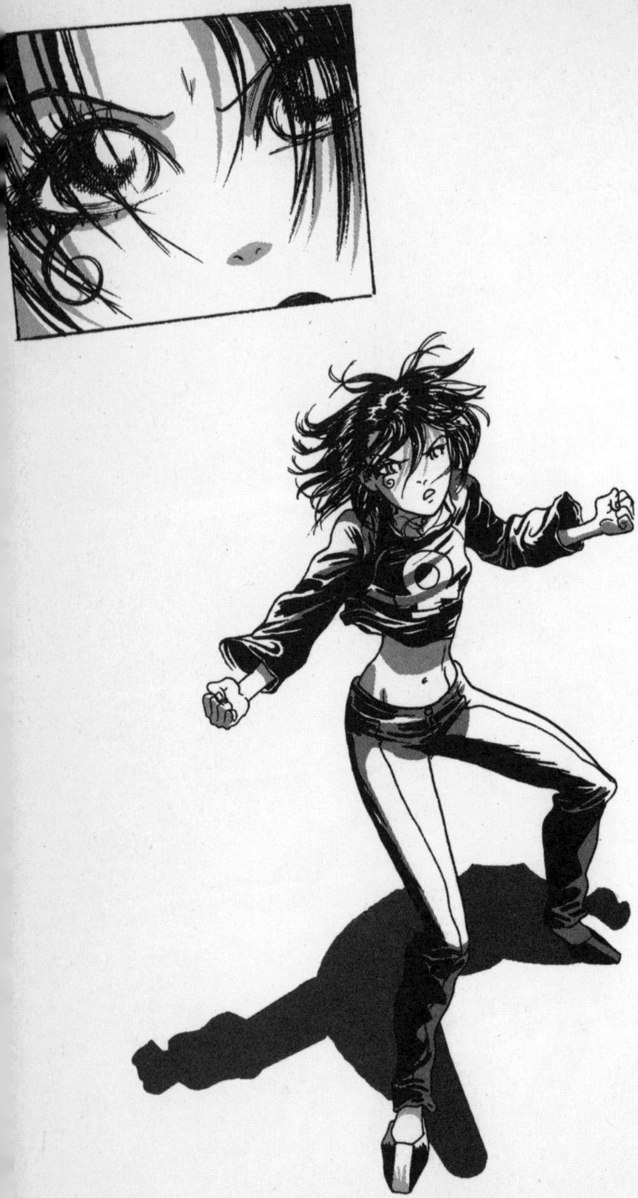

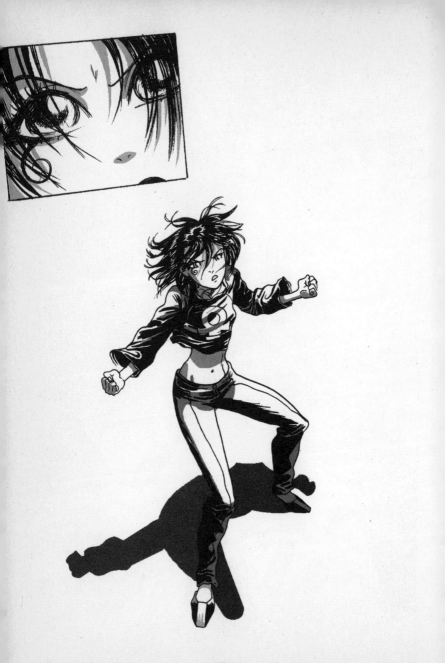

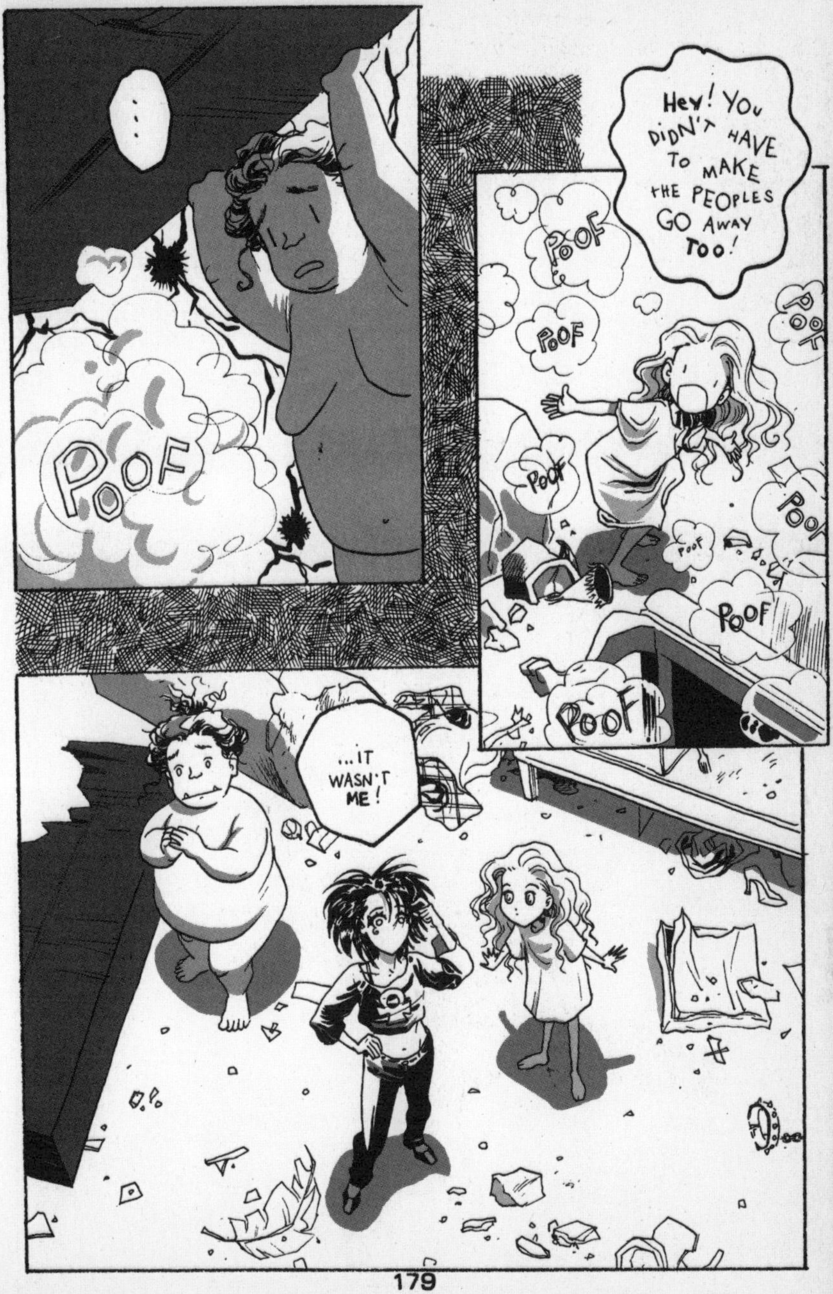
...
POOF
HEY! YOU DIDN'T HAVE TO MAKE THE PEOPLES GO AWAY TOO!
POOF
POOF
POOF
POOF
POOF
POOF
POOF
POOF!
...IT WASN'T ME!

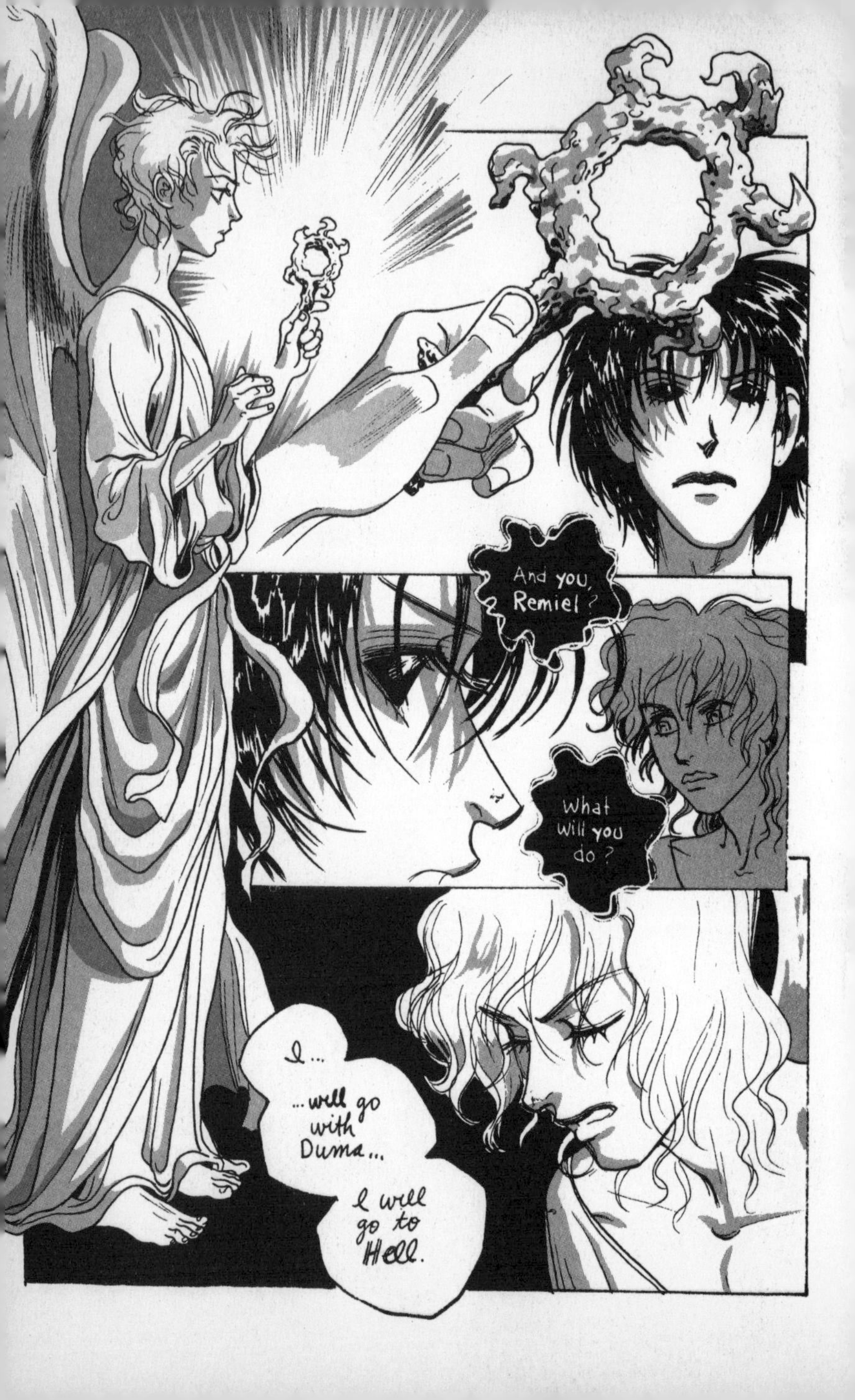
And you, Remiel?
What will you do?
I...
...will go with Duma...
I will go to Hell.

The war between Heaven and Hell is over. We have taken back the Key.
The damned have been returned to Hell and they will be punished.
The demons may once again take up residence there and will be expected to play their part in the rehabilitation of the Damned.
I thank you all for coming here. I trust that you understand my position.
I hope it will not cause any of you undue distress.

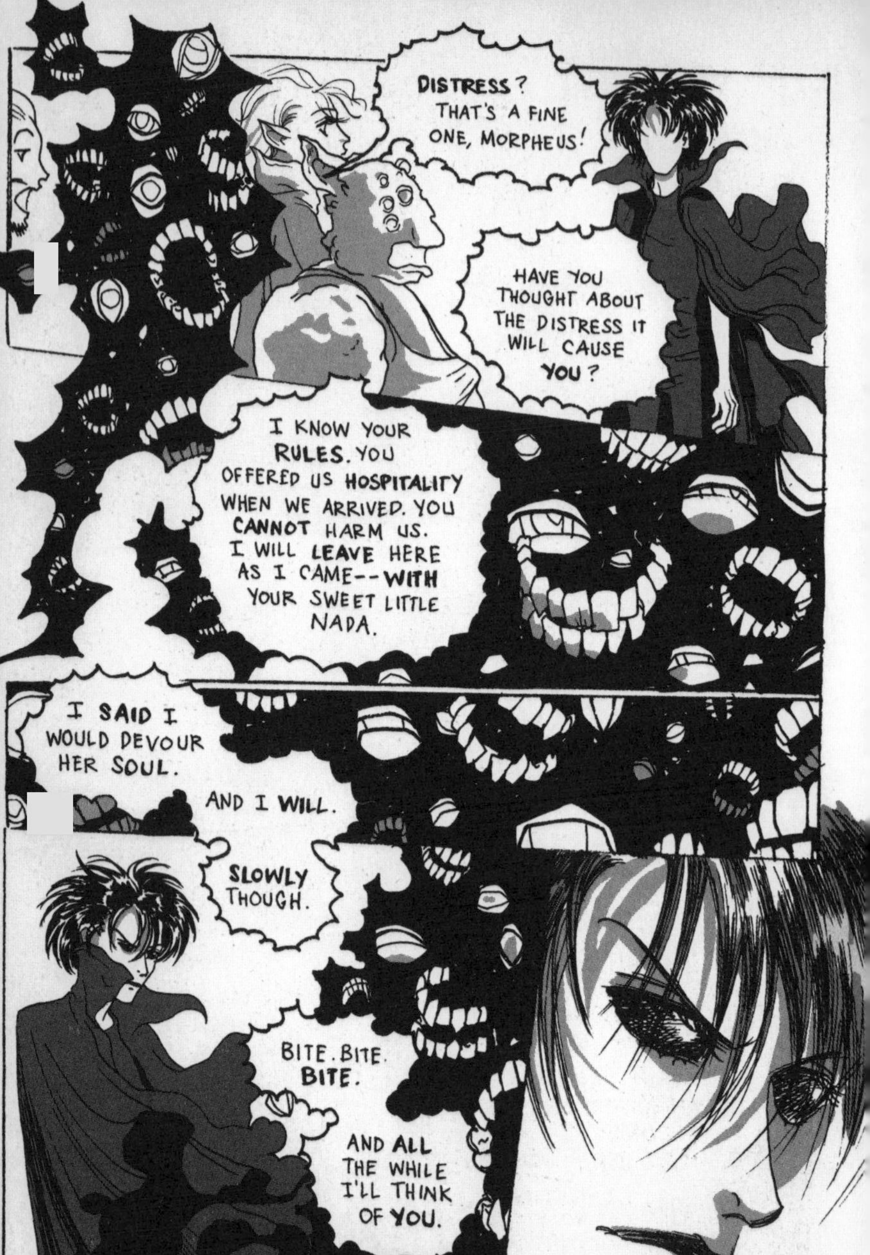
DISTRESS? THAT'S A FINE ONE, MORPHEUS!
HAVE YOU THOUGHT ABOUT THE DISTRESS IT WILL CAUSE YOU?
I KNOW YOUR RULES. YOU OFFERED US HOSPITALITY WHEN WE ARRIVED. YOU CANNOT HARM US. I WILL LEAVE HERE AS I CAME--WITH YOUR SWEET LITTLE NADA.
I SAID I WOULD DEVOUR HER SOUL.
AND I WILL.
SLOWLY THOUGH.
BITE. BITE. BITE.
AND ALL THE WHILE I'LL THINK OF YOU.

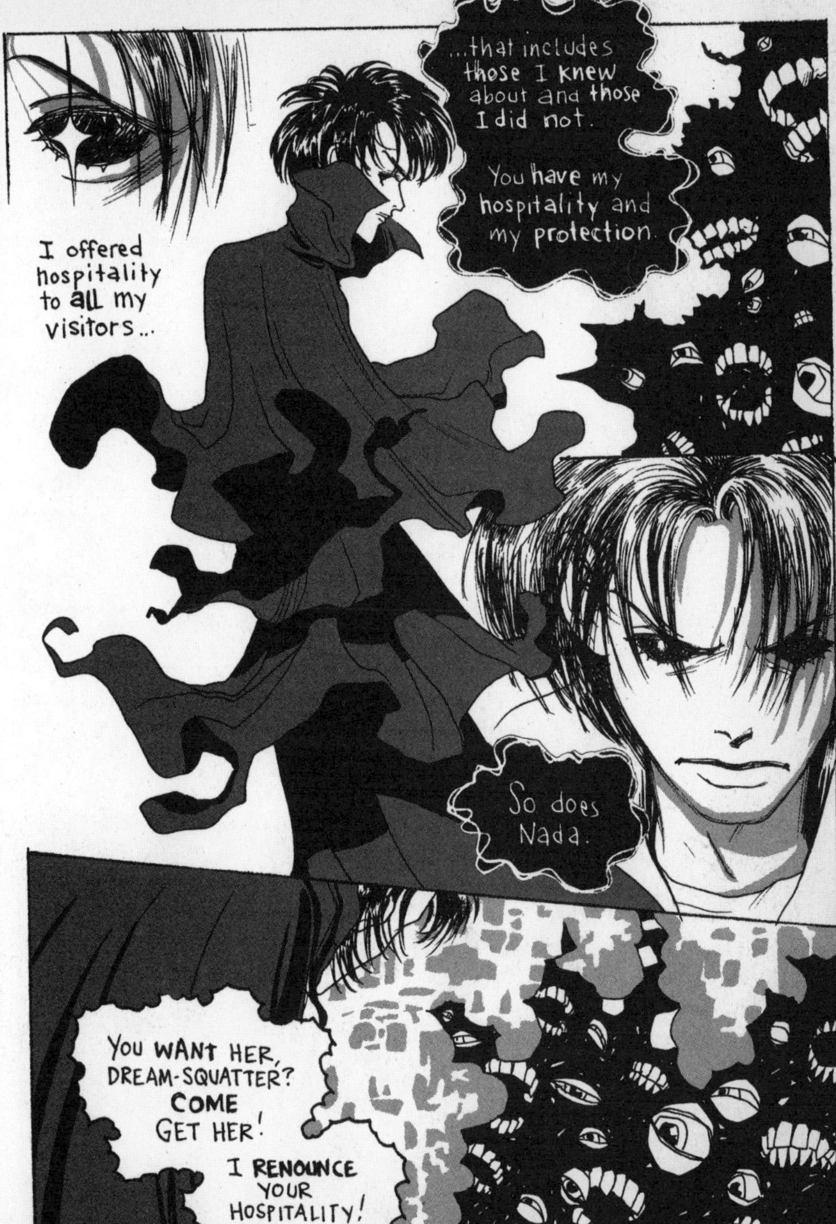
I offered hospitality to all my visitors...
...that includes those I knew about and those I did not.
You have my hospitality and my protection.
So does Nada.
YOU WANT HER, DREAM-SQUATTER? COME GET HER!
I RENOUNCE YOUR HOSPITALITY! PTUI!

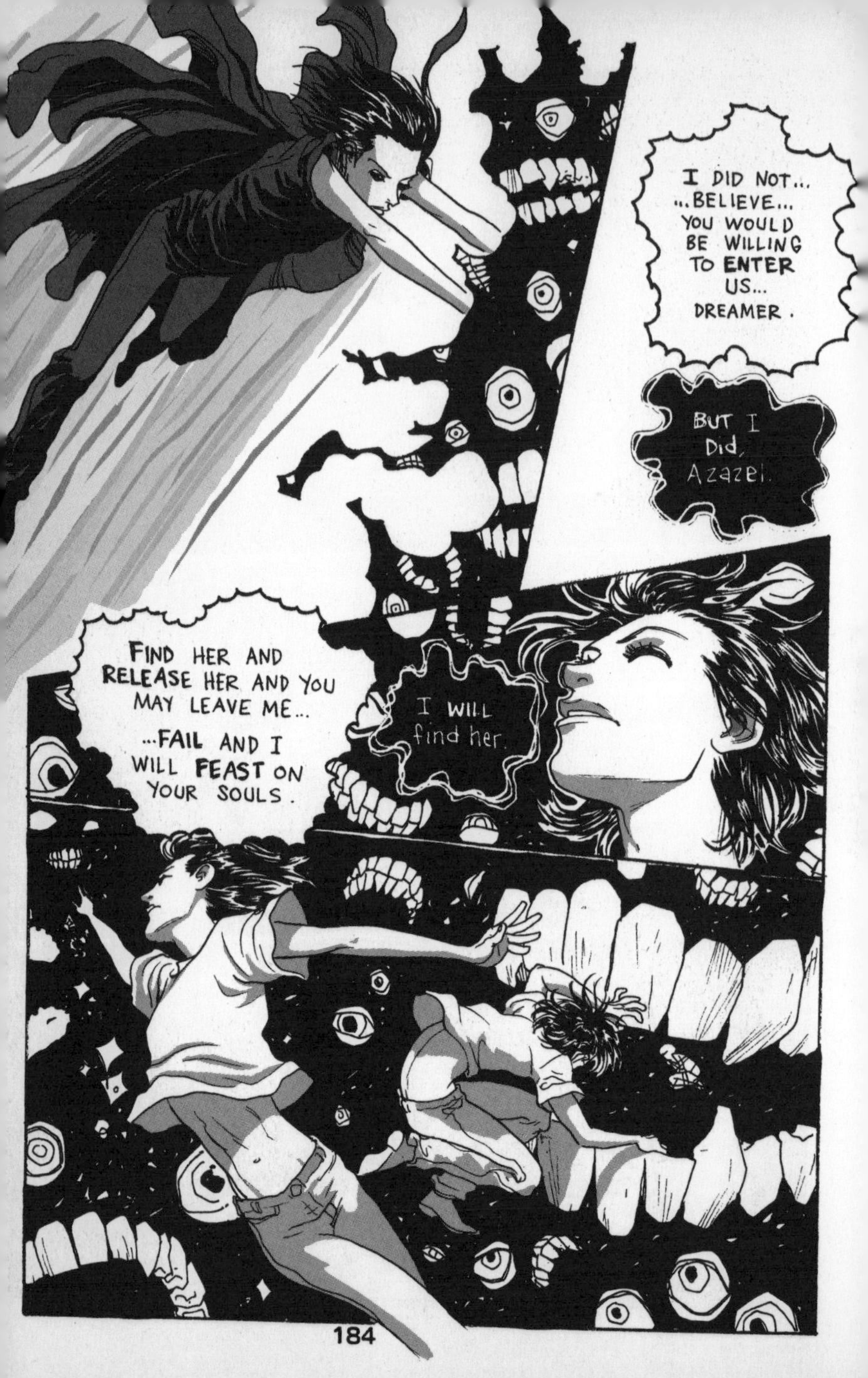
I DID NOT... ...BELIEVE... YOU WOULD BE WILLING TO ENTER US... DREAMER.
BUT I DID, AZAZEL.
FIND HER AND RELEASE HER AND YOU MAY LEAVE ME... ...FAIL AND I WILL FEAST ON YOUR SOULS.
I WILL find her.

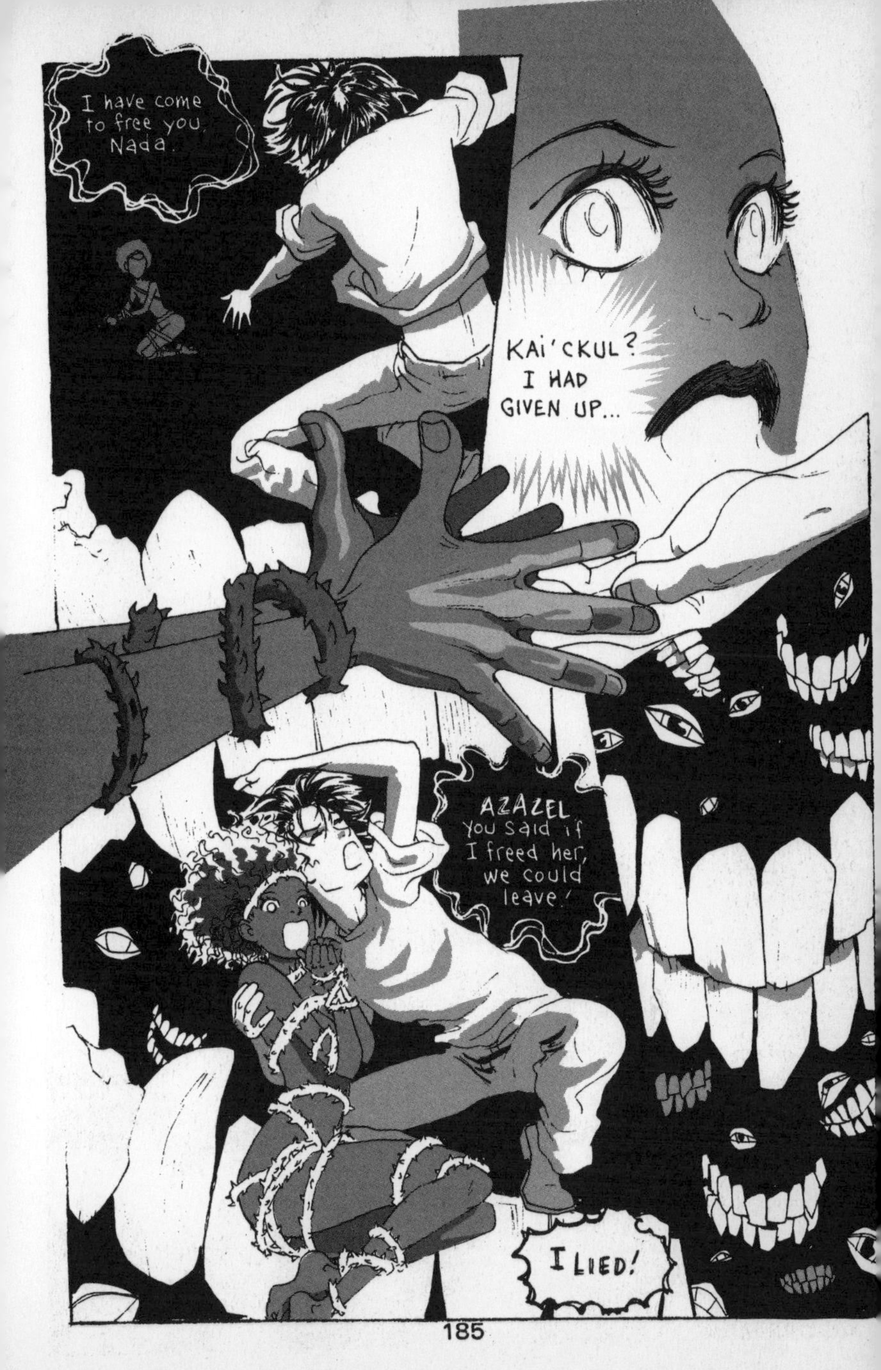
I have come to free you, Nada.
KAI'CKUL? I HAD GIVEN UP...
AZAZEL you said if I freed her, we could leave!
I LIED!

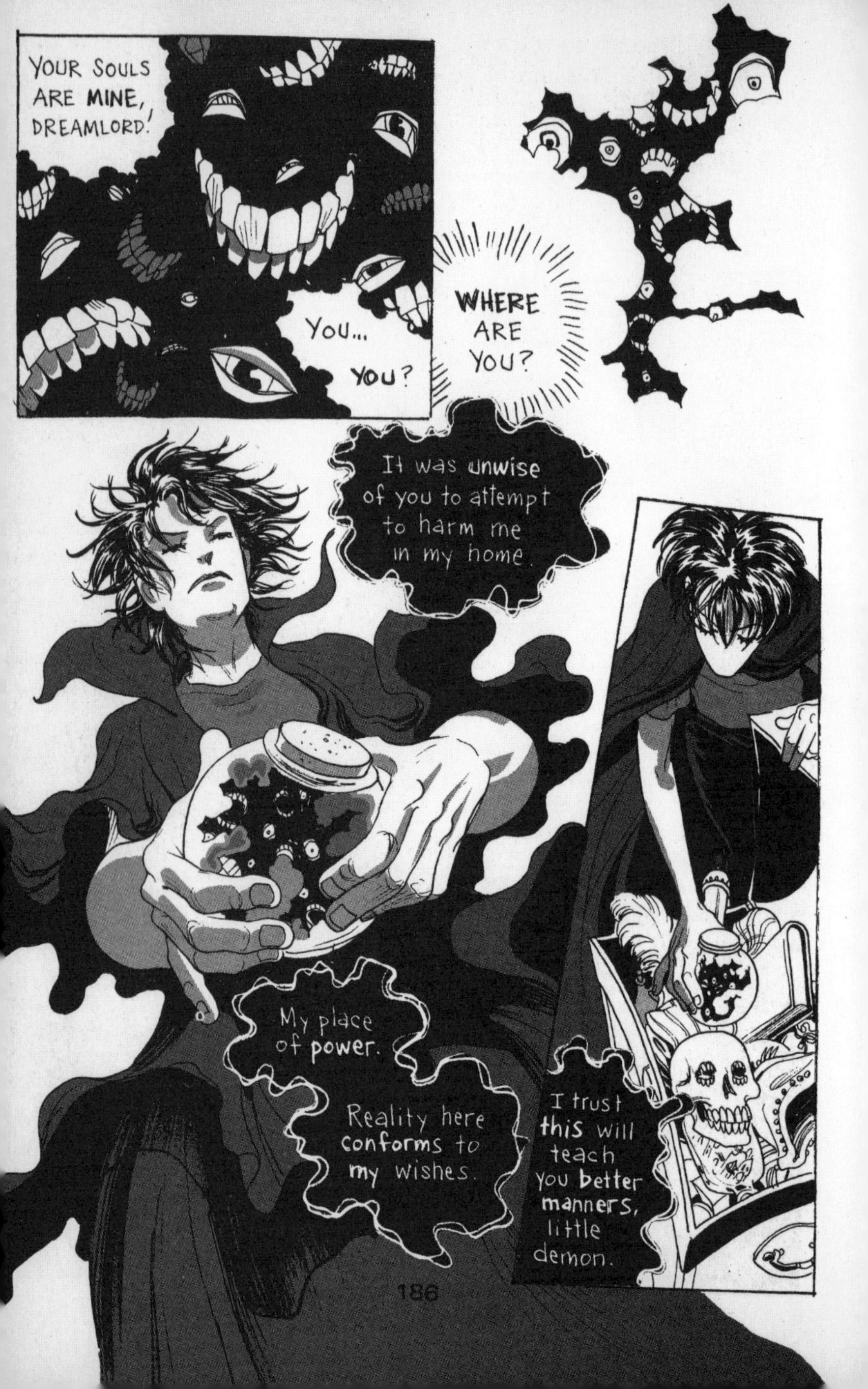
YOUR SOULS ARE MINE, DREAMLORD!
YOU...
YOU?
WHERE ARE YOU?
It was unwise of you to attempt to harm me in my home.
My place of power.
Reality here conforms to my wishes.
I trust this will teach you better manners, little demon.

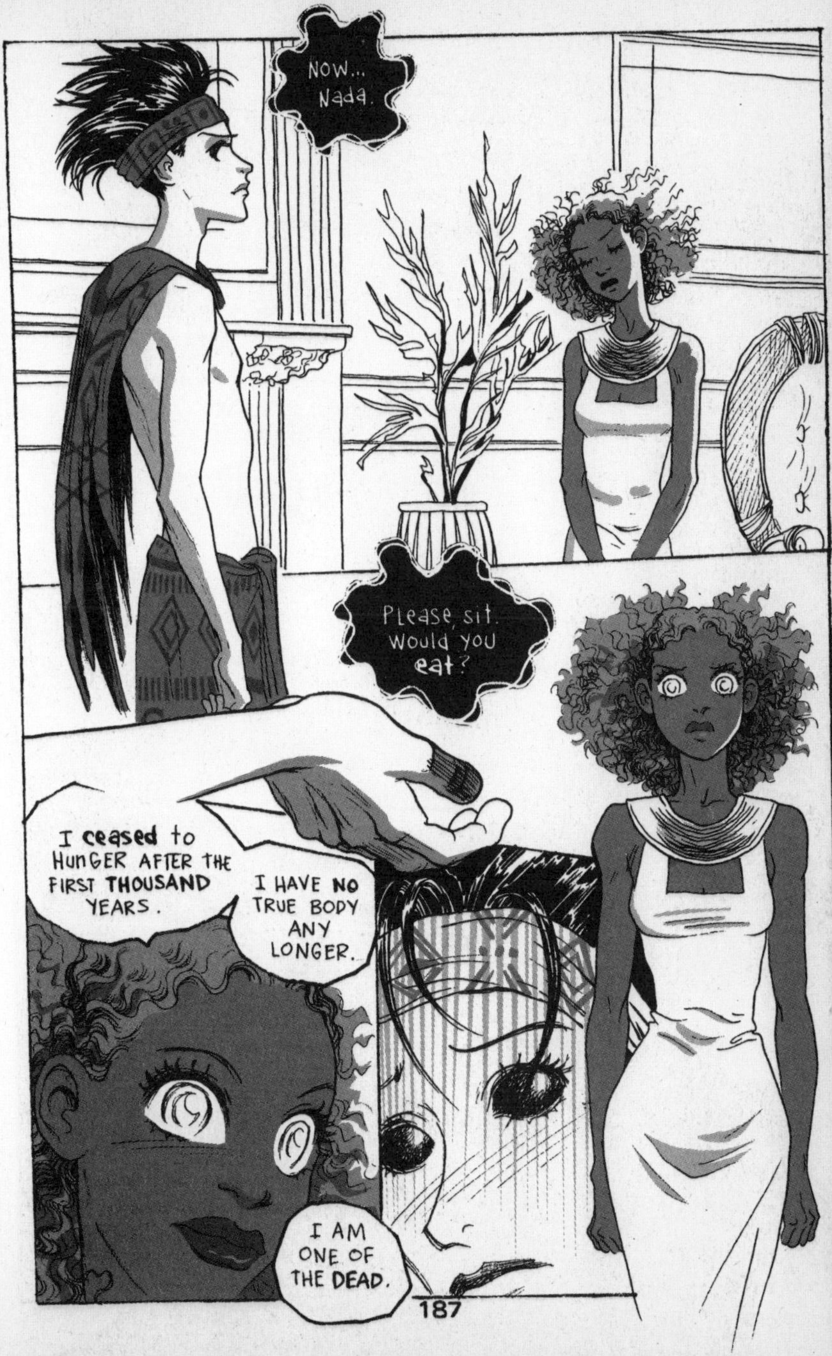
Now...
Nada.
Please, sit. Would you eat?
I ceased to HunGER AFTER THE FIRST THOUSAND YEARS.
I HAVE NO TRUE BODY ANY LONGER.
I AM ONE OF THE DEAD.

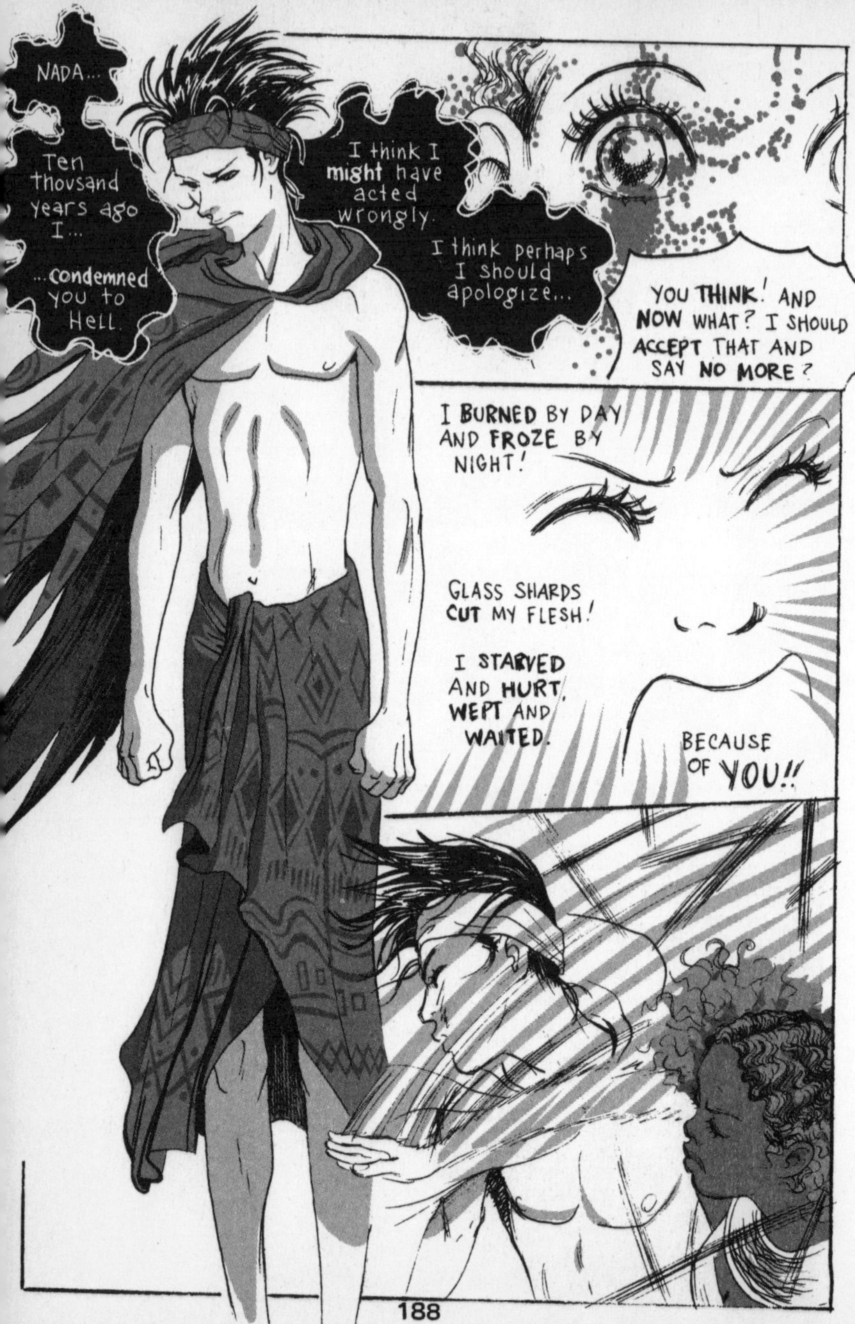
NADA...
Ten thousand years ago I...
...condemned you to Hell.
I think I might have acted wrongly.
I think perhaps I should apologize...
YOU THINK! AND NOW WHAT? I SHOULD ACCEPT THAT AND SAY NO MORE?
I BURNED BY DAY AND FROZE BY NIGHT!
GLASS SHARDS CUT MY FLESH!
I STARVED AND HURT, WEPT AND WAITED.
BECAUSE OF YOU!!

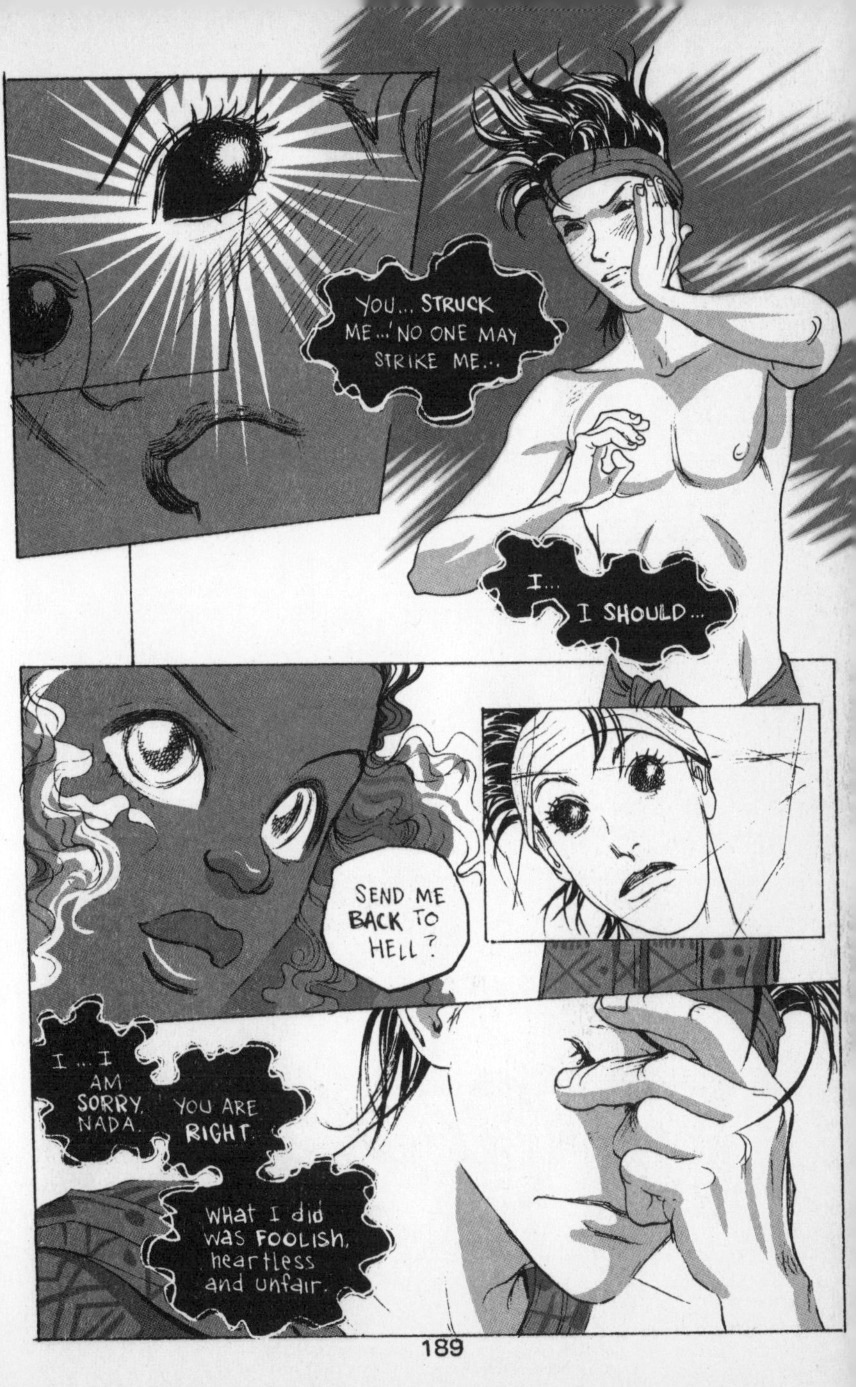
YOU... STRUCK ME...! NO ONE MAY STRIKE ME...
I... I SHOULD...
SEND ME BACK TO HELL?
I... I AM SORRY, NADA.
YOU ARE RIGHT.
What I did was FOOLISH, heartless and unfair.

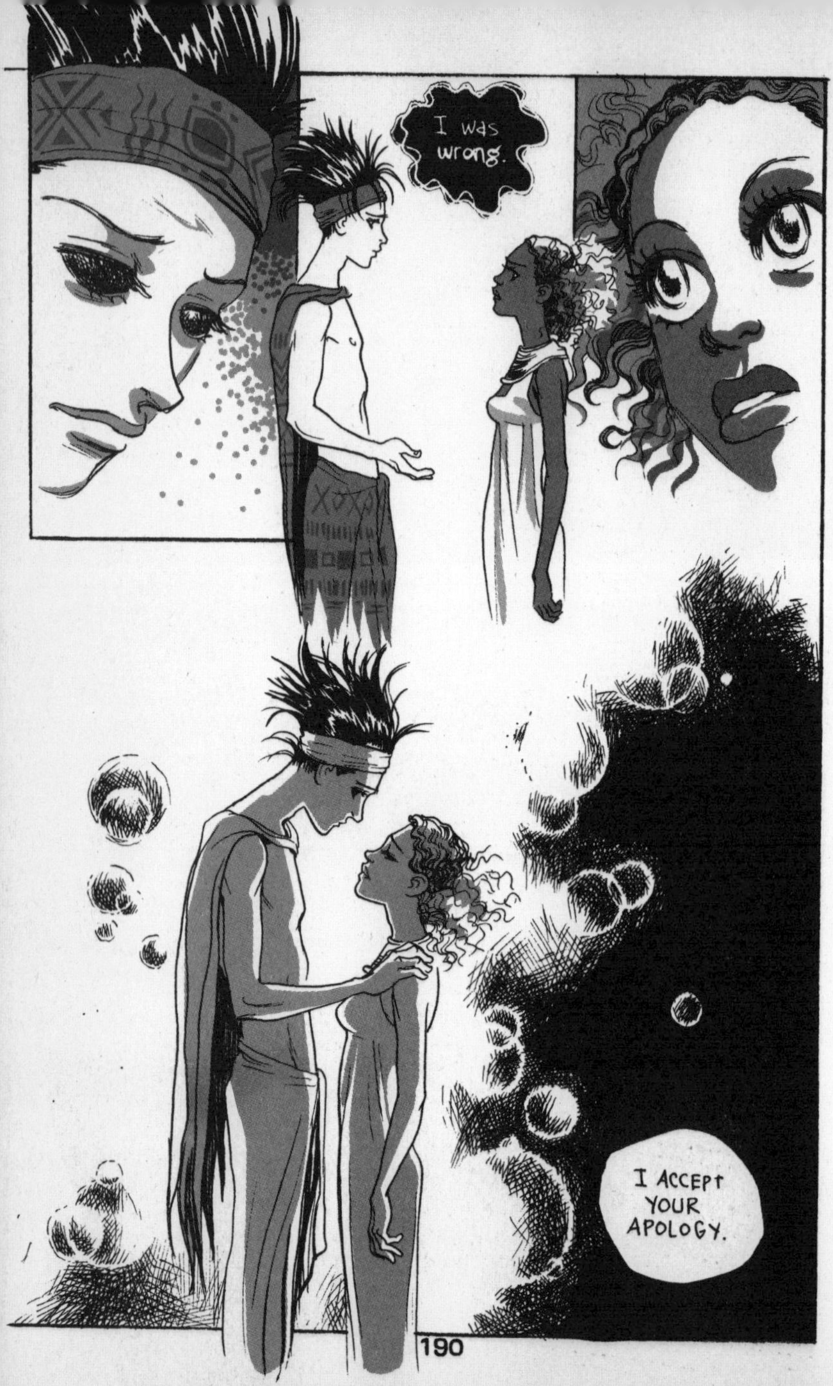
I was wrong.
I ACCEPT YOUR APOLOGY.

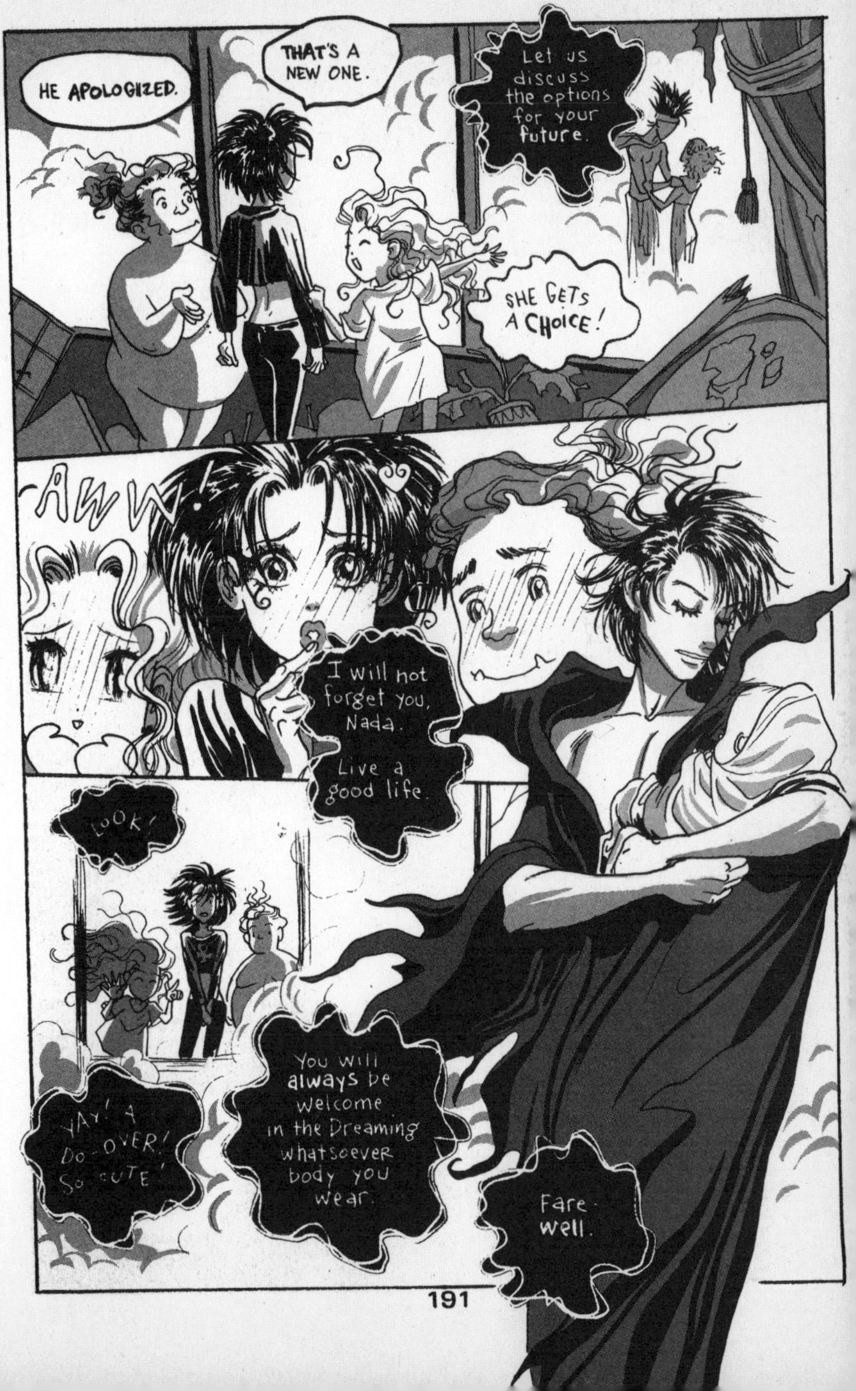
HE APOLOGIZED.
THAT'S A NEW ONE.
Let us discuss the options for your future.
SHE GETS A CHOICE!
AWW!
I will not forget you, Nada.
Live a good life.
LOOK!
YAY! A DO-OVER! SO CUTE!
You will always be welcome in the Dreaming whatsoever body you wear.
Fare-well.

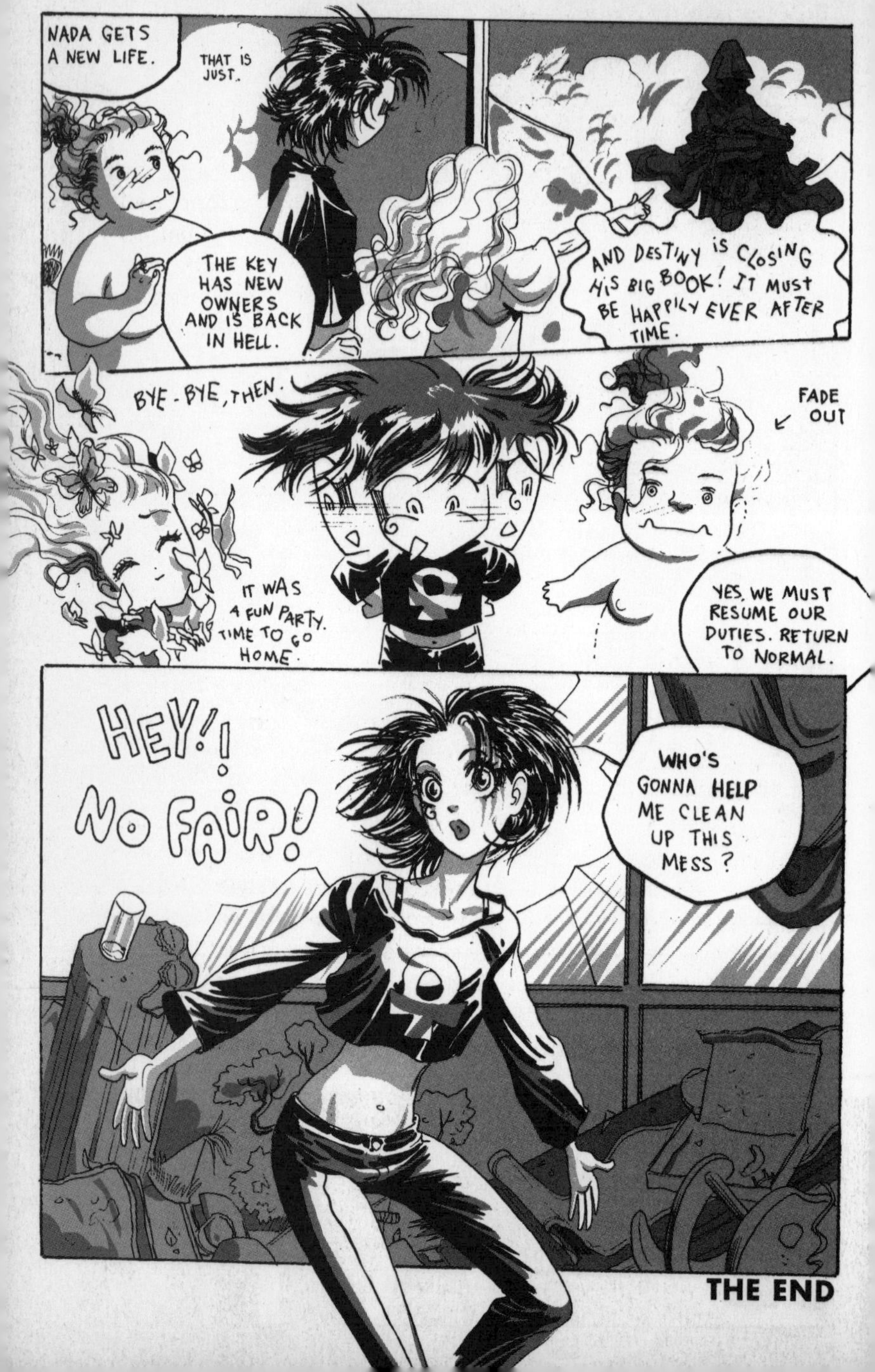
NADA GETS A NEW LIFE.
THAT IS JUST.
THE KEY HAS NEW OWNERS AND IS BACK IN HELL.
AND DESTINY IS CLOSING HIS BIG BOOK! IT MUST BE HAPPILY EVER AFTER TIME.
BYE-BYE, THEN.
FADE OUT
IT WAS A FUN PARTY. TIME TO GO HOME.
YES, WE MUST RESUME OUR DUTIES. RETURN TO NORMAL.
HEY!! NO FAIR!
WHO'S GONNA HELP ME CLEAN UP THIS MESS?
THE END

Chris Bachalo

OF COURSE I KNOW WHAT HAPPENS WHEN YOU DIE, SEXTON. I DO.

I'M DEATH.

The Sandman is the most acclaimed and award-winning comics series of the 1990s for good reason. A smart and deftly brooding epic, *The Sandman* is elegantly penned by *New York Times* best-selling author Neil Gaiman (*American Gods, Coraline*) and illustrated by a rotating cast of comics' most popular artists. A rich blend of modern myth and dark fantasy in which contemporary fiction, historical drama and legend are seamlessly interwoven, the saga of the Sandman encompasses a 10-volume series of tales. Unique in graphic literature, it is a story you will never forget.

Within the *Sandman* series, the often Byronesque main character Dream sometimes needs a little help from his family. He turns most often to his older sister, Death. One of the most enduring comic-book characters ever created, Death is as popular today as when she first appeared in the late '80s. Beautiful, perky, and the epitome of duty, she remains the most famous of The Endless siblings and the coolest Goth girl ever invented.

If you've ever wondered what Death was like, this is where you find out. Not a skeleton, not an old man with a scythe but a devoted-to-her-job girl with an impeccable sense of style. Death is beautiful, Death is wise, and Death cares about you, whoever you are, great or small. Death is one of the members of The Endless, a loose-knit family of seven: Dream, Desire, Despair, Destiny, Delirium and Destruction. Roughly as old as time, they are not gods or patron saints: they are the things themselves, personified.

DEATH

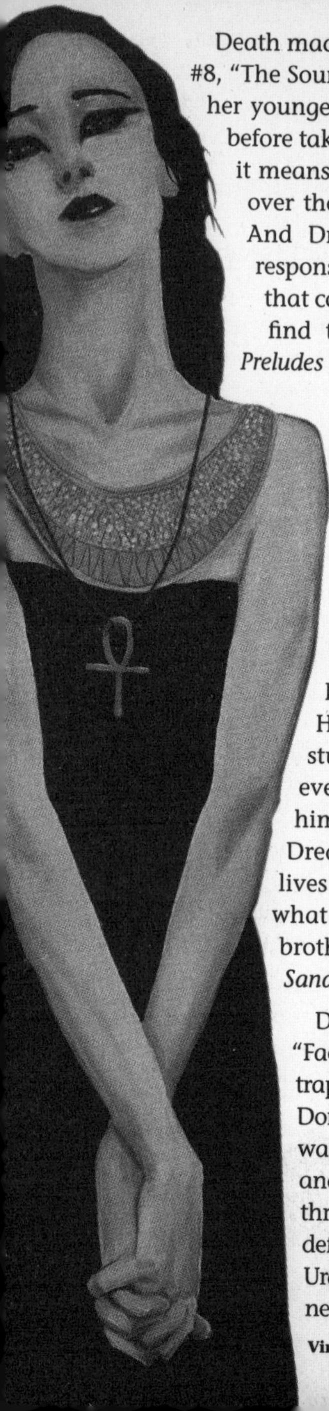

Death made her first appearance in 1989 in *The Sandman* #8, "The Sound of Her Wings," in which she soundly scolds her younger brother Dream for his moping and self-pity before taking him on a tour of duty, to remind him what it means to be one of The Endless. She escorts him all over the city, taking the dead with pragmatic grace. And Dream learns from his older sister — what responsibility is, what purpose means, and the peace that comes with the soft sound of her wings. You can find the story in the trade paperback *Sandman: Preludes and Nocturnes.*

That perky, pretty girl gained immense popularity after her debut and charmed her way into other appearances throughout the monthly Sandman series. In *Sandman* #12's "Men of Good Fortune," by Gaiman and artists Michael Zulli and Steve Parkhouse, we learned that while Death takes her job seriously she will sometimes bend the rules. Observing tavern life in 14th-century London, she and Dream take special notice of Hob Gadling, a soldier who boasts that his stubborn refusal to die will keep him alive forever. Amused by his impertinence, Death grants him immortality. Over the ensuing centuries, Dream strikes up a friendship with this man who lives forever. Again, Death's light heart enriches what might otherwise be a bleak existence for her brother. "Men of Good Fortune" can be found in *Sandman: The Doll's House.*

Death next appeared in *The Sandman* #20, in "Façade," the tragic story of an immortal woman trapped by life, by Gaiman and artists Colleen Doran and Malcolm Jones III. Urania Blackwell was transformed into the super-hero Element Girl, and no one can kill Element Girl. When danger threatens, she transmutes into an appropriately defensive element... voluntarily or not. But Urania wants to die. When Death claims her neighbor, Urania begs to be taken as well, but Death

Vince Locke

cannot oblige. She does, however, take pity on Element Girl, and helps Urania find her own solution. "Façade" is available in *Sandman: Dream Country.*

In *Sandman: Season of Mists,* Death displays her willingness to stand against her brother when he is wrong (*The Sandman* #21, by Gaiman and Dringenberg) and an unexpectedly flexible approach to her job when circumstances warrant. This story, of course, is referred to in this digest but we recommend that you check out the actual volume for the complete picture.

In *The Sandman Special* #1, by Gaiman and Bryan Talbot, Death exempts another: Dream's son, the Orpheus of myth, who wishes to enter the realm of the dead unscathed to rescue his beloved Eurydice. As a dark result of her boon, Orpheus survives his own beheading by centuries. This and *Sandman* #31, in which Gaiman and artist Shawn McManus introduce us to Death's favorite king, can be found in *Sandman: Fables and Reflections.* Every *Sandman* graphic novel contains an appearance by Death including *A Game of You, Worlds' End, The Kindly Ones* and *The Wake.*

Death's immense popularity inspired two miniseries. *Death: The High Cost of Living* by Gaiman, Chris Bachalo and Mark Buckingham shows us how for one day, every hundred years, Death becomes human; for to fully understand the lives she takes, Death must experience what it means to live. This involves hot dogs, bagels, crazy hermits, a depressed teenaged boy and a search for Mad Hettie's lost heart — basically just another day in the life. In *Death: The Time of Your Life* by Gaiman, Bachalo and Buckingham, we revisit Hazel and Foxglove from *A Game of You* and *Death: The High Cost of Living* a few years after their son Ralphie has been born and Foxglove's music career has taken off. Hazel made a deal with Death: In order to save the life of her son, she told Death that she would die in his place after a few years, and that time is now. Foxglove follows Hazel into Death's realm in an effort to redeem all three of them.

She is Death of The Endless. You no longer have to fear the divider of the living. She gives you peace. She gives you meaning. ♀

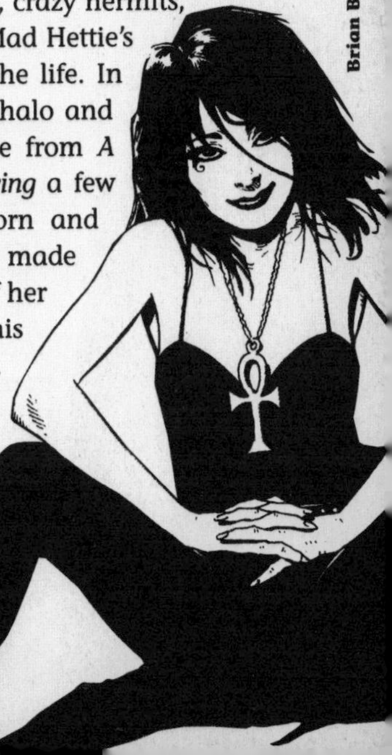

Brian Bolland

Here's a sampling of Jill Thompson's sketchbook which contains her early Manga drawings of Death and The Endless. ♀

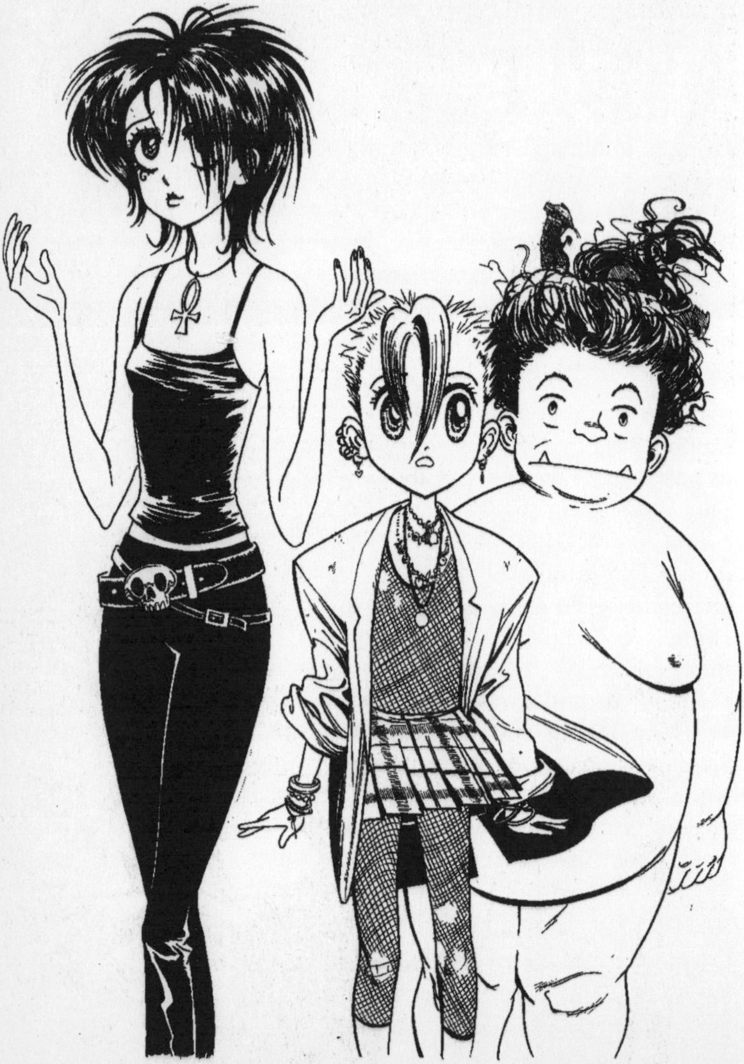

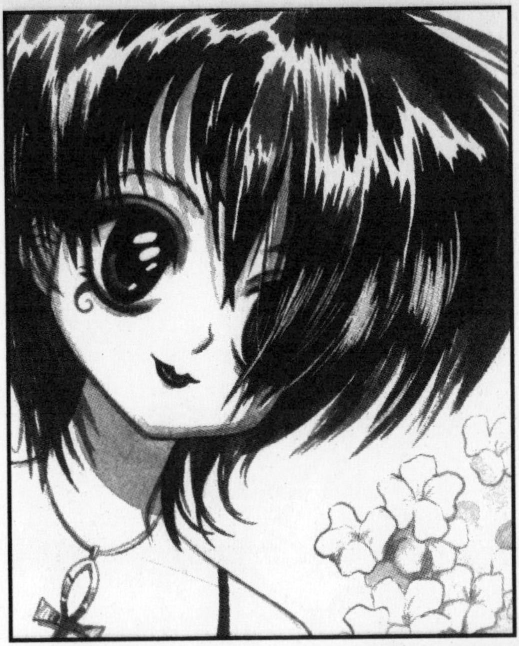

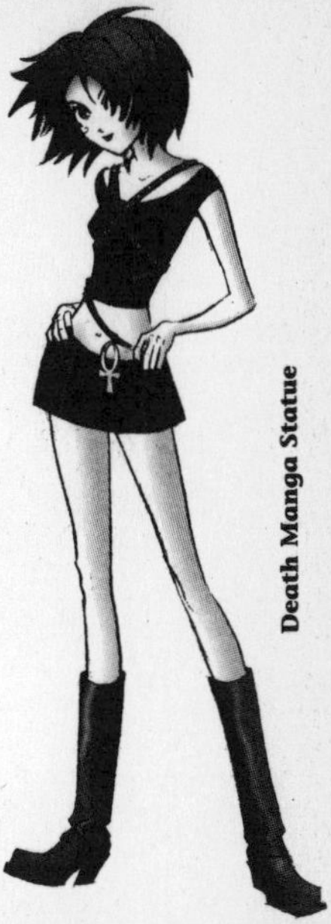

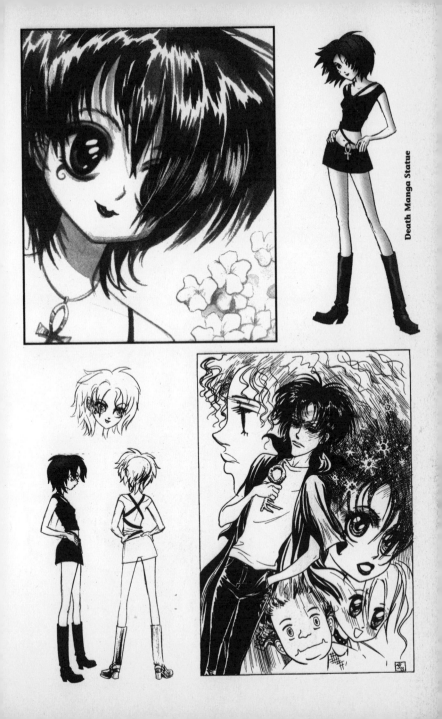

Death Manga Statue

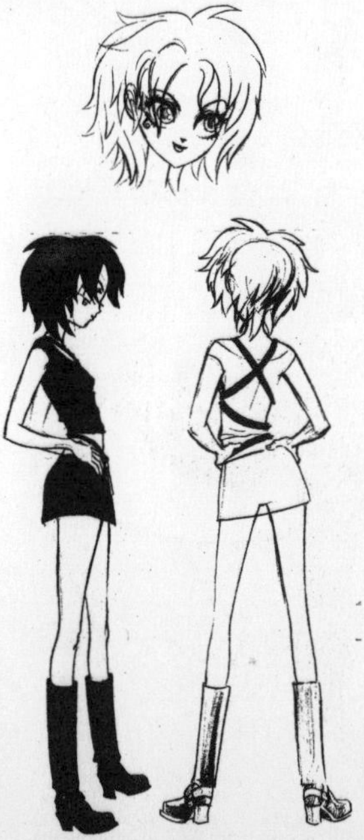

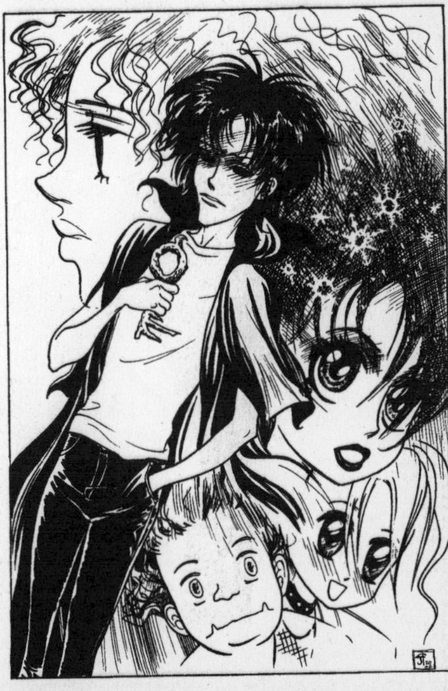

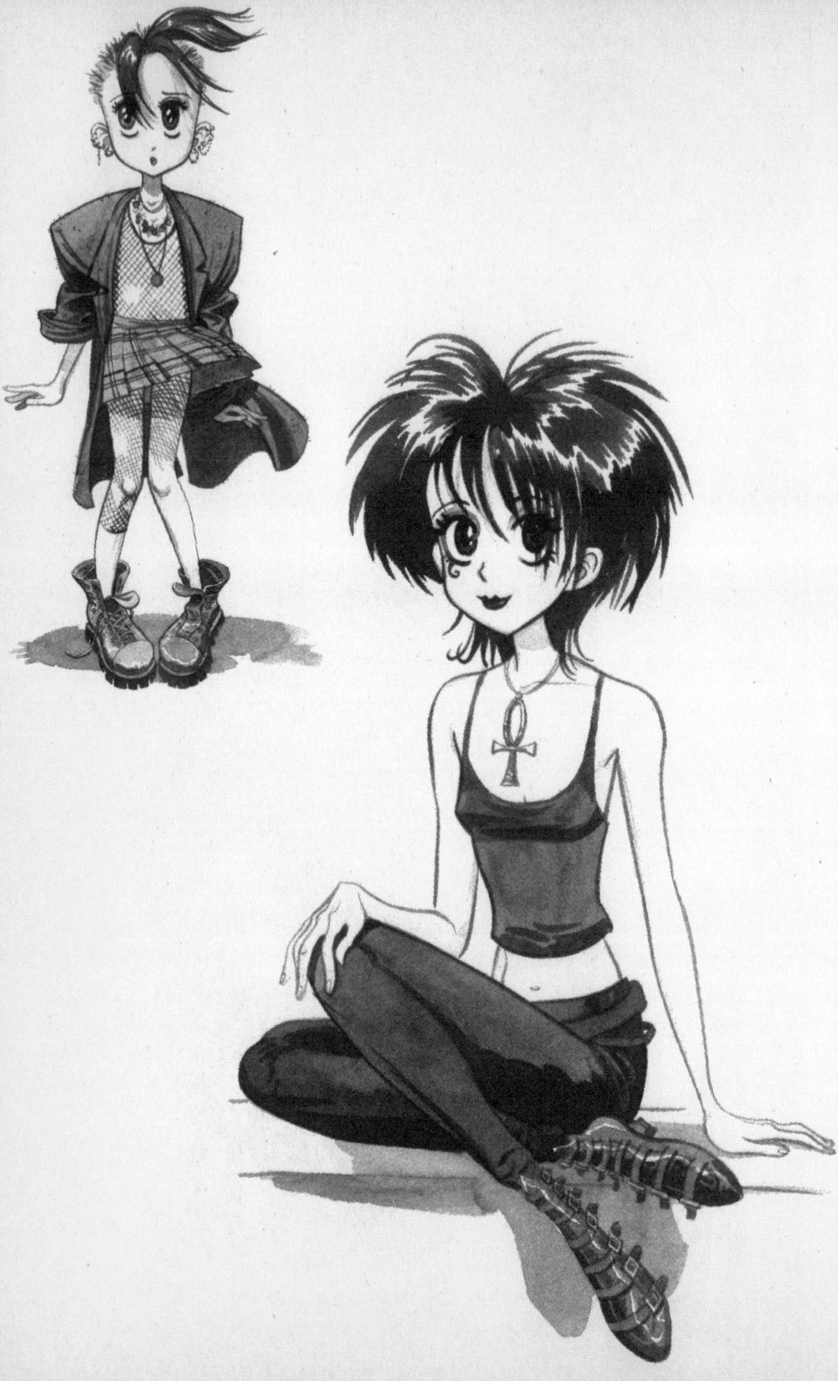

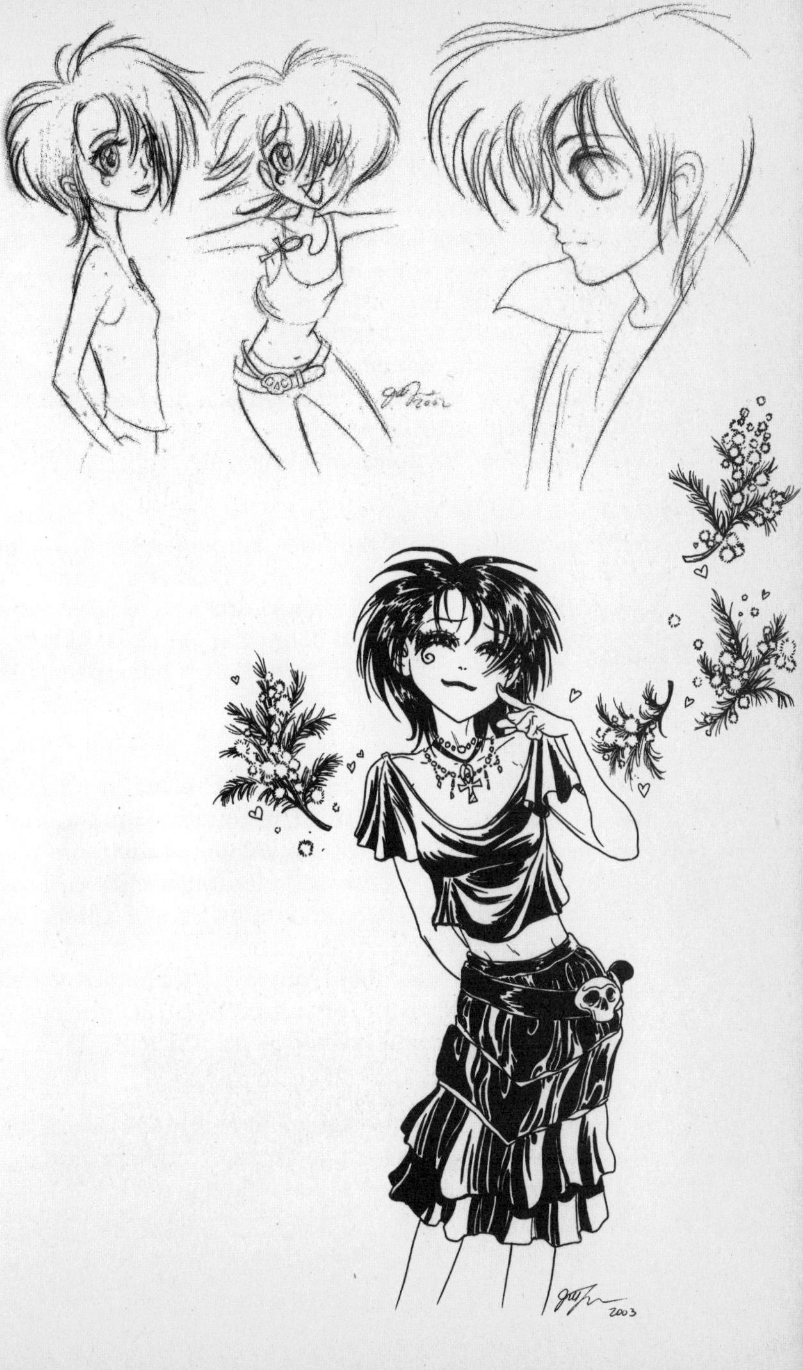
2003

If you've enjoyed this book, you should seek out these graphic novels from the 10-volume SANDMAN library:

PRELUDES & NOCTURNES

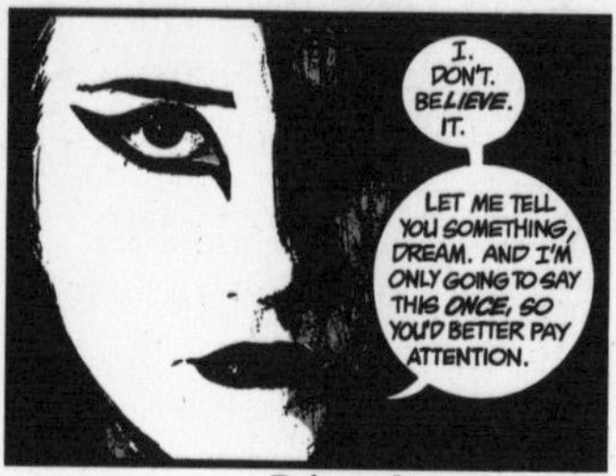
I. DON'T. BELIEVE. IT.
LET ME TELL YOU SOMETHING, DREAM. AND I'M ONLY GOING TO SAY THIS ONCE, SO YOU'D BETTER PAY ATTENTION.

Dringenberg/Jones III

Dream of the Endless, also known as the Sandman, had been trapped for 70 years when an attempt to capture his sister, Death, was spectacularly botched. After he escapes, the Sandman must reclaim his realm, The Dreaming, as well as his articles of power: his helmet, his pouch and his amulet.

THE DOLL'S HOUSE

Rose Walker finds more than she bargained for including long lost relatives, a serial killers' convention and, ultimately, her true identity. The Master of Dreams attempts to unravel her mystery, unaware that the hand of another, far closer to home, is pulling the strings. This collection also boasts the first appearance of Death.

DREAM COUNTRY

These four chilling and compelling tales include "A Midsummer Night's Dream," The World Fantasy Award-winning story of the first performance of the William Shakespeare play with art by Charles Vess... "Calliope," a beautiful muse enslaved by a novelist to feed his need for stories... "Dream of a Thousand Cats," revealing a cat's-eye view of the tyranny of mankind... and "Facade," a strange tale about an immortal, indestructible woman who only wants to die. This collection also features part of Neil Gaiman's original comic book script for "Calliope."

SEASON OF MISTS

Ten thousand years ago, the Sandman condemned his one true love to the pits of Hell. When his sister Death convinces him that Nada was unjustly imprisoned, Dream journeys to Hell to rescue his lost lover... just as Lucifer Morningstar decides to abdicate his throne... leaving the Key to Hell in the hands of the Sandman.

A GAME OF YOU

Barbie, from THE DOLL'S HOUSE, used to dream of being a princess in a lush, private kingdom with strange animals as her subjects. But Barbie has stopped dreaming now that her imaginary world has been threatened. In one desperate attempt to save the dying kingdom, Martin Tenbones journeys to the waking world to find Barbie and enlist her help in a story about gender and identity.

FABLES & REFLECTIONS

Dreams of power, dreams of darkness. Follow Morpheus, the Lord of Dreams, from the mists of the past to the nightmares of the present. Dream touches the lives of Haroun al Raschid, King of Ancient Baghdad, Lady Johanna Constantine, spy and adventuress, Joshua Norton, self-styled emperor of the United States, as well as ravens, actors, explorers, storytellers, werewolves and children in nine remarkable stories that will take you beyond your wildest imaginings.

BRIEF LIVES

Delirium, youngest of the extended family known as The Endless, prevails upon her brother Dream to help find their missing sibling, Destruction. Their odyssey through the world of the waking and the final confrontation with Destruction—plus the resolution of Dream's painful relationship with his son, Orpheus—will change The Endless forever.

WORLDS' END

Caught in the vortex of a reality storm, wayfarers from throughout time, myth and the imagination converge on a mysterious inn. In the tradition of Chaucer's Canterbury Tales, as the travelers all wait out the tempest that rages around them, they share stories of the places they've been, the things they've seen...and those that they've dreamed.

Dringenberg/Jones III

THE KINDLY ONES

They were never called the Furies. Instead, frightened people called them The Kindly Ones. Implacable, unstoppable in their mission of vengeance, they would not rest until the crime they sought to punish had been avenged, had been washed clean... with blood. Now Dream of the Endless, his family, his friends, and his enemies find themselves caught up in a dark conspiracy. A child has been stolen. Someone must pay. Someone will die.

THE WAKE

The King of Dreams is dead—long live the King of Dreams. Ancient gods, old friends and enemies gather to pay tribute, and to remember, in the strangest wake ever held. The echoes of the death reverberate: we see them touch a man who will not die, and a Chinese sage whose path into exile takes him through a desert of dreams. And, at the end of his life, William Shakespeare fulfills his end of a very strange bargain.

THE SANDMAN: THE DREAM HUNTERS

A solitary monk lives in a temple, surrounded by woods and peace. A fox and a badger wager that one of them will be able to drive the monk out, and then the temple will become the winner's den. But when the fox falls in love with the monk, she discovers that a local lord plans to harm him. The fox journeys to see Morpheus, the Dream King, to strike a bargain to save the monk's life. Set in Japan, this adult fairytale is told in prose by Neil Gaiman, and is lavishly presented with full-page illustrations by legendary artist Yoshitaka Amano.

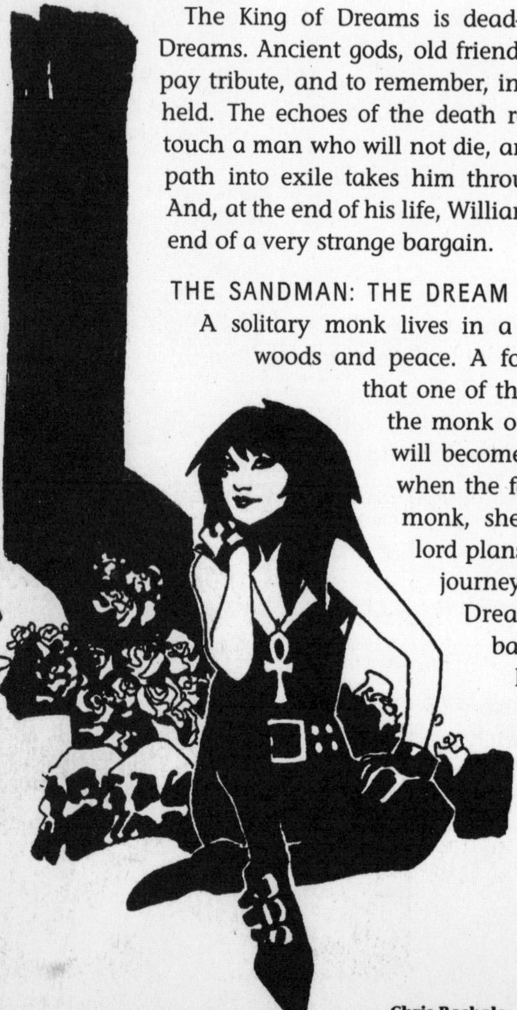

Chris Bachalo

THE LITTLE ENDLESS STORYBOOK

For years fans have demanded to see more of Jill Thompson's Little Endless, the diminutive versions of the Endless characters that made their first appearance in *The Sandman: Brief Lives*. Written and painted by Jill Thompson, this story follows one puppy's search through the strange and precarious realms of the Endless to locate lost Little Delirium. Recommended for readers of all ages, the characters are also available as cold-cast porcelain statues based on designs by Thompson.

Jill
Thompson

ENDLESS NIGHTS

Whether haunting, bittersweet, erotic or nightmarish, the seven stories in this book — one for each of the Endless siblings — reveal strange secrets and surprising truths. The stories are illustrated by some of the greatest comics artists from around the world.

♀ P. Craig Russell draws the story of DEATH and one day, two hundred years ago, on an island in the Venice lagoon — a day that goes on forever.

♀ Milo Manara paints a story of love and DESIRE in ancient times as a beautiful young woman gets everything she wants … at a price.

♀ Bill Sienkiewicz shows us who gets to enter DELIRIUM's realm to perform a strange rescue mission.

♀ Miguelanxo Prado takes us back for a DREAM of the dawn of time, when stars spoke and even The Endless were young.

♀ Barron Storey creates fifteen heartrending portraits of DESPAIR.

♀ Glenn Fabry draws a story of archaeologists uncovering the future and learning a little too much about DESTRUCTION.

♀ Frank Quitely draws a final commentary on the DESTINY of these Endless Nights.

P. Craig Russell

DATE			